MW01001481

Published by the PBIC, Inc. (Pet Bird Information Council)
Sponsored by the Pet Bird Report: The Companion Parrot Magazine
Alameda, California, USA
http://www.petbirdreport.com

Blanchard, Sally 1944 -
Riebe, Jeff 1969 -
Companion Parrot Handbook by Sally Blanchard
with drawings by Sally Blanchard and Jeff Riebe

ISBN 0-9671298-0-X

Library of Congress Catalog Card Number: 99-62131

1. Companion Parrots
2. Parrot Behavior
3. Companion Parrot Care

♺ Printed on Recycled Paper by Abbey Press, Oakland, California

FIRST PRINTING April 1999   9 8 7 6 5 4 3 2 1

Sally Blanchard's
COMPANION PARROT HANDBOOK

USING *NURTURING GUIDANCE* TO CREATE THE BEST COMPANION PARROT POSSIBLE

AKA
The Happy Bappy Fun Book

by Sally Blanchard

Illustrations by
Jeff Riebe and
Sally Blanchard

This book is dedicated to *Bongo Marie* — a remarkable African Grey who, as my companion for over 20 years, taught me more about living with a parrot than anyone ...

... and to all the committed people with companion parrots, behavioral consultants, parrot breeders, pet shop personnel, and avian veterinarians who put the birds first, ahead of profit and ego. These are the people who are doing the *right thing* for the parrots and remain open to the process of learning and sharing.

Thanks to everyone who has helped me with this project including Jeff Riebe, Pam Clark, Phoebe Linden, Jane Hallander, Gail T. Doyle, Pat Hill, Sam Foster, Joel Blumberg, DVM & Sandy Black of Abbey Press. A percentage of the profits from this book will go to worthy parrot-related causes for both wild parrots and companion parrots.

TABLE OF CONTENTS

.....➤

FOREWORD

**By Phoebe Linden,
Santa Barbara Bird Farm**

*Phoebe &
Josserlynn*

Information, Influence, Inspiration

The publication of Sally Blanchard's Companion Parrot Handbook provides parrot caregivers a new, important, and exciting information source. Anyone previously unfamiliar with Sally Blanchard's parrot behavior work will delight in not only her artistically rendered drawings, but also in her extensive knowledge. Companion Parrot Handbook is further enlivened by the brilliantly funny cartoons of Jeff Riebe. Sally and Jeff give their readers a volume replete with analysis, advice, humor, and insight.

For over two decades, Sally's work with parrot behavior has shaped thinking, spurred debate, and forced a closer scrutiny of the methods used to raise parrots and the standards for their keeping. Within the pages of Companion Parrot Handbook, Sally's three main contributions to avian behavior reaffirm themselves. These are *information*, *influence*, and *inspiration*.

Sally is known for her ability to provide good *information* to caregivers of companion parrots. In print, during seminars, at conferences, and via consultations, Sally's information has helped pet owners build trust between themselves and their parrots. Seriously dedicated to improving the welfare of captive companion parrots, Sally conveys her knowledge effectively, and with humor. Her entertaining presentations, like this book, are crafted to educate. During a presentation by Sally, for instance, audience members laugh uproariously, scribble pertinent notes, exchange knowing glances, shed tears, and radically rearrange their concepts about parrot keeping.

Sally's *influence* in avian behavior was felt in 1991 when she established the Pet Bird Information Council and began publication of *Pet Bird Report: The Companion Parrot Magazine*. *PBR* provides parrot owners with creatively conceived, functionally oriented, and well-documented articles that illuminate what it's really like to have parrots as day-to-day companions. For the writers of *PBR*, Sally is a sounding board, mentor, and source of encouragement. For *PBR* readers, she embodies authority, reason, and solutions. For both, and for the readers of this new book, Sally's information and influence will inspire happier relationships between people and parrots.

Sally is an *inspiration*. Webster's Dictionary says that to inspire is "to have an animating, enlivening effect upon; to motivate, encourage, impel." Indeed, Sally consistently motivates us to treat our parrots as sentient feathered companions. While she encourages us to analyze parrot behavior, she impels us to understand the whole parrot. She animates us to activity (make glop, hang toys), to think (no "quick fixes!"), and to impart essential skills to our avian companions. At the same time, Sally challenges us to understand our vital role as caregivers.

Companion Parrot Handbook will extend the reach of Sally's information, broaden the scope of her influence, and infuse her readers with inspiration. You'll want to share it with your family, friends, bird club members, avian veterinarians and their staffs, with anyone who may be thinking of adopting a first parrot, or with those who care for large flocks. The information, influence, and inspiration contained within the Companion Parrot Handbook are unmistakably Sally's.

INTRODUCTION

LIVING WITH A PARROT SHOULD BE FUN!

I like to think of my theory of *Nurturing Guidance* as a *recipe*. Through articles, seminars, the media, and behavioral consultations, I share the ingredients of this recipe with many people who live with companion parrots. Over the years, they have successfully used this recipe to create and maintain positive relationships with their companion parrots. It is very gratifying to hear how successful these people have been using *Nurturing Guidance*.

There are many possible ingredients for working with a companion parrot. Some are very successful and others doom the parrot owner to a life of *behavioral indigestion*. There is a dividing line. On one side of the line is information which is *trust-building*. On the other side of the line is information which is *trust-destroying*. Knowing the difference makes a tremendous advantage in the relationship people establish with their parrots.

In writing this book, my goal is not only to provide *the what* of mutually contented cohabitation, but also explain *the how* and *the why*. If readers begin to understand the basics of their parrot's behavior, they will be able to apply this understanding to almost all of the complexities of their psittacine companion's behavior.

I would have called this book **The Happy Bappy Fun Book** except that not everyone knows what I am talking about unless they subscribe to the Pet Bird Report or read the book first. (See page 64 for an explanation of the word Bappy.) Some people seem afraid of all the *work* it will take to share their life with a parrot. Truth is — it shouldn't be work. The more we think of our lives with parrots as a chore, the less likely we are to do what is necessary to establish *Nurturing Guidance*. Basically, the *work* we have to do is actually *instructional interaction* which involves relating to our parrots in a positive way, which makes them happier and, therefore, makes us happier. Generally speaking, **a contented parrot is a well-behaved parrot.**

The people who know the positive aspects of living with wonderful companion parrots are those who are open to learning. They accept the challenge of life with an animal whose complexities may be even more involved than living with another human being. I both chuckle and cringe every time I read anything that presents parrots as an *easy-care pet.* Perhaps they seem to be for some people — those who sling seed at them, keep the cage minimally clean, and don't interact emotionally or affectionately with their parrots. These people will never understand what delights me and so many others about life with parrots.

THE HAPPY BAPPY FUNBOOK

Life with a companion parrot may also seem easy to those who have established the kind of relationship with their bird that makes their care enjoyable. *The more fun the person has, the more fun the parrot has, the more fun the person has* ... keeping parrots should be fun. The hard work of their physical and environmental care should be balanced with the mutual pleasure we get from interacting with them.

Consider the focused time you give your parrot as play time, or the *flock interaction* your parrot deserves. Parrots are a lot of fun to play with. Special focused attention can be spent teaching your pet new tricks or new words, or singing and whistling favorite tunes. You accomplish a lot more if both of you are having fun.

Companion parrots are still instinctively wild and not domesticated in the sense that most other companion animals are. This fact, combined with their intelligence, makes their behavior more complex for us to understand. They are highly social animals and having one in our life implies that we spend quality time interacting with them. Much of that interaction should be instructional to stimulate their sense of security and independence. A parrot with a trusting bond with his or her people is secure and, therefore, content as a human companion.

I believe people who think it takes too much time or involves too much work to have a necessary positive interaction with parrots shouldn't have them. They will never know what those of us who do take the time know about how wonderful it is to have a parrot as a lifelong companion.

Read It From Start To Finish Or Use It As A Reference

The <u>Companion Parrot Handbook</u> is meant to be read in more than one way. You can read it from start to finish or use it as a reference to look up specific topics such as "First Aid For Broken Blood Feathers," "Towel Training," "Excessive Screaming," or "The Neutral Room." In reading this handbook from the beginning to end, you will notice some repetition of important points as each topic is also meant to stand alone.

I sincerely hope this book will help you realize how special a companion parrot can be — if you are up to the challenge. Most of all, please, share your knowledge about this book with other parrot caregivers.

Sally Blanchard

People who are interested in sharing their lives with a parrot need to understand that the rewards in the relationships with companion parrots come with accepting and meeting their unique challenges. Those who don't take the time and energy will never understand what is so special about the human/parrot bond.

the more fun the parrot has, the more fun the person has ...

WHAT IS THE PBIC?

The PBIC, Inc. is the Pet Bird Information Council, an organization established in 1991 and incorporated by Sally Blanchard to publish the Pet Bird Report and provide other companion parrot education endeavors. These include:

➲ The PET BIRD REPORT Magazine —
Edited by Sally Blanchard and published by the PBIC Inc. 6 times a year since 1991 and affectionately known as the PBR by its many subscribers and readers.

➲ Pet Bird Report Back Issue and Reprint Sales

➲ Publication of companion parrot-related books.
Planned Sally Blanchard books include: Companion Parrot Personalities© and Grey Matter© a book on Companion African Grey Parrots

➲ Publication of a series of booklets geared toward sale in bird shops and pet shops on the most common companion parrot behavioral problems and their prevention and solutions.

➲ An Educational Web Site at (www.petbirdreport.com)

➲ PBIC/PBR Behavioral Annual Convention

➲ Co-sponsorship of Sally Blanchard Seminars and Programs

➲ Co-sponsoring of Companion Parrot Behavioral Videos

➲ Sally Blanchard Behavioral Consultations (limited to PBR Subscribers)

➲ Reviewed Advertising for Products, Services, and Breeders

➲ Educational Appearances on Television & Radio

➲ Fund-raising Raffles & Promotion of Worthy Avian Endeavors

➲ Sponsorship of an On-line Parrot Behavior Discussion List

The Pet Bird Report/PBIC, Inc.
Alameda, CA 94501
510-523-5303 FAX 510-521-6475
www.petbirdreport.com   e-mail: sallypbr@ix.netcom.com

(The Full-color Cover Illustrations (Front and Back) by Jeff Riebe
Are Available on High-quality Pet Bird Report T-shirts)

Nurturing Guidance Tip: Monomorphic Psittacines

Parrot Genders

Most companion parrot species are basically monomorphic — both sexes look alike. A few are dimorphic which means there are major differences in the appearance of the genders. Of course, parrots know the differences, whether they are obvious or not to us. When ornithologists first discovered the Eclectus Parrot, they falsely identified the male and female as two different species, because the males are predominately green and the hens are mostly red. Sometimes there are subtle differences like the shape of the beak, the color of the eyes, and the shading of the feathers which can be used to make fairly accurate guesses. It is helpful to learn the gender of our companion parrots so we can begin to have a better understanding of gender-related behaviors in companion parrots. DNA sexing makes it easy and certainly less invasive than surgical sexing.

I believe in referring to parrots (and all animals) by the pronouns he or she rather than *it*, especially if I know their gender. To me, the word *"it"* is far too impersonal because parrots are so personal. They are too beautiful and full of life to be referred to with the inanimate term *it*.

To All The Parrot Hens, especially *Hen Libbers*:

I apologize for the use of male pronouns unless I know for sure the parrot I am referring to is a hen. It just makes the book easier to write and easier to read. I wish there was a better word to describe collective or unknown gender than *it* or always using the male pronoun, but no one has come up with one that doesn't sound even more awkward.

WHAT'S SO SPECIAL ABOUT PARROTS?

Sharing My Life

I could start out by proclaiming my love for parrots but in many ways, the word love has become a "sound bite." After all, I also love a new pair of shoes, a good movie, or a gourmet meal because they fill my particular need for them at that moment. There are other words that define my involvement with parrots: respect, awe, fascination, amazement, wonder — but none of these adequately expresses my feelings.

I have shared my life with companion parrots for over a quarter of a century and yet, I still cannot provide a definitive answer about what has made these relationships so special for me. Yes, there is nothing quite like having my African Grey Parrot, Bongo Marie, greet me with an enthusiastic, "Good to see ya!" when I come home. She chatters on incessantly during the day. Sometimes she just jabbers and sometimes she makes incredibly appropriate statements about life. She will ask some absurd question like "Where's your poodle?" and then laugh like a maniac. I never taught her that — honest! Anyone walking by my house would think a deranged family lived here. The chatter of my two Double-yellow Heads, Paco and Rascal, either squabbling or joyously sweet-talking each other with compliments in my words ("Oh, you're so pretty Paco. What a handsome Rackleburger!") and laughing together as they allopreen is amazingly entertaining. My Black-headed Caique has ambition to learn new tricks limited only by my inability to teach them to him. Spike hops on command, rolls over on his back when I ask him if I had too much garlic on my pizza, and readily does a somersault over and over in my hand, then bows with wings spread in response to applause.

Is it simply the greetings, the often appropriate laughter, the hopping, the beauty, the intelligence, and the acrobatic personalities that so endear them to me? It is far more than that but it seems too esoteric to put into words. Each and every day, from the very first moment I spent with a parrot in my life, I have stopped and marveled at the joy and fascination they provide me. I am so enriched by their presence that I chose to make their study, and sharing my knowledge of that study, my life's work.

I have almost always had dogs and often had cats in my life. They provide me with tremendous joy and will always be an important part of my life. I love them and they love me (although I'm not always sure about the cats). As long as I am around to take care of them, our bond remains positive. More than any other relationship, including ones with fellow human beings, dogs provide us with that fervently sought, yet usually unattainable, *unconditional love*. However, the love of a companion parrot is conditional. We have to earn their trust every day of our lives with them — and that can be a lifetime. Without trust, there is no bond. They are a challenge to live with. I have always been the type of person who reveled in a job well done and meeting a challenge has always been important to me. Exploring the many ways to meet a challenge is one of the most rewarding processes of my life.

Parrots As Teachers

Because they reflect our energy and mood, parrots teach us a great deal about ourselves — if we pay attention to their lessons. They often let us see a side of ourselves that we may not always want to see. I never realized how outrageous I sounded when I was angry until Bongo Marie learned to use my words which she says with my exact inflection. She often uses these words when she bangs her toys around with a vengeance. I am not someone who generally wakes up ready to go. Bongo is my mood barometer. Before I am even aware of my own energy, I stumble out in the living room, uncover Bongo's cage, and find out what kind of mood I am in. If I am in a good mood, Bongo provides me with a cheery greeting. Otherwise, she is as grumpy as I am. She always lets me know when I am stressed. Living with parrots has taught me to slow down and respond with more patience and consistency than I ever had before.

Sometimes one of my parrots does make me angry. From time to time, they nag at me with their screaming, especially if I am too slow getting breakfast ready. They become impatient or aggressive with me if I don't pay enough attention to them, or if I try to make them do something they simply are not in the mood to do. Even though they are all quite capable of entertaining themselves, they become withdrawn and agitated with me if I don't spend enough time with them. Because they are so reactive to my emotional output, my parrots have taught me to take the responsibility of defining my relationship with them.

Working With Parrots

For years, I tamed wild-caught parrots. Each one was unique. The sense of achievement in earning their trust and bringing out the potential they had as human companions kept me fascinated and motivated. As a wild-bird watcher and a conservationist, there was always a conflict for me. It has and will always disturb me that so many parrots were taken from their native habitat for the pet trade. If each one had received the care and respect they deserve, I would not be so upset. But then, if each and every parrot, imported or human-raised, received quality physical and emotional care, no one would need to champion their welfare. Much of my passion for parrot education comes from anger and frustration. Perhaps unrealistically, I want to create a world where parrots receive the respect they deserve, both in the wild and in captivity. But I have to maintain a compromise between idealism and reality. I know not everyone will care or learn. I can't become lost in the frustration and futility of trying to save them all. However, maintaining my idealism is essential toward dealing with that reality. I know that those who do care and are open to learning will make a difference in the world of parrots. Without a balance between my idealism and reality, I could not do the work I do. Every day I hear about parrots in appalling situations. I constantly read aggressive, quick-fix advice which destroys the fragile trust parrots have with the people in their lives. But I also talk to many people who are dedicated to doing the right thing for parrots. I hope, through this behavior guide and my theories of *Nurturing Guidance*, to provide information which will inspire others to develop a positive point of view and a passion for parrots.

NURTURING GUIDANCE FUNDAMENTALS

The Basics Of
Nurturing Guidance
As They Relate To
Companion Parrot Behavior

⮑ All interaction should be trust-building, not trust-destroying.

⮑ *Behavior* is a response to situations (also known as a stimulus) occurring in a companion parrot's life and home environment.

⮑ The foundation established with a young companion parrot by the early caregivers (including the breeder, handfeeders, and new human flock) determines lifelong pet potential.

⮑ Parrots are instinctively wild birds and need our guidance to adjust to life in our living rooms.

⮑ Negative behaviors can be changed if the caregivers have the knowledge to work with their parrots in a positive, consistent, nurturing manner.

⮑ Without positive guidance, parrots will develop substitute behaviors for unsuccessful natural responses. It is the conflict between natural behaviors and an unnatural environment that causes confusion and inappropriate, nonproductive behaviors.

⮑ Parrots are highly empathic and often mirror our energy and mood. Our high energy and/or bad moods can negatively affect a parrot's behavior. Lowering our energy can help the parrot relax and respond to us with less energy.

⮑ Punishment, abandonment, aggression, and quick-fixes destroy trust and are not effective toward changing behaviors in a positive manner.

⮑ We actually teach, or at least encourage, many of the negative behaviors our parrots develop as companions. Many problem behaviors are a reaction to our behaviors.

⮑ A great deal of companion parrot is reactive. If we don't change our behavior towards our parrots, they won't change their behavior.

⮑ Aggressive biting, excessive screaming, phobic fears, behavioral feather picking, and other common companion parrot problem behaviors are symptoms of greater problems. These problems may be that a parrot in control of his life is doing a bad job of it, or that a parrot is not receiving proper emotional and/or physical care. Treating the symptoms with quick-fixes only acts as a distraction and does not teach the bird anything about not biting, screaming, feather picking, or other negative responses.

⮑ Companion parrots can be *drama addicts*, often perceiving any dramatic response, even if it is negative, as a positive reward. We need to be aware of our behavior around our parrots as part of figuring out why they do the things they do.

◌ Parrots are more likely to learn from people and be less aggressive in a *neutral room.* This is an unfamiliar room (or area of the house) where they can not see their cage and where they have not established a sense of territory or need to display territorial protective behavior.

◌ Losing hand control of a companion parrot is the first step in losing tameness. Maintaining the ability to handle a parrot is essential for continued pet potential.

◌ We must establish ourselves as the *flock leaders* in the cage territory and be able to easily take our parrot out of his cage with the "UP" command. If we share the territory as members of the flock, we can avoid aggression due to territoriality.

◌ We must be decisive and assertive with our parrots without being aggressive and overbearing.

◌ We should never force our parrots to do anything that makes them frightened or traumatized, unless it is an emergency situation. We must gradually introduce new objects, people, and situations so they become familiar and acceptable.

◌ It is our responsibility to protect our parrots as much as possible from dangerous and traumatic situations.

◌ We must learn to sort all advice and information with common sense and a cause-and-effect logic. Anticipation and preparation are the best ways to avoid problems and dangerous situations. Think about your parrot's possible response before you do something involving him. (If I do this ... this could happen.)

◌ Establishing a positive lifelong relationship with a parrot requires the person to take responsibility for the parrot's behavioral development.

◌ **Behavioral problems are <u>NEVER</u> the parrot's fault.**

EXPLAINING *THE BRICK WALL* DIAGRAM

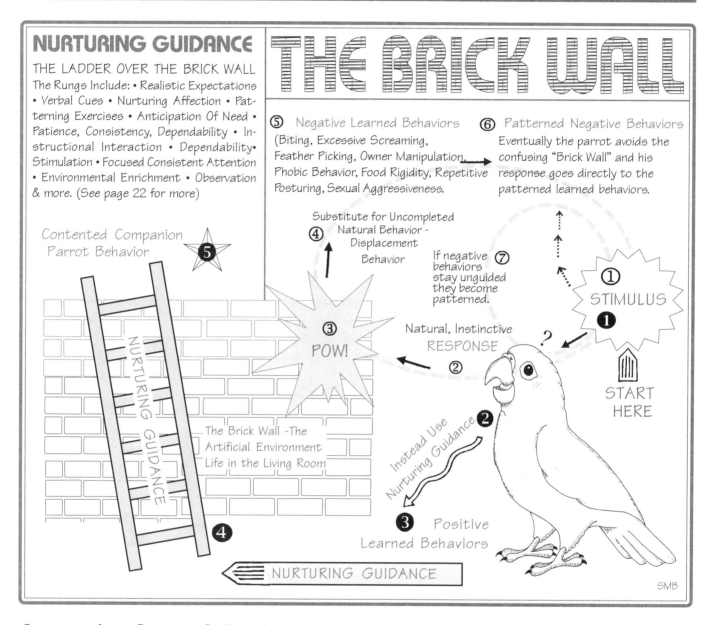

NURTURING GUIDANCE

THE LADDER OVER THE BRICK WALL
The Rungs Include: • Realistic Expectations
• Verbal Cues • Nurturing Affection • Patterning Exercises • Anticipation Of Need •
Patience, Consistency, Dependability • Instructional Interaction • Dependability•
Stimulation • Focused Consistent Attention
• Environmental Enrichment • Observation
& more. (See page 22 for more)

THE BRICK WALL

⑤ Negative Learned Behaviors (Biting, Excessive Screaming, Feather Picking, Owner Manipulation, Phobic Behavior, Food Rigidity, Repetitive Posturing, Sexual Aggressiveness.

⑥ Patterned Negative Behaviors
Eventually the parrot avoids the confusing "Brick Wall" and his response goes directly to the patterned learned behaviors.

Contented Companion Parrot Behavior ⑤

④ Substitute for Uncompleted Natural Behavior - Displacement Behavior

⑦ If negative behaviors stay unguided they become patterned.

① STIMULUS

START HERE

③ POW!

NURTURING GUIDANCE

Natural, Instinctive RESPONSE ②

The Brick Wall -The Artificial Environment Life in the Living Room

Instead Use Nurturing Guidance ②

④

❸ Positive Learned Behaviors

NURTURING GUIDANCE

SMB

Companion Parrot Behavior Without Guidance From People

Behavior is a living organism's response to a stimulus. Some behaviors are instinctive and some are learned. The more developed and intelligent animals are, the more complex their behavior becomes. Since parrots are intelligent animals, it is clear that we can influence their behavior in a positive manner.

① A stimulus occurs. A stimulus is an observed or sensed thing, event, or situation which causes and encourages a response or reaction. A stimulus is rarely simple and may elicit a complex array of reactions. The parrot generally responds along the path of least resistance — responding in an automatic, familiar, patterned manner.

② The instinctively wild, domestically-raised (not domesticated like dogs and cats) parrot reacts with a natural, instinctive response.

③ The natural response is blocked by the "brick wall" (unnatural environment) and cannot be completed as it would in the natural habitat. For example, in the wild, a parrot who is frightened by a predator will either fly away, freeze and hide, or fight. In captivity, the bird can't respond naturally and may throw himself around the cage thrashing in fear. If a person approaches him too aggressively and he can't escape by flying away, he may bite. If biting makes the person go away, this behavior can become patterned as a new learned response.

④ The parrot has to *make up* a new and different reaction as a substitute for the blocked natural response. This is called displacement behavior — an unnatural response when the natural response is not possible. Not all displacement behaviors are negative. For example, the fact that companion parrots are capable of bonding so strongly to their human caretakers is a positive displacement behavior. Many of the play behaviors of companion parrots may also be a displacement for natural foraging behaviors.

⑤ Displacement behaviors are often confused behaviors which cause many of the common problems people have with their companion parrots, including excessive screaming, aggressive biting, and behavioral feather picking.

⑥ If the natural behavior is continually blocked and the displacement behavior *seems* to meet the parrot's needs, the new displacement behaviors will become patterned. As intelligent as they are, parrots still do not understand that these displacement behaviors are not actually creating the optimum situation to get their needs met.

⑦ Once displacement behaviors become patterned, they replace the natural ineffective responses. The parrot has an investment in continuing the behaviors as long as they are rewarded. This is especially true when the bird receives attention (negative or positive) for the patterned behaviors from the people in his *human flock.* Once these new behaviors become automatic, they are more difficult to change.

This whole process results in a continual cycle of confusion for the companion parrot.

If People Establish *Nurturing Guidance,* The Pattern Is Changed

Much of a parrot's behavior and personality depends on early socialization and learning. With a knowledge of *Nurturing Guidance,* people can actually override many of their parrot's natural behaviors, helping the parrot adjust to a life which has little similarity to his natural life. Patterning positive behaviors requires understanding, patience, and consistency. The results are a positive relationship with a companion parrot.

❶ A stimulus occurs. The parrot has been taught new positive responses.

❷ He reacts with his learned positive responses and avoids "crashing into the brick wall" in confusion by heading to the "ladder over the brick wall."

❸ The bird has been guided to positive learned behaviors and "climbs the ladder."

❹ The "rungs of the ladder" nurture and guide the parrot and his behavior.

❺ A well-nurtured bird is a contented companion with generally predictable behaviors.

THE *RUNGS OF THE LADDER*

The Components of *Nurturing Guidance*

⊃ **Realistic Expectations:** Parrots are not easy-care pets. They are intelligent birds with complex behavior which is greatly influenced by their interaction with people. While they can be excellent companions, we must never forget that they are parrots with the special needs of parrots. If people have unrealistic expectations about their behavior and capabilities, they will always be disappointed. When choosing a companion parrot, it is critical to cut through the species stereotypes and generalizations about their behavioral characteristics.

⊃ **Dedication To Learning:** The best parrot owners stay open to learning and remain fascinated by the intricacies of parrots. Companion parrot behavior is a complex jigsaw puzzle with new pieces to put in place all the time.

⊃ **A Strong Human/Parrot Bond:** In order for a parrot to form a strong lasting bond with a person, that person has to have a strong lasting bond with his or her parrot.

⊃ **Rules:** A few basic rules include:
•Use the "UP" command to take a parrot out of his cage.
•A parrot is not allowed to run up his owner's arm to his shoulder.
•A parrot is not allowed to be out of his cage without supervision.
•Greet your parrot when you first come home.
•Say good-bye when you leave the room and let your parrot know you will be back.

⊃ **Verbal Cues and Commands:** These should be simple, clear, and concise.
•Up — Use the "UP" command to ask a parrot to step onto your hand.
•Down — Use the "DOWN" command to ask a parrot to step off of your hand.
•OK — A command to release a parrot from your direct control.
•No — A simple, short command to express immediate disapproval.

⊃ **Instructional Interaction:** Much of the time spent with a companion parrot should be spent teaching, patterning, and rewarding new positive behaviors.

⊃ **Nurturing Authority:** Nurturing is teaching and should be an integral part of parenting and love. Whether it is called dominance or being *flock leader*, the owner needs to establish the authority to guide the parrot's behavior. There is no such thing as a submissive leader.

⊃ **Physical Interaction:** Most parrots are highly social animals who are physically affectionate with each other. Cuddle time, petting, and mutual preening are important elements in keeping a parrot tame.

⊃ **Observation: Eye Contact and Body Language:** In addition to sounds and calls, parrots communicate through eye contact and body language. Pay close attention to what they are telling you. Eye contact is one of the best ways to communicate with your parrot. A soft, loving eye expression (what my friends and I used to call *cow-mooney-eyes* when I was in college) is a very effective way to communicate affection and to calm a parrot. When a parrot misbehaves, an immediate, quick, dirty look is one of the best ways to express disapproval. This *evil eye* should not be maintained for more than a few seconds or it may be interpreted as aggressive confrontation.

⊃ **Lowering Energy:** Parrots reflect our energy and mood. Lowering our own energy is an effective tool to lower the parrot's energy.

⊃ **Patterning Exercises:** Gradually patterning a parrot to accept new situations and objects will help him become more comfortable. The more familiar a parrot is with a particular behavior, the more likely he is to repeat it.

⊃ **Anticipation of Need** (The Parrot's and Yours): Knowing what a parrot will do in a specific situation and either avoiding the situation, or planning it for the maximum welfare of the parrot and the household is important. For example, if you know that your parrot will be frightened when large objects are carried past his cage, keep yourself between the object and the parrot, or cover his cage. If it is something very threatening, move him to another room before the situation occurs.

⊃ **Stimulation:** The wild parrot's natural habitat keeps him busy and alert. For their emotional and physical health, we need to provide companion parrots with activity, exercise, attention, and safe, gradual introduction to new adventures.

⊃ **Social Interaction:** Companion parrots learn through social interaction with their human flock. For example, parrots learn to talk much more readily from people conversing with them appropriately than they do by listening to meaningless repetitive phrases on recordings.

⊃ **Attention:** There are three basic levels of attention:
•Focused/In-Your-Face Attention: Your total attention is focused on the parrot with no distractions.
•Casual Attention: The parrot is with you but you are also reading, watching TV, talking, etc.
•Ambient Attention: The parrot is on his playgym or in his cage and you call back and forth.

⊃ **Positive Personality Traits Of A Successful Parrot Owner:** These include consistency, patience, predictability, dependability, common sense, compassion, a sense of personal responsibility, a calm demeanor, and a dedication to learning. Parrots normally respond well to people with these traits.

⊃ **A Sense of Humor, Fun and Play:** *The more fun the person has, the more fun the parrot has and the more fun the parrot has, the more fun the person has ...* A contented parrot is one of the best forms of entertainment.

⊃ **Environmental Enrichment:** This includes a spacious clean cage with multiple perches, a fun activity-filled playgym, good lighting, clean air, stimulating toys, a nutritious varied diet, and frequent bathing opportunities.

⊃ **Quality Physical and Health Care:** Cause-and-effect prevention of accidents and traumas, proper veterinary care, and medical treatment are essential to a healthy, happy parrot.

"Maybe the cassette tape was not such a great idea after all".

"Want a cracker Want a cracker Want a cracker Want a cracker Want a cracker Want a cracker Want a cracker Want a cracker..."

WHAT IS SOCIALIZATION?

The Process Of Learning

Socialization is the process by which all intelligent young animals learn their social and survival skills. Most parrots, particularly the larger species, are what ornithologists call a K-select species. These birds raise only a few chicks at a time who require extensive long-term parental care as they mature and become independent. The behavioral development of the young parrots is greatly influenced by parental and/or flock guidance. While many of their behaviors are instinctive, the intricacies are most likely learned from example and instruction. Flying may be something that comes naturally to parrots, but it appears that the intricate skills of maneuvering, navigation, and landing are learned from observation and practice. It is certainly natural and necessary for any animal to eat, yet diet specifics, food sources, and techniques of food manipulation are developed as the young parrot watches and learns from the example of his parents and flock until he

"I Know It's A Scary World Out There But I'll Teach You What To Do Until You Get The Hang Of It!"

becomes food independent. The language and calls of the family flock are learned from listening, mimicking, and associating the proper meaning of sounds. Without the ability to reproduce these calls, the chick could not communicate properly with the other parrots. There is evidence that individual flocks even have their own dialects. The finesse of preening technique may be honed from observing adult birds of the same species. Skills to recognize and avoid predators are only partly instinctive. There have been studies which clearly show that the chicks of many birds innately recognize flight silhouettes of predators. Despite this, parrots clearly need to learn many of their skills in avoiding predators from their parents and the flock. Evidence of this is shown in the overwhelming difficulties trying to reintroduce domestically-raised parrots into the natural habitats of their species — few of these birds survived due to predation. The attempt to reintroduce Thick-billed Parrots into Arizona was an example of this difficulty. Without the opportunity to learn flock traditions, the young Thick-billed Parrots became very expensive hawk food.

Flock Traditions

All-important flock traditions are carefully taught and learned by eager young parrots. The closer a young parrot comes to independence, in many ways, the more dependent he is until he becomes secure enough to transition away from parental care. There is constant calling as the chick wanders farther and farther from the parent. Parrots have their own language — calls with specific meaning. It is as if the chicks are asking, "Am I OK?" with the parent answering, "Yes, you are fine!" If there is danger, the youngster is called closer to the security of the flock. Even as adults, because they are prey animals, parrots depend on their flock for safety. There is safety in numbers. Parents instinctively want their chicks to mature and to become independent so they teach them to the best of their ability. If a wild parrot chick does not successfully learn his social and survival skills, he does not survive. If too many offspring of a species don't survive, the continuity of the flock, and even the species, is threatened. If the mortality is consistently higher than the birth rate, the species is doomed and extinction is forever. **THIS IS HOW CRITICALLY IMPORTANT EARLY SOCIALIZATION IS.**

Also Critical For Domestically-raised Parrots

Companion parrots have not yet become domesticated. Parrots will have to be bred in captivity for many, many more generations for us to see enough difference in their genetic makeup for them to be considered domesticated. Domestically-raised chicks come out of the egg with the same complexities of instinctive behavior as their wild counterparts. If eggs laid in captivity were flown down to the rainforest and hatched by the same species in their natural habitat, the young chicks would fit right in with the wild flock. People raising baby parrots must become the surrogate parents, providing them with early socialization, which helps them adjust to life as human companions. Otherwise, parrots respond to what goes on in their lives on an instinctive level, which does not result in getting their needs met. If they have not been taught new behaviors, when their instinctive behaviors are continually blocked, parrots develop displacement behaviors as a substitute. These displacement behaviors come out of confusion, with the results often creating problems such as excessive screaming, aggressive biting, and behavioral feather picking. Signs of poor early socialization may not be readily evident in birds who have not fledged or weaned. Poorly socialized companion parrots begin to exhibit behavioral dysfunction as they mature and reach their independence stages. The socialization process to help baby parrots successfully adapt to life as human companions is just as important to their success as the teaching of flock traditions is to wild parrot chicks.

"I Know It's A Scary World In Here But I'll Teach You What To Do Until You Get The Hang Of It!"

Once, after I gave a bird club program, a critic dismissed socialization as being insignificant. "After all," she said, "if early socialization was so important, there would be thousands of people having serious behavioral problems with their young parrots." She evidently had not noticed that there are, and this was becoming one of the greatest problems facing aviculture. After all, it is satisfied customers who continually encourage a healthy retail market. Far too many people *get rid of* their parrots when they experience the serious behavioral problems that have their origins in production-breeding and poor early socialization.

Education is needed to acquaint people with the complexity of their parrots. The purpose of the <u>Companion Parrot Handbook</u> is to provide the information needed to socialize bappies in a way that prepares them for life as successful human companions in an environment that is totally alien to where they naturally evolved. It is intended as a guide to establishing the *Nurturing Guidance* necessary to develop and maintain long-term pet potential.

SMB

FUN AD *by Sally Blanchard*

(This cartoon advertisement is only for fun and NOT for a genuine product or service.)

BirkenZygos

Comfort Footgear For Parrots Who Are Always On Their Feet
Ergonomically Designed For The Zygodactyl Foot • 100% Natural Supple Leather

Recommend by

Psittacine Podiatry Practitioners

The "Macaw"
The Original
BirkenZygos™
Basic Half Toe
PsittaPeds™

The "Cockatoo"
Thong-Toe
ZygoZandals™

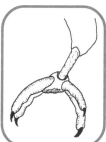

The "Amazon"
Sturdy Ankle High
Full Toe *ZygoBoots*™

The "African Grey"
High-Lace Roman
ZygoZandals™

NEW! "ZygoZlippers"
Winter Weather
Foot Warmers

SMB

Walking, Climbing, Standing Flat Or Perched: Flexi-ProtectaPed™ Arch Support Keeps Its Shape

Nurturing Guidance Tip: Do Your Homework

Impulse Buying

Do your homework before you buy a parrot. Educate yourself first so you choose the right source and the right species. Buying a parrot impulsively or for the wrong reasons may result in unrealistic expectations, disappointment, and a tremendous loss of pet potential in your new bird. Buying a lifelong companion parrot is not a time to be looking for a bargain. The $1,000 parrot you buy from an excellent breeder or bird shop is always a better bargain than the $500 parrot of the same species you find from a questionable source. Not only does poor socialization diminish pet potential, the parrot from the questionable source may require extensive veterinary care exceeding the cost of a bird from the quality source. The extra money spent with a breeder or bird shop concerned with both the physical and psychological development of their chicks is a valuable investment in lifelong pet potential.

A PET PARROT ISN'T FOR EVERYONE

An Easy-care Pet?

Is a parrot the right pet for everyone? Absolutely not!

For the last decade or so the media has been giving the impression that parrots are easy-care pets. Whoever wrote these articles either never lived with companion parrots or, if they did, they didn't know how to properly take care of them. To have a well-behaved parrot who lives a long, healthy life requires remarkable intuition, common sense, and/or a great deal of specialized knowledge.

I am certainly not saying that parrots don't make excellent pets — they can and do all of the time! But ... great companion parrots don't just happen. They are

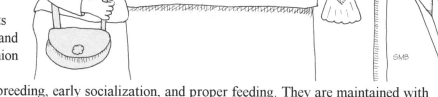

"I just love that little pink and gray one — he matches our drapes so beautifully!"

"Life's Short Bite HARD!"

created with a combination of quality breeding, early socialization, and proper feeding. They are maintained with good parenting and *Nurturing Guidance*. The rewards are worth it if the work is done properly.

Before even considering a parrot, a person should thoroughly research the world of companion parrots, the different species, and their proper care. Everyone who sells parrots has their own particular bias depending on the parrots they love, breed, or sell. If the seller gives advice solely based on what they have available, the recommended bird may not be appropriate for the buyer. Some people who sell parrots are afraid to mention the downside of keeping parrots for fear of losing a sale. They may not mention required veterinary care, or the cost of necessary accessories. The buyer may not hear about how messy and demanding parrots can be. Most of all, the seller may not provide essential information needed by the owner to create positive pet potential, for fear it sounds too complicated.

People who are planning to buy a parrot should talk with people who have parrots, to avian veterinarians, and to breeders about the traits and needs of each species. Unfortunately, much of the parrot information readily available to novices is inaccurate, out-of-date, or based on pet industry "mythology." Many pet industry books contain atrocious information, much of it based on a time when most parrots being sold were wild-caught. Although there are quality pet shops that give excellent information, some still provide information solely based on the profit motive. Joining a local bird club often provides access to a wealth of information, but again some of it may be questionable or biased to special interests. The Internet and World Wide Web can overload a person with so much conflicting information that a novice may have no idea what to believe. It is essential for a prospective bird owner to learn to judge the source and accuracy of information.

Parrots are Messy

Buying and preparing a nutritious, varied parrot diet can be costly and time consuming. But it is an essential ingredient for the health and happiness of a companion parrot. Knowing this, the caring owner slaves *over a hot stove* all morning preparing a gourmet delight for their eagerly nagging parrot. The parrot excitedly runs to the food bowl and takes the first five beakfuls and throws them on the living room carpet. Parrots coevolved with the plants in their habitat which provide them sustenance. In the wild, their messy eating habits sow the seeds of plants for the parrot flock's future generations. Bird owners do not want to cultivate these plants on the living room rug, but that won't deter the parrot from wasting food by flinging it around the house. My African Grey's record for food flinging is about 10 feet. That sticky glob of food landed on my glasses when I was across the room reading. Food flinging should be a sport in the Parrot Olympics. There are logistical ways to get around this — hooded bowls and acrylic partitions can help. Water bottles keep a parrot from making *soup du jour* in his water bowl. A varied, healthy diet is messier than a diet of seed or pellets, but it is also necessary for the physical and emotional health of a companion parrot. It is unfair to deprive a parrot of soft foods just because they are messy. Don't let anyone convince you that parrots are easy-care pets. Just keeping their environment clean requires a lot of work. Cages need to be cleaned every day and scrubbed weekly. Cage paper needs to be changed every day. Bowls need to be scrubbed and disinfected daily. Perches and toys need to be cleaned or replaced frequently.

Poop Machines

I have talked with a number of people who have purchased parrots and returned them within a few days complaining that the birds pooped all of the time. There is no denying it — parrots poop a lot. Whatever they eat goes right through their system, and sometimes comes out in just a few minutes. It is wet and warm but it rarely has any odor. The color will depend on what the parrot has been eating. If parrots are on a good diet with lots of mashes, fresh veggies and fruits, their droppings can be pretty messy. Personally, I don't find parrot poop to be that offensive and it cleans up fairly easily with a paper towel. A discerning person can always tell when a parrot is about to poop. The bird usually gets restless, shifts his weight, squats down a bit and raises his tail. Being observant and fast enough, and keeping a paper towel or a waste basket nearby can usually keep anyone from being soiled. Potty training a parrot is fine as long as the training does not become so rigid that the parrot will not go in his cage or without a command — rigid potty training can cause health problems for parrots (see page 127).

Care Is Expensive

Quality care from an avian veterinarian tends to be expensive, but not because the bird doctor is trying to take advantage of his or her clients. There are several reasons for the expense; one is that avian medicine is so specialized. Quality cages, toys, and accessories can also be expensive, and parrots need a lot of *stuff* in their lives to keep them happy and healthy. A variety of toys help keep a parrot stimulated. Most parrot toys are meant to be destroyed and have to be replaced regularly. Parrots should have at least one sturdy playgym and a portable T-stand. The price of all of these items can add up very quickly.

Behavioral Problems

Even the most compliant, well-behaved, delightful parrot will be a pain in the neck from time to time. I adore Spikey and can't imagine life without his bouncing personality ... but there are times when I think I'd sell him for a quarter. This negativity passes quickly enough and I am again delighted with him, but if I expected him to be on his best behavior at all times I would be pretty disappointed. I recently did a consultation with a woman who had lived with a Blue-fronted Amazon for eighteen years without a single aggressive incident. One day, he bit her viciously. Not only did it cause her physical pain, it hurt her feelings and complete confusion. Luckily, she was committed to working with him. It took about a month for him to settle down and return to his normally loving personality.

Parrots scream ... I don't consider most parrot vocalization and/or screaming to be a problem. However, manipulative excessive screaming for attention becomes problem behavior. Even contented companion parrots scream as a way to communicate. Some can be quite loud when they are letting the world know they are happy to be alive. Some make high-pitched beeps just because it irritates us. Some parrots talk or chatter incessantly. This verbal communication is usually a normal part of being a parrot but may be very annoying to noise sensitive people.

The Right Reason

A **lifetime** is a long time to commit to a parrot but that is the necessary commitment. People shouldn't buy parrots to impress their friends, because they saw a movie with a cute parrot, because parrots have become a fad, or because of their decorative value. Parrots are far too intelligent and gregarious not to be thought of as close companions. Every minute of time and energy spent interacting positively with a companion parrot will be generously rewarded. Like all close relationships, there will be difficult times but they will be worth it.

CHOOSING A PARROT SPECIES

The Importance of the Source

Phoebe Linden, a parrot breeder I have learned a great deal from, once told me that if she was going to give one piece of advice to someone buying a parrot it would be, "Choose a quality source for the parrot first and then buy the healthiest, best socialized, most abundantly fed young parrot they have." I have echoed this message many times. The truth is that the source of the parrot is usually far more important than the species you buy. Even if I really wanted a Blue and Gold Macaw, I would rather buy a properly nurtured Scarlet Macaw bappy than a poorly socialized Blue and Gold. The pet potential of companion parrots is greatly determined by their early development and their physical and emotional health. Any parrot species, from budgie to macaw, can make an excellent human companion if he has been socialized properly as a chick and if the owner establishes and maintains *Nurturing Guidance.*

Black and White Thinking

Many people are attracted to a certain parrot species. Perhaps they want a grey because of his talking ability, but they may shy away from these generally sensitive birds because they hear **all** greys are neurotic and don't like to be cuddled. One woman was totally talked out of buying a grey because the behaviorist she talked to had little or no experience with greys, and therefore, didn't like them. After talking to me at great length, she was confident enough to find an excellent African Grey breeder. People miss the point when they believe stereotypical thinking and generalizations. If they concentrate only on the positive absolutes, such as **all** *greys are excellent talkers,* they are apt to have unrealistic expectations and not appreciate all the other traits that make greys such delightful human companions. If they hear only the negative absolutes, such as **all** *greys are neurotic feather pickers,* they may reject a species that would actually make an excellent companion for them.

There are many generalizations which give a species its reputation. These stereotypes simply do not apply to all the parrots within the species. People may choose an eclectus because of its color and beauty, an Amazon because of its comical reputation, or a cockatoo because they think it will always be a "love sponge." Some people want a macaw because of its mistaken image as a big macho parrot. Others stick with a smaller (and therefore, more manageable?) parrot-family bird because they don't think they could handle a larger parrot. People have been warned about certain species, hearing that they are **all** biters, screamers, are not cuddly, or have an innate tendency to feather pick.

Too Many Personality Generalizations

It is important to realize that there are many generalizations about parrots and there are varying degrees of truth about all of these. Most Amazons can be pretty comical, but the continual warning is that they become aggressive as they mature. Yet, I know a lot of Amazons who have stayed delightfully tame and remain comical and cuddly throughout their lives. While many greys do talk, some do not. Well-socialized greys who have nurturing owners rarely pluck their feathers and some are quite cuddly. Not all cockatoos remain "love sponges." It takes consistent nurturing interaction for many cockatoos to remain predictably loving. Poorly raised cockatoos may grow up and try to chase the whole family around the house. As delightful as they are, some smaller parrots like lovebirds, parrotlets, caiques, and conures can be just as *macho* as any large macaw. In fact, if raised properly, macaws can be one of the most gentle "love sponge" companion parrots. **Regardless of species, the best companion parrots are the ones who have been properly socialized and raised with consistent guidance.**

All Parrots Species Have The Potential

There are far too many black-and-white generalizations about parrot species. All parrots have the potential to be excellent companions. It is their interaction with the human beings in their lives which encourages or discourages that potential. Do your homework before you buy a parrot. Make sure you get accurate information about the species and its potential, but remember that everything you hear is one person's opinion. Before you accept an opinion, try to figure out if the person giving it really has the experience needed to form that opinion for the entire species. I read so many posts from people on the Internet making sweeping generalizations about parrot species — based on the fact that the person has owned one bird, sometimes for less than six months. The opinion is valid for that person's individual parrot but not for all the parrots of that species. I have often heard about a particular breeder or pet shop that has bad-mouthed a certain species of parrot, saying they make horrible pets — often because they don't sell them or had other parrot species they wanted to sell.

Mission Possible

Almost anyone can develop a positive relationship with their parrots if they are have a thirst for knowledge, a modicum of common sense, and are willing to implement quality information in the way they interact with their parrots. In choosing your companion parrot, find an excellent source and buy the healthiest, happiest bappy you can find. Raise him with *Nurturing Guidance* to maintain his lifelong pet potential.

This book is intended to explain how to look for and create quality pet potential with any parrot species. *ƒ*

CAVEAT EMPTOR AVIS

Bird Buyer Beware

Purchase your bappy from a reliable source, whether it is an excellent breeder or a quality pet shop. The seller should be concerned about both the physical and emotional health of their bappies. Unfortunately, there will always be unscrupulous money-oriented people who sell smuggled, stolen, poorly socialized, production-raised, and/or sick, stunted birds. Be careful about any suspicious situation — buying young birds from the back of someone's van or a newspaper advertisement is always suspect, especially species of Mexican origin. Bargain birds are rarely a genuine bargain. I don't usually recommend buying birds at bird shows because of stress and possible disease contagion. However, a bird show may be a place to make contact with a good source for a bappy. Interview the seller — ask for credible references. Ask the questions on pages 36 & 37. Not all quality breeders want people trooping through their aviaries to see the breeding birds. This is justified as there is an incredible number of bird thefts and many breeders don't want their breeding birds upset or exposed to potential disease. *ƒ*

If Parrots Had People For Pets

"After seeing Bobbie, I sure wish I had bought a beak-fed bappy!"

HOW ABOUT AN OLDER PARROT?

Rejecting Some of the Best Parrots

People often reject some of the best parrots available because they have heard a parrot needs to be very young to bond to them. For some reason, the concept of *imprinting* has become embedded in our thinking about parrots. Imprinting implies that birds bond forever to the first living creature they see when they open their eyes. This is one of several reasons many breeders erroneously presume that an incubator-hatched chick who is handfed and raised from day one will make the best human pet. In fact, if that day one chick is not raised with exceptional competency and quality socialization, the parrot may have seriously diminished pet potential. Imprinting suggests that parrots form an unchangeable lifelong bond to the person who nurtures them as a chick. This concept simply does not apply to parrots. The proof is the number of wild-caught adult parrots who formed strong bonds with nurturing people. Parrot bonding is not engraved in stone. These intelligent birds are capable of forming new bonds throughout their entire lives. A parrot comfortably handled and consistently nurtured will usually form a strong bond with their caregiver regardless of the bird's age.

Contrary to the misguided advice which says, "buy an unweaned chick so it will bond," the best parrots on the market are those who are beyond fledging and weaning and have been raised with proper early socialization. Unfortunately, in some situations, pet potential is diminished as young birds are rarely handled after weaning if they are not sold. Knowledgeable people who provide enough nurturing can overcome some of the loss of pet potential due to lack of proper early socialization. If socialization and handling are maintained after weaning, the pet potential continues to develop. An older bappy from a quality shop or breeder where the parrots have been continually nurtured can be an excellent companion, even if he is way past weaning age. One advantage to buying an older parrot is that you may be better able to determine the parrot's personality than with a younger bird.

Parent-raised Chicks

A parent-raised chick is one who has been raised completely by his natural parrot parents. In the past, many wild-caught parrots had been socialized in the wild by their parents before capture. With the proper handling and care, some imported parrots made exceptionally good pets. I believe that a totally parent-raised chick has the potential to be a better human companion than a poorly socialized chick raised by a breeder with *production values*. The captive-bred, parent-raised chick has experienced the parental socialization necessary to his healthy emotional development. The chick raised with a production mentality has not. A parent-raised parrot may need some taming from a knowledgable person who will do the nurturing work needed to win trust in humans. Because of the lack of quality early socialization, the production-raised chick may not have been nurtured (by parrots or people) enough to even develop the long-term ability to trust.

Co-parenting Of Parrot Chicks

Many breeders leave the chicks with the parrot parents for a few weeks and then pull them from the nest for feeding and human socialization. Early parenting from the natural parents usually provides a healthier beginning for a bappy's immune system. More and more breeders are experimenting with actual co-parenting, which involves simultaneous parrot and human parenting. The advantage of this process is that the chick learns skills both from parrots and people. He knows he is a bird, yet is still comfortable with being a human companion. Many people consider this the best of both worlds, but it may not be practical with every chick, every species, and every breeding situation. Normally the parents have to be tame, trusting, and used to being handled by people for this to work. The breeder or handfeeder leaves the chicks with the natural parents but handles them a few times a day for handfeeding and human socialization. In some situations, co-parenting is all one big happy family with successful interactions between the adult parrots, the people, and the chicks. The greatest success with co-parenting seems to be with smaller parrot-family birds such as cockatiels and budgies, and with cockatoos, eclectus, and African greys.

Buying A "Used" Bird

Previously owned parrots are, unfortunately, a growing market. Impulse buying accounts for a large number of bird sales. Too many people "fall in love" and buy their bird on a whim without having any idea what owning a parrot is all about. These people often want to *get rid of* their parrot within the first year when they discover they are in totally over their heads. Some keep their parrots until the birds exhibit major behavioral problems. Unappreciated birds continually show up in pet shops and in the newspaper classified ads. Often the people selling their parrots are angry with the birds and take no responsibility whatsoever. They have determined that all the problems are the parrot's fault, yet some still want to sell their parrots at full value. These people may also deny that their parrots have any behavioral problems in an attempt to sell them for as much money as possible. To make a bad analogy, if a person drove a new automobile out of the car lot and crashed into a telephone pole, they would know the car had lost value immediately. While parrots must always retain their *intrinsic* value, why should they retain their financial value for the people who have ruined them with neglect, lack of guidance, and in some cases, abuse? "Used" parrots from homes where they did not receive quality care or guidance need a knowledgable new owner to straighten them out. I would not recommend these parrots for a novice unless the person is willing to seek excellent information and is dedicated to the parrot no matter how much time and patience it takes to make the necessary changes in the bird's life. I recently worked with the new owners of a screaming, biting, feather picking Nanday Conure who was rescued from a neglectful situation. The bird was about two years old and had been kept in a garage with his cage mostly covered for the last year or so. Armed with good behavioral information on building trust, my clients were able to turn this behavioral nightmare into one of the most delightful characters I have ever met. He is tame and will happily accept attention from almost anyone. He stopped feather picking, biting, and screaming (except for when he just has to let the world know how happy he is to be alive). He is one lucky bird! In other situations, people may have to find a new home for their beloved and well-behaved parrot due to circumstances beyond their control. These parrots have often received quality care. There is usually an adjustment period in the new home, but well-nurtured parrots usually make good pets for the people who buy them, no matter how old they are. I have worked with 40 year old Amazons and other older parrots from several species who transferred their affections to a new person in their life. Patience and *Nurturing Guidance* from the beginning are essential.

Rescue Parrots

Unfortunately, there are more companion parrots in need of a good home than there are good homes for them. This sad truth is becoming more of a reality all of the time. If you have the knowledge, patience, and the inclination to work with an older parrot in need of a good home, I would highly recommend contacting a reputable parrot rescue, adoption, and/or rehabilitation organization. There are several of these organizations with a growing need for more all the time. Many of the parrots adopted out by these organizations need special care and handling. Some are physically or emotionally handicapped. Far too many parrots have been poorly socialized and some have been severely neglected and abused. Some people find it very rewarding to work with emotionally or physically damaged parrots because incredible positive changes are often possible with long-term good care and nurturing.

SHOULD I GET MORE THAN ONE?

Room In Your Heart

If you are thinking of getting more than one or adding a new parrot to your household, the first step is to ask yourself, "Why do I want more than one bird?" If the answer is because you enjoy your first parrot and have both the time and the room in your heart (and house) for another one, then, by all means, go ahead and get another bird. If, on the other hand, you were told by someone that buying a new bird would solve the problems you are having with your first bird, that you need to have another bird to keep your first parrot company, or that it is not fair to keep any parrot as a single pet, then you are being misguided. Getting another bird rarely solves any problems. In fact, it often aggravate the behavioral problems the first bird has. Life with multiple birds is more complex than life with just one because you are not only adding more care time, but you are creating a different set of dynamics in the relationships.

Parrots bond to us primarily because another parrot is not available. In many ways, we are simply a substitute for what would be a normal parrot-to-parrot relationship. Because parrots form a strong bond with people, they make desirable companions, but the bond is also the reason for some of the problems people have with parrots. Remember that parrots, even if they are domestically-raised, are not domesticated animals. They still operate with basically the same instinctive behaviors that work for them in the wild. With rules and guidance established by a caring owner, a parrot can become well-adjusted to life as a human companion. Without rules and guidance, the parrot's life can be very confusing because of the conflict between natural behaviors and life as a pet. The more guidance owners provide for each parrot, the more likely all of the parrots in a multiple bird home are to stay bonded to their human caregivers. Before you even consider buying another parrot, make sure you are providing quality emotional and physical care for the first one.

Compatibility Or *Combatibility?*

Buying another parrot to provide a friend for the first one may not always work. Some parrots turn out to be more *combatible* than they are compatible. Some birds in a multiple parrot household will simply not like each other. They will not exhibit compatibility no matter how much the owner wants them to like each other. Some incompatible parrots will ignore each other as if they don't exist, while others will fight. Care must be taken that these *combatible* birds do not interact physically with each other. I always advise that each companion parrot should have his own cage so that the primary bond remains with the human flock. Usually, there is little harm in allowing birds to play on the same gym if they get along. Don't leave them together unless you are absolutely certain they are compatible. Unless you provide consistent *Nurturing Guidance* plus exceptional and individual focused attention, two parrots housed in the same cage will usually form a strong bond with each other and may not stay tame to the people in their lives.

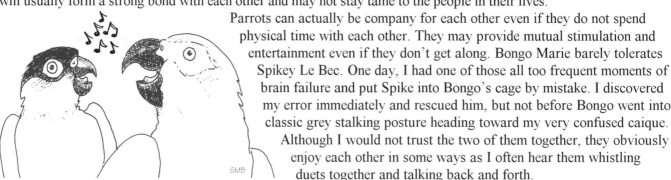

Parrots can actually be company for each other even if they do not spend physical time with each other. They may provide mutual stimulation and entertainment even if they don't get along. Bongo Marie barely tolerates Spikey Le Bec. One day, I had one of those all too frequent moments of brain failure and put Spike into Bongo's cage by mistake. I discovered my error immediately and rescued him, but not before Bongo went into classic grey stalking posture heading toward my very confused caique. Although I would not trust the two of them together, they obviously enjoy each other in some ways as I often hear them whistling duets together and talking back and forth.

Multiple Bonding: Parrots and Humans

Simply because companion parrots form strong bonds with the people in their lives does not mean that they can't bond to other people and other birds on some level. There are many situations where two birds who relate to each other can still remain good human companions. The key is to know when this is possible and when it will create problems. With multiple birds, a caregiver has to work harder to develop and maintain his position of "flock leader." People who do not set rules and provide the guidance for their birds to remain bonded to them will have a difficult time with multiple birds, especially as the birds reach sexual maturity. Most parrots are flock birds who will form bonds of varying degrees to several other members of their group. However, the most intense bonds are with their mates, especially during breeding season. At this time, most wild parrots form strong pair bonds that exclude other birds from their nesting territory. If companion parrots are allowed to form strong bonds with each other, people may experience aggressive behavior from the birds when they become sexually mature, especially during breeding season. This is particularly true of birds of the same species and opposite sex, and most frequently seen when parrots are paired together in the same cage. When establishing a multiple parrot household, it is important to ask yourself if you want to be a breeder. If the answer is yes, then providing parrots with partners of the same species and opposite sex is the right thing to do. However, if you really want to maintain a close relationship with companion parrots, pairing is not advisable. Many people who have sweet young parrots do not realize that they may lose a great deal of that tameness if their bappies are allowed to bond strongly to other birds as they mature.

Every time I address this topic, I get letters from people who tell me that their birds are the exception, that they birds stay tame despite being housed with other birds and despite the formation of strong bonds. It is important to realize that these situations are exceptions, usually true only because the owners have worked diligently with each parrot to create one big happy flock. Just as with people, parrots are certainly individuals, and generalizations are not always true. However, it may be easier for certain species (such as budgies, cockatiels, eclectus and some cockatoos) to co-habitate without serious problems, while others (such as Amazons and macaws) have a tendency to form more intense bonds and be more protective of their perceived territory and mate. Another generalization that may be true (but not always) is that two males of the same species may be more aggressive if housed together while females of many species tend to be more compatible if kept in the same cage. In certain parrots, such as eclectus and some of the *Psittacula* species, the opposite may be true.

Addicted To Parrots?

Too many people let their enthusiasm run away with them and end up buying several bappies — one right after another. After all, most baby parrots are compliant and seem to present few behavioral problems for their owners. Unfortunately, these people rarely realize that as their parrots mature and go through various developmental stages, each parrot will present unique and, in many ways, difficult, challenges. With multiple parrots of the same age, these challenges may become overwhelming for the parrot owner. It is better to start out slow with a realistic knowledge of what lies ahead.

How Many Is Too Many?

The answer to this question depends on the life-style and dedication of the people who have the parrots. As a generalization, I think 2-3 companion parrots is the most the average person can manage and still give them what each needs. Many more than that and each parrot may not get the care and focused attention he or she needs. There are, of course, exceptions but it is important to know first if you are really the exception and not get in so far over your head that your parrots suffer.

"C'mon Honey! One more couldn't be that much more work for you?"

QUESTIONS TO ASK

THE INTELLIGENT PARROT PURCHASE

Sadly, it often seems as if some people give more thought to buying a new automobile or refrigerator than they do to buying a lifelong companion parrot. Almost all baby parrots are cute and sweet, but they may not stay that way if they have not been socialized and handfed with individual concern and respect. The homework you do choosing a breeder or a pet shop is essential toward determining the pet potential of the parrot you buy. Make an intelligent parrot purchase and interview breeders and pet shops before you buy a companion parrot. The following are some of the questions you should ask the breeder or pet shop owner or manager:

➲ HOW MUCH ATTENTION DO YOU GIVE YOUR BABIES?

The answer should be "lots," but it should be qualified with explanations of how the breeder encourages exploration and teaches the babies to accept change and new adventures. Stay away from breeders who say, "I don't pay any attention to my babies when I feed them because I don't want them to bond to me and/or I don't want to spoil them." Babies need frequent handling, instructional interaction, and attention. This kind of nurturing does not spoil them. Breeders with this attitude are ignorant about socialization and a chick's psychological development. Parrots are capable of bonding on many levels to many different people throughout their lives. Even if a baby has bonded to the breeder/handfeeders, well-socialized bappies easily transfer that bond to any nurturing buyer who is comfortable handling them. I believe that all handfed baby parrots should be taught to step on a person's hand before they are sold as a human companion. The minimal time it takes to teach this basic skill is well worth the added pet potential.

➲ AT WHAT AGE DO YOU WEAN YOUR BABIES?

The answer should be, "It depends on the individual bird." Parrots who are forced to wean to a rigid timetable with no regard for their individual needs can experience serious traumas which may cause insecurities and eventual behavioral problems. Weaning is a gradual process where handfeedings are gradually replaced by the young parrot eating on his own. *Deprivation* is instinctively equated or experienced by the bappy as *starvation*. Parrots should not be forced to eat on their own. This will not wean them any sooner. In fact, parrots who are fed abundantly wean sooner and more securely. Just because a parrot has started eating on his own does not mean he is weaned. True food independence may take weeks, or even months for the larger macaws, after a parrot starts to eat anything on his own. Because of possible insecurities from relocation, even a weaned baby may need special feedings of hand held food when he goes home with his new family.

➲ DO YOU SELL UNWEANED BABIES?

The answer should be "No." In some cases, if the breeder provides extensive on-the-job handfeeding instructions to a competent buyer and remains available for questions at all times during the handfeeding and weaning process, buying an unweaned bird *may* be acceptable. If you have no experience handfeeding baby parrots, you have no business buying an unweaned baby and trying to feed it yourself. The myth that a parrot won't bond to you if you don't hand feed it is nonsense. Parrots are capable of bonding and rebonding throughout their lives and a parrot develops a strong bond with anyone who handles him in a nurturing comfortable manner. Inexperienced handfeeders may starve babies, puncture the throat or crop, cause infections, burn the crop, aspirate the baby, cause mortality, and create traumas which can destroy pet potential. The handfeeding process should be left to the experts.

⊃ DO YOU ROUTINELY GAVAGE (TUBE) FEED YOUR BABIES?

The answer should be "No." Gavage feeding involves inserting a tube down the chick's throat and pumping the formula directly into the crop. Usually this practice indicates that the breeder raises more chicks than can be socialized properly. While handfeeders should know how to tube feed in case of illness or emergency, gavage feeding for expediency is non-nurturing. This unnatural method of feeding does not teach a bappy anything about eating and the manipulation of foods. Many gavage-fed parrots experience weaning traumas which can result in serious behavioral insecurities as they mature. Another non-nurturing method of feeding is called power-feeding. This technique forces food into the back of the throat and crop using a syringe. Normal syringe-feeding, spoon-feeding, bottle-feeding, and/or finger-feeding soft globs of warm food are far more acceptable methods for nurturing developing bappies.

⊃ ARE YOUR CHICKS ROUTINELY INCUBATOR HATCHED?

The answer should be "No," except with parents who routinely damage their eggs, maim their chicks, or don't raise their chicks successfully. Incubator hatching involves taking freshly-laid eggs from the parents and placing them in a temperature/humidity controlled environment until they hatch. There is absolutely no contact with the parents. There is evidence that chicks are much healthier if they are initially raised by their natural parents and then pulled after a few weeks for hand-raising and feeding. Chicks left with their parents develop a stronger immune system and show healthier physical and emotional development than do incubator hatched chicks.

⊃ DO YOU LET YOUR CHICKS FLEDGE?

"Yes" is the best answer, but not all sellers have the facilities to do this. Chicks who are allowed to fly even for a short time before their wings are gradually trimmed are more secure and independent than those who never fly.

⊃ WHAT FOODS DO YOU WEAN YOUR BABIES TO?

The answer should be "a variety of foods including pellets, vegetables, fruits, nutritious soft mixtures or mashes, a small amount of seed." A seed-only diet is a "death" diet because seed lacks many of the nutrients essential to parrot health. Do not believe the pet industry propaganda that any seed mix (even if it is vitaminized) is a nutritious, balanced, or complete diet. Parrots learn about their lifelong foods when they learn to eat. It is generally difficult to get parrots weaned to a narrow diet (seed or pellet only) to eat other foods as they mature.

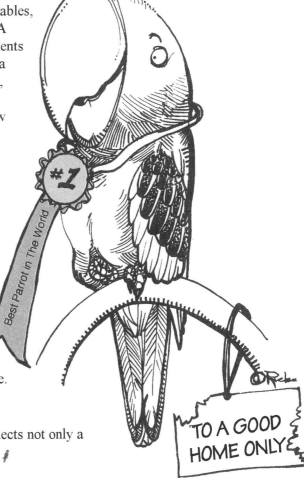

⊃ WHAT INFORMATION ARE YOU WILLING TO PROVIDE ME ABOUT MY NEW BAPPY?

A concerned seller will want to provide you with good information for the care of your new parrot. Because you can't learn everything from them, they will direct you to sources for quality information. They will also recommend a competent veterinarian with knowledge about parrots.

⊃ WHAT DO YOU WANT TO KNOW ABOUT ME?

A quality breeder or pet shop will want to know about the kind of home their babies will be going to. They are proud of the bappies they raise and want them to go to the best home possible.

⊃ WHY DO YOU RAISE PARROTS?

Throw this one in for fun and hope for a genuine answer that reflects not only a love of parrots but a respect for their physical and emotional needs. ⨍

EMOTIONALLY HEALTHY BAPPIES

Curiosity And Exploration

Emotionally healthy chicks exhibit curiosity and have a well-developed sense of exploration. They want to be a part of what is going on around them. If well-socialized bappies are approached calmly in a nonthreatening manner, they should react without fear. There is a difference between initial shyness and excessive fear. A well-socialized chick may show initial shyness but will still be inquisitive about what is going on in the environment.

Poorly socialized parrots seem insecure and withdraw from unfamiliar situations. In some cases, they may fling themselves around and act as if they fear for their lives. In others, they may just seem blank and uninvolved.

Either On Or Off

Emotionally healthy baby parrots play with great energy and intensity but when it is nap time, they usually *crash* just as hard. Nap time is not usually the best time to judge the emotional health of a bappy. At this time, most will seem like real duds with no interest in being around people at all.

Do not judge young parrots by whether they immediately take to you or not. In my teens, I got to pick out the family puppy and chose the one who excitedly waddled over to me, climbed in my lap, and then peed on me.

"Look Ma ...
No Hands!"

Unlike puppies, even well-socialized, friendly bappies may not take to strangers immediately (although they may poop on you). I have been told about buyers who unrealistically rejected extremely well-socialized young parrots because they did not feel there was an immediate bond.

These folks were missing the point. It is not normally in a parrot's natural makeup to bond quickly. A well-socialized chick may delight in attention but he may also attempt to bite a person who picks him up too aggressively or, in the case of novices, too awkwardly. While he may be curious about a person, a real bond takes time, patience, and trust to develop.

Emotionally healthy baby parrots are very responsive to the mood of the people around them and calm down around people who are comfortable with them.

Make friendly eye contact with the chicks. Most well socialized baby parrots are not threatened by a friendly gaze. Look for a strong sense of security and independence — a young parrot who is *full of himself*. Well-socialized youngsters will certainly appreciate attention and affection but will also be happy entertaining themselves with new toys. A few years ago, I spent an afternoon with a young Moluccan cockatoo who had been raised with positive social interaction and *Nurturing Guidance*. The bappy was very content just sitting on her playgym manipulating her toys, but if I wanted to give her a hug, she was more than happy to accept it. She was secure enough not to be needy.

If new objects, people, and situations are introduced in a nonthreatening manner, emotionally healthy bappies do not react to them as if the world is full of alien predators.

Bappies who are doing a lot of food begging may not have been fed abundantly or weaned properly. Food begging consists of whining, crying or repetitive *gronking*, rocking back and forth, flicking of the wings, and excessive head bobbing. These are signs that a chick is hungry and, in some cases, insecure. If you visit the breeder or pet shop just before feeding time, you will probably see some of these behaviors in the bappies. Normal food begging behavior from otherwise healthy chicks should not be a problem. However, if the babies are frantic and act like this all of the time, even after they have been fed, this is excessive food begging. Excessive food begging is a sign of a serious problem. Some poorly fed chicks continue food begging either because they are not getting enough to eat, the food source is not providing adequate nutrition, or they are desperate for handling.

Pay Close Attention To The Seller

With some baby parrots, it will be difficult to determine if they have received proper socialization by just interacting with them for a short time. The signs of poor early socialization may be very subtle in some young bappies. Serious behavioral dysfunction in intelligent animals usually does not show up until babies start to reach their independence stages. How many human babies seem like juvenile delinquents at 6 months or even 2 years of age? Some medium-sized parrots do not start to show signs of serious behavioral problems until they are about 6 months to a year old.

You may actually get a better sense of what is going on by spending time visiting with the breeder. However, I have talked with quite a few breeders who *talk the talk* and profess to be caring but don't actually do what they say. I think a better gauge is watching how they actually relate to their bappies. Listen to the way the seller talks about their bappies and pay close attention to the way they interact with and handle them. It is important for them to love the chicks they raise, but it is more essential for them to respect the babies and their complex needs for proper early development.

An ethical seller will probably want to know all about you before they sell you one of their beloved bappies. If the baby has established a comfortable bond with the person who has raised him, he will easily transfer that bond to you within a few days after you bring him home.

Unfortunately, ordering parrots from an advertisement in the back of a magazine seems to be a popular way to buy birds. The more credible an ad seems — the bigger or cuter the ad is — the more assured some people are that they will be getting a physically and emotionally healthy bird. It doesn't usually work that way. Even I have been fooled into thinking some breeders I talked to on the phone were sources for healthy, happy parrots, only to find out I was wrong. I would never recommend buying a bird sight unseen unless you also have recommendations from credible sources who have no hidden agenda. I personally know of several quality breeders whom I would recommend buying from sight unseen because I know these breeders do an excellent job.

Do your homework before you buy a bappy. Buy from a quality source — it DOES make a tremendous difference in your pet's pet potential. ✦

PHYSICAL HEALTH

Careful Examination

Your new parrot's physical health at the time of his purchase can play an important part in both his physical and emotional development. Sick bappies may miss out on the nutrients needed for healthy normal growth. They may also spend so much time in survival mode they miss out on a great deal of the learning needed for successful socialization. Carefully examine a parrot before you buy him.

This section may also be very helpful in evaluating indications of health throughout your parrot's entire life. Remember that many birds hide their illness as a survival strategy so symptoms may not be immediately obvious unless you are paying close attention. Parrots **do** show signs of illness before they become seriously ill, but we have to observe our parrots carefully on a daily basis so we know what is normal and what is not. Any physical symptoms or change in normal behavior warrants a trip to an avian veterinarian. The vast majority of bird diseases are not self-limiting (as with humans and the flu or a cold). This means parrots will not get better without proper medical treatment.

The following should help you determine whether the young parrot you are looking at is a healthy bappy or not:

⊃ **Watch his energy level.** An emotionally and physically healthy parrot chick is energetic, robust, and ready to go unless it is just after feeding or nap time when he usually sleeps soundly.

⊃ **Check the chick's posture.** If it is not nap time, fluffed feathers, and a drooping head can indicate a health problem. Many bappies have not yet developed their balance skills so they may still be quite clumsy, but frequent loss of balance, sitting with feet far apart, or an inability to perch should be questioned.

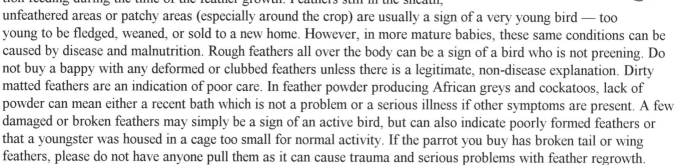

Nap Time

⊃ **Check the feathers carefully.** The *virgin* feathers on a baby parrot are usually the most beautiful — soft, bright and velvety. Feathers should be clean and shiny without streaks, breaks, holes, and discoloration. Breaks in the feather growth and discolorations can be a sign of malnutrition, illness, use of antibiotics, or deprivation feeding during the time of the feather growth. Feathers still in the sheath, unfeathered areas or patchy areas (especially around the crop) are usually a sign of a very young bird — too young to be fledged, weaned, or sold to a new home. However, in more mature babies, these same conditions can be caused by disease and malnutrition. Rough feathers all over the body can be a sign of a bird who is not preening. Do not buy a bappy with any deformed or clubbed feathers unless there is a legitimate, non-disease explanation. Dirty matted feathers are an indication of poor care. In feather powder producing African greys and cockatoos, lack of powder can mean either a recent bath which is not a problem or a serious illness if other symptoms are present. A few damaged or broken feathers may simply be a sign of an active bird, but can also indicate poorly formed feathers or that a youngster was housed in a cage too small for normal activity. If the parrot you buy has broken tail or wing feathers, please do not have anyone pull them as it can cause trauma and serious problems with feather regrowth.

⊃ **Look at the skin and crop.** Skin areas should be smooth and supple with good color. Gently move the feathers apart to check the skin on the crop at the upper breast; discoloration, and a scaly, hard, or scarred area can be a sign that the crop was burned during handfeeding.

⊃ **Watch the bappy's breathing.** Normal breathing should be relaxed and barely noticeable. After a period of high activity, normal breathing will resume within less than a minute or so. If the breathing stays labored or rapid, with increased tail pumping and wheezing, or whistling in the breath, the bird is likely to have compromised health. With extreme stress there may be a "thunking" sound in the breathing.

⊃ **Check the weight.** Feel the keel bone in the middle of the upper breast. Although it is true that a chick may lose weight before fledging and during the weaning process, he will still have a healthy weight. A sunken breast with a sharp keel bone is usually a sign of an underfed chick. However, there is a great deal of difference between the breast area of different species. For example, a well-fed Amazon will be more rotund than a well-fed cockatoo.

⊃ **Look carefully at the eyes.** Eyes can provide an excellent indication of a parrot's health. If the bappy is playing and full of energy, his eyes should be shiny, bright, and alert. Dull, lifeless, *half-mast* eyes during activity are signs of a sick bird. The eyes of tired, napping bappies will often be half shut with the lower lid coming up to meet the upper lid. This is not a problem, especially if a fully satiated baby becomes sleepy after feeding. However, half-mast eyes in an active bird are usually a sign of a health problem. Swollen, puffy, red eyes, a teary discharge, matted feathers around the eyes, and frequent kicking at the eyes with the foot are signs of an infection. Bulging eyes may be a sign of a stunted baby.

⊃ **Check the cere and nostrils.** The soft area above the beak, the cere, should be soft and fleshy with clear, round, and well-formed nostrils. In some parrots, the nostrils are covered with feathers, in others the cere is naked. There is a little piece of flesh in each nostril that may look like a small seed — it is normal. Any redness, clogging, or discharge can be a sign of an infection. Beak grooves running from the cere or misshapen nostrils can be a sign of a chronic respiratory problem.

⊃ **Look at the vent.** This is the *all-purpose* opening where the combined body wastes come out of the parrot. The skin and feathers around the vent should be clean. The area should not be soiled or pasted with wet or dried droppings. Missing feathers around the vent may be a sign of a chronic problem.

⊃ **Check the droppings.** Parrot droppings have three components: 1) the toothpaste consistency fecal matter in the center which may be a greenish color or the color of whatever the bird has been eating; 2) the urates which are usually just a little more moist than the fecal matter; and 3) the surrounding liquid wastes called urine. A bappy who has been weaned to a varied, nutritious diet will have droppings that reflect the various foods the bird has been eating. Healthy droppings do not necessarily look like the classic *alien fried egg* photos in many books. For example, yams and carrots may create a brownish-orange dropping, beets and berries make the poop reddish, and broccoli droppings are green. Fruit and some veggies can cause droppings that reflect their liquid content. These are wetter than normal but still healthy. Droppings that are excessively watery or contain undigested food matter may be a sign of a problem. Droppings in which the normally-white urates appear pasty and lime-greenish can be an indication of psittacosis (chlamydia). Any consistent change in droppings not related to food intake should be discussed with an avian veterinarian as soon as it is noticed.

⊃ **Check wings, body, legs, and toes.** Look for bruises, scrapes, swellings, lumps, or bumps. Make sure the chick has full range of motion with his legs and wings. If a baby is still resting his weight on his ankles and not on his feet, he is too young to purchase.

⊃ **Recognizing stunted birds.** Check the size of the head and feet in proportion to the body. Undernourished, poorly-fed parrot chicks who have been weaned too soon usually have heads and feet that are out of proportion to their bodies. Feathering is usually sparser than with other parrots of the same species and the same age. The bird may look unbalanced and top-heavy. Their eyes are bulgy. They are often dehydrated and their skin may be reddish in color and not as supple as a well-nourished chick. This is more apt to happen with incubator hatched, day-one handfed chicks, especially the large macaws. These undernourished chicks usually end up underdeveloped both mentally and physically, and often have continuing health problems. Parrots who are at least partly raised by their natural parents are less likely to be stunted.

⊃ **Rescuing a sick parrot.** Many people have a tendency to want to help parrots in bad situations. While admirable in many ways, rescue often perpetuates the sale of poorly cared for parrots. The disreputable seller will usually just replace the sick bird sold with another sick bird to be sold to someone else — too often a person who has no idea what a sick bird looks like.

On the other hand, a parrot may have some health problems that a reputable seller will be totally honest about. If the seller works something out with you because he or she knows you will do the right thing by the parrot, buying a bird with a solvable problem which is not life-threatening may be the right thing to do. Just make sure that you understand what the problem is and can afford the veterinary care and time required to improve the parrot's health. ∮

FUN AD *by Sally Blanchard*

(This cartoon advertisement is only for fun and NOT for a genuine product or service.)

T-Joy Parrot Products Introduces Their New
POLLY PORTA POTTY

Are you tired of indiscriminate droppings throughout your house?
Are your dry cleaning bills *for the birds* because of the birds?
Is your parrot too shy to evacuate without privacy in public?
Does your parrot need a comfort station when you travel?

❱ Easy Grip Carrying Handle
❱ Pressure Activated Talking Comfortagrip™ Perch
  Says "Go-potty" when bird steps on
  "Good-birdie" when bird steps off
❱ Self-contained self-cleaning patented Scatray™
  Saniflushes with Bioergonomic Fresh Pine Scent
  (Can be attached to existing home plumbing)
❱ Decorative parrot head Peek-a-potty™ viewer
  Front and back windows
❱ Comes in three sizes for all pet birds
  Extra tall for birds with crests
  Extra wide for tail wagging
❱ Privacy door —
  Macaw size has opening in back for added tail length
❱ Contains specially designed play objects
  to occupy parrots who procrastinate
❱ Dual side roof air flow filtration ventilation system
❱ Constructed from Indestructible Space Age materials
❱ Five exterior designs:
  Victorian, Hacienda, Ranch, Cape Cod & Taj Mahal

SMB

☽ HALF MOON DIVISION ☾
T-Joy Parrot Products

Nurturing Guidance Tip: Gentle Handling

Predator And Prey

Don't ever let anyone handle your parrot in an aggressive manner. Aggressive handling results in a loss of trust which damages the parrot/human bond. Even if you are not present during mishandling, the parrot may still develop a negative response towards you and the other people in his life. Always remember that parrots are prey animals and anyone who threatens their sense of security with aggressive handling may be perceived as a predator. Once the parrot develops this type of response towards people, it is essential for his human flock to approach him slowly and indirectly with great patience until he begins to relax and accept attention from people again. (Please see page 189 for more information on phobic behavior.)

While a veterinarian will most likely have to do examinations, testing, and/or procedures which will make your parrot uncomfortable or even cause him pain, the general atmosphere should always be one which is protective and benevolent towards the parrot.

THE FIRST AVIAN VETERINARIAN VISIT

A PRE-EXAM FEEDING TIP

If your new parrot is eating pellets and soft foods such as mashes, vegetables, and fruits, it is a good idea to feed him only pellets the night before and morning you take him in for his veterinarian visit. If he will only eat the soft foods in the morning, then go ahead and feed them so he does not go hungry. While most soft foods are very healthy and should be fed on a regular basis, sometimes they will create a higher bacteria level in the mouth which may not give your vet an accurate appraisal of whether or not your bird has a bacterial infection. Most avian veterinarians are aware of this but some are not.

Almost all food has some bacteria in it, but if the parrot has a healthy immune system and has been on a good diet, potentially harmful bacteria in small amounts will pass right through the system and not build up to harmful levels. Too many young parrots are routinely and sometimes prophylactically placed on antibiotics. Ask to make sure your parrot actually has a problem that needs to be treated.

The First Thing You Should Do

Even if your weaned bappy seems healthy to you and the seller says he is fine, it is an excellent idea to establish a relationship for him with an avian veterinarian. The cost of the first visit to the veterinarian should be considered just a part of the money you will spend on a new companion parrot. It is impossible for us to know if a bird has a health problem by just looking, so an expert eye will help determine what tests need to be run. For example, if new parrot owners are concerned that their baby is sleeping too much, they may be reassured by another bird owner that baby parrots normally sleep a lot. But when does "a lot" become "too much" and what are the signs of a sick bird? It is always a good idea for new parrot owners to get an expert perspective on the health of their new babies. Don't let your veterinarian get away with saying, "Gee, he looks fine to me." This is a disservice to both you and your parrot. Even if he looks and proves to be healthy, basic tests create a basis for his new doctor to determine what his normal results are for future reference.

Although they may not be willing to share the details, some avian veterinarians may determine how extensive their testing needs to be according to where you bought your parrot. Most veterinarians are aware of the general health of birds sold by the various pet shops and breeders in their area.

Your vet should start by asking you a lot of questions about all aspects of your parrot's purchase and care. You should mention anything that concerns you, whether you think it sounds silly or not. Let your veterinarian know that you want to know what is going on and are concerned about the health of your parrot. Many people seem afraid to ask simple questions for fear they will seem stupid, but some seemingly silly questions have very important answers. Your veterinarian should ask you about the diet your parrot is on and how much he is eating. Be prepared to provide details about special treats and supplementation. Hopefully, you have taken along the paper from the cage bottom so the vet can observe the consistency and number of droppings over a 24 hour period.

The next step is careful examination of his entire little body, including eyes, nares, beak, mouth, and vent. The vet should check feather condition and palpate the chest and belly. The particular tests a veterinarian will run during a first visit checkup may vary. Avian medicine is changing all the time and more accurate diagnostic tests are becoming available. Most avian veterinarians will start with:

1) CBC — a blood count,

2) a basic chemistry panel, and

3) gramstains and cultures

Some veterinarians routinely test for psittacosis (chlamydia), PBFD (Psittacine Beak and Feather Disease), and aspergillosis depending on the part of the country you inhabit. If there is an indication of any problem, they may want to run other tests to determine what the causes may be. The Polyoma vaccine is available now and as avian medical research tackles more parrot diseases, as with other companion animals, more vaccines will become available to help guarantee the health of your parrot.

Remember, you are ultimately in control of what happens to your parrot at the vet's office. Don't try to save money by skipping essential care for your parrot's health at the veterinarian. While there may be some veterinarians who overtreat with little respect for your pocketbook, the majority are quite fair in their treatment of both your parrot and your checkbook. This is not to say that avian medicine is not expensive. It is, at least partly because the testing and procedures are so specialized, and mostly because there are not nearly as many parrots as there are dogs and cats.

If Your Parrot Is Sick And/Or Needs Treatment

Take an active interest in what is going on. Ask questions and expect answers to be given in a manner which helps you understand what is happening with your parrot. If you don't understand, ask the veterinarian to explain it from a less technical viewpoint. If antibiotics are prescribed, be sure to find out why they are needed. Antibiotics should not be prophylactically or routinely given unless there is an actual or strongly-indicated infection to be treated. Ask about any special care you should be providing your parrot if there is a problem. Should any treatment be started before the test results are back? Will there be any side effects from the examination, treatment, or medicines your vet has prescribed? Several years ago, I took a rescued parrot to the veterinarian late on a Friday afternoon. That evening, fresh, red blood was coming from her vent — not a lot but enough to cause me to worry. My veterinarian was not available so I took her to an emergency vet clinic. Unfortunately, they knew very little about parrots. They examined her and ran some tests. I was there until past midnight and the examination and tests cost me over $100. Neither of us realized at the time that, sometimes, when a cloacal swab is taken just inside the vent, it is not uncommon for the area to bleed a little bit. I sure wish I had known that before I left the vet's office.

"So Angel, all we need now is a cloacal swab."

"Gee, she's smiling. It must be fun!"

Make sure that before you leave the examining room you clearly understand what is expected of you if any medications or specific treatments are required. If you need to medicate your parrot, ask your veterinarian or one of the technicians to show you how to properly administer oral or injectable medication. If you get home and are confused or unsure of what you are supposed to do, call and ask again. Write the information down so you can reference your notes. Giving your parrot some types of medicine through injection may actually be easier, more efficient and, in some cases, safer than medicating the bird orally.

If you are apprehensive about medicating your parrot, ask if there is someone qualified in your area who can help you until you get the hang of it.

Ask if there will be any side effects from the examination or treatment. Follow the treatment to the letter. Ask what you should expect to see with your parrot as the treatment progresses? What conditions could occur which should alarm you enough to bring the bird back immediately? Should you be giving supplements to support the bird's body from the effects of antibiotics? Don't stop giving medication just because the bird starts to look better — antibiotics are not effective unless the treatment cycle is completed. Be sure to schedule a follow-up visit to make sure your parrot has gotten over what he was being treated for.

Most bird diseases are not self-limiting — parrots won't just get better with time. Never give your pet bird any over-the-counter pet shop medications (such as diarrhea or cold remedies). Besides being ineffective, these products can be very dangerous because they may disguise an actual illness in such a way that your veterinarian will have no way to know what is really wrong with your parrot.

How About Your Veterinarian's *Perch Side* Manner?

The best veterinarians are aware of how traumatic aggressive handling can be to a companion parrot, but some are not. While a vet will most likely have to do examinations, testing, and/or procedures that will make your parrot uncomfortable or even cause him pain, the general atmosphere of the veterinarian's office should be protective and benevolent. You have a right to supervise the handling of your avian companion. However, parrots readily pick up their owner's energy, so if you are extremely apprehensive about what is being done, it may be best that you are not in the room for examination, tests, and treatment. Some procedures may be done in an area which may not accommodate you, but you have every right to know what is going to happen to your parrot. Make it clear that you do not want anything done with your bird without your approval. One client told me how angry he was when his veterinarian pulled out several broken tail feathers on his young macaw during a routine examination — without his approval.

If you believe the handling of your parrot is too aggressive, you have the right to request that he is handled more gently. Communicate your concerns with your veterinarian. If they will not listen, you may need to look for another avian veterinarian. While a good *perch side* manner is not necessarily evidence of a veterinarian's skill in diagnosing and treating his avian patients, needless traumatic handling can cause some serious problems for your parrot. If your parrot is traumatized by handling, it is best to go slow with him to let him calm down for at least a few hours after you get him home, then approach and handle him very slowly and gently. Parrots are prey animals which means that aggressive or traumatic handling may cause an extreme fear response. If he has gone into "prey mode," you may need to behave very submissively with him so he will not be afraid of you (See page 189 for information on preventing and dealing with phobic behavior).

You can help your avian veterinarian by working with your parrot at home to get him used to being handled in a towel (see page 102). If you can towel your parrot in a friendly manner and then pass him to your veterinarian, it will save the parrot the trauma of being toweled in a more threatening manner by someone he may not trust as much as he trusts you.

Having a positive relationship with an avian veterinarian will be a major plus in the life of your companion parrot. *

SERIOUS CONSIDERATIONS

Serious consideration should be given before accepting or allowing any of the following treatments or procedures:
- Routine preventive treatment of a baby parrot with antibiotics without indication of an infection or illness.
- Any surgical procedure, including surgical sexing, performed at a bird mart or other location lacking quiet and sterile surroundings.
- The immediate presumption that a problem is behavioral.
- Pulling of any feathers (especially wing or tail feathers) for any reason, particularly for cosmetic reasons.
- Trimming of the secondary wing feathers close to the body or trimming of any flight feathers too close to the follicle.
- Trimming just one wing. This can create serious balance problems.
- Pinioning or permanent immobilization of the wing.
- Trimming toenails back to the quick so they bleed.
- Using a cautery tool to burn toenails.
- Placing a parrot in a collar for chronic feather picking.
- Excessive reshaping of the beak through beak grinding or beak notching for biting or feather picking.
- Aggressive capture or threatening toweling, including chasing the parrot around a darkened room with a flashlight.
- The use of tranquilizers or mood altering drugs without serious consideration of other possible causes or treatments.
- Surgery to stop screaming or removal of vocal apparatus.
- Surgery to neuter a parrot without life-threatening egg laying.

FINDING A *REAL* AVIAN VET

Understanding The Initials

How do you know if the veterinarian you are taking your parrots to is really qualified to treat birds? Looking in the yellow pages won't help (unless you understand all those initials) because any veterinarian can advertise that they treat birds. Even business cards and phone book ads can indicate they see birds. Talk to other people with parrots and ask them what veterinarians they use and if they are satisfied with the way their parrots are handled. If your local pet/bird shop or aviary is a good one, ask them who treats their parrots. Don't ask a questionable pet shop about their veterinarian. They either don't have one, or they have may have worked a deal with the cheapest (perhaps not the most qualified) one around in exchange for references.

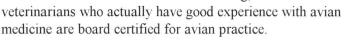

"D.V.M." means Doctor of Veterinary Medicine and all veterinarians who have graduated from veterinary schools in the United States have this title — except for "V.M.D." who are graduates of the University of Pennsylvania (just to confuse us?). Board certified (American Board of Veterinary Practitioners) avian veterinarians use the title, "D.V.M., Dip-ABVP, Avian Practice," which is quite a mouthful. These notations indicate that recipients have passed tests which qualify them as *real* avian veterinarians. At the time of this writing, not all the veterinarians who actually have good experience with avian medicine are board certified for avian practice.

What other factors should you investigate to know if a non-certified avian veterinarian is really qualified to treat your parrot? At least 25% of their practice should be birds. Do they consult with other avian veterinarians on a regular basis about avian cases? Do they handle your parrot comfortably? Do they handle your parrot in a trust-building manner or are they rushed, aggressive, and/or threatening? Do the people in their office handle your parrot with respect and gentleness? Do they really listen to you and answer your questions with words you can understand? Do they belong to the A.A.V. (Association of Avian Veterinarians-http://www.aav.org) — the professional organization for veterinarians practicing avian medicine?

With research and shared experiences, avian medical information grows constantly. It is essential for avian veterinarians to further their education to stay on top of new techniques in diagnosis and treatment. Those who don't may fall behind quickly in being able to provide your parrot the competent care he needs and deserves. 🖋

CERTIFIED AVIAN SPECIALISTS?

What is a C.A.S.?

P.I.J.A.C. (The Pet Industry Joint Advisory Council) offers four hour classes in bird husbandry followed by an open book test. After completing minimal requirements, people are eligible to use the designation C.A.S. (Certified Avian Specialist) after their names. It is important for readers to realize that these initials signify no specialized qualifications to either provide health examinations for parrots or give advice about their medical treatment. It is unethical (and most likely illegal) for a C.A.S. to give information or provide services that may be misunderstood as coming from a qualified avian veterinarian. While any educational endeavor that will teach us more about the proper care of parrots should be respected, it is important to know that the C.A.S. certification, *by itself,* implies no specialized knowledge about either avian medicine or parrot behavior. Before accepting someone's authority or credibility based solely on a C.A.S. designation, check to see what other experiences he or she has with parrots.

QUARANTINE ISSUES

Honey, I'm going to go in and feed the new bird...

BIOHAZARD

Make Sure *Everybirdy* Is Safe

Any parrot purchase should involve an immediate visit to an avian veterinarian. Your vet will provide an accurate assessment of your new parrot's health and will explain the necessity of quarantine if you have other parrots. A bappy's immune system is not yet fully developed. The younger the parrot is, the more susceptible he is to infectious disease and many avian diseases are highly contagious. If one of your present birds has compromised health, you will need to take special precautions to guarantee that your new bappy does not come in contact with contagion from this bird.

How long and where should a new bird be quarantined? This often depends on the health and condition of your present birds and where you bought your new bappy. If you have purchased your new parrot from a high quality breeder with a *closed aviary* or an exceptional store where there is little potential for exposure to unknown birds (and their possible diseases), your quarantine procedures may not need to be totally restrictive. A closed aviary is one that has a stable population of parrots with no new birds (except for babies bred and raised there) coming in and out of the facility. Most closed aviaries do not allow visitors into their actual breeding facilities. I know of only a few sellers I would buy a bird from without providing some sort of quarantine situation. The key is exposure to unknown birds. If all sorts of birds go in and out of a seller's location (for grooming, boarding, or for resale), your parrot could have been exposed to any disease from one of those unknown birds.

How Do I Quarantine My New Parrot?

During quarantine your new parrot will be kept in a separate area of your home to guarantee that he will not infect your current birds or be compromised by the birds already in your house. Total in-home quarantine is almost impossible as there is usually air flow from room to room but it still creates fewer chances of contagion than putting the birds in the same room or the same area of the house.

Just as important as placing parrots in a separate area is the protocol with which you feed the birds and clean the cages. The infectious organisms of many contagious bird diseases can be transmitted on your hands, or articles that carry germs (fomites) such as clothing, shoes, food and water bowls. If your new bird is a baby, you should always feed him before feeding the other birds. Make sure you wash your hands thoroughly before feeding the other birds. If you know one of your parrots has an infectious disease, that bird should be fed **last**. It will be necessary to change clothes and shoes after handling him before entering the room where the other parrot is located.

If you decide <u>not</u> to quarantine your new parrot, be sure your decision is based on common sense and knowledge instead of on convenience. If you do keep the new and the old birds in separate areas of your house, the new bird should also be in an area where there is a good amount of activity. It is important that he becomes used to your normal routines. Always remember that baby birds need a lot of protection, guidance, and socialization. Quarantine from your other birds should not mean separation from the human flock. Also, it is critical not to deprive your first bird of attention just because there is another parrot in the household. *

DISEASE & TAKING CHANCES

Taking A Chance

Every time you expose your parrot to situations where there are unknown parrots, especially with exposure to multiple birds, you are taking a chance of infecting him with disease. This is most true for young parrots who do not yet have a fully developed immune system. The immune system of most medium to large parrots may not be completely developed before the bird is 2 to 3 years old. Taking your parrot to bird club meetings, bird shows, or bird marts may be fun and serve as a wonderful opportunity for your pet to meet lots of friendly people and other birds. However, socialization as a trade-off for your parrot's health is taking a big chance. Although it may be easy to tell if some parrots are sick, many sick parrots look just fine but may be highly contagious. You can't presume that everyone there with a parrot is as conscientious as you are. At bird marts, I have seen too many people with their pets on their shoulders standing right next to obviously sick birds. Before your parrot meets any other parrot, you must be relatively sure that bird is healthy and disease free. For example, if you have a friend with one or two healthy, long-term, stay-at-home parrots, there should be little chance of any contagion if you visit that friend with your parrot.

Fomites As Disease Transmitters

If you attend bird club meetings where people bring their birds, go to aviaries or pet shops that do not take proper care of their parrots, or visit bird marts where there are a lot of birds for sale, you take a chance of bringing home highly infectious diseases on your clothes and shoes. Infectious organisms can be transferred from a bird mart, bird club meeting, aviary, or pet shop to your home on what are called fomites, which are any substances that can absorb, hold, and transport infectious germs. These can include your body, hair, clothes, shoes, and even items you buy at the events. Shoes are one of the worst offenders because they pick up whatever is on the floor. When you come home after any situation populated with unknown birds, take off your shoes, take a shower, and change clothes <u>before</u> greeting your parrots.

This information is not intended to discourage people from buying bird products from quality bird shops or bird shows. However, we need to be careful with items we bring into our homes. Most food sold in packages is usually problem-free once it is placed in new containers. Hard goods purchased at a bird show can be left outside on a sunny day (the sun is an excellent germ fighter) and/or washed and cleaned. Some vendors sell bird toys in clear wrapping at bird shows. This excellent idea allows us to remove the wrapping before bringing the toys in the house.

"Officer, Please try to understand.
We just got home from a BIRD SHOW and we didn't
want to expose our parrots to some disease!"

"Put your clothes on! We can discuss this at the station!"

SMB

TRIMMING WINGS: YES OR NO?

An Unnatural Situation

While it is true that trimmed wings are an unnatural situation for parrots, most aspects of their lives as human companions are unnatural. Because of this, we must provide an incredible amount of guidance and a benevolent, stimulating environment for our caged parrots. When their emotional, nutritional, and environmental needs are properly met by the people in their lives, most parrots adapt well to their lives as companions and most adapt well to having their wings trimmed. This said, I occasionally talk to people who have a parrot that I believe would be far more secure if he did not have clipped wings. However, I only recommend this when I believe the owners have the common sense to understand ALL the implications of living with a flighted parrot.

Parrots with trimmed wings are far more dependent on their owners than are untrimmed birds. We must become their wings. We must take them from place to place and keep them with us when they want to be a part of our lives. Sometimes this dependence is at least a part of what encourages a stronger bond between bird and human. Some parrots have been traumatized by botched wing trims and I can understand why their owners would not want to have their birds' wings trimmed again. If an unclipped parrot is well-behaved (and it appears as if he will stay that way with continued guidance), I am not concerned about people having serious behavioral problems because he is flighted and therefore he has the potential to be far more independent. In some cases, with some parrots, whether it is because they have not been provided proper guidance or because they are just more willful birds, it may be essential to trim their wings to keep them tame as pets. I received a phone call from a woman who wanted to know what she should do because her Sun Conure would fly at visitors' faces and attack them. The answer, in this case, was quite simple. The bird needed to have his wings trimmed to settle him down and to create a more dependent parrot. The woman answered that she could not do so because he was so beautiful in flight, yet she was seriously thinking of "getting rid of him" because he had become so aggressive. Clearly, trimming the wings to help her manage the aggression was a better alternative than finding him a new home. I suggested she have the wings trimmed and then work diligently to establish better behavioral guidance with him as his wings grew out. Then, perhaps, he would be less aggressive being flighted.

If a person takes exceptional care of his or her parrot, is concerned with his welfare, and uses quality *Nurturing Guidance*, the parrot can become an exceptional companion. The key word I am using is "exceptional." If a person has carefully thought about the positive and negative possibilities of having a flighted parrot with a common sense, cause-and-effect logic, he or she may become "the exception to the rule." Of course, the established rule is that all companion parrots should have their wings trimmed. More and more thought is being given to the idea that companion parrots should be allowed to fly. Unfortunately, many bird owners who have not thought this out carefully, and do not provide guidance for their parrots, are asking for problems if they do not trim their parrot's wings.

A Few Exceptions

I used to believe that it was essential for ALL birds to have their wings trimmed. That was until I met several owners of flighted birds who were the *exception* to the rule. One, a very tame and loving blue-fronted Amazon, lived in a converted warehouse in San Francisco. He was fully flighted and the only problem was that he would not always come down from the high ceiling beams. By bribing him down with a treat, the owners were able to establish verbal commands for him to follow. The key was that the owners were always aware of where their Amazon was whenever doors were opened. Behavioral consultant, Liz Wilson, has an elder Blue and Gold, Sam, whose wings are not trimmed. Sam always comes out with a sort of Tarzan yell before flying, and Liz is always aware when Sam is out of her cage. Liz also believes that she is less likely to let Sam fly away because she is always aware of the flighted condition of Sam's wings. Phoebe Greene Linden of Santa Barbara Bird Farm allows all her babies to fledge and learn to fly with mastery before gradually trimming their wings a few feathers at a time. As part of their flight training, they are pre-introduced to mirrors and windows. Phoebe's companion Hawk-headed Parrot, Hawkeye, is fully flighted. Her time out is structured and supervised because, as an independent and somewhat opinionated parrot, Hawkeye does not particularly appreciate all visitors to her house. Chris Shank of Cockatoo Downs, now lets all her 'too bappies fly. She finds that they are much more secure and independent than the babies she raised without letting them fledge. My Double-yellow Headed Amazons, Paco and Rascal, live in their own bird-safe porch and are fully flighted yet I have rarely actually seen either of them fly in their room. When I do bring them into the house, I make sure all the doors are shut and locked first so that no one opens a door and provides a venue for their escape. The birds in the house are trimmed. I usually have far too many things on my mind to trust myself to allow fully flighted birds free in my home.

Are You Really The Exception?

In considering leaving a parrot flighted, it is essential to analyze the situation carefully. Is everyone in the family aware of the potential dangers of the parrot escaping? Do you have children (or their friends) who might forget (or not know) the family rules about where the parrot is when they go in and out of the doors? It is not usually the owners of flighted birds who let them fly out the door; it is usually someone else who is not as careful or even aware of the bird's presence. When I was a child, my visiting grandmother walked out the door with our beloved flighted budgie, Micki Finn, on her shoulder. Micki was quite a talented talker and had several phrases he repeated frequently in his squeaky little voice. One was "Shut the door stupid, the bird's out!" It was only when Micki uttered these words that my grandmother realized Micki was on her shoulder. She quickly backed into the house and shut the door. We were very lucky. Many people are not this lucky. Over the years, I have talked with hundreds of people whose birds have flown away. Many of these people never found their beloved companions. In most cases, people didn't think their bird could fly with his wings trimmed or had not realized the wings had grown out.

The truth is that some birds can fly quite well with trimmed wings. This is particularly true of slim-bodied birds like budgies, 'tiels, cockatoos, conures, and macaws — especially the mini-macaws. I believe that people should not have their avian pets outside, whether the wings are trimmed or not, unless the birds are in a harness or carrier. When a bird has been safely and gradually accustomed to being in a harness and the owner supervises the bird properly <u>at all times</u>, a harness can be a wonderful way of allowing pet birds time outside.

Obviously, I would not tell everyone that they must trim their parrot's wings. Owners of flighted birds must remain vigilant so that an accident doesn't happen that will injure or threaten their parrots. The rule to trim wings still applies to the majority of parrot owners and I am not going to give the advice to everyone that it is OK to leave their parrots flighted. Before you decide you are the exception and you can safely keep your parrots flighted, you must carefully evaluate your own situation. Is your household a safe place for a parrot to fly? Is it large enough for parrots to maneuver in flight without crashing into things? Can you realistically prevent everyone who does not pay attention to what is going on from indiscriminately coming in and out of your house? Do you have the knowledge to fledge a bappy or teach your older bird to fly? Are you tuned in enough to be able to always be aware of what your parrot is doing? Do you have the time, energy, and ability to carefully supervise your parrot at all times when he is out of his cage? Can you logically think about dangerous situations that would threaten your parrot and then make common sense plans to prevent or avoid those situations? Are you already providing enough *Nurturing Guidance* so that you are in control of your parrot's life? At this time, can you prevent and/or deal with any aggressive behavior from your parrot in a way which does not escalate the aggression? If you are in control now, do you provide enough behavioral guidance so that you will still be in control of your bird if he is flighted?

Are you really the exception to the rule about trimming wings or are you fooling yourself about the eventual endangerment of your parrot? If you can truthfully answer all of the above questions from a positive point of view, you may be an exception to the rule. If not, I would encourage you to keep your parrot's wings trimmed. 🪶

POTENTIAL GROOMING PROBLEMS

Psychological Trauma/Physical Harm

⤳ Improper handling and grooming techniques can cause psychological trauma to a parrot (especially a bappy) by seriously affecting his sense of security and by possibly creating long-term phobic behavior, or even permanent behavioral dysfunction. Find a gentle, competent groomer you can trust, or learn to groom your own birds in a gentle, nonthreatening manner.

⤳ Toenails should NEVER be cut back to the quick unless there is a medical reason (see diagram page 54). Only the tips should be filed or trimmed. Bappies should only have their toenails slightly filed to remove the sharpness. Cutting toenails too short can cause serious balance problems, particularly for young parrots. Bappies may fall, damaging their feathers, injuring themselves physically, and/or creating fear patterns in their behavior.

⤳ Improper wing trimming can result in permanent damage to the wing, balance problems, blood feather problems, and feather destructive behavior. Don't clip into the secondaries, even on heavy-bodied birds. Clipping feathers too short on the shaft up under the coverts (which are intended to protect emerging blood feathers) can create serious problems with blood feathers when the new feathers start to grow. Clip both wings for balance. I do not recommend leaving P10 and P9 since many birds can fly with these feathers remaining (See page 54 for trimming diagram). These long unprotected feathers can also get caught in cage bars and are vulnerable to breakage (See page 137 for information on blood feathers).

A Bad Grooming Job Is Much More Traumatic To The Recipient Than A Bad Haircut.

⤳ Don't allow anyone, even an avian veterinarian, to pull multiple tail or wing feathers at one time. New growth of many feathers at one time can deplete the *raw materials* (nutrients) needed, and new feathers will most likely have problems or growth flaws. In some cases, the feather sheath may develop improperly and may not be strong enough to prevent breaking or bleeding. Because there will be no feathers along the side of the emerging blood feathers, there is no protection and the chance of these breaking is very high. Pulling many feathers at one time can also cause balance problems and aggravate feather picking problems.

⤳ The beak is very sensitive and is used not only to eat but also as a "hand" both to grasp objects and to explore them. Grinding a parrot's beak too short can cause pain and debilitation. Routine beak trimming (except for minor cosmetic filing) should not be necessary for healthy birds on a nutritious diet. Because of the beak's sensitivity, I am opposed to the use of a Dremel type rotary grinding tool to reshape the beak — especially on a bappy. The beak should not be trimmed unless there is a specific problem with beak growth and should be done by someone with experience. Some birds, like Grey-cheek Parakeets, Slender-billed Conures and Corellas have naturally longer upper mandibles.

⤳ Aggressive or rough handling (i.e., swooping down on a parrot from the back like a *harpy eagle looking for lunch)* can cause psychological trauma in parrots. There is absolutely no reason that a tame parrot cannot be gently and calmly wrapped in a towel from the front. Do not allow anyone to capture your bird by chasing him around with a towel or turning off the lights and using a flashlight to startle the bird and then grab him.

⤳ Pay close attention for signs of stress in your bird. Excessive pressure on the head or chest can cause serious injury, shock, or even death. Heavy breathing combined with a "thunking sound" in the chest is an indication of serious stress. Stressed birds should be released immediately and allowed to rest.

⤳ Don't let <u>anyone</u> (professional groomer or veterinarian included), no matter how experienced they are supposed to be, handle your bird in a manner that can be injurious to his physical or emotional health.

⤳ Never attempt to remove a leg band by yourself. Serious injury to the foot and leg may result. This procedure should only be done by an avian veterinarian (and his staff) who has special tools for the safe removal of leg bands. ⨍

"EAGLE BOY!"

Easy-To-Establish Grooming Routines

People buying a bappy have a great advantage in establishing grooming patterns and routines. They can start out by making a game of having their young parrot raise his wings for trimming or raising a foot for nail filing. Most bappies will enjoy the game and delight in being groomed if the owner maintains a calm, confident attitude. Using cue words like "Be an Eagle" or "Shake hands" makes it easy to let your parrot know verbally that you want him to raise his wings or foot for grooming. This way, grooming can become a routine part of attention and affection rather than a traumatic seasonal torture session. When a healthy new feather is developed beyond the blood feather stage, the owner can give their bird the "Eagle Boy" command and just snip the one long feather at the trim line (see next page). Weekly gentle filing of sharp tips on the toenails with an emery board or file means the nails should never have to be cut back — especially short enough to cause bleeding or balance problems. If toenails are too short, it may cause serious perch insecurity and balance problems for bappies. Except for the cosmetic gentle filing of rough spots, beak trimming should not be necessary with most parrots and should only be done by an avian veterinarian.

BEAK GRINDING, BEAK NOTCHING, TOENAIL BURNING

Lessons From Wood Carving

For over two decades, I created bird sculptures out of rare hardwoods. I ended up with far more scars on my hands from wood carving than I ever did from taming parrots. One of my most useful woodcarving tools was a rotary grinder. I probably owned ten different Dremel tools. I also had an assortment of motorized flexible shafts with various grinding and cutting bits on them. I used them both for heavy grinding and delicate shaping. Some of the birds I carved, such as hummingbirds and chickadees, were small enough to require delicate attention so I would hold them in my left hand while I used the grinder in my right hand. I would be concentrating on the detail work and suddenly the grinder would slip and touch a finger nail on my left hand. It hurt and it burned. Occasionally, I would use a wood burning tool and, if it slipped, it also hurt and burned when it touched my finger nail.

Why would I write about this in a parrot care book? Because many groomers and veterinarians routinely use rotary grinders on a parrot's beak even if the beak doesn't really need trimming. The beak is not just a hunk of plastic-like dead material hanging off the front of a parrot's face. The beak has sensitive nerve endings and a blood supply. From my experience with these tools grinding and burning my fingernails, I can imagine the use of these tools can be painful to parrots if they are used to grind beaks and toenails. The sound can also be quite frightening ... and what if the grinder slips and damages an eye?

I do not recommend the use of a rotary grinder or a cautery tool for the routine grooming of beaks or toenails unless there is an absolute reason (such as a beak deformity), and then it must be done by a competent avian veterinarian. I am absolutely opposed to having a parrot's beak notched as a *cure* for biting or feather picking. There are many other health-related and behavioral steps that can be taken before the beak is mutilated to stop the bird from using it to pick feathers.

YOUR BIRD WILL STILL LOVE YOU

There's Always A First Time

When I was new to parrots, I was terrified of grooming my own pets. I was not afraid they would bite me — I was afraid I would hurt them with my incompetence. I was friends with a wood-carver and his wife who had more than a dozen *rasty* imported Amazons. The woman was less than 5 feet tall and weighed about as much as the largest male Double-yellow Head. Yet she would towel her parrots one at a time, and trim their wings and beaks all by herself without any problems. I even watched her groom them with her right wrist in a cast. I figured if she could manage these wild Amazons, I could groom my own parrots. She taught me her basic techniques and I have groomed parrots ever since — my own and hundreds of others. I never have to worry about someone else doing a bad grooming job or traumatizing my parrots with aggressive handling. I also learned to trim wings according to the parrot's body size and shape — clipping a few more feathers for the slim-bodied birds than the chunkier ones.

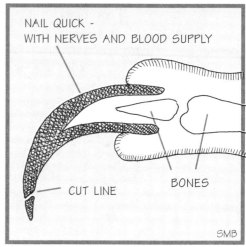

NAIL QUICK - WITH NERVES AND BLOOD SUPPLY

CUT LINE

BONES

SMB

For several years, I groomed parrots professionally. I found one thing to be consistently true. If I approached the parrot gently and calmly from the front with a towel, they were much more relaxed with me. They rarely struggled or fought the towel as I quickly trimmed their wings and clipped their toenails. After I was through, the tame parrots almost always melted into my neck for a good cuddle. Even wild-caught birds were rarely traumatized when I used calm, yet decisive handling techniques.

COVERTS

TRIM LINE

P10

PRIMARIES

P1 S1

SECONDARIES

S10

SMB

Trimming flight feathers down from the coverts rather than up under them protects emerging blood feathers with strong feather shafts on each side. The number of flight feathers to trim depends on the body shape and weight plus the shape of the wings and the tail — slim-bodied birds with long tails usually need more flight feathers trimmed; heavy-bodied birds with square tails need less trimmed. Trim so the bird can still glide to the floor rather than injure itself falling like a lead balloon. Do not ever trim S5 to S10 (the secondaries next to the body).

Wing Trimming Patterns

I have successfully used the trimming pattern shown to the left for years. I remove fewer primaries for heavy bodied birds and, in some cases, trim just a few of the secondaries in addition to the primaries (never the ones close to the body) for slim bodied birds. Although other people may make a strong argument to do so, I believe the flight feather shafts should never be trimmed up underneath the coverts. This way each emerging feather shaft is protected with strong feather shafts on each side as the new feathers grow (See blood feather information on page 137).

I have seen many problems when most of the primaries are trimmed and p10, p9, and p8 are left. Many parrots can fly quite well with this trim called the Vanity Clip. The outer untrimmed flight feathers usually become ragged or broken. Many parrots also fly easily with every other flight feather trimmed. I trim both wings equally so the bird does not develop balance problems.

GROOMING & GROOMERS

No Professional Guidelines

As the popularity of companion parrots continues to increase, more people are involving themselves professionally in their care. With more and more bird grooming services available, how do we know who to trust with our parrots? At the time of this writing, the field has no accredited training or professional guidelines for methodology. The field is wide open and anyone can call themselves bird groomers. This means that the bird owner looking for help with his parrot grooming must determine whether the parrot groomer has legitimate expertise. The basic rule applies — are they working with parrots in a trust-building, gentle manner or are they working with them in a trust-destroying, aggressive manner? Do not allow anyone to handle your parrot in an aggressive manner.

Is the groomer overstepping his or her boundaries and providing care that should really be given by a qualified avian veterinarian? I have heard about groomers who have recommended treatment for health problems. This is unacceptable unless the groomer is also a qualified avian veterinarian. For over a decade, I groomed other people's parrots as part of my behavioral consultation services. As part of that service, I gave each parrot a thorough visual exam and looked for problems the owner might have missed. I always made it very clear that my examination was no substitute for a visit with an avian veterinarian. If I found anything at all questionable about the parrot's health or condition, I always insisted the owner make an veterinarian appointment as soon as possible.

"I don't know what her problem is - I just nipped her a little and she grabbed the towel and scissors and came running after me muttering something about me being Samson and her being Delilah."

SMB

Calming The Parrot

In my years of grooming, I rarely had any problems. I always relaxed and slowed the parrot down before I wrapped him in a towel for grooming. I would take a few deep slow breaths, shut my eyes for a few seconds, and droop my head and smile. I found that most parrots matched my energy and I was able to handle them easily without stress during the whole grooming procedure. Once they were in the towel, I worked as quickly as possible so the job would not take too long. If they became stressed or had any difficulty in breathing, I immediately let them out of the towel to relax again before I re-toweled them to finish the job. After the grooming, the parrot and I would have a cuddle and skritching session. Very few parrots held a grudge because I had groomed them.

Groomers should also know how to deal with emergency situations. With a few parrots, I found they stressed so easily I was sure there was a serious health problem. I refused to groom these birds until they had been examined by an avian veterinarian. In other situations, the owners were so worried or stressed about their parrots being groomed that I had to ask them to leave the room. The parrot was picking up the owner's stress which made it almost impossible for me to get him parrot to relax.

I have groomed hundreds of parrots, and I only had problems in two situations. Both were with wild-caught birds. The birds went limp and *passed out* while I was working. There had been no signs of immediate stress and the parrot came around in only a few seconds. In each case, I called my avian veterinarian for advice. He suggested that all of the bird's energy reserves had been expended, causing problem with low blood sugar. Although the birds did seem fine afterwards, I recommended that they should be taken to their vet to be checked for some underlying problem.

BIRD SITTERS

A Great Challenge For Many Parrot Owners

One of the most challenging problems for parrot owners is finding a competent situation for their bird's care when they need to travel or go on vacation. Parrots, especially bappies, should not be left even overnight without someone checking on them and providing them with interaction. The ideal situation is to have a relative or close friend, someone who forms a caring bond with the bappy, and who enjoys having your parrot visit when you are gone. If you don't have family or friends who are able to bird sit, I recommend finding another person in your area who has both similar birds and bird care philosophies. Make a bird sitting arrangement that is mutually advantageous — you take care of their birds when they are gone and they take care of yours when you are gone. I know of several situations where people plan the timing of their vacations so they can watch each others parrots. But this is not possible for many people so they have to find other arrangements. While professional pet sitters and boarding situations are readily available for dogs and cats in most areas of the country, there are far fewer appropriate alternatives for companion parrots. Many of the dog and cat sitters who come into people's homes simply do not have the know-how to work with parrots. Some do, but it is essential to know first if they really have the knowledge necessary to handle parrots and, especially, if they are competent enough to handle them in an emergency.

Special Needs

In many areas of the country, there are few, if any, quality bird boarding possibilities. Call your avian veterinarian for references because some clinics have knowledgeable employees who will bird sit for extra money. A quality pet shop may also be able to recommend people for bird sitting or may have separate facilities for bird boarding.

As parrots become more popular, hopefully there will be more specialized boarding facilities for them. A well-run boarding facility is concerned about keeping your parrot separated from birds who may not be healthy. They want to know all about your parrot's diet and special needs and want to give him his normal level of attention and affection. They want you to bring his special toys so he keeps himself busy. They will also require an avian vet check, a health certificate, or detailed knowledge of your parrot's health before they watch your parrot. It may cost more money this way, but it is assurance for you that they do the same thing with the other parrots they watch.

Don't wait to introduce your parrot to the bird sitter until moments before you leave. Preparation and introduction help insure that he will not be placed in an entirely new situation or traumatized while you are gone. Make sure your parrot gets to know and is comfortable with the new sitter before you leave him in their care and most of all make sure you are comfortable with the care your bird will receive. Interview the bird sitter carefully — sharing similar bird care philosophies is critical. You won't want someone taking care of your parrot who doesn't care about his emotional needs or believe in his intelligence. If your bird has special needs, make sure you relate them to the sitter. When I used to bird sit, I had my clients provide me with detailed information about their parrot's food likes and dislikes, when he liked attention, what his favorite games were, and any special health considerations. I think it is essential that the sitter cares about how much your parrot means to you.

QUALITY BIRD SHOPS

In Need Of Good Information

The first experience most people have with parrots is in a pet shop that sells birds. Often, the novice *falls in love* with a bird in the store and purchases it on impulse. I had budgies as a child and, as an adult, purchased my first bird on impulse. I was told the cockatiel was handfed and sweet. After a week or so, I thought it must be my fault I couldn't handle him. But he talked up a storm, so I was happy. The pet shop sold me seed, told me <u>not</u> to give him toys or he would bond to them and not me (*nonsense!*), and emphasized one piece of advice, "Don't put him in a draft — it will kill him!" I was told to carry a lighted candle around the room. If the candled flickered anywhere, that would not be a good location for the cage. The candle flickered almost everywhere so I didn't know what to do. Now I know that drafts are overrated as bird killers, but if a parrot had health problems shortly after being sold, the seller could always blame it on drafts. As a new bird owner, I trusted I would be given good information from the store where I bought my bird. I wasn't. I believe it is the responsibility of the seller to give the bird buyer good basic information. Certainly sellers can't possibly provide everything new caregivers need to know, but they can at least point them in the right direction.

How Do You Know If You Are Dealing With A Quality Bird Shop?

⮑ The shop owner, management, and employees have a genuine interest in making sure their parrots go to good homes. They want to know as much about you as you want to know about them.

⮑ Employees are knowledgeable and willing to help. They take time to know you rather than just push you into buying a parrot. Personnel are willing to recommend avian veterinarians, publications, and other information sources.

⮑ Store personnel are honest — if they don't know the answer to a question, they don't just make something up to try to impress the customers. Their information is based on common sense, logic and trust-building.

⮑ Birds in the store are always handled with respect, quality care, and gentleness.

⮑ The individual needs of the parrots are respected.

⮑ The physical environment of the store is clean and positive with good lighting and comfortable temperature and humidity. Dark, dirty, dingy pet shops should be a thing of the past. No store can be immaculate all the time because birds are messy, but cleaning is done as part of the daily routine.

⮑ Cages, water bowls, and food dishes are cleaned at least once daily.

⮑ No stalagmite droppings in the cages. Filthy cages give an accurate idea of the total care the birds receive.

⮑ All cages are clean and roomy with good lighting and toys for each parrot.

⮑ The cages are the proper size for the birds in them. Each bird can move about comfortably and smaller, high-energy birds have the lateral room to go from perch to perch.

⮑ Every bird has the chance for activity or exercise. Older weaned bappies who have not yet been sold are handled and come out on a playgym on a daily basis.

⮑ Customers do not have direct access to young babies without close employee supervision.

⮑ Customers have to wash their hands before handling bappies.

⮑ Customers can't just grab at or handle any of the birds without employee supervision.

⮑ There are not too many birds and too few employees to give each bird proper care and attention.

⮑ Cages are not stacked everywhere on top of each other and on the floor.

⮑ The birds are fed a nutritious, varied diet of pellets, mashes, greens, vegetables, some fruit, and some seed. (If the store still has parrots on a seed-only diet, they are in the dark ages and do not deserve your business.)

⮑ The store is recommended by people with knowledge about parrots and their proper care.

⮑ **Vote with your money!** Don't spend your money in a store that provides substandard care for parrots. If you are lucky enough to live near a quality pet shop where the personnel genuinely care about both their birds and their customers, be sure to support them with your business, even if you have to drive a distance. Keeping good stores in business is the best thing we as consumers can do to guarantee a quality bird industry! ⚡

BEHAVIORAL CONSULTANTS

Qualifications & Credentials

At the time this book was written, anyone can call themselves a parrot behavioral consultant. Lots of people who are fascinated with parrots because of their own birds are calling themselves "behaviorists." But do they really have enough long-term, in-depth experience with many parrots to have the knowledge to work with other people's birds? So how do you know if someone is really qualified to help you with your parrot's behavioral problems? Ask them how long they have been working with parrots and how many parrots they have worked with. Of course, this is not a fool proof test — some people have been doing the wrong things with parrots for years. Ask about their background with parrots. Did they work in a pet shop, for an avian veterinarian, or as a bird show trainer? All of these jobs provide multiple exposures to parrots and can provide valuable learning experiences. But again, these learning experiences may not always relate to the relationship between a person and his or her companion parrot. This may be particularly true of people who come from a bird show training background. Training parrots for a bird show is vastly different than keeping parrots as companions. However, people with a bird training background who also have companion parrots may have a solid understanding of live with pet parrots.

Have you read any-thing they have written and did it make sense to you? Were they referred to you by a respected bird shop, breeder, or avian veterinarian? What are their behavioral theories and techniques for working with your parrot? Do they take your parrot with them and promise you changed behaviors when they bring it back? That rarely works because if the owners have not been educated to behave differently with their parrots, then the negative behaviors will return very quickly. The competent behavioral consultant knows that train-ing the owner to work with his parrot is actually more important than training the parrot.

Is their approach based on creating a contented parrot using non-aggressive, non-threatening techniques which take the parrot's needs and intelligence into consideration; or is it based on ineffective, punishing, or even aggressive quick-fixes and stereotypical generalizations which have no place in the world of companion parrots? Can they tell you **why** their advice works? If they can't, perhaps they don't understand it themselves. If they don't have a grasp of what makes parrots *tick*, their advice may not come from common sense. If they dismiss your grey (or Amazon ...) as having behavioral problems simply because he is a grey (or Amazon ...), then look for help elsewhere. The behavioral advice must apply to your specific parrot in your particular family and individual home. Telephone consultations can be effective if the behavioral consultant asks you a great number of questions before he or she provides advice.

Really working to change your parrot's negative behaviors involves time and patience. Don't let anyone convince you that his or her advice is some sort of miracle quick-fix that will work overnight.

Most of all, when you really think about the advice you have received, you need to use common sense to deter-mine if following it with your parrot will be trust-building or trust-destroying. If the advice is punishing, aggressive, or confrontational, it is trust-destroying and should not be used if you want to earn your parrot's trust and bond.

RESCUE/REHAB/ADOPTION

A Great Need

Over the past few years, it has become evident that there is a great need for nonprofit organizations to work with the rescue, rehabilitation, retirement, and placement of companion parrots. Many people mistakenly think parrots maintain their financial worth. However, this is rarely the case, especially if the owner has not provided consistent behavior guidance, in addition to proper physical care. Behavioral nightmares abound. In some cases, parrots who have been neglected or even severely abused are lucky enough to find their way into a quality rescue organization. Many of the imported birds who for years sat in pet shops without being sold, and those who have become too old to breed, present a special challenge for parrot *rehabbers*.

Unfortunately, some people present themselves as rescue centers but are really brokers trying to get free parrots they can sell for a profit. Not everyone who rescues a few birds is actually a legitimate rescue organization. The true sanctuaries are dedicated to the welfare of parrots.

How Do You Know The Difference?

Most genuine organizations have established a nonprofit status. Any organization that presents themselves as a nonprofit organization that does not actually go through the proper channels is in violation of the law. Ask to see their paperwork before you support them. A genuine rescue organization allows you to visit and inspect their facilities by appointment. Too many rescue organizations are started by people with big hearts who too soon end up with more birds than they can care for properly. Unfortunately, sometimes the birds need to be rescued from these places. I believe that genuine rescue organizations will not breed birds as they have all they can do to care for their rescued parrots. They will not buy parrots with the intent of selling them for profit, but will definitely need to charge an adoption fee to cover their veterinary, feeding and housing expenses. They may also do fund-raising or sell products to help raise money.

The parrots in the care of an ethical sanctuary are well-housed and well-fed. Knowledgeable people work with the birds to evaluate and improve their health and behavior. Decisions are based on the best interests of the parrots — some birds are maintained by the sanctuary, others are adopted as companions by qualified caregivers, and a few are placed with respected breeders to be paired with a mate. Trustworthy rescue organizations aspire to educate people interested in parrots about the complex needs of our feathered friends through focus on their psychological, physiological, environmental, and nutritional needs. They also want to generate continuing awareness of the big picture: the natural habitat of parrots and their conservation and captive breeding.

Qualified parrot sanctuaries and rescue organizations can be an excellent place to find a companion parrot. Some parrots who enter the "throwaway cycle" had ignorant owners and only need consistent care and nurturing for their pet potential to shine. A quality rescue group may also be a solution for placement if you can no longer care for your parrot. A trustworthy organization will be more concerned about placing your parrot in a quality home than making money off of the transaction. Talk to them and read their adoption policies to see if you trust them to make the right decisions about finding your parrot a quality living situation.

SMB

PARROTS & COMPUTERS

The Internet — An Incredible Information Opportunity — Yes and No

Never before have so many parrot-interested people had access to sharing information, ideas, and opinions with so many others than now, on the Internet. While this is wonderful, it can present information overload — so much information a novice has no idea who or what to believe. Unfortunately, along with excellent information given by concerned knowledgeable people, you can also find some of the worst, punishing, quick fix, and trust-destroying advice I have ever read. Parrot-related interactive lists often present some intriguing human dynamics. Some are monitored and supervised, while others allow a totally free exchange of opinion. Computer lists are a chance to be "published" (to see one's opinions in print) without the restrictions of an editor or any kind of immediate censorship. In some cases, people make up "handles" and you never really know true identities. Although on many lists people use their actual names, most writers still remain faceless. This anonymity and lack of personal accountability can lead to some volatile exchanges.

Sadly, a dedicated student of parrot behavior and care may also occasionally encounter some very mean-spirited people on the Internet. Computer lists also bring out strong opinions and argumentative personality tendencies in otherwise more genteel people. Lies, exaggerations, and gossip can be and often are interlaced within seemingly credible information. I have seen some people use the various lists to berate others, simply because of professional jealousy. Some people with little actual experience express their opinions freely with what seems to be great authority. For this reason, it is best to proceed according to the old adage, "Forewarned is forearmed." When using the Internet as a learning tool, readers must figure out whether a writer is truly knowledgeable or not. The computer message boards are just another cross-section of humanity, and information given therein should be judged carefully before using it with a companion parrot.

Take What You Can Use — Leave The Rest

There are many web sites offering a vast amount of information about parrots. Some of these sites are quite professional sources of information, some advertise products or baby parrots, and others are the personal sites of people who love parrots. Again, there is a tremendous range in the quality of the information in web pages. I have found some very delightful web sites that I love to visit over and over. The ones where people are just bragging about their birds are usually great fun. They provide a personal view into how people live with their parrots.

As with all commercial enterprises, you will have to decide for yourself which web site aviaries really have well-socialized, healthy baby parrots for sale, and which products are made with the quality you want for your parrot. You cannot always determine quality by how flashy the web site is.

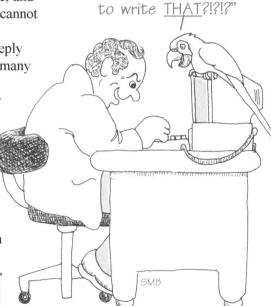

"Are you allowed to write THAT?!?!?"

The Internet is a great adventure and many of the people on it care deeply about the welfare of not only their birds, but also all parrots. Because so many people share their knowledge and feelings about their own parrots, the Internet provides a remarkable opportunity for learning. So, don't let any negative experiences or people you might encounter ruin the learning experience for you. *Surf* with an open mind, but learn to make appropriate judgements about the information you read, based upon your feelings about what is right for you and your parrots.

The *Pet Bird Report* web site is dedicated to providing information you can trust about the behavior and care of companion parrots. The popular site contains several articles from the *Pet Bird Report* magazine, a content list of all the back issues, plus a lot of fun stuff and information about quality bird-related products. Please come and visit:

http://www.petbirdreport.com

JUDGING INFORMATION

Think About The Advice & Information You Receive

The world of birds can be a confusing place for bird owners. Although there has been a vast improvement in the quality and accuracy of the information available about the care and behavior of parrots, there is still a great deal of bad advice out there. Because of the swift growth in our knowledge of parrot behavior, many of the books on the market today have out-of-date information, underscored by the advocating of aggressive handling techniques. Even bird club newsletters may have questionable information. The popular media (both local and national) usually *goes for the cute* and continually perpetuates inaccurate information about parrots, because the reporters simply do not know enough to make proper judgements about the information they give. There are many opinions in the world of birds and a great deal of variance in what can be termed as good information. Unfortunately, there is still a vast amount of nonsense being disseminated everyday about parrots and their care.

How Can We Determine If Information Is Valid Or Not?

➲ **Could the person giving the information have a "personal agenda"?** If a breeder negates the pet potential of every species he or she does not have available, you need to question whether their advice might be calculated to sell the birds they do have. The same thing is true for parrot related products.

➲ **Is the advice given in a truthful, understandable way?** When a potential buyer questioned one breeder about her practice of gavage feeding all chicks, the breeder replied that she didn't gavage feed, but used a system of "modified tube feeding." Gavage and tube feeding both involve putting a tube into the crop to deposit the food therein and neither teaches the parrot anything about eating. The response that her method was "modified" was confusing and clouded the truth.

➲ **Is the advice contrary to what makes sense?** In a bird club newsletter, a breeder recommended spitting into the handfeeding formula while mixing, in order to provide *beneficial bacteria* to the chicks. Given what we know about parrots and bacterial contamination, this advice is in direct opposition to what would be optimal for the health of any chick.

➲ **What is the bias of the article or program?** Many magazine articles and television programs dealing with parrots are biased toward an animal rights agenda and therefore contain negative and inaccurate information about the parrot industry.

➲ **When was the publication printed?** The information in many parrot-related books is often archaic, simplistic, stereotypical, inappropriate, and misleading. Many of the commonly sold books are reprinted from European sources. They may contain valid species descriptions or even decent breeding information, but the behavioral information is often atrocious. Look at the copyright date; if the book was first published more then 5 years ago, the information should be interpreted with a critical eye and assimilated with caution.

➲ **Is statistical information based on valid criteria or a small sampling?** Surveys based on a small sampling of information in one area usually provide invalid statistical samplings and inaccurate interpretations.

➲ **Is the advice based on an absolute or a "black and white" generalization?** Any use of the terms *All* or *Every* when applied to parrots should be questioned.

➲ **Does the person giving the advice have experience in the area in which they are giving advice?** Many people give generalized advice, based only on their experience with their parrots. Behaviorists and breeders should not give medical advice and not all breeders are qualified to give behavioral advice. Behaviorists may not be qualified to give breeding advice. Some veterinarians give questionable behavioral advice and so on.

➲ **Does the advice actually apply to your parrot and your situation?** Advice given about a biting 10 year old cockatoo may not apply to an 8 month old African Grey. An Amazon usually plucks for different reasons than a cockatoo.

➲ **Does the advice make sense to you?** Think about the advice — if it doesn't make sense, don't follow it.

➲ **Can the person giving the advice tell you WHY it works?** If he or she can't tell you in a clear, logical way why you should do something or why the advice works, don't pay attention to them.

➲ **Is the information based on punishment or quick fixes?** Quick-fixes distract a parrot from the immediate bout of screaming but do not deal with the underlying cause or teach a parrot anything about not screaming (see page 145).

➲ **Is the advice trust-building or trust-destroying?** This is the ultimate question every parrot caregiver must ask himself when evaluating any advice he comes across, no matter what the source. Advice advocating any aggressive, punishing techniques must be discarded, because these will not foster the trust needed in a parrot/human bond. ƒ

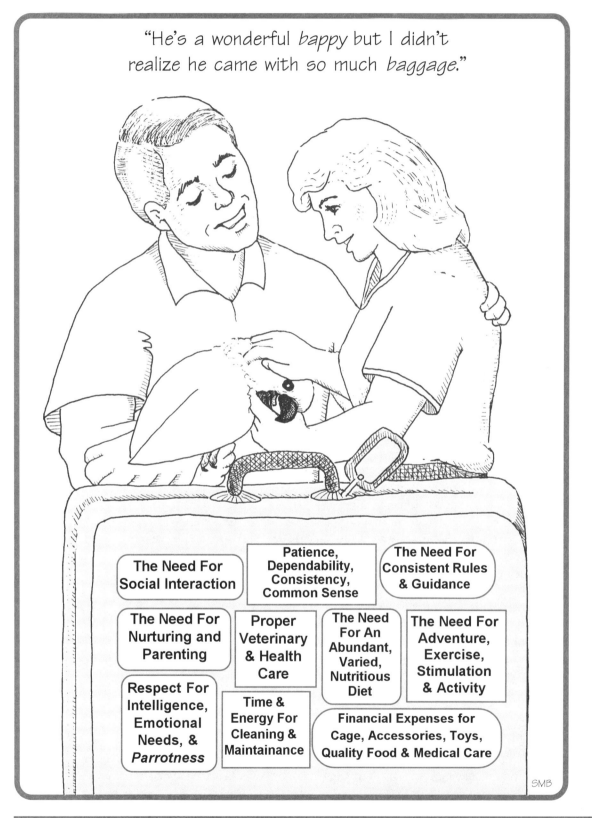

Chapter Four:
PREPARING FOR YOUR BAPPY ·····➤

Nurturing Guidance Tip: Be Prepared

Prepare Your Household Before Your Bappy Comes Home

Be Prepared! The more prepared you are, the more readily your bappy will adjust to his transition from the breeder or bird shop. Have his cage all set up with a few familiar toys with which he played where he was raised. Make sure you have foods on hand he is used to eating even if you plan on changing his diet. Remember he is a baby and don't let him climb too high on a play gym or cage unless he is already quite an acrobat with all his balance skills. Many young parrots injure themselves quite severely when they try to fly and fall to the floor. Some birds split the skin on their keel bone when they land and this can be a difficult injury to treat. Go slow at first — if he is a bappy, he will need his rest but he will also need some affection and attention.

REMEMBER HE'S A BAPPY

Extensive Parental Care

If you are bringing a newly weaned parrot home, the most important thing you need to remember and continually convince yourself about is that your new companion is still a baby. In the wild, large macaws maintain parental care and supervision until the chick is as old as two years. With most medium sized parrots, some parenting is continued until the chick is a year or older. Your new parrot will most likely still need to develop his balance, climbing, eating, social, and talking skills, and will need your help and guidance for these important parts of his development. Don't unrealistically expect him to be everything you

wanted from a parrot right away. His eventual pet potential depends on the parenting and instructional interaction you provide for him. Do not be impatient with him. Even if he seems like a big bird when you bring him home — respect and take responsibility for his needs as a constantly developing and maturing young parrot.

THE ORIGIN OF THE WORD BAPPY

I have found after years of working with parrots that many people think a weaned bird is no longer a baby mostly because, to the untrained eye, he looks much like an adult bird. This is the main reason that I developed the word *bappy* a few years ago.

Puppies, Kitties and ... Bappies? There is nothing cuter than a frisky little puppy, except maybe a furry ball of a kitten. I've often heard folks lament, "the trouble with puppies (kittens) is that they grow up to be dogs (cats)." The same reality is absolutely true with human babies that are *oh so cuddly,* but eventually grow up to be either well-adjusted or juvenile delinquent teenagers (or something in between) on their way to adulthood. Mammal babies are quite different in appearance and behavior than their adult counterparts. It is very obvious when they are babies and quite evident that they will not continue to look or act the same as they mature. There are even words for the babies of dogs and cats which we humans often keep as pets. Despite the fact that some people love the word "bappy" and some hate it, I do believe that there needs to be a word like 'puppy' and 'kitty' to distinguish young companion parrots.

I think the fact that there is no special term for a baby parrot may create some misconceptions, especially for the novice bird owner. We obviously know that a *silly-putty blob* of a parrot before he has his feathers is a baby. But too many people presume that once a bappy is feathered out and eating on his own, he is no longer a baby. Novices may not realize that a baby parrot is soft and cuddly with velvety shiny feathers, clumsy little rubbery feet, and innocent inquisitive eyes that can melt the heart of all but the most production-oriented breeders. The new caregiver may expect too much too soon and not treat his or her new parrot like the *bappy* he is.

Some people love the word bappy, some are ambivalent, and others despise the word. My purpose was to change the way people think about the young, developing parrots who come into their lives — that is what matters.

BRINGING BAPPY HOME BASICS

⮑ Remember your new parrot is a bappy — even if he is weaned and looks almost like an adult. Respect his limitations and encourage his healthy development. Patience and consistent nurturing are essential.

⮑ Plan ahead and set up the cage area, cage, and cage environment before bringing your new bird home. Remember that parrots are social birds and it is important that your bappy be part of the flock and live in an area where his new "human flock" spends time.

⮑ Even if your baby has been fully weaned, he may become insecure in his new environment. It helps to offer him soft, moist, warm foods such as cooked sweet potatoes with your fingers. Some birds may actually need to be handfed again with a spoon or syringe to help their sense of security. Foods such as pureed vegetables, cooked oatmeal, and organic baby foods are wonderful for this purpose. (African Grey breeder, Pam Clark suggests making convenient feeding spoons by dipping plastic spoons in very hot water to soften the plastic, then molding the sides upward by pressing the spoon between two fingers. They should cool before using.)

⮑ Baby parrots DO need more attention when they are young simply because they are babies. It is not the amount of attention that spoils a parrot — it is the kind of attention. Do more than just cuddle your new bappy. He needs lots of *instructional interaction* and structured play time with you, in addition to cuddling.

⮑ Take it slow at first but give your baby the level of attention he is used to. I have often read that new parrots should be left alone in their cage for a few days to adjust to their surroundings. This is simply not true. However, it is very important that his life is not too busy and that he has plenty of naps and adequate sleep at night.

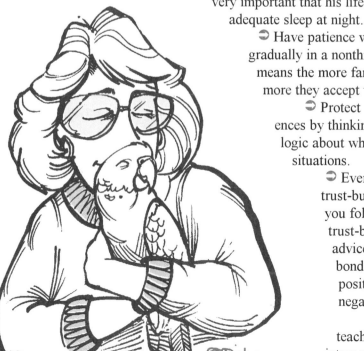

⮑ Have patience with him. Introduce new people and objects gradually in a nonthreatening way. Parrots learn by patterning which means the more familiar they are with someone or something, the more they accept that person, object, or situation.

⮑ Protect him as much as possible from traumatic experiences by thinking ahead and using a cause-and-effect sense of logic about what could happen if you put him into specific situations.

⮑ Everything you do with your young bird should be trust-building for a positive parrot/human bond. Before you follow any advice, carefully determine whether it is trust-building or trust-destroying. Follow only the advice that builds trust and makes the parrot/human bond stronger. Teach him the right way to behave with positive interaction rather than punishing him for negative behavior.

⮑ Be his *surrogate parent*, his friend, and his teacher. The foundation of guidance and instructional interaction you provide for your young parrot has a profound effect in determining his lifelong pet potential. ✎

PREPARING THE HOUSE

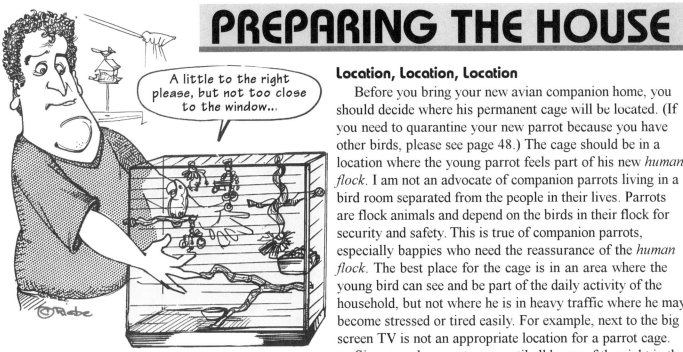

A little to the right please, but not too close to the window...

Location, Location, Location

Before you bring your new avian companion home, you should decide where his permanent cage will be located. (If you need to quarantine your new parrot because you have other birds, please see page 48.) The cage should be in a location where the young parrot feels part of his new *human flock*. I am not an advocate of companion parrots living in a bird room separated from the people in their lives. Parrots are flock animals and depend on the birds in their flock for security and safety. This is true of companion parrots, especially bappies who need the reassurance of the *human flock*. The best place for the cage is in an area where the young bird can see and be part of the daily activity of the household, but not where he is in heavy traffic where he may become stressed or tired easily. For example, next to the big screen TV is not an appropriate location for a parrot cage.

Since people may stay up until all hours of the night in the household activity area, I usually recommend getting young parrots used to a smaller sleeping cage in a quieter part of the house. This way, if the family wants to stay up late watching television or talking, the bird can be placed in his *night-night* cage in the evening and still get the rest he needs. If your household is hectic during the day, you might even need to put the bappy in his sleeping cage in the early afternoon for an hour-long "siesta."

Environmental Concerns

There are many aspects of your household that need to be taken into consideration in placing the cage. Good lighting is essential. While some parrots may enjoy being next to a window, others may find it threatening if there is a great deal of activity going on outside the window. Make sure that the cage is not placed in an area where the sun beats down on it through the window. Even placing the parrot's cage in a sunny location does not guarantee him the essential light he needs. Normal glass used in windows filters some of the color ranges of light needed for health. Because of this, I highly recommend the use of a full-spectrum light above the cage. Full-spectrum lighting should be kept on during daylight hours only. Ask the manufacturer or retailer about the specifics in location and duration they recommend.

Most parrots can tolerate a fairly wide range of household temperatures if they become used to them gradually. Parrots can be comfortable with temperatures of about 60°F to 90°F but may have problems with extreme fluctuations in short periods of time. Do not place the cage in an area of the house which receives intense heat or heavy cold drafts. While normal air flow is not a problem, cages should not be placed near drafty windows in winter or air conditioner vents in summer. Parrot cages should not be placed next to west facing windows, heater vents, or fireplaces.

I would not recommend placing the cage next to the front door for a variety of reasons. If your household is busy, with lots of people coming in and out, especially strangers and kids, this placement could be very threatening to a sensitive bird. A location near the front door could also expose your parrot to extreme temperature changes. Placing the cage next to the front door or a front window where the parrot can be viewed by strangers may also create a security risk since there is a market for stolen companion parrots.

Another consideration is avoiding areas of the household where the bird might be exposed to dust, exhaust fumes, cigarette smoke, cleaning agents, aerosol sprays, or other toxic fumes.

If your parrot is going to live in the kitchen area, you should first test all gas appliances to make sure they are in working order and do not have the potential for leaking gas fumes. I recommend buying a gas leak and/or a carbon monoxide detector. Some cooking fumes can be dangerous for your parrot, especially if anything is overheated or burned. If you have any cooking utensils with PTFE nonstick coating, please consider replacing them with pans that do not have a coating. It will be more work in the kitchen but could save your parrot's life.

PREPARING THE CAGE

Set The Cage Up Before Your Bappy Comes Home

Make sure the cage material is safe without a possibility of heavy metal toxicity (lead and zinc) from chipping or paint. Decorative scroll work is dangerous if the parrot can access it from inside the cage. The width of a parrot's cage is far more important than the height. Cages should be wide enough to allow a parrot a great deal of space to move from side to side rather than up and down. High energy birds need ample room for moving around and cage size should accommodate multiple perches for climbing and exercise.

If possible, set up everything in the cage before you bring your new pet home. Place the perches, bowls, and toys in the cage so they are ready. Some perches should go from front to back with others going from side to side. The material and size of the perches should vary so parrots are not standing with their feet in the same position all of the time. If you choose to use a concrete or nail-trimming type perch, make sure it is not too abrasive (rub your hand tightly on it and if it scrapes you, it is too sharp), and do not use it on the highest perch or the perch your parrot uses most frequently. Parrots will usually only use a swing if it is the highest perch in the cage. Once they are used to them, most parrots love their swings. The cage should have three or four bowls — one for clean water, one for dry foods (pellets, etc.), one for moist foods, and even one as a toy box for foot toys and other play objects. Getting a young parrot used to a water bottle can help keep his water clean and free of chewed debris. Other greatly appreciated cage accessories include a climbing ladder, rope type perches, corner platforms, a privacy shelter, and a sleeping tent or tube.

Potential Problems With The Grate

With young birds who have not completely developed their balance and climbing skills, be sure to place the perches low. For some young parrots, it also helps to put food and water in crocks on the cage floor so they have easy access to them. I highly recommend <u>not</u> using a grate in the bottom of a bappy's cage. Many young parrots are injured when they fall from their perches and get their wings or tail caught in the grate at the bottom of the cage. If your new cage

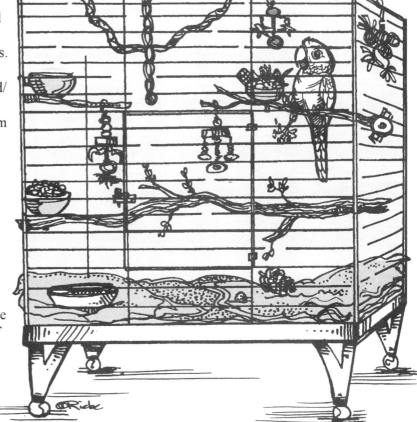

doesn't have a removable grate, place a folded blanket or towels directly on the grate and then cover it with newspaper, newsprint, or unwaxed white butcher paper. Even without a grate, the bottom of the cage should be padded for bappies. Many young parrots will spend a great deal of time on the cage floor, so put some textured and/or colorful foot toys there and make sure you change the papers frequently. Hanging toys from the lower perches also creates fun play time on the floor.

As your new parrot matures and develops his balance and climbing skills, gradually raise the perches and start putting food and water in the bowls on the sides of the cage. Whether or not you use the grate after your parrot matures will be your choice. I personally do not use a grate in the bottom of my birds' cages. I find it much harder to clean a cage with a grate, and also prefer for my birds, especially Bongo Marie and Spike, to be allowed to play on the floor of their cages. (Cockatoos also appreciate cage floor time.) Contrary to popular mythology which says grates are essential, my parrots do not walk around or play in their poop. 🪶

PLAYGYMS, T-STANDS & TOYS

The Price Of A Parrot

When considering the purchase price of a parrot, certain costs besides the cost of the bird should be obvious — a roomy cage and all its accessories and an initial well-bird exam with an avian veterinarian. The cost of a good playgym and a T-stand should also be considered. If you purchase a playgym for your new parrot, it is very important that you supervise his play on it for the first few weeks unless he is already a secure little acrobat. Again, I have heard about far too many injuries sustained when a bappy falls or 'flies' off of a new playgym before he had developed the balance and climbing skills to be on one.

Multiple stands and gyms in various locations around the house lessen the possibility that the parrot will form a strong territorial imperative around his cage or one particular playgym. Because of the possibility of height dominance issues with a strong-willed parrot, the highest playgym perch should be no higher than human eye level. A multiple parrot household may need more than one playgym, because not all parrots happily share a gym with other parrots.

Several Types Of Stands And Gyms

There are several types of stands and playgyms on the market today, each with a different purpose. A basic T-stand is a perch on a pole and may have food bowls, a tray, and rollers. This stand is convenient for training in the "neutral room" (see page 158) and provides a *parking place* for your parrot when he is with you while you are working nearby during *casual attention times*. The basic T-stand is too boring to be thought of as a playgym. There is not enough to do on one. Some T-stands have multiple perches and toy holders and provide more avenues for activity than a basic T-stand, but are not as large as a playgym. The ring-style perch provides more activity than a basic T-stand, but the most play and exercise activity opportunities are with multiple perch playgyms.

Manufactured playgyms and multiple perch stands can be made from several materials including wooden dowels, natural branches, and PVC. Some utilize multiple materials in their construction. Several manufacturers have given a great deal of consideration to the perch material, texture, and shape. The materials and design should be safe and have multiple places to hang toys, several perches of various thickness and textures, swings or rings, and bowls for food and water. Most have trays below the perches, both to keep the parrot on the stand and to keep the floors clean. A good playgym setup will have enough activity centers to keep a parrot entertained for a few hours at a time.

Not A Substitute For A Cage

A playgym should not be a substitute for a cage. A large, quality cage with lots of toys and perches provides far more safety, security, and activity than a playgym. Even parrots who have never climbed down from their gyms or stands eventually will, for one reason or another, and can end up injuring themselves. Chewing on electric cords seems to be a favorite pastime of errant parrots. Parrots should not be out of their cages, even on their favorite playgyms, without close supervision.

CAGE ETIQUETTE

Sharing The Cage Territory

It is essential to establish and maintain "cage control" as one of the major ways of guiding a parrot's behavior. I've talked to many parrot owners who can no longer handle their parrots because they never established cage control, then lost hand control, and subsequently became afraid to handle their parrots. If a parrot establishes control of his cage, that control will eventually transfer to all aspects of his life. From the time parrots are first perching, I encourage people to use the "UP" command to ask them to step onto the hand. I also emphasize the importance of consistently bringing the bird out of the cage by announcing your presence, reaching in the cage, saying a firm but friendly "UP" so the bird steps on your hand, and then bringing the bird out. This is all done in a nonthreatening, non-aggressive manner and I recommend a nurturing verbal reward of "very good" or "what a good bird" once the bird is out on your hand.

Flock birds share territory on one level or another with the other members of their family and flock and tend to only be intensely defensive of that area with strangers and intruders. In a positive parrot/human bond, the human is viewed as a close and trusted flock member — hopefully as the flock leader and not an adversarial threat to the territory. Consequently, for the trusted human members of the parrot's family or flock, the cage becomes a **shared** territory and not the parrot's stronghold against perceived intruders. However, in some cases when a parrot has not formed a trusting bond with humans because it has either been poorly socialized as a youngster, spoiled without any rules, neglected, abused, or in some way threatened by humans, establishing a positive cage relationship may take patient development on the part of the people in that bird's life.

While a contented companion parrot will generally have no trouble when one of its "human flock" approaches the cage, it is understandable why some parrots will respond aggressively to strangers or perceived intruders to its cage territory. Unless your parrot is one of those extremely well-socialized, laid-back birds who doesn't mind being approached by strangers, it is unfair to allow new people to approach the bird's cage and try to pick him up from the cage. In fact, with many parrots, allowing a person who is not a member of the bird's accepted "human flock" to try to take the bird out of or off of its cage is a major mistake which can result in territorial aggression. New people in the bird's life have a much greater chance of being accepted as a new "flock member" when they are introduced in a neutral room where the cage can not even be seen and the bird has no perceived territorial imperative.

Punishment and Time-Out

There is a vast difference between time-out in a cage and punishing a bird by putting him in his cage. I do not believe a parrot should ever be threatened in his cage or placed there aggressively for punishment. Throwing objects at a cage or banging on it with a stick for whatever reason is childish and totally unacceptable human behavior and will eventually result in a breakdown of the trust necessary for a positive human/parrot bond. Parrots should never be teased or threatened while they are in their cage. The cage should be a roomy, safe haven — a place for rest and independent entertainment. If a parrot truly feels comfortable in his cage, then the bird should feel no threat being placed back in it even if it is to *chill-out*. Sometimes because of their high excitability, parrots may go into overload behavior. They may turn life into a challenging game for their owners by insisting on climbing off of their playgym and chewing on the furniture over and over and over. They may simply become demanding and *pest-chevious* from time to time when they are out of their cage. Sometimes this is because they are tired and cranky and need a nap, or they may be hungry or thirsty and want to eat — in the security of their cage. Their insistence on behaving in a negative manner may be just a way of asking to go back to their cage. Whatever the message the parrot is giving, time-out in the cage is usually the way to deal with this type of behavior.

SLEEP IS ESSENTIAL

A Consultation About A Sleep-deprived Cockatoo

A previously well-behaved young Moluccan started screaming, biting, and feather picking. Several things had changed. The woman had started a new job, the family had moved to a larger home, and they had recently purchased a big screen television. After a few minutes of discussion, I knew what was causing the 'too so many problems. The woman worked days and the man worked nights. When they weren't working, each one watched a lot of television. The new TV was in the living room right next to the cockatoo's cage. It was on day and night. So was the 'too, even though his cage was covered at night. The TV was still under warranty but it had already been repaired three times. The cause was cockatoo dust — perhaps an appropriate, but coincidental revenge for so many sleepless nights. The room was bright and noisy all day and almost all night. Parrots are prey animals which means they are very wary when there is activity in their sleep area. Deep sleep only occurs in a partially dark, quiet, safe place. During afternoon naps, parrots remain very alert even if it appears as if they are sleeping. Watch how quickly a napping parrot's eyes open when any activity occurs in the room. The cockatoo was clearly sleep-deprived and this was causing all sorts of behavioral problems. The solution was simple. I did not recommend moving the cage out of the living room because it was obvious the 'too liked to be where the action was, but not twenty-four hours a day. I recommended buying a small, yet comfortable, cage as a sleeping cage. They spent about a week getting him used to being in the new cage by playing with him in and around it. Then every night a few hours before the man went to work, he spent some quality cuddle time with the cockatoo and then put him to bed in the quiet guest room. In the morning, a few hours before she went to work, the woman got him up and spent some time with him in the living room. Within less than a week, the Moluccan's behavior improved dramatically.

A Secure, Dark, Quiet Place To Sleep

A good night's sleep in a safe, dark, quiet room is essential for parrots, especially young birds. I recommend covering the cage as a nighttime ritual. It helps to establish a period of time when the parrot knows he should rest and most of all, it establishes a specific time when he can start making noise in the morning. I usually work late at night and appreciate the fact that my parrots don't carry on in the morning until I get up and uncover their cages.

Not all parrots have the same sleeping habits. Many like to roost on the highest perch in their cage at night. Others (especially macaws and conures) may hang onto the side of the cage to sleep. Some birds like to sleep in a secure enclosed area in the cage and others burrow under their cage papers. Most, but not all, sleep with one foot tucked into their body and their head tucked into their back feathers.

Some parrot-family birds (including cockatiels and greys) have occasional night frights and thrash around their cage. With some birds, a dim night light may help alleviate night frights. If there are windows in the room, car lights should be kept from reflecting on the walls. Parrots have bundles of nerves in their joints which may act as vibration detectors to warn them of night predators. Trucks rumbling by on a nearby highway, people walking around on the floor above the parrot's room, and minor earthquakes may also be contributing factors to night frights. A small sleeping cage can help avoid injury and may provide a more steady sleeping area than the larger daytime cage.

The Sleeping Cage

The nighttime sleeping cage is one perfect solution to guarantee a night's undisturbed sleep for a companion parrot. Some parrots are perfectly happy sleeping in a carrier or travel cage. Place the cage in a secure, quiet area of the house. In earthquake areas, a sturdy sleeping cage in a safe room may make a big difference in keeping your parrot out of danger. Be sure and get your parrot used to the sleeping cage gradually by making it a special fun place so he feels confident and secure there before he is placed in it for bedtime.

PREPARING THE FIRST BIRD

Preparation For Sharing Time

If you already have a strongly bonded parrot, it is a wise idea to prepare him properly for the addition of the new bappy. **The major threat to the first bird's security usually has more to do with timesharing than jealousy.** The best way to get the first parrot used to sharing your time is to set the new bird's cage up a few weeks before he comes home. When you clean or service your first parrot's cage, do the same things with the new parrot's cage. Fiddle with the food dishes, the paper, the perches, and the toys on a daily basis. One *Pet Bird Report* reader wrote about introducing her new grey into a home with a well-loved Moluccan cockatoo. She fashioned a grey sock and a red sock to look like an African Grey doll, then took it out of the cage on a frequent basis in front of her 'too to help him adjust to the new grey. When the grey bappy actually came home, the cockatoo pretty much took his presence for granted and barely reacted to him. Planning ahead and introducing the new routines gradually, instead of suddenly, prevented some adjustment problems with her cockatoo.

What Parrots Get Along With Each Other?

I am often asked which species of parrots get along best with others. This is an almost impossible question to answer due to individual personalities within a particular species. It also has a lot to do with the ages and genders of the birds, environmental considerations, and personalities of the owners. Although many birds adjust to each other if introduced properly, some may never readily share space with others. The best way to introduce the two is to hold the first bird with one hand and the new bird with the other hand in a neutral area away from the cages. Talk to each of them, telling them that everything is OK ... and bring them closer together. Watch their body language carefully and don't push the introduction. Be in control of the situation. Have a towel handy to place over either bird — just in case there is a problem. A few weeks may pass before the first bird settles down, so be patient and remember that if your new bird is a vulnerable baby, you will need to be his protector. Before any birds are left alone together or without close supervision, you must be absolutely sure there will not be a problem between them.

Although most birds will adjust to each other if introduced properly, some may never like each other. Others may seem to get along but will not readily share space with each other. Remember to establish rules and provide guidance for your new bird so that he forms the strongest bond with you instead of with your other parrot. Whatever you do, don't neglect your original bird just because you have a new bappy. Provide him with as much time as before the new bird so he does not feel displaced by the new parrot. Although this process may sound complicated, choosing a new bird carefully and introducing it properly can guarantee you a harmonious, secure multiple bird home. Your companion parrot flock will usually form its own hierarchy. Generally, you can tell who is the dominant parrot in your multiple-bird family. He or she is usually the one who gets preened but rarely returns the favor. They also prefer and usually get the highest perch. Although the people may not always be aware of it, the parrot who perceives himself as being the leader may also have convinced his owner to let him out of his cage first. 🪶

PREPARING OTHER PETS

Guess what?

People who have happy, well-behaved dogs usually have well-behaved parrots. These people know how to set rules and provide *Nurturing Guidance.* Most companion animals will be very curious about a new addition to the household — especially a first parrot, who is probably unlike anything they have seen in their living area. No matter how well-trained your other animals are, I think the first rule should be absolute — make sure you are in control of everyone and everything before you attempt any introduction. Disasters can happen very quickly if you're not. Usually it helps to have at least two people around for introductions, or at least one to closely supervise each animal. Expect the unexpected. Even animals with fairly predictable behavior can react differently in unfamiliar situations.

I know my animals fairly well. I have three dogs, two cats, and four parrots. My silky terrier, KT, the cutest and most submissive dog with me, is actually the one I trust the least around my birds. She becomes very excited around my parrots when they are out of their cages. Sometimes, if Spike is in the bottom of the cage, KT will jump at him. Dewey, my 70 pound dog is a pushover and my grey, Bongo Marie, often feeds him the foods she decides not to eat by throwing them at his head. Still, I am not going to trust him or any of the other mammals around the birds without very close supervision. Cats are particularly intrigued by smaller, active parrots. My cats are usually afraid of the large parrots, but that doesn't mean a bird couldn't be injured by one of them if there was a confrontation.

My mammalian animals live in the back of the house, especially when I am not home. One day a few years ago, I had not shut the door to the living room tight enough and my cat, Nimbus managed, with a great deal of work on his part, to get the door open. He sauntered into the living room where Paco and Rascal, my Amazons, were sitting on a playgym. I was talking on the telephone. As Paco cheered him on, it took less than 10 seconds for Rascal to jump off the stand, and doing *his* imitation of a harpy eagle looking for lunch, he landed right on top of Nimbus. I have never seen the normally nonchalant Nimbus jump so high and run so fast. Of course, Rascal wasn't going to let it go at that and went racing after him. Nimbus ended up backed into a corner ready to defend himself with teeth and claws. Since I was nearby, I managed to scoop one overloaded Amazon up before anyone was injured.

Some parrots will form a very strong bond with the family dog (or cat). It is not uncommon for parrots to share their food with expectantly waiting dogs. I have also seen situations where phobic parrots, who are afraid of almost everything, will form a trusting bond with the mild-mannered friendly family dog.

Always remember that dogs and cats are both instinctively predators. Although domesticated for years, instincts can still be strong, like the instinct to protect the dog pack. A bonded dog may harm a parrot trying to protect his owners. **Close supervision is always essential.** Regardless of all the cute photographs we have all seen of canine/feline/avian cohabitation and cooperation, **do not place your parrot in jeopardy by assuming your friendly mammals can be trusted.**

I'll bet he tastes like chicken...

KIDS & BIRDS

DOES HAVING A HUMAN BABY MEAN YOU HAVE TO FIND A NEW HOME FOR YOUR COMPANION PARROT?

Guess what?

People who have happy, well-behaved kids usually have well-behaved parrots because they understand the importance of setting rules and providing *Nurturing Guidance*. How well your parrot gets along with your kids depends a great deal on the personality and behavior of the children. Parrots may bond strongly to a quiet, confident child but become overstimulated by an active or exuberant child. Some of the things that curious children do can be quite threatening to a bappy. The cage should be the parrot's safe place so if children poke at a parrot in his cage territory, it can easily lead to fear behavior and defensive biting. The ideal situation is to introduce the kids and the bappy in a controlled family get-together in a neutral room, making sure that children understand the handling rules you set for them. If you want the parrot to stay tame to the children and they are old enough to understand and obey the rules, kids should be a part of the family's *warm potato* game. If a child is exceptionally trustworthy with the new bappy, he or she can spend time developing a strong individual bond with the bird in their own room. With *ambient attention*, the parrot can be quite happy on a T-stand while the child does homework or plays nearby.

One important rule in a household with parrots and children — don't let your kid's friends mess with your parrot, especially without close supervision! Excited behavior in the cage territory, or teasing by children who are not a part of the human flock and are, therefore, viewed as intruders or predators, is a leading cause of phobic behavior in companion parrots. ✦

Of course not! But there are people who do it all the time. Perhaps their parrot is totally out of control. Hopefully they have learned some lessons about parenting. If not, they may wish they could get rid of their new kid in a few years. The expectant couple has close to nine months to work on getting their parrot used to a baby in the household before the baby is born. The first step is to establish *Nurturing Guidance* with your parrot. The second is helping him adjust to time sharing by setting up the baby's furniture and accessories ahead of time. As silly as it sounds, getting a doll and spending some time in front of your parrot with it can help him learn to share time. The sound of crying can aggravate screaming in some parrots. Gradually getting him used to the sound of a crying baby by playing a tape can also help you control his responsive screaming before the baby actually comes home. Even after the baby comes home, try to give the parrot at least 10-15 minutes a day of focused attention. Giving him the attention he deserves will make all the difference in the world in his acceptance of the new human baby. Whether or not you trust your parrot near the baby with supervision will depend on his gentleness and your ability to guide his behavior. ✦

"I like to think of it as keeping them out rather than keeping me in."

FOOD INDEPENDENCE

The Difference Between Weaning and Food Independence

Weaning is the process by which a young parrot learns to eat on his own. In the wild, food independence is a gradual process started long before a chick has fledged. However, no young bird could possibly be weaned until he has learned to fly and can travel with his parents and the flock. During these travels, a young parrot learns from instruction and example about foraging and gathering his own food. While he is still in the nest, his parents (and in some species, other caretaker birds) are responsible for filling all of his nutritional needs. Breeding season usually comes during and just after the rainy season, which guarantees abundant food for parrot babies when they hatch.

Chicks are fed whenever the parents have food to give them and not according to some arbitrary timetable. Wild parrot babies are not deprived if there is abundant food available. At first, most of the food is partially predigested by the parents and then regurgitated into the baby's beak as pabulum. As the chick matures, the variety and consistency of the food changes. Gradually he learns to manipulate larger pieces and different types of food. By the time he fledges, he is familiar with many of the foods that will be available to him throughout his life but he does not yet know how and where to find them. He does not know where foods grow and how to take them from the plant and manipulate them for his consumption. These lessons take longer. Although he reaches a point where he is pretty much eating on his own, his parents continue feeding him until his food independence is evident. While the odds are against the successful raising of every parrot chick, wild parrots have evolved to be good parents. It is their biological imperative to raise their young as well as possible for success and survival of the species.

Domestically-raised Chicks And Abundance Weaning™

Almost from the beginning of aviculture, it has been acceptable to deprive domestically-raised baby parrots of food to force them to wean. It seems that over the last few decades aviculturists came up with protocols for the breeding and handfeeding of parrots that had much more to do with the convenience of the people involved than the developmental needs of the chicks. Some parrots are forced to wean long before their natural weaning time. Years ago, someone decided this was the way to do it and few breeders challenged this accepted method. In the mid-80's, as most of my work shifted from taming wild-caught parrots to working with domestically-raised parrots, I began to see a correlation between weaning trauma and behavioral dysfunction. **Weaning trauma is the insecurity and dysfunction caused by deprivation and/or forced weaning, gavage feeding until weaning, and inadequate nutrition.** The more handfed parrots I worked with, the more obvious this cause-and-effect connection became.

In the early 90's, I met and visited Phoebe Greene Linden of Santa Barbara Bird Farm and was amazed at the innovative common-sense way she nurtured and handfed her chicks. Her ground-breaking theory of Abundance Weaning™ was first presented in the *Pet Bird Report*. Phoebe does not deprive her chicks to wean them. Rather than feed her parrots a limited amount of food on a strict timetable, Phoebe feeds her bappies an abundant variety of healthy foods frequently during the day. Most of the soft, moist, and warm foods are fed with her fingers simulating the beak feeding of an adult parrot. Deep yellow-orange sweet potatoes are a favorite. Phoebe developed the concept of Handweaning Foods for Marion Zoological's Scenic Bird Foods. These nutritionally dense pellets are soaked in warm/hot water and then finger fed to eager chicks. When I visit Phoebe, I am fascinated with the way she interacts with her chicks. With a bowl of warm/hot foods, she walks by the clean and stimulating cardboard boxes the babies are raised in. The chicks pop their heads up for a few morsels and happily go back to their play. There is never any desperate food begging or excessive hunger. As Phoebe further developed her special techniques of feeding parrot chicks, she found that they weaned more readily if they were abundantly fed instead of being deprived of food in an effort to force them to wean. Parrots who have been abundantly weaned with this nurturing technique clearly are more secure and contented, and have much greater pet potential than chicks weaned with deprivation. ✶

FOOD INSECURITY

Excessive Food Begging and Regression Weaning

Hopefully you have purchased a secure, well-socialized, fully-weaned baby parrot. Even if this is true, you may have some problems with immediate adjustment. Many recently weaned birds become a bit insecure in a new location and will begin food begging again. Some parrots even become excessively aggressive when they get too hungry. I have worked with more than one hyperactive baby grey who was not getting enough to eat and was throwing himself out of the cage when someone opened the door.

Excessive food begging beyond weaning is common with several species but happens with young macaws on a regular basis. I believe far too many handfed macaw bappies have not been fed well enough or long enough. In the wild, these large parrots are still being fed by their parents up to a year of age or older, yet many macaw chicks are *weaned* and expected to be food independent before

they are 4 or 5 months old. Some parrots who are forced to eat on their own become insecure because they don't even have the physical skills to successfully manipulate their foods. A macaw, or any other parrot who normally holds food in a foot to manipulate it, can't possibly be food independent until he has developed the dexterity and balance skills to hold food in his foot. Therefore, working with other skills will also encourage food security.

Several years ago, I bird-sat a newly weaned Green-winged Macaw. The owners were appalled when they returned and discovered that I had to start handfeeding him again. No amount of logical explanation would calm their unreasonable anger. With all the confusing changes, the bird had become quite insecure and started food begging almost incessantly. He needed some extra handfeeding and cuddling to feel secure again, but they felt that since he was weaned, he was no longer a baby. He <u>was</u> a baby and was still going to be a baby for close to a year. Even though they seemed unwilling to follow my advice, I tried to convince them that they needed to watch him closely for the next month or so and handfeed him if he became agitated or exhibited any food begging behaviors.

Be Prepared

Food begging from a weaned bird is not necessarily a sign that the bird was force-weaned or weaned too young, although parrots with handfeeding trauma are likely to become insecure in a new situation. When you bring your bappy home, it will be important to have some of what he has been eating on hand, even if it is not what you plan to continue feeding him. The first few days in a new home is not the time to begin converting birds to another diet.

Don't ignore your baby if he becomes insecure and wants to be handfed some more. The old adage "Do not pay attention to a screaming bird" does not apply to an insecure, recently-weaned parrot. While you do not want to reward him for begging by running up to him and grabbing him up to cuddle, it is advisable to "regression wean" him by offering food with your fingers, a spoon, or syringe a few times each day until he is more relaxed and secure in his new situation. Do not let anyone convince you that a food begging bird should not be handfed again or he will never be weaned. This is nonsense. I don't recommend regressing a weaned parrot to complete handfeeding again or getting him to "pump on the syringe." Hopefully, he will accept some warm, soft foods from your fingers. If this doesn't seem to work, try a spoon with the sides bent up or ask your breeder, veterinarian, or bird shop to provide you with a syringe and some handfeeding formula and have them show you how to use the syringe to just dribble some formula into his beak. Then gradually transition him to take food from your fingers. As he becomes more secure, offer him a crock of nutritious steamed veggies and show him how to eat from the bowl. This activity helps his sense of security and also helps him develop a healthy appetite. Most regression weaned chicks will readily wean themselves once they are more secure. If not, gradually reducing the amount of food being handfed will encourage weaning.

Recovery Support Groups For
The Overly Dependent Companion Parrot

HEALING THE BAPPY WITHIN

Balancing Dependence & Independence

We know it isn't your fault you are so dependent on human affection and attention. We understand your obsessive-compulsive need to constantly be with a human being. Yes, it was the way you were raised but it is time now to self-actualize and discover your own inner power.

◇**Find Your Own Sense Of Security Within**◇
(Detaching your emotional velcro)

◇**Dealing With Flock Separation Anxiety**◇
(Is there really a Harpy Eagle hiding under your cage?)

◇**Learning The Daily Primal PsittaScream**◇
(Learning to scream only once to get it all out of your system)

◇**Achieving A Healthy Relationship With People**◇
(You're good enough, you're smart enough and by golly, you deserve it)

◇**Establishing Basic Communication Skills With Humans**◇
(You're OK — They're OK — They just need help understanding you)

◇**Getting Needs Met With Socially Acceptable Requests**◇
(Biting and excessive screaming tend to discourage intimacy)

◇**Seeking Harmony Within The Entire Human Flock**◇
(It is not acceptable to chase the family out of the house)

◇**Playing Happily By Yourself Is Healthy**◇
(Your off button shouldn't be on just because no one is there to entertain you)

◇**Building Your Confidence and Sense Of Security**◇
(But you need an astronomy lesson ... the world revolves around the sun)

◇**Rehatching Regression**◇
(Healing through reliving the traumatic struggle of pipping)

Sponsored by the
PPPPP (Psociety of Psittacine Psychological Pathology Practitioners)
Call 1-800-555-TJOY for location and dates

SMB

Nurturing Guidance Tip: Realistic Expectations

Don't Expect More Than You Should

Having unrealistic expectations is one of the most detrimental problems undermining the human/parrot bond. Unfortunately, there are so many generalizations and so much stereotypical thinking about parrot species, it is often difficult to know what can realistically be expected from a companion parrot. If the new owners of baby parrots expect too much too soon from their birds, or expect their birds to live up to the personality of another parrot they have met, they can put unrealistic pressure on their companion. For example, far too many people expect their baby African Greys to talk loquaciously in just a few months, but many greys don't really talk until they are a year or older. Some greys don't talk at all but have other delightful qualities.

Having unrealistic expectations about such things can lead to serious problems in the relationship. The human flock members can become unrealistically disappointed if they have not done their homework about their parrot's pet potential. It is unrealistic to expect bappies to embody all the personality and skills of more mature parrots. These have to be developed with the guidance of the "human flock." It is also unrealistic to expect a parrot to stay a bappy forever. While a well-guided parrot can stay sweet and tame, he will no longer have the wide-eyed innocence of a baby as he matures. It is the new caregiver's responsibility to insure their parrots will be the kind of companions they want. Each parrot is an individual, but parrots who are raised with concern and guidance always make the best human companions. ∮

"THE GETTYSBURG ADDRESS:
Four score and seven years ago our fathers brought forth on this continent a new nation, conceived in liberty and dedicated to the proposition that all men are created equal. Now we are engaged in a great civil war, testing whether that nation or any nation so conceived and so dedicated can long endure. We are met on a great battlefield of that war . . .

Don't be disappointed if your African grey parrot doesn't recite the Gettysburg Address by the time he is six months old!

THE FIRST DAY

©Riebe

The Big Day

You've got the cage all set up and ready. The toys are in place and you've done everything you can think of to ready your home. The big day has come to bring your bappy home. If you have not done so already, make an appointment to have him seen by his future avian veterinarian. I believe a parrot should be seen by a vet on the way home, but if that is not possible, he should be seen within the first three days after he comes home, whether or not the seller recommends seeing a veterinarian.

When you actually bring your new bappy home, how much attention you give him the first day or so will depend on him and your household. The idea that he should not be handled until he becomes used to his new surroundings is inappropriate for handfed babies who have been handled frequently by the breeder or by people in the pet shop. (This is also inappropriate advice for older parrots who will quickly become comfortable enough to reestablish previous behavior patterns which may be what got them in trouble in their previous homes.)

Body Language

Pay close attention to your bappy's body language to give you clues as to how to proceed with him. Careful observation will also help you pick up information about his health, energy level, and times when he is receptive to play and handling. Young parrots will need some closely supervised time out of their cage to explore their new surroundings. They will also need some cuddle time. However, it is extremely important they have play time in their cage and lots of quiet time to rest and nap. Do not overdo the attention or expect him to have the confidence and energy to accept too many adventures or to meet a parade of new people the first day. If he spends a lot of time food-begging or is noisy and hyperactive, he may need to be hand fed for a few days or longer to help his sense of security (see page 75). I highly recommend providing parrots with a wide variety of food so they have many choices. Of course, you should feed some of the foods he is used to even if you are not planning to continue feeding them. The first few days in a new home is not the time to try to change a parrot's diet. If your parrot naps all the time and does not have any periods of playfulness, a trip to the veterinarian is recommended. This is especially true if his feathers are fluffed up most of the time.

From the very beginning, time should be spent giving him *instructional attention*. Do not worry about giving him too much attention as long as he gets his rest. Do not listen to the nonsense that giving him too much attention will spoil him — babies need lots of attention. **The amount of time you spend with him is not as important as what you do during that time.** Just cuddling a parrot will result in a "spoiled" bird but teaching him to play by himself and patterning him with exercises to encourage good behavior will create a well-behaved parrot. Start from the beginning using the "UP" command consistently when you take him out of the cage or pick him up and the 'Down' command when you ask him to step off your hand onto his perch. You are not only patterning him to respond positively to these verbal cues, you are also patterning yourself to the consistent use of these instructional commands which provide a clear message. Setting rules and providing guidance from the very beginning will be helpful in maintaining his trust and tameness throughout his entire life. ✒

Sally Blanchard's COMPANION PARROT HANDBOOK

THE FIRST WEEK

The behavioral foundation you establish for your bappy from the very beginning will determine his pet potential as he matures.

Go Slow — Establish Positive Introductions

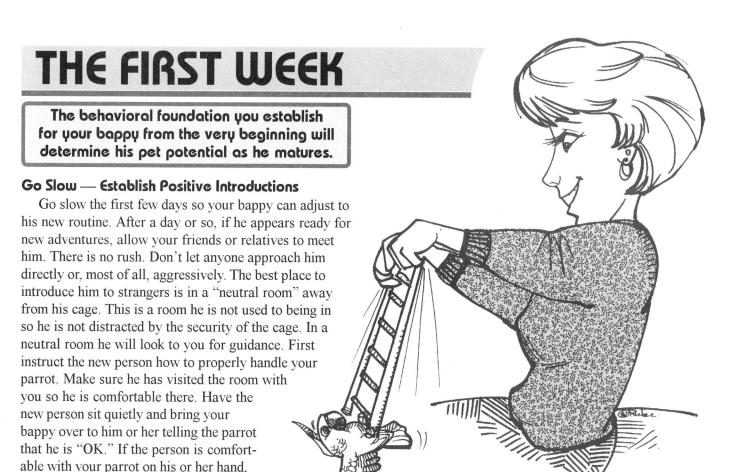

Go slow the first few days so your bappy can adjust to his new routine. After a day or so, if he appears ready for new adventures, allow your friends or relatives to meet him. There is no rush. Don't let anyone approach him directly or, most of all, aggressively. The best place to introduce him to strangers is in a "neutral room" away from his cage. This is a room he is not used to being in so he is not distracted by the security of the cage. In a neutral room he will look to you for guidance. First instruct the new person how to properly handle your parrot. Make sure he has visited the room with you so he is comfortable there. Have the new person sit quietly and bring your bappy over to him or her telling the parrot that he is "OK." If the person is comfortable with your parrot on his or her hand, place the bird there. If not, place the bird on his knee and let your friend approach the bird more gradually. It is important for everyone to be calm and move slowly during their introductions. If a person is afraid or won't listen to your instructions, it is usually better to not have him or her handle the parrot. Mishandling can create stress and trauma for a young bird. Winning and maintaining trust through nurturing and guidance are the best ways to establish a wonderful parrot/human bond.

A few days into the first week is the time to start encouraging your bappy's curiosity and sense of adventure. Playing games (page 104) such as warm potato, bappy picnic, and real estate agent will go along way in establishing a strong mutual bond. It is also important to begin guidance and patterning exercises. Patterning exercises are just as important to establish consistent routines with the human flock as they are for the parrot. People who learn to handle their parrots comfortably and deal with their parrots consistently will have much less confused parrots. While consistency and predictability are critical for a young parrot's sense of security, rigid routine may set up serious problems with him accepting change and new adventures in the future. Always doing everything the same way at the same time may make the parrot uncomfortable with any deviation from the rigid routine.

Basic Skills For Confidence

During the first week, cuddling is very important but it is even more important to start instructional interaction. Besides playing the games mentioned above with your parrot, spending time teaching basic skills will result in a more confident parrot. While some parrots may be active little acrobats, others may need help in developing their balance skills. Playing with a bappy on the carpeted floor, bed, or couch will allow him a soft landing if he loses his balance. Teach him to climb up his towel and then stretch it out like a thick tightrope for him to walk from one hand to the other. Have him climb up a ladder, then turn the ladder so he can walk from side to side, and then slowly turn it upside down.

The first week is the time to introduce healthy new foods and finger feed an abundant variety of healthy foods. If he was weaned to a narrow diet, this is the time to gradually replace unhealthy foods and start him on new, more nutritious foods. You will probably waste a lot of food but it will pay off in the long run. Adequate rest and sleep are still very important, with quiet time in the cage even if you are there. ✿

THE FIRST MONTH

Settling In

During the first month, your parrot will become comfortable in your home and start to develop his individual behavioral patterns. Also, you will most likely begin to be comfortable with him as you to understand his individual personality quirks as he responds to your personality and the activities in your home. Although it is important to be aware of the special needs and generalizations about a particular species, make sure you do not anticipate any negative traits so strongly in your parrot that they become self-fulfilling prophecies. Some species of parrots, particularly eclectus, may become a bit bitey during this time. Being bitey is often part of an independence stage where the parrot tests the owner to determine if he or she is really an adequate flock leader. This is also a time during which the young parrot begins to establish a territory. Greys may go through a stage where they seem a little afraid of new things. With a well-socialized bappy, you can usually cajole him to accept new situations by continual reassurance or more gradual introductions. Patience is essential. The mistakes you make in managing your parrot's behavior during the first month of his life with you can establish patterns that cause serious problems as he becomes older. Young parrots are *learning sponges* but life can be confusing in our environment, so alien from their own natural habitat. Try to stay calm to avoid overexciting the youngster and do not use aggression to try to stop any biting or screaming. Lower your energy and speak softly with gentle eye contact. Establishing the principles of *Nurturing Guidance* with your parrot during this time will make all the difference in creating and maintaining your parrot's pet potential.

Time In The Cage

During the first few weeks, it will be essential to define positive time in the cage. Don't get into the habit of banishing your parrot to his cage as punishment or if he misbehaves. His cage should be his happy home where he feels secure, entertains himself, and has the quiet-time he needs. Don't let him out of the cage for attention each time he squawks. Instead, call to him from across the room with a short, calm response such as, "Be a good bird, Charley." Establishing the concepts of *ambient attention* (see page 95) are critical to help your parrot remain a part of the flock while he is in his cage. Pick a time when your parrot needs to stay in his cage even if you are home. If he calls to you, respond from where you are to his contact call with a friendly question or statement like "What are you doing?" or "Have fun — keep playing."

If a relative or close friend wants to be a part of your new parrot's human flock, the first month is the time to start going for short car rides and visiting their homes. Maintain his security and make sure he is safe at all times. Over the years, I have heard many horror stories about parrots being injured while riding in the car. A sturdy travel cage secured with a seat belt in the back seat is essential. Parrots have been killed by air bags opening in the front seat. In the new place he visits, be aware of and in control of as many variables as possible. For example, if your friend or relative has a curious dog, make sure the dog is in another room or outside so you can be in control of the introduction. If your parrot relaxes and is comfortable in the new location with his new acquaintances, you could leave for a while to test his comfort level while you are gone. If everything goes well, the next time you visit he could even spend the night in his home-away-from home (see Pajama Party pg. 105). This is a gradual way to teach him to accept your absence and trust other people in other locations.

THE FIRST YEAR

Independence Stages

There will be many changes in the first year of life as your bappy matures and goes through his independence stages. All living creatures grow up and change. We cannot expect our young parrots to stay bappies forever. With *Nurturing Guidance* and instructional interaction, you will have a direct effect on how well he goes through these stages. I have often heard people dismiss negative behavior by saying, "It's just a stage and he'll get over it." This is absolutely true, but whether he gets over it with his pet potential intact will depend on how you handle these stages. A domestically raised companion parrot can be experiencing a great deal of conflict at this time. We are asking him to remain totally dependent on us for just about all of his needs at a time when his biological urges are pushing him to become increasingly independent.

Most young parrots have bonded to us as their parents, but this is the time that the natural parental bond begins to lessen. Yet, the paradox for a young parrot is that to become independent, he actually becomes more dependent

on the reassurance of his parents to brave the world on his own. People need to be aware that although their parrot seems to be asserting and even demanding his independence, this is a time during which the bird needs a great amount of gentle reassurance. In the wild, young parrots are continually being reassured by their parents as they venture farther from them. They have continual contact calls which are the chicks' way of asking "Am I OK?" and the parents' way of replying "Yes, you are fine." If the answer is "No, there is danger" the chicks, parents, and even the flock, are quickly reunited because there is safety in numbers. We need to provide our companion parrots with the same sort of reassurance during the independence stages of their lives. We must encourage their independence enough for them to learn to be contented when they do not have our attention, yet at the same time, we must let them know they can depend on us to meet the majority of their needs. During these independence stages, some parrots will start shifting their bond from the previously most favored person to another. In most cases, the parrot will transfer the strongest bond to the person who has provided them with the clearest guidance. After all, this is the person who has caused them the least confusion.

Characteristics Of Independence Stages

A critical independence stage usually starts at about 6 to 9 months of age with the medium to large parrots and is often characterized by increasing noncompliance and, in some cases, increased insecurity. Guidance and parenting through neutral room patterning exercises and instructional interaction is particularly important to keep your parrot on-track. Other independence stages may occur at about 6 month intervals until the parrot is two to three years old.

Because of the need for continual reassurance and guidance from the perceived parents during this critical independence stage, I encourage my clients not to plan a vacation when their young parrot is 6 to 9 months old. This seems to be particularly true for more sensitive birds like African Greys, but other species may also develop insecurities during this time if the people they look to for reassurance are gone. Because of their sense of abandonment, it seems to be classic for greys to start feather picking if their owners leave them at this age. If you must leave your parrot, try to make sure that he goes to stay with someone he is comfortable with, someone who knows how to handle him and give him affection and reassurance.

While most parrot species seem to go through similar stages, certain species exhibit particular behaviors during these independence stages. Some parrots may not naturally form a strong parental bond once they have fledged. In their eagerness to form a looser bond with other juveniles in the flock, these young birds may actually transfer their bond to a person who has paid little attention to them. This seems to be particularly true of Rose-breasted Cockatoos who would rather be exploring the world around them than having close contact with the people in their lives. In the wild, they are raised and weaned in a creche (nursery) past fledging. It is wise not to pressure these parrots during this time of increased independence — guidance, instructional attention, and play — yes — but don't try to force them to be velcro birds. This may be true of greys and some of the *Poicephalus* such as Senegals, Meyers, etc. Do not take the fickle bond of a young parrot as personal rejection. Generally when people just relax, accept changes, and continue to pay attention to the young bird without forcing affection on him, the bond will become stronger again with time. Even the cuddliest parrots may go through a stage where they seem to reject the people in their lives. Again, it is critical not to let this dampen your affection for your parrot. Just accept it as a normal part of the maturation process and continue to provide guidance and nurturing.

During the fledging and weaning stages, well-socialized parrots are like little sponges absorbing all of the experiences they are safely introduced to. This is part of their normal learning cycle. With some species and/or individuals, we need to continue to cajole them to accept new adventures and experiences throughout their independent stages. Without this continual gentle coaxing, they will begin to narrow their acceptance. This seems to be particularly true of some African Greys and other African parrot species. One of the major mistakes people make with greys at this time is to back off completely if the parrot seems afraid or anxious about a new toy, playgym, or situation. Instead, the owner should desensitize the parrot to new objects and situations by finding clever ways to gradually and safely introduce them. For example, new objects to be placed in the cage such as toys and perches are much less threatening if introduced in a play situation in a neutral room, then placed near the cage or hung outside of the cage, and then finally placed into the cage.

Increased Aggression and Cage Territoriality

While some parrots may become less adventuresome, others may try to become the supreme commander of the household during the first year. The dutiful human servant opens the cage door and the parrot climbs out and up to the top of his cage where he is in control of all he surveys. I have met countless adorable little Amazon dictators who only needed someone to gently remind them who was really in control of the household. Another predictable situation occurs with many macaws when they hit their critical independence stage at about 9 months to a year. Some (especially those without established rules and guidance) can easily become the king of the cage and you had better not try to get them out with your bare hands. No matter how sweet a young macaw has been, if he gets cranky and his owner becomes even the least bit intimidated by the size of his beak, the macaw can quickly establish control. Actually, I only remember being severely bitten by one or two macaws in the quarter of a century I have been around them. I always found that making direct friendly eye contact and watching them carefully has prevented them from getting the best of me. When that didn't work, I held an unfamiliar object in my other hand to distract the macaw (see pg. 159) while I took him out of his cage.

I encourage my clients to stick train (see pg. 94) their young parrots since many of them regularly test their owners with aggressive behavior during their independence stages. If a parrot is used to stepping on a stick, the owner doesn't have to be afraid of being bitten. Aggressive behaviors can be lessened and even remedied with proper guidance. Always taking the parrot out of his cage with the "UP" command, not letting him hang out on the top of his cage, and neutral room patterning exercises are the best ways to establish and maintain hand control of a less compliant parrot.

THE FIRST FIVE/TEN YEARS

Positive Daily Interaction

By the time your parrot is a year old, you will have ample evidence to determine whether or not you have actually established a positive behavioral foundation. No matter how much we want our young parrots to stay bappies forever, they do grow up. However, because of their dependence on us, their maturation process can be confusing to both themselves and the people in their lives. Balance is the key to their success — we guide their maturation so they stay tame and sweet without an emotional dependence on us. They need to welcome our company and attention yet still know how to keep themselves stimulated and entertained when we are not available for them. We must allow our companion parrots to grow up but not away from us.

"Look! Down there! There it is! Neverland where you'll never have to grow up!"

SMB

The more consistent and nurturing our handling is, the more positive the bond will be. For most parrots, allopreening (or mutual preening) helps maintain a strong pair bond. Petting, skritching, gentling exercises, and nurturing towel cuddling are important ways to keep parrots tame to their human flocks. Sometimes people get lazy or become too busy for their parrots and may not continue the positive interactions which guarantee a lifelong tame companion. Preventing behavioral problems is easier than solving problems. Consistent positive daily interaction and focused attention make parrots wonderful lifelong companions.

With many companion parrots, the ages from 1 to about 5 can be the most difficult for the people in their lives. The logical reason is because this is actually one of the most difficult times of a companion parrot's life. This is particularly true for people who thought their bappy would always act like a bappy. In this time span, parrots may become somewhat unpredictable. Caregivers are often terribly confused by mixed messages such as "I love you — go away!" which, with a parrot may translate as, "I want your attention but it has to be on my terms or I will bite you." Parrots do not know how to ask politely to get their needs met. Often, they ask in ways which give them the exact opposite of what they need. Parrots may learn to bite aggressively or scream excessively if they are not getting their social needs met. Most people, who do not understand that this may be the way a parrot is telling them that there is a problem, respond negatively to these misbehaviors. People who patiently try to understand why their parrot has started misbehaving and work with him by increasing focused attention and neutral room patterning exercises will be rewarded with improved behavior. If a person has established a strong relationship created with *Nurturing Guidance,* and pays close attention to his or her parrot's body language, these years will not be so difficult.

The Onset Of Sexual *Immaturity*

The majority of companion parrots will most likely exhibit sexual behaviors by the age of five. Some develop problem behaviors — others do not. In fact, many competent caregivers spend a great deal of time anticipating the problems of sexual behavior only to realize their parrot is past the time the problems would have started. Even so, with many parrots and their people, this time can be very confusing. Do not give up on them — **just because they are behaving sexually does not mean they would be happier in a breeding program.** The more guidance a parrot has from his human flock, the less likely he will be to become *obsessed* with sexual behavior. With normally well-behaved parrots, these difficult behaviors lessen with time. (See pgs.180-182.)

THE REST OF YOUR LIFE

The Best Is Yet To Come

A lifetime is a long time — especially to live with a companion animal. If you take very good care of your parrot, he could outlive you. If you establish *Nurturing Guidance* and maintain a positive mutual bond with your parrot throughout his life, does that mean it will always be smooth sailing? Of course not. After living with a parrot for a decade or so, his behavior becomes pretty predictable and there are few surprises unless some drastic change occurs in your life and routine. Most changes in the parrot's behavior are in response to changes in the life of his human flock. Human kids grow up and move away. Older mammalian pets die and new ones are introduced. Jobs change. People move to new houses. Divorces happen and/or new significant others move into the parrot's life. Along with the parrot, people get older and their energy level changes. The parrot is often a barometer of how well the human flock adjusts to the changes in their lives. If the parrot's needs are considered during these changes, he remains fairly consistent and predictable. If his needs are forgotten in the stress and chaos, the parrot adds to the stress and chaos.

Like A Good Marriage

Parrot behavioral consultant, Liz Wilson, has appropriately compared her long-term relationship with her Blue and Gold Macaw, Sam, to that of a good marriage. There have been many ups and downs in her over thirty years with Sam. I have lived with Bongo Marie for almost a quarter of a century. I would be lost without her, but sometimes she really irritates me and, at times, I am sure she feels the same way about me. But the positive aspects of my relationship with her balance it all out. Often, the very aspects of my relationship with her that make her so dear to me, are also the aspects that irritate me. Bongo is very loquacious and jabbers almost nonstop. Much of what she says is coherent and totally appropriate to the situation, but sometimes she just makes repetitive obnoxious noises that eventually get on my nerves. She knows it, too.

There are times when I have not been able to give her all the attention she needs. Although I am usually aware of my shortcomings, it has never occurred to me to find her a new home. I know that life will eventually settle down and I will be able to spend adequate time with her. When Bongo Marie is not receiving her normal level of appreciation, she acts out to get my attention. She has developed a high-pitched call (which seems to be intended to shatter my cerebral cortex) to let me know my shortcomings. When I make the association between my decrease in attention and her increase in obnoxious noises, I increase the quality and quantity of my attention. Bongo Marie is forgiving and our relationship quickly becomes positive again.

I don't believe the saying, "You can't teach an old dog new tricks" when it comes to dogs or people, but I can tell you for sure, it is absolutely not true with regard to companion parrots. Parrots are capable of learning throughout their lives so their behavior can be improved, and they can always learn new behaviors and tricks if they live with people who are willing to teach them.

A BELOVED PARROT'S FUTURE

Long Potential Life-span Creates A Need For A New Home

Because of such a long potential life-span, well-cared-for parrots may outlive the people who love them. What happens then? Have you made arrangements to guarantee your parrot will live out his life in a home where his emotional and physical needs will be taken

> **The better behaved your parrot is, the more likely he will be to find and stay in a quality, caring home if for some reason you can't keep him.**

seriously? My nightmare is that my parrots could possibly end up in some throwaway cycle with poor care and little interest in their welfare. How could they adjust after receiving such good care living with me — especially since they are so used to the *craziness* that often goes on around here? One of the best ways to guarantee your beloved parrot a loving home in the future is to use *Nurturing Guidance* to help him adjust well to life as a companion parrot. The better behaved your parrot is, the more likely he will be to stay in a good home if for some reason you can't keep him.

Plan ahead for your parrot's future. Create a trust fund. Put him in your will. Try to find an heir for him — someone who will care as deeply for him as you do. In some cases, a relative may be delighted to assume the bond with your parrot. Keeping the family involved in his life is one way to do this. Sometimes, the bird will just be a burden for a son or a daughter. Make sure the person you have made arrangements with really wants the parrot and that he or she is responsible enough to maintain that bond regardless of problems. It is best, if possible, that the heirs for the parrot get to know him before an emergency arises so the bird has some comfort level with them. All parrots are capable of rebonding to another nurturing person who is comfortable with them; however, many parrots will go through a difficult transition period as they bond to a new person. The new caregiver needs to understand there may be some problems at first. The strongly-bonded parrot will miss you and I believe he or she will need to go through a period of grief. The more positive the relationship is with the new people in his life, the less time it will take to build the trust needed for the parrot to bond to them.

Keep Notes About Your Parrot

Even if new owners want to do the right thing, they may not have the information to do so. Keep a journal of your parrot's special needs and likes. Write down his favorite foods and toys. Describe his individual personality quirks, and the special interactions you have with him. Write down as much about him as you can. What time of day is his favorite time to spend with the people in his life? What words does he say and what does he mean when he says them? What makes him happy? What makes him afraid, moody, or aggressive? What are his bad habits? The more information the new owner has, the easier the adjustment will be for both the bird and humans.

New owners need to be patient and consistent in trying to provide the same level of attention the parrot is used to. Guidance should be started immediately and gradually strengthened. If possible, start handling the parrot right away. Letting him adjust to the new situation before anyone in his new home handles him may actually make the bonding process more difficult to achieve. Parrots are creatures of patterning and they will quickly develop their own patterns before the new human flock has a chance to provide the guidance the parrot will need in a new household. With proper planning, your parrot can make a successful transition.

FUN AD *by Sally Blanchard*

(This cartoon advertisement is only for fun and NOT for a genuine product or service.)

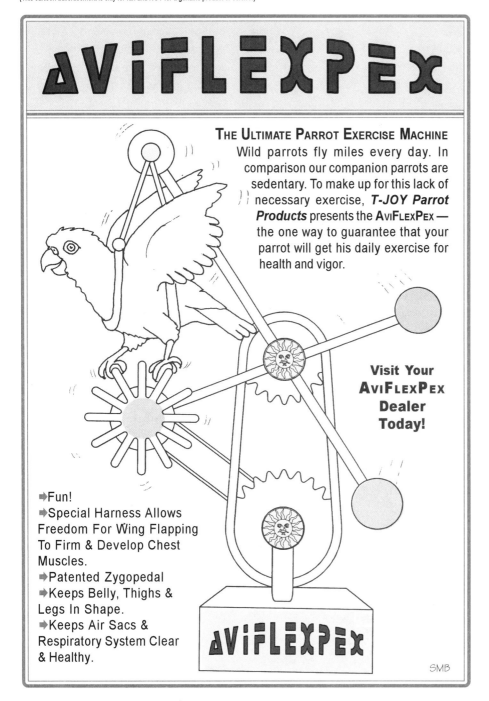

AViFLEXPEX

THE ULTIMATE PARROT EXERCISE MACHINE
Wild parrots fly miles every day. In comparison our companion parrots are sedentary. To make up for this lack of necessary exercise, *T-JOY Parrot Products* presents the AViFLEXPEX — the one way to guarantee that your parrot will get his daily exercise for health and vigor.

**Visit Your
AViFLEXPEX
Dealer
Today!**

➡Fun!
➡Special Harness Allows Freedom For Wing Flapping To Firm & Develop Chest Muscles.
➡Patented Zygopedal
➡Keeps Belly, Thighs & Legs In Shape.
➡Keeps Air Sacs & Respiratory System Clear & Healthy.

SMB

AViFLEXPEX

Chapter Six:
SKILLS TO TEACH YOUR BAPPY ⋯⋯➔

Nurturing Guidance Tip: Maintain Hand Control

Use Verbal Commands or Cues

Loss of hand control is one of the first steps in losing pet potential in a companion parrot. Establish and maintain hand control with consistent use of the "UP" and "DOWN" commands. Always use the "UP" command when you are asking a parrot to step onto your hand and the "DOWN" command when he is stepping off your hand. When you take a parrot out of his cage, let him know your intent by asking him, "Do you want to come out?" Always approach in a calm and friendly manner. Put your hand into the cage and with your finger at his belly level say the "UP" command. Push gently into his belly and have him step on your hand to come out. Consistent use of the "UP" command to get him out of his cage will help you become a part of his cage territory and will prevent him from becoming territorial with you around his cage.

Ways To Get Your Parrot Off Of Your Body If You've Lost Or Never Had Any Hand Control

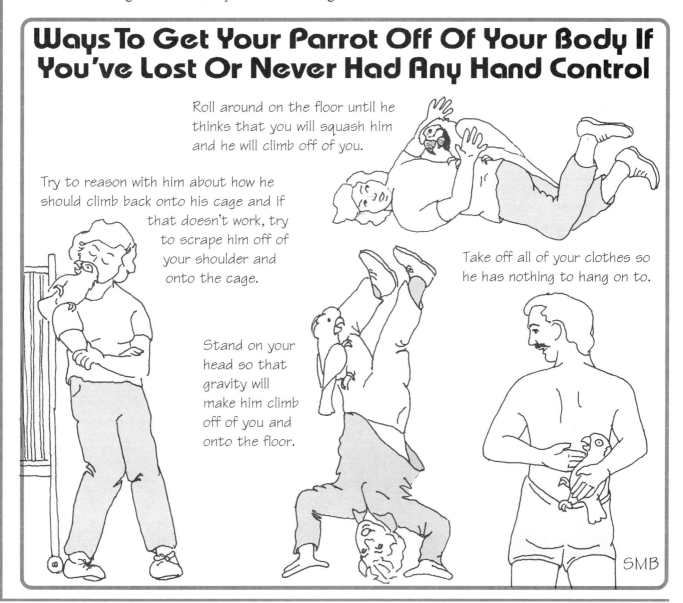

Roll around on the floor until he thinks that you will squash him and he will climb off of you.

Try to reason with him about how he should climb back onto his cage and if that doesn't work, try to scrape him off of your shoulder and onto the cage.

Take off all of your clothes so he has nothing to hang on to.

Stand on your head so that gravity will make him climb off of you and onto the floor.

SMB

BASIC BEHAVIORAL PRINCIPLES:

Many of the following concepts which are so important in understanding companion parrot care and behavior are closely related. For example, the fact that parrots are prey animals has created a strong flock response in many species. Flock closeness, a high degree of empathy, and interaction — all these provide security if there is a threat to an individual or the flock. A close flock structure includes social foraging and eating.

➲ **PARROTS ARE MORE COMFORTABLE WITH PEOPLE WHO ARE COMFORTABLE WITH THEM:** This may be the only absolute behavioral observation with companion parrots. Although parrots probably can't read our minds, they certainly reflect our energy. A companion parrot quickly learns to sense or read the body language of the people around him. A parrot will be unlikely to relax with a person who is uncomfortable handling him. Parrots will also bond more readily with people who provide them with clear, consistent guidance. If you are afraid or apprehensive around your parrot, chances are he will not be comfortable with you. He will either be afraid of you or may react with aggression to get you to leave him alone. Focused attention, gentling exercises, and comfortable cuddle time help to keep a parrot tame throughout his life.

➲ **PARROTS ARE HIGHLY EMPATHIC:** This is the basis of the concept, "Parrots are more comfortable with people who are comfortable with them." Parrots are very responsive to us and often mirror our energy. Aggression is usually met with aggression or fear, depending on the bird. Fear is often met with fear which may result in an aggressive response from a parrot. People who know how to calm themselves down will usually be able to calm down an overexcited parrot by slowing down their own energy before attempting to interact with the bird. If you want a parrot to relax with you, you will need to relax with him. If you have had a bad day or are simply not in a good mood, unless you can calm down first, you will be better off not handling your parrot.

Because of their empathic responses, parrots can actually teach us a lot about ourselves. If Bongo Marie has a negative response to me, I usually stop and pay attention to my own mood. In this manner, she often provides me with a much-needed attitude adjustment. Many people try to return their parrot to his cage when they are in a hurry. The bird simply will not cooperate, and the more upset and rushed the person becomes, the more the bird becomes frenzied and even aggressive. If you have this type of problem, it will be much easier if you just walk away, and do some relaxation exercises to calm down — shut your eyes, drop your head, and take a few slow, deep breaths for a minute or two — slow down your energy. Then, go back to the bird and approach him calmly and decisively. He will be much more likely to cooperate than when you are hurried.

➲ **PARROTS ARE SOCIAL FLOCK ANIMALS:** Companion parrots are not happy off in a room by themselves unless there are other parrots they consider to be a part of their flock. Parrots rely on their flock for safety and security. They like to be where the action is. It is unnatural for most parrots to be isolated from their group. Abandonment from the flock can mean death. In fact, in the scheme of nature, the flock may abandon an individual who presents a threat to the safety of the rest of the birds. Because of their social needs, I always recommend that parrots live in the room of the house where the family lives and not in a separate bird room. This way they know what their flock is doing and they receive ambient attention from the human flock just from being in the same area.

Sally Blanchard's COMPANION PARROT HANDBOOK

HOW THEY APPLY TO OUR PETS

⊃ **PARROTS ARE PREY ANIMALS:** In the wild, parrots are prey animals. Predators hunt and eat them. Parrots rely on their flock for safety and protection. Despite being domestically-raised, a pet parrot has the instinctive fears and responses of a prey animal. A sustained threat can create fear responses and even long-term phobic behavior in sensitive parrots. We should not create or allow situations that seriously threaten our parrots. For example, swooping down on a parrot from behind with a towel seems to create a fear response in a parrot similar to that caused by a "Harpy Eagle looking for lunch." You can't sneak up on a wary parrot from the back — they have eyes in the sides of their head and always know if they are being "attacked."

As a prey animal, parrots pick up every little nuance from the flock and sentinel birds. For example, watching the synchronicity of a large flock of Bare-eyed Cockatoos clearly shows how in tune they are with each other. They move together as if they have been choreographed, yet no single bird seems to be directing the flight pattern. Each individual parrot's life depends on heeding the warning to survive a predator attack. Because parrots are so tuned into emotion, any rise in our emotions can create a flight response in our companion parrots. For this, and other reasons explained later in this book, yelling at them, becoming agitated at them, and punishment are ineffective.

If a companion parrot has been in a traumatic situation and develops a strong fear response, it is best for the owner to be patient with the bird. Some phobic parrots seem to go into "prey mode" around their previously trusted owners. Being too direct while interacting with a phobic parrot may cause more fear. People need to move slowly and establish a submissive posture to win back the trust of the frightened or phobic parrot.

⊃ **MOST PARROTS ARE PHYSICALLY AFFECTIONATE:** In the wild, most species of parrots express physical affection within their family groups. Bonded pairs allopreen (mutual preening) and parents fuss with the chicks to keep them secure and clean. Physical affection in the form of touching, skritching, and cuddling are an important part of a companion parrot's attention. (See pages 98 and 99.)

⊃ **IT'S NOT THE BIRD'S FAULT:** The pet potential of domestically-raised parrots depends on their innate personality and the interaction they have with people in their lives. It is amazing that they are as well-behaved as they are in such an alien environment. Inappropriate behaviors are usually caused by a conflict in their natural behavior and their maladjustment to life in our living room. Clear guidance from humans can avoid this confusion. We must take responsibility for both causing and changing problem behaviors.

⊃ **ALL INTERACTION SHOULD BE TRUST-BUILDING AND NOT TRUST-DESTROYING:**
Strong bonds between parrots and humans are based on mutual trust. In working with our companion parrots, the most important consideration is whether or not what we do will be trust-building or trust-destroying. The majority of punishment techniques used with parrots are trust-destroying. Quick-fix or aggressive discipline are generally ineffective anyway because parrots do not have the cause-and-effect logic to understand them.

⊃ **PARROTS NEED EARLY SOCIAL-IZATION TO LEARN THEIR SUR-VIVAL AND SOCIAL SKILLS:**
While some basic parrot behavior may be instinctive, the finesse of social and survival skills is learned

from parents and flock members. Parrots mature slowly and require a great deal of instructional attention to reach their independence stages. Young handraised parrots depend on people to teach them the skills they will need to survive as pet birds, just as wild parrots learn the skills they need to survive in the rainforest from their flock members. Poorly socialized chicks will develop behavioral problems as they mature.

⟳ **PARROTS ARE CAPABLE OF BONDING AND REBONDING ON DIFFERENT LEVELS THROUGHOUT THEIR LIVES:** The concept of the **One-Person Bird** is certainly not engraved in stone. *It is nonsense to believe that you have to handfeed a baby parrot so it will bond to you.* Young parrots transfer their bonds from the handfeeder to anyone who is comfortable and nurturing in handling them. We can use patterning exercises to keep companion parrots tame to several people within their household throughout their lives. Individuals who want parrots to stay tame to them need to establish their own individual relationships with their birds. It helps if each person can provide the parrot with a special event (like a shower) or treat (like an almond in the shell) that no one else is allowed to give the bird. The "warm potato" exercise patterns the bird to allow handling from everyone in his life. This exercise involves slowly passing the bird from person to person with each one giving him attention for a few minutes at a time.

⟳ **EVEN DOMESTICALLY-RAISED PARROTS ARE STILL INSTINCTIVELY WILD:** We have not bred the vast majority of parrot family birds for enough generations in captivity to make changes in their genetic makeup. Therefore, they come out of the egg with a full complement of instinctive behaviors. Most of these natural behaviors are inappropriate for life in our living room and can create serious conflict and confusion for young parrots as they mature. Since parrots are capable of learning, it is up to us as their "surrogate parents" to teach them new behaviors to help them adjust to life as human companions.

⟳ **PARROTS SPEND A GREAT DEAL OF TIME AND ENERGY FORAGING FOR FOOD IN THE WILD:** Although some nutritious food should always be available during the day in a parrot's food bowl, we should also make them work for their food — especially for their favorite treats like nuts and seed. Placing these high in their cage or on their playgym so they have to climb to get to their favorite foods at least gives them a little exercise.

Activity foods or foods *in packages* (whether nature-made or devised by humans) also add more activity to foraging in the cage or on the gym. Nuts in the shell, peas in the pod, washed and baked yams in the skin, small winter squashes, and a corn/bean mix wrapped in a tortilla are all excellent activity foods.

⟳ **PARROTS ARE SOCIAL EATERS:** A bird owner who eats in front of a parrot, without offering the bird a healthy tidbit first, will usually be screamed at and, in my opinion, he deserves it. Healthy treats kept near the cage can be fed as part of a greeting ritual, or to encourage a strong social bond. Occasional "junk-food" treats may be OK, but remember the size of a parrot in regards to food consumption when you give treats like pizza, nuts, or other high-calorie foods. The best way to get parrots to eat a new food is to prepare it in front of them and let them see you eating the food as you share pieces with them. If there is more than one person in the parrot's human flock, it is possible to use "model-rival" behavior to intrigue a parrot into eating new foods. One person feeds healthy foods to the person who the parrot has the strongest bond with in front of the bird. Many parrots will try new foods after seeing the person they are bonded to being fed the food just a few times. The main reason people are not successful in getting their parrots to eat healthy new foods is because they don't try hard enough or give up too soon.

"C'mon! His breath isn't that bad!! You know he loves his Pizza with Garlic, Onions, and Anchovies!"

⮑ **PARROTS ARE WASTEFUL, MESSY ANIMALS:** There are few reasons for a parrot to be fastidious in the wild. Parrots are often referred to as seed predators. They often destroy and discard the whole plant or fruit just to get to the seeds. Parrots naturally consume only part of what they are eating and throw the rest down. This way they often plant the food for future generations. They naturally destroy branches, leaves, and most anything they can get their beaks around. There is no reason for them to hold their droppings and they usually evacuate whenever they need to. These droppings are used by nature to enrich the rainforest floor.

⮑ **PARROTS ARE CREATURES OF PATTERNING:** Parrots like their routine and become so used to the patterns of their life that they will manipulate their owners to maintain those patterns. However, the best way to change their behavior is through distraction from the established pattern and gradual repatterning to more acceptable behavior. The basic concept of patterning is that the more a parrot does a certain behavior, the more likely he is to do it again. If we consistently use the "UP" command when we ask a parrot to step on our hand, then he will become patterned to step on our hand whenever he hears the "UP" command. Repetitive patterning exercises can be effective in achieving many positive behavioral patterns. A few of these include patterning a bird to step out of his cage with a command, to accept handling from several people, and training basic tricks for stimulation.

⮑ **PARROTS ARE INTELLIGENT BUT ...** Parrots do understand at least part of what we are saying. They are clearly smart enough to associate specific words with people, objects, and even events. Some parrots, with proper instruction and interaction, have shown the ability for basic abstract reasoning. Most pet parrots are clever enough to manipulate our behavior. Despite this, sometimes I think we may give them too much credit for intelligence, perhaps for our own convenience? It has been shown that a 2 to 3 year-old child does not understand the cause-and-effect logic of punishment. A child who is made to stand in the corner does not relate his misbehavior to standing there. If this is true, how can we expect parrots to understand punishment? I doubt sincerely that a parrot who is put in a dark "naughty box" has any concept at all about the behavior that made his owner put him there. He may, however, relate the exciting drama of being swooped up to be put in the box with his screaming, which may actually reinforce the negative behavior.

⮑ **PARROTS CAN BE TERRITORIAL:** In a parrot's natural habitat, choice nest sites are usually at a premium. There is often great competition for nesting sites within the flock, from the other birds, or from other animals in the environment. Because of this, companion parrots can become territorial around their cage and their perceived mate. Trying to work with a parrot around his cage may result in aggressive behavior. The best place to work with a parrot who is starting to develop behavioral problems is in a "neutral room." This is an unfamiliar area of the house where the parrot has no territorial agenda. When you become the most familiar aspect in the neutral room, the parrot is likely to pay close attention to you. Patterning exercises, introducing strangers, working to reestablish bonding after a problem, and the handling of an aggressive parrot are best done in the neutral room.

·····➤

⮊ **PARROTS WERE BUILT FOR CHEWING:** The parrot beak was made for ripping, shredding, digging, slicing, chomping, sawing, and other types of chewing. Among its many functions, this all-purpose tool is used to manipulate food, hull and husk seeds and vegetable matter, extract insects and grubs from bark, dig roots, excavate nest sites, and, in some cases, fashion tools (see page 113). Companion parrots (and breeding birds) need lots of chewing material to keep them busy and stimulated. Packing an area of the cage or aviary with safe, unsprayed tree branches is one way to keep a busy beak happy.

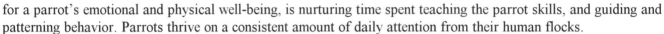

⮊ **IT IS NOT THE AMOUNT OF ATTENTION THAT SPOILS A BIRD, IT IS THE KIND OF ATTENTION:** Because they are social animals, parrots (especially bappies) need a lot of attention. But it shouldn't be just cuddle time. Instructional interaction, essential for a parrot's emotional and physical well-being, is nurturing time spent teaching the parrot skills, and guiding and patterning behavior. Parrots thrive on a consistent amount of daily attention from their human flocks.

⮊ **QUALITY ATTENTION IS ESSENTIAL:** As our companion parrot's human flock, varied interaction with us is essential. There are three levels of attention we can provide our parrots: **1.** **Focused/In-Your-Face Attention** is essential for keeping a parrot tame. This is the time when you should provide instructional attention and teach basic tricks. Hugging and "skritching" is part of in-your-face time. **2.** **Casual Attention** is that which you might provide your parrot while he is perched on or near you, on a chair or stand, while you are otherwise engaged in other things like watching television, reading, or holding a conversation. Only a part of your attention is directed at him in an intermittent fashion. **3.** **Ambient Attention** is the indirect contact you and your parrot have while you are in the same room together. Occasional chirps and "Hi, what are you doing?" back and forth contact calls and are important for a bird's sense of security. (See page 95 for more information on attention.)

⮊ **QUICK-FIXES AND PUNISHMENT ARE NOT EFFECTIVE IN CHANGING BEHAVIOR ON A LONG-TERM BASIS:** If you want to change a parrot's negative behavior, you need to work with the underlying causes — not the symptoms. Quick-fixes, such as squirting the bird with water, putting him in a dark room or a box, and/or *thunking* him on the beak only treat the symptoms and act as a short-term distraction. Most punishment is totally ineffective because a parrot does not have the ability to understand the cause-and-effect reasoning of the punishment. Some quick-fixes are aggressive enough that they cause a loss of the trust which is necessary to maintain a strong parrot/human bond. The major cause of behavioral problems in companion parrots is *a parrot in control of his own life doing a bad job of it.* The more we guide our parrot's behavior with rules, verbal commands, instructional attention, and positive patterning, the more likely the negative behaviors will change on a permanent basis.

⮊ **PARROTS ARE ACTIVE ANIMALS WHO NEED A GREAT DEAL OF STIMULATION:** In the wild, parrots spend a great deal of time flying and foraging for food. This takes a tremendous amount of energy and calo-

ries. We do not need to feed our companion parrots as many high-energy foods as a wild parrot naturally eats. Most importantly, we need to provide our parrots with as much physical and mental stimulation as we can. A large cage plus a playgym, both with multiple perches, toys, swings and platforms, are essential. For many parrots, supervised floor time for running and acrobatic exercises is a must. The more they learn to keep themselves entertained, the happier everyone will be.

○ **PARROTS COMMUNICATE VERBALLY:** Parrots are verbal animals with a 'language' of their own. They use specific sounds, ritual greetings, and contact calls to communicate with each other. Since parrots bond so strongly to us in captivity, our language becomes the language of the flock and many birds will mimic our words to become part of our flock. In many cases, the parrots use our words appropriately to get their needs met. They also clearly understand the meaning of certain key words and phrases we use frequently with them. Parrots use contact calls to stay in touch with us and it is a good idea to get into the habit of responding with our own contact call. Some elements of screaming and loud vocalization must be accepted by the "human flock" because they are an integral part of being a parrot. Excessive screaming for manipulation or self-stimulation becomes a problem.

○ **YOU CAN TEACH AN OLD BIRD NEW TRICKS:** People often ask me if their bird is too old to change his behavior. As long as the person is willing to do the work necessary to establish new patterns, parrots can learn. I have worked with parrots who were in their teens, twenties, thirties, forties, and even older and we have established new behaviors. In many cases, parrots who have not been handled for many years can be worked with in a gradual nurturing manner and will become tame and trusting again. It all depends on the knowledge and dedication of the people in the parrot's life.

○ **TRICK TRAINING IS VERY DIFFERENT FROM WORKING WITH COMPANION PARROT BEHAVIOR:** While some trick training concepts work well with parrots, many of them are inappropriate for life with a companion parrot. A pet parrot should never be deprived of food to get it to do tricks. I believe in teaching companion parrots simple tricks as a way to provide focused attention and much needed stimulation. For my Caique, Spike, tricks are a way to get attention, hugs, verbal rewards and applause. In fact, one of his favorite tricks that he developed himself is to spread his wings and sway when he is being applauded by his audience. Tricks may also be a positive way to distract a bird from negative behaviors. For example, if we teach a parrot to raise his wings with a certain verbal command and he enjoys the positive attention he receives for doing this, it is often possible to use this trick to distract him from screaming.

○ **PEOPLE NEED TO CHANGE THEIR BEHAVIOR TO CHANGE THEIR PARROT'S BEHAVIOR:** Parrots are highly reactive to our energy and behavior. By responding to negative behaviors with *drama rewards*, we actually teach our parrots many of the behaviors which we find to be so disturbing. If we are unable to change our actions which reward the parrot's negative behavior, we will never be able to change the parrot!

○ **PATIENCE IS ESSENTIAL (Rome Wasn't Built In A Day):** The major reason that people are unable to change their parrot's negative behaviors is because they do not do the right things consistently for long enough. Trying *everything* for short periods of time is ineffective. Parrots are creatures of patterning and it takes time, patience, and consistency to establish new behavior. For example, converting *seed/junk food junkies* to a nutritious diet may take months of wasting food and will often be an ongoing process over the lifetime of the parrot.

○ **IF ANYTHING CAN GO WRONG — IT WILL!** This is an extremely important concept for the companion parrot owner to understand. From the very beginning of our relationship with our companion parrot, we must establish ourselves as his protector. If raised properly, a young parrot has an almost insatiable sense of curiosity. Well-socialized bappies usually grow up to be very adventurous parrots who are eager to explore the world around them. They use their beaks to investigate textures and shapes. Sometimes they use their beak as a tool to rip and shred objects. Curious parrots who are allowed on the floor may graze through the carpet and find all sorts of dangerous items. They may find a live electric cord. They may chew on unsafe materials and swallow them. Many common household items are toxic to parrots. Potential danger is everywhere for an unsupervised parrot. If allowed to remain unclipped, they may fly out the door. As parrot owners, we need to continually learn and enhance our cause-and-effect logic and common sense to make sure we keep our parrots safe and healthy. ✦

TEACHING BASIC SKILLS

There a re a few basic skills that should be taught to all companion parrots. Teaching these skills to your bird will improve the quality of the parrot/human experience for you, and will make interactions with your parrot safer and more enjoyable.

⮑ BASIC VERBAL COMMANDS

From the very beginning of your life with your new bappy, teach him to step on your hand with a firm and friendly "UP" command, and to step off with the "DOWN" command. As you develop confidence with your parrot you may find a need for other verbal commands. Use them consistently.

⮑ FULL BODY HANDLING

While some parrot species are not usually comfortable with full-body handling, others delight in being held. A well-socialized bappy should enjoy being handled, but as he gets older, he may balk at full-body handling. This does not necessarily mean he doesn't ever want to be handled again. It may just mean he is being more particular about when he will accept handling. Without forcing him to accept your affection, continue to gently handle him from the top of his head to the tips of his toes as much as possible on a daily basis.

⮑ WING & TOE EXAMS

While your bappy is perched or playing in the towel, play "this little piggy" with his toes while you touch and handle each one with your fingers. Encourage him to play 'Eagle Boy' (or Girl) by gently lifting each wing with your fingers. When he is comfortable with both wings spread, touch each flight feather individually, smile, and say "Eagle Boy" (or whatever does the trick for you) so that he knows to spread his wings and let you touch his flight feathers.

⮑ TOWEL HANDLING

To get your parrot used to being handled in a towel, prepare the neutral room first. Lay the towel flat on the bed and then bring the bappy in and place him on it. Gradually pick the corners up and play peek-a-boo. Once he is used to that, gently and playfully wrap him in the towel to pick him up and cuddle him. Make a practice of handling him in the towel on a regular basis to keep him used to it. It will help tremendously to make his trips to the vet easier, if he will allow you to gently towel him and then hand him to his veterinarian for examination.

⮑ STICK TRAINING

Lay a branch or dowel (appropriately-sized for your parrot so he can wrap his toes around it) on the bed while you are playing with your parrot. Let the bird get used to it and, without poking it at him, encourage him to step on it while it is flat on the bed. As he steps on it, gradually lift the branch up. Once he is used to it, ask him to step on it with the "UP" command. Pick him up with the stick from time to time to keep him used to it. This way, if you have any trouble handling him in the future and become afraid of reaching for him with your hand, you will feel safe asking him to step on the stick. You can maintain hand control of a stick-trained parrot even when he is a bit "frisky."

⮑ BALANCE SKILLS

Work with your young parrot on the carpet, bed or a couch. Let him climb onto a towel and slowly and gently move the towel to help him develop his balance skills. Have him walk on it like a tightrope. You can also use a parrot ladder.

⮑ SPOON OR SYRINGE FEEDING

A few times a week, feed your bird some warm (not hot! 102-108°F) baby food (sweet potato is great!) with a syringe or spoon. If you microwave it be sure and stir it to avoid hot spots. Don't let him pump on it — just dribble it in his beak. Keeping your parrot used to taking treats from a spoon or syringe will make it much easier to medicate him in the future. ⸙

ATTENTION: THE 3 LEVELS

As our companion parrot's human flock, varied interaction with us is essential. There are three basic levels of attention we can provide our parrots:

1. FOCUSED/IN-YOUR-FACE ATTENTION

Essential for keeping a parrot tame, this is time when the caregiver is totally focused on the parrot — with no distractions such as TV, reading, conversation with others, or other pets vying for attention. While hugging and *skritching* are part of in-your-face time, focused time should also be the time when you provide instructional attention. Teaching basic tricks is part of focused attention. Neutral room patterning exercises are an essential part of focused attention. When a parrot first starts behaving in ways which negatively impact the owner, the first step should be consistently providing daily in-your-face time. This will make positive changes, often within only a few days.

2. CASUAL ATTENTION

This is time spent with the parrot either on you (preferably your arm, knee or lap), the arm of the chair, or a nearby stand. Your focus is on the parrot much of the time, but he is busy, perhaps playing with a toy, and you may be occasionally distracted by the television, conversation, or reading. Casual attention time can include having your parrot hanging out on a playgym or his T-stand in the kitchen with you while you do the dishes, or the bathroom while you take a shower or put on your makeup (avoid using potentially harmful products such as hairspray or perfume). Casual attention provides your parrot interaction while you are otherwise engaged in another relatively mindless task.

3. AMBIENT ATTENTION

This level of attention is critically important to your parrot (and vitally important for African greys.) Ambient attention involves greeting your parrot when you come in the room and saying goodbye when you leave. It is also the indirect contact you and your parrot have while you are in the same room or area. Ambient attention may just be occasional chirps from your parrot with a "Hi, what are you doing?" response from you. In the wild, parrots stay in touch with contact calls. This interaction is important for a bird's sense of security. When you are in the same room with your parrot — even if you are very busy with another task — your response to his contact call will usually stop him from increasing his volume to get your attention. If he calls to you when you are in the other room, just call back with a simple response to let him know you are aware of his presence.

"Hi Tiki, What are you doing?"

HOW TO PICK UP A PARROT

⮑ **The Importance of Hand Control:** This is not advice for the lovelorn parrot about finding a mate in the Tree-Top Lounge, but a guide to help parrot owners maintain or regain hand control of their tame companions. Being able to have your pet easily step on your hand is an essential part of a successful relationship with a parrot.

⮑ **The "UP" Command:** Decisive, but not aggressive, is the key attitude to maintaining hand control of your parrot. Parrots need to be given a clear message to step onto your hand. Using direct, friendly eye contact and the verbal "UP" command will establish authority with your parrot. Say "UP" once with a friendly but firm and clear voice in the same way you might give a dog a "SIT" command. Be assertive but not aggressive. If the bird does not respond, say it again as a new command.

PACO'S TREE-TOP TAVERN

OOO! check out the drumsticks on that chick!

She's looking at me! Look how she shakes her tail when she walks!

⮑ **Ineffective "UPs":** Don't say "uuuuuuuuuupppppppp" too softly or "???up?" as if you are asking a question. The motor boat command, "upupupupup" is also confusing and ineffective. Neither is the 5 syllable word "uuu-uuu-uuu-uuu-uup." Saying "!!!!UP!!!!" too loudly or aggressively will have an undesired effect as aggression is often met with aggression. Placing the command in the middle of a sentence is also not a clear message. Using the "UP" command at the wrong time, for example, before you present your finger to your parrot or after he has already stepped on your hand, gives a confusing message.

⮑ **The Golf Swing:** Many people make the mistake of trying to pick up a parrot by just placing their hand in front of him and expecting the parrot to automatically step on — some parrots will but many won't. Just as they always say in a perfect golf swing — follow through. Make direct friendly eye contact and push your fingers gently into his lower belly, say a clear "UP" and follow through by getting your parrot on your hand. Don't push him or move too fast, but make a continuous motion.

⮑ **Fish Bait:** Just wiggling your fingers around in front of a parrot does not give him a clear message. Expecting him to step onto your moving hand is unrealistic. The parrot may become confused or agitated, and that wiggling finger can be too tempting. Just as a fish can't resist a wiggling worm, your parrot may not be able to resist biting your wiggling finger. If you do it often enough, fish bait biting may become a patterned game your parrot plays with you.

SMB

⊃ **Hands Should Bring Pleasure:** Finger-feeding treats can be one of the best ways to get a hand shy parrot used to being approached by hands. If your parrot is afraid of hands, move slowly and try not to approach him from above. Parrots bond to our faces and holding your hands near your face is one way to let a hand shy bird know that your hands are part of you.

⊃ **Announce Yourself First:** Be sure and check a parrot's mood and activity before attempting to pick him up. If he is busy eating or excitedly playing, it may not be a good time to pick him up. It is best to greet him first by saying something like "Hey, what are you doing?" before you attempt to pick him up.

⊃ **Distracting Or Redirecting The Behavior:** Sometimes you will need to pick a parrot up and he will be uncoopera-tive, either because he is playing a game about coming out of his cage, he is in overload behavior, or he is busy playing or eating. Some parrots are very possessive about food and play objects. Rather than just reaching in and trying to get him, you can distract him by holding a nonthreatening object like a magazine or a potholder in the other hand and then use the "UP" command to ask him to step on your hand.

⊃ **Playing The Game:** Parrots can be incredible game players and it doesn't take too many inappropriate re-sponses from people for a parrot to set his own rules for a new game. If your parrot reaches out with his beak and you pull back, this routine may become your bird's favorite game to let you know he is in control. Using the "UP" com-mand properly changes the rules of this game and turns you both into winners.

⊃ **Left-footed?:** Watch to see which foot your parrot uses to hold food and toys. A left-footed parrot will gener-ally be more comfortable stepping onto your right hand and a right-footed parrot is more likely to step on your left hand without hesitation.

⊃ **Back steppers:** Some parrots are far more comfortable stepping back onto your hand. If you consistently have trouble picking your parrot up from the front, try approaching him from the back. Use the same decisive techniques and the "UP" command. Giving a "back-stepper" the opportunity to step on your hand in this manner may give him less opportunity to be a "beak-stabber."

⊃ **Not Wrist Tame:** For good hand control, your parrot should step on the ridge of your fingers and not onto your wrist, arm, or the back of your hand. Gently placing your thumb over his toes can act as a *psychological barrier* to keep him on your fingers. If you have small hands and a large parrot, it may be uncomfortable for him to remain on your fingers. Give him the "OK" command to allow him to go to your wrist after he steps on your fingers.

⊃ **Shoulder Runway:** Once they are on your hand, many parrots will try to run up your arm to your shoulder. If a parrot gets into this habit it can be difficult to change. The best way to prevent this behavior is not to let it happen. If your parrot starts running up your arm, just bring the other hand over in front of him and have him step on with the "UP" command.

⊃ **Ladder Your Parrot:** To reinforce the "UP" command, make a friendly game out of laddering your parrot. Transfer him deliberately from one hand to the other, saying "UP" each time. Go slowly — the purpose is not to wear his little legs off. I do not recommend laddering a parrot as a discipline or punishment. Many parrots interpret this as confrontation or may become overstimulated by aggressive laddering.

⊃ **It's Your Choice:** Many people lose their parrots' hand tameness because they take it for granted. Bring your parrot out of his cage with the "UP" command instead of just letting him come out by himself. To establish guidance, make it your choice instead of his. Always use the "UP" command to ask him to step onto your hand. Keep it friendly and clear. Don't let him run up your arm to your shoulder. If you want him there, place him there with the "DOWN" command. Do not force him in an aggres-sive manner. Always keep your commands decisive and friendly.

CUDDLING A PARROT

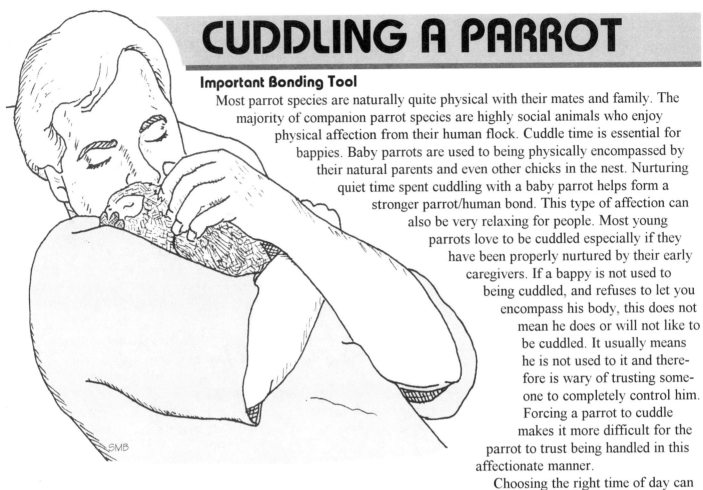

Important Bonding Tool

Most parrot species are naturally quite physical with their mates and family. The majority of companion parrot species are highly social animals who enjoy physical affection from their human flock. Cuddle time is essential for bappies. Baby parrots are used to being physically encompassed by their natural parents and even other chicks in the nest. Nurturing quiet time spent cuddling with a baby parrot helps form a stronger parrot/human bond. This type of affection can also be very relaxing for people. Most young parrots love to be cuddled especially if they have been properly nurtured by their early caregivers. If a bappy is not used to being cuddled, and refuses to let you encompass his body, this does not mean he does or will not like to be cuddled. It usually means he is not used to it and therefore is wary of trusting someone to completely control him. Forcing a parrot to cuddle makes it more difficult for the parrot to trust being handled in this affectionate manner.

Choosing the right time of day can make a big difference in whether or not your parrot enjoys cuddling. Many parrots love to be cuddled just before bedtime, but others may prefer it around their afternoon siesta. Cuddling should be introduced gradually to a reticent parrot. One way is to start petting the parrot in ways that he will accept readily, such as gently skritching the skin around the beak, then gradually moving your hands to the back as described on the next page. Once the parrot is comfortable with you gently touching his back, each time you work with him, put a little more pressure on his back with your hands and gradually bring your hands around his whole body. This may take a only few attempts before your parrot will accept cuddling or, in some cases, it may take many times before he trusts you enough to have that much control of him. Occasionally, there will be a stubborn parrot that actually will not enjoy being cuddled regardless of whether he trusts you or not. Once you determine that no amount of gradual introduction will work, it is best not to push him any more. My male Double-yellow Head Amazon, Rascal, never would let me get past skritching his neck. He has always been an independent sort of guy and I decided to appreciate the other aspects of his personality. I would not say this is a particular trait associated with male Amazons, as I know of many who love cuddling. Some species of parrots have a reputation for not liking to be cuddled — these include eclectus and *Psittacula* species (Alexandrines, Derbyans, ringnecks, moustaches, etc.). Even though this may be true of some of these species, I have certainly known exceptions to these generalizations. So it is best to give it a try on a nurturing level, without forcing it on them, before accepting the generalization as a self-fulfilling prophecy. (See Trust-building Towel Handling Techniques on page 102 for information on a gentling exercises to help keep your parrot tame.)

Instructional Interaction Is Also Essential

As essential as cuddling is, if it is the only kind of attention your parrot receives, he can become seriously spoiled rejecting most other attention and demanding to be cuddled all of the time. Cuddling time should be balanced with instructional interaction such as patterning exercises, working on improving skills, teaching basic tricks, and playing games. All of these interactions create a companion parrot with optimal pet potential. ∮

SKRITCHING A PARROT

Another Important Bonding Tool

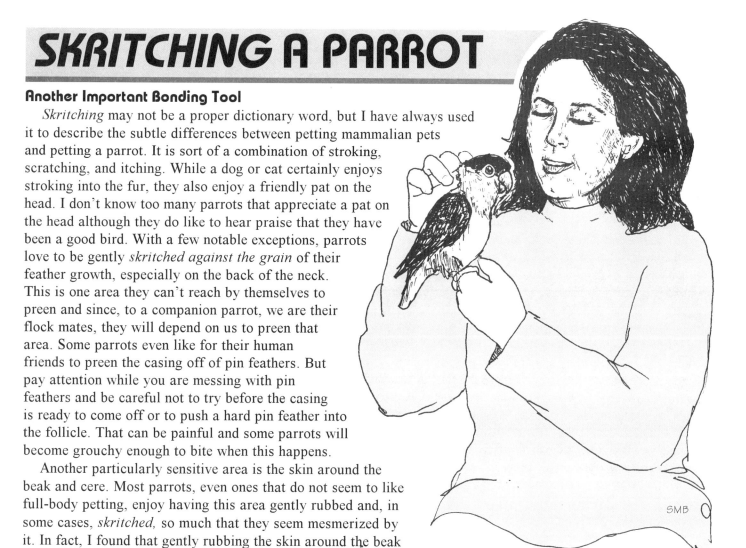

Skritching may not be a proper dictionary word, but I have always used it to describe the subtle differences between petting mammalian pets and petting a parrot. It is sort of a combination of stroking, scratching, and itching. While a dog or cat certainly enjoys stroking into the fur, they also enjoy a friendly pat on the head. I don't know too many parrots that appreciate a pat on the head although they do like to hear praise that they have been a good bird. With a few notable exceptions, parrots love to be gently *skritched against the grain* of their feather growth, especially on the back of the neck. This is one area they can't reach by themselves to preen and since, to a companion parrot, we are their flock mates, they will depend on us to preen that area. Some parrots even like for their human friends to preen the casing off of pin feathers. But pay attention while you are messing with pin feathers and be careful not to try before the casing is ready to come off or to push a hard pin feather into the follicle. That can be painful and some parrots will become grouchy enough to bite when this happens.

Another particularly sensitive area is the skin around the beak and cere. Most parrots, even ones that do not seem to like full-body petting, enjoy having this area gently rubbed and, in some cases, *skritched,* so much that they seem mesmerized by it. In fact, I found that gently rubbing the skin around the beak was one of the best ways to tame and win the trust of wild-caught parrots.

While most baby parrots will come into their new household loving to be touched and skritched, occasionally a parrot will not seem to like it. As previously noted, some parrot species are not known for enjoying a lot of physical handling, among them eclectus and the *Psittacula* family. However, I have certainly known individual parrots in these families who have learned to enjoy an occasional cuddle and a good skritch, although they prefer that you stroke them in the direction the feathers grow. If your parrot does not seem to like petting, do not try to force him to accept it immediately. Start slowly around the sensitive beak area and gradually move to the top and back of the head. Some parrots may become relaxed enough to accept petting within a few sessions, while others may take longer. In some cases, you may need to start by gently rubbing the toes and work up the body. If you are gentle and patient, as the parrot gets to know you better, he will trust you more and allow you to touch him on more areas of his body. Once he is comfortable having the back of his neck skritched, you can gradually start moving your fingers down his back. If he gets grouchy with you, wait until next time and try to go just a little farther each time. Eventually, most parrots who trust the people in their lives will enjoy being touched and/or petted all over their heads, under their wings, on their chests, and even down their backs.

Pay attention when you are skritching your parrot. I have been asked by many pet owners why their parrots suddenly bite them during a good *skritching* session. After some discussion, they have usually admitted they were watching television or talking to someone while they were petting the parrot. Their attention had wandered and even the most docile parrot can become upset when someone starts wearing grooves into his head. While *skritching* and petting is an important part of a parrot's emotional care, they aren't everything. Make sure your parrot also receives instructional interaction along with affection.

GIVE YOUR PARROT A JOB

What Do Parrots Do For A Living?

For years, I have had daily conversations with my companion animals about one thing or another. Obviously, these conversations are not too profound, but I really like to ask them questions. Bongo is the only one who routinely gives me a verbal answer, but her answer rarely makes a lot of sense. One of my favorite questions to ask is, "What do you do for a living?" I usually follow this up with the question, "Well, why aren't you doing it?" When my mother is visiting, she always provides the answer, "Well, they make you happy, don't they?" My answer is, "Most of the time," and that is certainly good enough for them to earn their room and board!

I never seriously gave what my parrots did for a living much thought until I was visiting a friend and fellow *bird person*, Barbara Jo Hinsz, in Seattle. She was telling me her border collie, Sarah, was so intelligent she always needed to have a *job*. Since the breed had been developed as working dogs, border collies need to be trained to work around the house to keep them mentally alert. Sarah's jobs include herding the backyard pet chickens and the cat (much to the cat's dismay), pointing at one of the parrots if he or she lands on the floor, plus watching every member of the family (human, feathered, and furred) and locating them on the "Go find ___" command. Of course, my part-time job while I was visiting was to keep Sarah busy by throwing toys for her to retrieve.

While I was performing this task, I suddenly realized one of the key ingredients to having a contented companion parrot is to give them a job to do. It seems to me that parrots are also too intelligent not to have a job. Their jobs can vary from simply chewing up a toy to more complex tasks such as doing basic tricks for verbal accolades. Once she thought about it and integrated the concept into her interaction with her parrots, Barbara Jo found a different way of relating with her avian companions. Within a few weeks, each one had been trained to do specific behaviors which keep them busy and alert.

Max, her Yellow-collared Macaw, learned that one of his job*s* was to be really cute instead of making noise. Whenever he starts acting out by being noisy for attention, Barbara Jo uses the simple cue *"TaaDah!"* to redirect his energy to raising his wings to show off. His payoff for this is verbal praise. It makes him feel appreciated and stops his negative behavior. Max naturally likes to raise his wings and all Barbara Jo had to do was consistently and emphatically use the verbal cue *"TaaDah!"* when he did it so he would learn to associate the words with the action. Now, instead of screaming for attention, Max will flick his wings and raise them. Understanding the importance of ambient attention, Barbara Jo rewards Max with verbal praise even if she is across the room doing something else.

Sophia, the Moluccan, has a small set of colorful plastic buckets. It is her job to find the right color bucket to ask for special treats, new toys, or pieces of wood to chew on. She doesn't get her reward unless she presents the bucket which is the right color for the task. It is quite hysterical to watch her sort through the buckets and then hold the right one up with her foot, trying to hold it steady. Of course, she has to make sure she is holding the bucket right side up so Barbara Jo can put her reward in it. Sophia's face shines with expectation and happiness as she receives her reward and takes it out of the bucket.

Barbara Jo has a new Rose-breasted Cockatoo bappy and is now in the process of finding just the right jobs for Emily. Being a Galah, Emily will no doubt need a job which requires a greater variety of less focused tasks. By teaching her parrots a few basic behaviors or tricks, Barbara Jo provides them with focused positive instructional interaction. She is also able to redirect undesirable behaviors and turn the situation into fun. Emily is young enough that she is still perfect but once she has learned her various jobs, she will most likely be too busy with them to get into a lot of trouble. Barbara Jo's parrots are happier with jobs to do and so is their human flock. *

PLAY & EXERCISE

SMB

Highly Active Animals

In the wild, parrots are active for much of the day. Most parrots fly many miles from their roosting or nesting areas to their feeding grounds. Then they spend hours foraging for food — acrobatically climbing around branches and flying from tree to tree. By comparison, captive parrots are sedentary and receive little exercise, even in large aviaries or cages. Some parrots develop serious health problems because of this lack of activity. Physical problems range from obesity to egg-binding in hens with poor muscle condition. Depression, repetitive behaviors such as rocking back and forth, and behavioral feather picking may also be a result of lack of activity and stimulation.

It is up to us, as concerned parrot owners, to provide our companion parrots with as much physical activity and exercise as we possibly can. This starts, but certainly does not end, with providing parrots with a large cage with multiple perches and activity items such as toys, swings, platforms, ladders, and spiral rope perches. In addition, parrots should have multiple perch playgyms which offer a great deal of play and exercise opportunities. A secure aviary-style enclosure outside can provide fresh air, sunshine, and extra exercise. Make sure that your parrots are safe and well supervised even if they are in cages outside.

Interactive Play Exercise

Without your help and interaction, it is doubtful that your parrot gets enough exercise on his own. My Amazons, Paco and Rascal, live on a bird-safe enclosed porch. Their cage is open all of the time unless they have to go in for a particular reason. In the summer, when the sun comes up at 5 a.m. and I (and anyone in the neighborhood) want to sleep in, I put them in their cage and keep it covered until I decide the sun should come up! This postpones their sunrise serenade. The Amazons have rope perches and various platforms around their room. They have easy access to their veggies and pellets, but if I give them seed, corn, or fruit, they have to forage for these goodies by climbing up one rope across a playgym to another rope and then down again.

There are many ways to help a perch potato parrot get healthy exercise. Parrots with trimmed wings benefit greatly from wing flapping which not only helps the muscle tone of their *pecs* and *abs*, but also benefits their respiration. Some parrots love to flap while hanging on to a playgym or their cage bars, but others need a little encouragement from their owners. As with most experiences, it is best to introduce flapping gradually. First of all, let him know you are in a friendly, playful mood. If he is the type of parrot who is easily handled in a physical manner, you can start right away to teach him to flap. While holding your parrot above you on your fingers with your thumbs gently over his feet, bring your arms down quickly so he raises his wings to catch his balance. If he is apprehensive, go slower until he is used to the flapping experience. Wing flapping should always be fun and never used as punishment. Some parrots may never enjoy flapping and you may need to provide these birds with other types of *amusement park rides*.

Many parrots, particularly macaws and conures, can be played with in much the same way as we play with puppies. Gentle cuddle wrestling, supervised time running on the floor, or climbing the stairs, are great exercises for most parrots. Paco loved to climb up or down the carpeted stairs with me when I lived in a house with two levels. Many companion parrots enjoy chasing a ball rolled along the floor or toys that are dragged on the bed. Some will play catch with a ball of wadded paper which is just the right size for them. Remember that these interactions may excite a parrot enough to put him in overload, so if he gets too excited, let him calm down first before handling him again.

NURTURING TOWEL HANDLING

➲ Parrots have no natural fear of towels — there are no *predator towels* in the wild. They fear being attacked from the back — the way a predator would. The fear of towels is usually based on the way they have been toweled.

➲ In the wild, when a parrot is swooped down upon from behind, he becomes a predator's meal. People who use towels to attack parrots like a *Harpy Eagle looking for lunch* often cause them significant trauma which can result in loss of trust and behavioral dysfunction. This is especially true for bappies who have never learned any predator skills.

➲ Don't kid yourself. You can't sneak up on a wary parrot. Being prey animals, parrots have eyes in the sides of their heads. They have excellent hearing and even have bundles of nerves in their leg joints which act as *vibration detectors*. Survival depends on them knowing what is going on around them.

➲ Don't let anyone traumatize your parrot by toweling him aggressively — including your veterinarian or groomer. Throwing a towel over a parrot from the back, or chasing him around the room with a towel, is aggressive and unnecessary (especially when done in the dark with a flashlight). Instead just kneel down, smile, talk softly, and gently towel the parrot from the front and then pick him up without trauma.

➲ There are many ways to make your parrot comfortable with towels, but the easiest is to start out by putting him on the towel rather than putting the towel on him. Place a large, light colored towel on the bed or couch in a neutral room (a room the parrot is not used to). This way he doesn't see you approaching him with a towel. Bring the parrot into the room and place him on the towel which is far less threatening than placing the towel over the parrot. Make this into a game of peek-a-boo by gradually and playfully bringing the towel up over his head and covering him in a safe, friendly way. Work with your parrot this way often to make this a fun, nurturing event and to keep him tame.

➲ When you want to towel your parrot, always approach him in a calm, friendly manner — smile and talk softly, reassuring him that everything is OK. Show him the towel by holding it loosely in your hand. Facing him, bring the towel up and around his side, then from the back place it over his head, and wrap his whole body loosely. Then pick him up with your hands securely but gently around his body, with your fingers together on his belly and your thumbs just below his head. Make sure his legs and body are gently supported in your hands.

➲ Some parrots love to be held in a towel and gently towel dried after a bath. Pat them dry rather than rubbing the feathers. Bath time is a great opportunity for cuddling with some parrots!

⮕ Every parrot should have his own friendly towel. When you are handling him in the living room or playing *warm potato*, pass the towel with your bird.

⮕ Play is one of the most important parts of any companion parrot's life. Playing with your parrot in a towel is one way to keep him comfortable with being toweled. It is also a great way to have fun with him. Parrots should not be allowed to play with the towel by themselves as they may become tangled or trapped.

⮕ It is often possible to get some parrots to cuddle and allow skritching more readily if they are securely wrapped in a towel and introduced to these activities gradually.

⮕ Routinely wrapping your parrot in a towel and holding him close to your heart for cuddling and skritching is one way to keep your bappy tame for his entire life (see below).

⮕ Parrots cuddled in towels often learn to associate their towels with affection and pleasure, so keeping your parrot's towel handy can help calm him down.

⮕ There are times when a parrot has to be toweled for grooming or examination. The way the parrot is toweled is crucial in keeping him from becoming alarmed and stressed. Parrots do associate the people who are handling them with being toweled. However, if the toweling is done carefully and gently, the association is a positive one and there should be no problems.

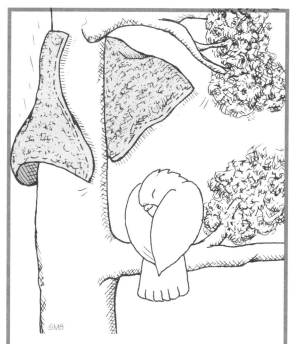

The unsuspecting Amazon sleeps unaware of the presence of his bitter foe, the deadly predator towel, preparing for its next meal.

⮕ Loosely covering a parrot's head during grooming or examination usually makes the event less traumatic. They are less afraid if they can't see what is happening to them. Be sure and stay aware of where the eyes and the beak are.

⮕ If your parrot is used to being toweled by you and trusts you, offer to towel him first and then pass him in the towel to your veterinarian or groomer. This can help prevent a traumatic experience.

⮕ Once again, DO NOT ALLOW ANYONE TO HANDLE YOUR PARROT AGGRESSIVELY! Aggressive handling can cause serious problems that take a great deal of time and patience to remedy.

A TOWEL GENTLING EXERCISE

One of the best ways to keep a parrot tame is patterning through consistent gentling exercises. One very effective exercise is towel cuddling. From the time he is very young, getting your parrot used to being wrapped gently in a towel helps to maintain your ability to handle and play with him. Once they know the towel means special focused time, most parrots readily allow themselves to be gently wrapped up and cuddled.

Pick a quiet time when both you and your parrot are mellow — usually before bed time is good. I recommend that my clients place the towel on a table or desk. Sit down in a chair and lean up against the table. Place the parrot on the towel and then slowly wrap him up, leaving his face open for skritching around his beak area to relax him. Apply a little pressure to cuddle him gently against your chest. Kiss the top of his soft head. Spend about 5 or 10 minutes relaxing with him this way before you put him to bed. Don't limit this experience to bappies. The important aspect of patterning exercises is to keep doing them. If you do this exercise consistently a few times a week, chances are your parrot will stay tame and cuddly!

INTERACTIVE GAMES TO PLAY

Games As Patterning Exercises

Using games as patterning exercises help socialize a young parrot and guide his behavior so he trusts his new human flock. Each game should become part of a daily or weekly routine for maximum learning potential. Make sure everyone is calm and relaxed — games are best played with laughter and smiles! Remember that you are the one setting the rules for these games. Playing with your parrot is a cycle — *the more fun the person has, the more fun the parrot has, and the more fun the parrot has, the more fun the person has ...*

⊃ **PEEK-A-BOO:** a patterning exercise to get your parrot used to being in a towel. Teaching a parrot to love snuggling and playing in a towel is one of the best ways to make sure he is not afraid of being toweled when he needs to be at the veterinarian or in an emergency. Use a large pastel or neutral-colored bath towel. Lay it down flat on a soft surface, such as a bed. If your parrot already has a mistrust of towels, it is best to place the towel on the bed before you bring him in the room. Bring the bappy into the room and place him on the flat towel. Gradually pick the corners up and play peek-a-boo. It may only take a few times to get him used to being enclosed in the towel or it may take a few weeks. Don't force him. Be patient. Once he is used to being in the towel, gently and playfully wrap him loosely and then pick him up and cuddle him. This game can be played as a gentling exercise to keep him used to being toweled in a friendly manner throughout his life.

⊃ **TOWEL ACROBAT:** an exercise to develop your parrot's climbing and balance skills. Encourage your bird to climb on a towel. Once he is securely on the towel, pick it up and gently twirl it vertically while he is climbing. Spread it horizontally between two hands like a tightrope for him to walk on. Let him go from one hand to the other on the towel. Make sure to play the game close to the carpeted floor or on a bed or couch so that if he falls, he will not hurt himself.

⊃ **REAL ESTATE AGENT:** a patterning exercise to acquaint your parrot with new adventures. Take your new bappy around the house and gently set him down in different locations. When he is comfortable, slowly move away from him just a foot or so. Continually reassure him that he is OK. Let him explore the objects around him. Make sure he is safe at all times. Parrots are usually far less wary of new objects introduced to them away from the cage than they are in or around the cage. This game should be played with parrots on a lifelong basis to encourage curiosity and keep them used to accepting change in their environment. With some parrots, it is a good idea to introduce new playgyms, furniture, decorations, and large items in the household in another room away from the cage first and then, once he is comfortable with them, bring them into his environment. The parrot can also be taken for walks in the yard as long as you are continually in control of him and aware of his safety needs. Some parrots will accept being put in a harness with a lead but you still need to hold on to him the entire time he is outside. Don't put him on your shoulder or just let him wander around — there are too many potentials for injury. Hawks <u>do</u> attack and kill parrots who are outdoors.

⊃ **WARM POTATO:** a patterning exercise to train your parrot to go to everyone in the human flock. Everyone (family, friends, relatives) who wants to relate to your parrot in a positive way should be involved — a few at a time. Make sure each person uses the "UP" command and knows how to handle the parrot properly. Gather in a comfortable room and slowly pass him from person to person. Each person spends a minute or so petting, cuddling, or playing, and then the next person uses the "UP" command to pick him up for a minute before passing him on. To keep a parrot tame to everyone, continue to play this game a few times a week throughout his entire life.

⊃ **BAPPY PICNIC TIME:** An exercise to encourage your parrot's sense of play and independence. This should be a supervised and interactive play time. Place a large clean sheet (or two for the bigger parrots) on the floor and lay several toys on the sheet. A blanket may not work as well because of the bappy's toenails getting caught in the loose weave. It is also not advisable to just have him play on the floor or the carpet due to potential contaminants. Many parrots who would normally spend time on the ground also like to graze and may pick up dirty or dangerous objects to chew on. The clean sheet also defines the boundaries of the play area. Drag a toy along the sheet (just like you would do with a puppy or kitty) to get him to chase after it. Roll a ball back and forth a short distance for him to chase. Parrots can be taught to retrieve items for you. Floor play is very important for parrots who normally spend time on the ground or in the tree canopy including cockatoos (particularly Rose-breasted 'toos), macaws, caiques, and greys but almost all parrots will enjoy this kind of play with their human flock.

⊃ **PAJAMA PARTY:** A way to help your parrot adapt to new environments and adjust to being without his immediate family. If you have a neighbor, trusted friend, or family member who enjoys your parrot and knows how to handle him and care for him properly, take him for visits. If he is comfortable in this home away from home, at least once a month take his sleeping cage and let him spend the night. Spend some time playing together before you leave and make sure you let him know you are coming back the next day. This makes boarding him a lot easier if you go on vacation or have to leave him for a few days.

⊃ **MAGIC FOUNTAIN:** Many parrots are afraid of water being sprayed directly at them with a spray bottle. To disguise the spray bottle, put it inside your blouse or a towel and adjust it to a fine mist. Don't ever shoot a stream of water directly at him, but spray from above the bird and let the water gently mist down on him. This is the way I got Bongo Marie used to being misted when she was afraid of the squirt bottle. Now she loves being sprayed and even squirted with the water bottle. Don't ever use the ineffective quick-fix of spraying a parrot with a squirt bottle as a punishment. Bathing is far too important for parrots to make them afraid of water.

⊃ **TEACHING TRICKS:** Teaching basic tricks like raising wings to a command, waving, shaking hands with his foot, turning in circles, saying yes with head bobbing, and somersaults can take advantage of a parrot's natural behaviors and help keep him stimulated. Teaching these tricks also encourages essential focused interaction. Just as getting a parrot used to a towel is helpful, teaching a parrot to lift or wave his foot or raise his wings with a verbal command can be an excellent advantage in grooming and examining your parrot. Basic tricks as learned behaviors can also be a positive way to redirect negative behaviors. ⨍

"Gimme Four"

ACTIVITY TIPS

A Busy Parrot Is A Happy Parrot

Parrots are highly intelligent animals who need a great deal of stimulation and activity to keep them content. An independent parrot who knows how to keep himself busy is usually well-behaved. Part of the key to having an independent parrot is to provide focused interaction. When people spend focused time interacting with their parrots with toys and play objects, the birds are more likely to keep themselves entertained at other times.

⮞ **Toys** are essential. New ones should be added on a regular basis and old ones can seem new if they are temporarily retired and returned again. If your parrot has an absolutely favorite toy, leave it in the cage all the time, but others can be removed, cleaned up, and then replaced in a new location after a week or so. I give my parrots many toys, but tend to put most of them on one side of the cage, leaving the other side fairly free for the birds to move around in. This gives them a choice whether they want to be in the *toy forest* or not.

Spikey Le Bec purposefully pulls many of the toys in his cage together and clusters them as close as possible to the entrance to his sleeping tent. I think it is his way of insuring privacy and a secure place to play, hide, and sleep.

⮞ Many **foods** come in natural packages and can be great fun — unshelled nuts, peas in the pod, pomegranates, chunks of coconut in the shell, organic oranges with peels, small pumpkins or squash, whole carrots with the greens on them, large sopping wet leaves of collard greens placed on a plate or shallow bowl, greens laced through cage bars, and baked sweet potatoes left in the skin stuffed with pellets can all provide behavioral enrichment. When Brussels sprouts are in season, I occasionally find a stalk of them and hang it in my Amazon's room. They love to rip the stalk and the Brussels sprouts apart. I doubt that they actually eat much of it but they have great fun. I also wrap various healthy foods in a flour tortilla and hang it in the cage "piñata style" with leather or 100% cotton strips. If you leave the skin or shell on any foods, make sure that they are thoroughly cleaned first. On citrus and melons, organic is preferable, as the rind of these foods can collect systemic pesticides and other toxic chemicals used in growing foods.

⮞ Provide **clean branches** from unsprayed trees to destroy. Check with your veterinarian, pet shop, or local poison control center to find what local woods are safe for your parrot. Keep the leaves on for additional entertainment in the cage or on the playgym. One good way to clean branches is to spray them with the hose and then leave them in the sun for a day or so, keeping them away from wild birds. Sunshine can be a very effective disinfectant.

⮞ Clean **pinecones** from unsprayed trees are also a special rip-apart treat.

⮞ Clean **cardboard** boxes are a delight for most parrots to rip apart. Empty cereal and cracker boxes are usually great fun. Egg cartons, paper towel rolls, and toilet paper rolls are also fun to rip up. It is important to make sure the cardboard is just being ripped apart and not ingested. Cardboard can contain glue, ink, dye, and chemicals that can be toxic to birds. Safe pressed cardboard rolls or special paper chewies are available from several bird toy companies.

⮞ **Paper bags, wadded-up paper towels, crumpled computer paper or unwaxed butcher paper** create some of the best bottom-of-the-cage or floor time fun possible. Rolls of unwaxed white or brown butcher paper can be purchased at most warehouse-type stores or paper supply stores. I use them on the bottom of the cages but also crumple up a few sheets for Spikey Le Bec to play under. Most conures would also have fun with crumpled paper.

⮞ Clean, untreated **pine blocks or sticks** provide inexpensive chew-um-up fun. You can buy wood pieces or scraps from several toy companies or purchase kiln-dried pine at a lumber store and have them cut the wood into strips. Make sure the wood from the lumber yard is untreated natural pine and does not contain any preservatives or coloring agents.

⮞ The **old style clothespins** without springs can be used to attach various chewing items on the sides of the cage and can also be safely chewed on.

➲ The use of **mirrors** as amusement for parrots is controversial. Certain birds may spend so much time with their own images that they may not be consistently tame with people. However, to most well-loved parrots who have a lot of interaction with their human flock, the mirror is usually another fun toy. Jing, Jane Hallander's Timneh Grey, talks to and gives herself noisy kisses in the mirror. All this self-adulation has not diminished her pet potential one bit although her intense self-infatuation seems to suggest a new *"subspecies"* of grey parrot: *Narci-psittacus erithacus timneh*?

➲ Many **toys made for babies and children** are wonderful for parrots. Avoid children's toys with brittle plastic or soft ingestible rubber. By law, children's painted toys must have nontoxic paints and dyes. Spike loves to wrestle with rubber action figures. He always wins even against the most menacing monsters. This is always supervised play — I watch him carefully since he almost always starts to chew the fingers off once he conquers his perceived enemy. (See page 132 for toy safety information)

➲ Placing a cage near a **window** can provide entertainment for a parrot during the day. A parrot in a window where easily seen from the street is a security risk, but a private window is fine. Some parrots enjoy watching wild birds feed at feeders outside the window. However, if something frightening occurs outside the window, the parrot may be traumatized by it. Parrots can become badly frightened by a hawk attacking birds at the feeder.

➲ Leaving the **television** on during the day can also provide stimulation for a parrot. Again, caution should be given about the shows the bird watches. Parrots do see images on television and while the nature channels can be great entertainment, shows on predators, especially raptors, can be traumatizing for parrots. One *Pet Bird Report* reader wrote to say that her Blue and Gold Macaw became quite alarmed when an automobile commercial showed a full-screen hawk flying towards the viewer.

➲ Leaving the **radio** on during the day can provide auditory stimulation for your parrot. Remember that music is not just mood altering for people. If you leave loud, raucous music on all day, your parrot may be pretty wound up when you get home. I recommend classical, jazz, easy listening, or soft rock, but some parrots seem to enjoy talk radio — make sure it is a show without expletives or you may be surprised what your parrot starts saying.

➲ **Reading** books, magazines, or the newspaper aloud to parrots can be great fun. It is amazing how responsive they become even though they may have no idea what you are reading.

➲ **Dancing and singing** with parrots is great fun for the parrot and the person. Paco loves to dance and sing with me. The sillier I become, the more fun she has. We can't dance for too long, especially if the music is loud and fast, because she becomes excited and goes into overload behavior (See page 170). We stop our fun and I put her back on her playgym — her head starts to bounce up and down, her eyes pin, and her body becomes rigid. My Amazons and caique love my singing, but Bongo Marie, my grey, shakes her head as if I am hurting her ears, especially if my voice becomes too loud or high-pitched.

➲ Parrots are social eaters and **sharing meal time** with a well-behaved parrot can be fun for the whole family. Provide him with his own plate of nutritious foods and set rules so he stays off of your plate! If you don't want him on the table, let him hang out on his T-stand with his own food bowl.

➲ Playing **"Real Estate Agent"** by taking your parrot for walks around the house or outside. Talk about what you see to keep him entertained. Closely supervise your parrot's safety at all times (see page 104).

➲ **Showering together** or going for safe walks in a warm rain are special treats for parrots.

➲ Time spent in a safe, partly-shaded **outdoor cage or aviary,** when you are home to supervise, is healthy and enjoyable for companion parrots. Do not leave parrots outdoors unattended unless you are sure the aviary is secure.

➲ Many parrots are **natural-born entertainers.** Teach your parrot a few basic tricks and behaviors to impress your friends when they come to visit.

➲ **Be creative** and come up with your own ways to keep your parrot busy and entertained. Remember to always consider his safety and well-being before embarking on any new adventure. Have fun!

TEACHING BATHING SKILLS

In the wild, excellent feather condition is essential to the survival of any bird. In addition to flight, feathers provide insulation and temperature control, water-proofing, and protection from the elements. Feather colors also serve both as camouflage and "advertising." It is a powerful instinctive behavior for our companion parrots to keep their feathers in good condition. Showering and bathing encourages them to preen. Poor feather condition can be caused by malnutrition and disease but is often due to poor hygiene resulting from lack of bathing opportunities. Most wild parrots bathe often and come from rain forest areas with high humidity. Even parrot-family birds who live in dry areas relish a good bath during the rainy season. Bathing or showering is also beneficial to the skin, body tissues, and respiratory system.

A highlight of a bird-watching trip I took to Costa Rica was watching a small group of Yellow-naped Amazons bathe in a small waterfall pool. Ducking in and out of the falling water, furiously splashing in the pools, and prancing about with spread wings, they were an exaggerated version (yet quieter) of my pet Amazons at home when they have their showers. After their baths, they flew with some difficulty up to a tree branch to preen, shake, and drip dry.

There is no doubt that most parrot species naturally love their baths and showers. If your parrot seems afraid, work slowly and gently to pattern him to accept bath time. Daily misting, spraying, bathing and weekly soaking are important parts of the routine that keeps our parrots in tip-top shape.

BATHING AND SHOWERING TIPS

➲ Bathing is often part of a wild parrot's daily routine. Parrots bathe in rain showers, small waterfalls, streams, shorelines, wet leaves, or in pools of water that form in the leaves in the tree canopy.

➲ Bathing encourages preening, which is necessary to feather health.

➲ Some people set their spray bottle on "stun" and shoot a direct stream of water at their parrot. Then they say, "My parrot doesn't like baths." Instead, parrots need to be introduced to bathing or showering in an indirect way so that they will learn to trust the event. Spraying to the side of the bird may waste water, but will allow them to make the decision to go into the water.

➲ Some birds are afraid of spray bottles. In some cases, it may be the red nozzle which alarms them, especially if the bird has red in his feathers as a "flash color." A spray bottle with a blue nozzle may be less threatening to some parrots. I do not recommend using a squirt gun because the spray should be gentle.

➲ If a parrot is tentative about new things around his cage, it is threatening to him to spray him with water when he is in his cage or around his cage territory. It is usually best to introduce new situations away from the cage.

➲ Do not punish a parrot by spraying him with water. This ineffective quick-fix can make him afraid of being sprayed for a shower or bath and does not teach him to behave.

➲ Some parrots like to take baths in their water bowls, especially when the vacuum cleaner is on. Perhaps the sound of the vacuum is similar to the sound of a rainforest downpour.

➲ It is a parrot-see, parrot-do world with companion parrots. If you have one bird who loves baths, it is helpful to let the hesitant bird watch the enthusiastic parrot shower or bathe.

➲ Many small birds will bathe happily in shallow bowls or "bird baths" available in pet shops. Keep the water shallow and make sure the bird can easily climb out if he needs to.

➲ Some parrots, such as lories and caiques, enjoy a good drenching. Once the birds become used to it, they delight in playing in the sink and even being held gently under warm running water. Be careful not to get water in their eyes, nostrils, and ears.

➲ One of the major causes of environmental feather plucking is infrequent bathing opportunities. Humidity and moisture are essential to good skin and feather condition.

➲ Most parrots love taking a shower with their owners. Put your parrot on a stand in the bathroom while you shower to add extra humidity which will improve his feather condition. If you want to take your parrot into the shower but don't want to hold on to him, there are several shower perches and stands available. Be sure the perch is securely attached so your parrot doesn't fall and become traumatized by showering with you.

➲ Use only clean, fresh water for your parrot's bath or shower. Additives or commercial preparations are unnecessary unless specifically prescribed by your veterinarian. Water can be room temperature to warm, but not hot or cold (some parrots, especially African greys, prefer cooler water.)

➲ Work with your parrot gradually to make being toweled a safe nurturing experience in all aspects of his care. Approaching him from the front in a friendly manner makes it possible to accustom him to being towel dried after his bath or shower. Pat him gently instead of rubbing him with the towel to avoid roughing up the feathers.

➲ Using a blow dryer can work well if the parrot becomes used to it. Some parrots, especially cockatoos, get excited with warm air blowing through their feathers. Don't put the dryer too close to the bird and continually check the heat level by directing the air flow towards your hand or arm. Make sure the temperature does not get too warm. (Caution: Because some new dryers have a coating on the heat elements to prevent rust, never use a new dryer with your parrot. This new coating can be toxic when heated, so make sure you use small appliances for the first few times outside and away from parrots. Some hair dryers also contain nonstick coatings which can cause serious problems, especially if they overheat. Check with the manufacturer to be sure.)

➲ Lots of things can make a parrot dirty. Wash your hands before handling your parrot to help his feather condition. Smokers create greasy nicotine stains on feathers if they don't wash their hands before petting their parrots. If you are a smoker, wash your parrot's feet frequently. One client of mine had a cockatoo that only picked the feathers on her back. It

turned out that the cockatoo was perpetually greasy because of the man's habit of watching TV, eating potato chips, and cuddling with his 'too all at the same time. Some wrought iron cage bars, or rolling in newspaper on the bottom of the cage can also create a dirty bird. I had to give one Maroon-bellied Conure a "real bath" after he had escaped from his cage and climbed down into a fireplace to roll in the ashes.

➲ Large sopping-wet leafy greens (collard, kale, mustard, turnip) placed in a shallow bowl or on top of the cage can provide a fun bathing experience while providing vitamin A nutrition if your parrot decides to eat them after his *leaf bathing* fun.

➲ The law of the jungle is to "preen until you're clean" and a very dirty bird may pluck his feathers if he can not preen them. However, parrots do not need to be given a "real bath" with shampoo or soap unless they have become very dirty or greasy. **Excessive use of soap or shampoo may eventually cause dry skin or even feather problems.**

➲ If your parrot is dirty or greasy, it is probably best to have help giving a "real bath," especially the first few times. Put a folded towel in the bottom of the kitchen sink so the bird has something to grip. Place him on the towel applying gentle pressure to his back to hold him steady. Wet him down thoroughly with a faucet spray attachment, being careful not to get water into his eyes, nostrils, and ears (those feather-covered holes on the sides of his head). Once he is sopping wet, methodically rub a quality, organic shampoo (or a gentle children's shampoo) into his feathers, concentrating particularly on the dirty, greasy areas. I usually start with the neck and work down to the tail and then do the head last — very carefully just dabbing the soapy water on a small area at a time. Then make sure he is rinsed completely! After you are sure there is no soap in his feathers, rinse him some more. Leaving soap on his feathers will cause problems with feather condition and may cause skin problems. Towel dry him as much as possible and let him thoroughly dry the rest of the way in a warm room. A blow dryer may be used but be sure to read the cautions presented earlier in this section.

➲ If a parrot is afraid of being misted with a bottle, there are creative ways to gradually acquaint him with the bottle. Bongo Marie was terrified of the spray bottle when she first came to live with me. She was actually terrified of almost everything, but just seeing the spray bottle caused her great fear. Most spray bottles have red nozzles and red is a "flash color" for greys so I looked all over and finally found spray bottles with a blue nozzle. After a few days of trying to show her that it was safe — I even sprayed myself in the face and acted like it was really fun — I set the bottle to a fine mist and placed it inside my blouse, with the nozzle just below the top button. I calmly walked up to her in a submissive posture with my head down. I smiled but didn't make direct eye contact with her. I sprayed the fine mist above her so it just sprinkled down beside her. At first she was surprised, but not really frightened. After trying three or four times, she moved into the spray. Within a week or so, she was actually enjoying the water coming gently down on her. After a few more days, I took the bottle out of my blouse. She had no problem with it. Eventually she learned to love her baths so much, she turned them into a special game. I approach her with the spray bottle behind my back and she says, "Gonna getchew!" I pull the bottle out and spray her and she yells, "Pow, Pow — ooh, ooh ya got me!" She loves her spray showers and sometimes will invite me to play by exclaiming "Gonna getchew," even when I don't have the spray bottle in hand. ƒ

LEARNING HUMAN FLOCK SOUNDS

Interaction Matters

Some parrot species have the reputation for being excellent talkers and others don't. Regardless of reputation, it is the interaction with people that creates a clever talking parrot. Most parrots can be taught a few words or expressions but may not say them clearly or develop a large vocabulary. Just as there are species differences, there are also differences among individuals. Among the individuals who possess exceptional aptitude for speaking, the ones who excel are the ones who receive a lot of social and verbal interaction from the people in their lives.

"I'll take 'Rude and Obnoxious Noises' for $500, Alex ..."

Acceptance In The Human Flock

Wild parrots learn the natural vocalizations of their parents to gain acceptance in the parrot family or flock. Companion parrots learn to imitate human sounds from their *surrogate* human parents to gain acceptance in the "human flock." The first words learned are usually simple sounds the parrot's owners have repeated often with enthusiasm like "Hello," "UP," "Hi!," or "Wanna Bite?" Some parrots start talking when they are bappies, while it is not unusual for others to talk after they are over a year old. Often people tell me their birds are not talking, but when I listen, I hear words. Parrots learn to talk much like small children do, practicing and mumbling new sounds before they get them right. When parrots hear certain words over and over, they start trying to imitate the sounds. At first, the sounds are simply incoherent mumbling but the proper inflections are often there. This is the origin of much baby-talk in humans. Just like small children need an adult to listen carefully to figure out what the child is trying to say, young parrots also need a human to reinforce the words they are trying to learn and to teach them to say the words correctly. Pay close attention to mumbling, especially the rhythm or cadence and you will begin to hear the words as they develop. Remember, although a bappy may be fully feathered and looks much like an adult, he is still learning a great deal. Don't expect too much. Your parrot will not learn to enunciate clearly or use words appropriately without social interaction from his human flock. Be patient and work with your youngster even though he may just be mumbling incoherently. Successful learning in intelligent species often requires more maturity. Once they start talking, they may say new words without any practice, especially if they are taught with enthusiasm. With instructional interaction, many parrots increase both their vocabulary and comprehension as they get older.

Can an older parrot learn to talk? If he says a few words, more verbal interaction may increase his vocabulary. It is rare for an adult parrot who has never talked to start talking but it does happen, especially in a new home situation where he receives proper care. Some previously-owned parrots will start talking once they become comfortable. I think older talking birds keep learning new words as long as they have positive social and verbal interaction. I have had my African Grey for over two decades and she still learns new words and sounds all the time.

Just because your parrot is not talking in our language does not mean he is not communicating with you in a verbal manner. Parrots have their own language of sounds and calls. While it is certainly not as complex as human languages, each sound has meaning. Listen carefully and you may learn to understand your parrot's communications. While we expect our parrots to learn our language, you too can become bilingual and learn to speak theirs.

TALKING TIPS

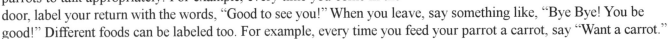

"How's it goin'?"

⮑ Do parrots really know what they are saying? The answer is yes and no. Like small children who begin to use sounds to label objects and activities in their lives, parrots are also capable of associating certain sounds with specific people, situations, and objects. This association is the most basic concept of language. Many parrots use words appropriately for common everyday situations and objects. Some seem to have a more complex comprehension of words. There is no evidence parrots possess any complex understanding of language, its grammatical construction, or its use.

⮑ Parrots learn to talk best in an interactive context when they hear words spoken to them with emphasis, clear enunciation, and enthusiasm.

⮑ Learn to use consistent words and expressions as labels for people, situations, and objects in your parrot's life. This is the best way to teach parrots to talk appropriately. For example, every time you come in the door, label your return with the words, "Good to see you!" When you leave, say something like, "Bye Bye! You be good!" Different foods can be labeled too. For example, every time you feed your parrot a carrot, say "Want a carrot."

⮑ If you are always saying, "I love you, Jing," your parrot will seem quite narcissistic. Phrase your expressions so they make sense coming from the parrot.

⮑ Continual, meaningless repetition of a word or phrase is not an effective way to teach parrots new words and phrases. They get just as bored hearing words over and over as we do saying them. Instead, parrots learn more readily from social interaction. Tapes and CDs usually serve only as a reinforcement for what they already have learned.

⮑ Speak clearly and a bit more slowly than normal — parrots often speak faster than we do.

⮑ Don't talk baby talk because that is what you will hear back *ad nauseam*.

⮑ If you have a deep voice, some parrots may learn to speak better if you raise the pitch of your voice a bit. However, if your changed voice sounds silly, that is the way your parrot will probably sound to you.

⮑ Watch what you say around parrots. It is easier for them to learn dramatic expressions and expletives than it is to get them to stop saying them.

⮑ Don't keep a talking parrot in your bedroom unless you want everyone knowing what goes on in there!

⮑ Parrots will not always learn what we teach them. Sometimes they just don't want to say something. They will take our words, learn them and then combine them or distort their meaning. This adds a new dimension to our use of language. Sometimes it is funny and sometimes it is embarrassing.

⮑ If you want a parrot to continue saying a certain word or phrase, you will need to reinforce it by either repeating it in context or providing a response when the bird says it.

⮑ Whistling and other sounds are great fun, but if a parrot learns to whistle first and gets his communication and social needs met in this way, he may not need to learn to talk. Teach parrots to talk first and once they are saying several words, teach them to whistle or make fun sounds like animal imitations.

⮑ Appropriate responses are fairly easy to teach some parrots. For example, say "Hi, how are you?" in a very quiet voice so the parrot hears it but it is not exciting enough to repeat. Then provide the answer in a dramatic voice, "FINE, HOW ARE YOU?!" The parrot most likely will not learn the boring first part, but when you say it, he will associate the second part with your words and say the second part with the same excited tone.

⮑ Old birds can learn new tricks — once a parrot has started to talk, he can usually be taught more words and expressions with the proper interaction. He may not seem to remember all of them, but will surprise you one day with what you thought was a long-forgotten word or expression because something causes an association for him.

⮑ If a normally loquacious parrot stops talking, there is a good chance there has been some sort of change in his life that makes him uncomfortable. If you suspect any physical problem he should be checked by his avian veterinarian. Be patient and increase both your focused and verbal interaction with him. Give him time. Bongo Marie has gone through periods of time when she has stopped talking, but she has always started again. ⸙

ARE PARROTS BIRDBRAINS?

By Whose Definition?

Insulting someone by calling them a "bird brain" may actually be complementing them when it comes to parrots (and many other kinds of birds). Only mammals have a proportionately larger brain than birds and the parrot brain is one of the most developed of all the birds. Asking if they are as intelligent as human beings is comparing apples and oranges. Parrots do not seem to possess many of the traits we assign to human intelligence, such as cause-and-effect logic and reasoning, a recollection of the past and its connection to anticipation of the future, or a complex sense or awareness of the use of language. However, we don't have to judge all intelligence by our standards and dismiss an animal as being unintelligent because his abilities do not have the same characteristics as ours. It is not anthropomorphic to give parrots credit for the intelligence and emotions they obviously possess.

Tool use is well-documented in wild parrots. Palm Cockatoos advertise for a mate by banging a specially-constructed stick on a hollow tree trunk. Hyacinth Macaws use a blade of grass or a leaf to help pry open a palm nut. Stories from companion parrot owners about their clever parrots' problem solving abilities abound. One of my favorites is about a cockatoo who chewed up a toy to make specially shaped wooden tools that he used to scratch the top of his head and the back of his neck — two places he couldn't reach with his beak. This was no coincidence, as he tucked the tool into a special place in his cage after each use. He even offered it to his owner when she was *skritching* his head. When he dropped the tool out of his cage, he fashioned another in the same shape using the same wooden toy.

I have watched parrots (particularly cockatoos) take wing nuts off of bolts. This, by itself, is not particularly noteworthy. I have also watched a very focused Lesser Sulphur-crested Cockatoo screw the wing nut back on the bolt. He figured this out by himself. I observed an Umbrella Cockatoo undo two dog leash snaps (not an appropriate toy without close supervision) that were snapped together, and then snap them together again. I know of many parrots who have been taught to correctly place children's plastic puzzle pieces in the appropriately shaped hole.

Companion parrots have a great deal of awareness and a basic understanding of their environment. However, a mistake is made if we expect too much understanding from a pet parrot, as it is a mistake not to expect enough. One of the frequent errors made in the interpretation of behavioral problems is that many people assign their clever birds motives according to their own thought process. Consequently, these people devise ways to change the behaviors that are guaranteed to fail because they are not based on the reality of the parrot's situation or capabilities. The most important aspect of a companion parrot's life is getting his needs met. However, he may not try to get these met in ways that seem logical to us. Although he needs more attention, he is unable to figure out that his misbehavior is actually having the opposite effect he desires when it makes his owners angry. Beyond the basics, his interpretation of these needs is often dictated by his early socialization and the way his needs have been met.

The attempt to deceive or manipulate other animals is expressed as one criterion used to evaluate the intelligence of animals. Taking this into consideration, it is obvious to me that parrots are extremely intelligent. I personally know of no animal as manipulative as some of the companion cockatoos I have met. There is no doubt in my mind that many of the ways companion parrots go about manipulating their human flock's behavior is just short of genius level, especially for a bird brain! Many of us with companion parrots spend a great deal of time trying to prove that we are, indeed, smarter than our parrots. ✒

GAMES PARROTS PLAY

Manipulators Extraordinaire

One of the criteria for animal intelligence is if they exhibit awareness of their capability to deceive other animals. Parrots are smart, and as bonded human companions, they learn to play some very manipulative games with us. Without realizing it, we play right along with lots of drama rewards and even help the parrot to set his rules for the games. Some of the games can be fun but some are not. Playing games with parrots is only fun if the person sets the rules or at least understands some of the rules of the game before the parrot gets to play!

In some cases, when the games become too rough and the parrot has too much control, the owner needs to take charge by gently distracting the parrot from his behavior. Then the person can start setting new rules for the games.

The following are just a few of the favorite games our parrots play with us:

☞ Boo!

Many tame macaws play a variation of *boo*. They lull you into a false sense of security by being sweet. The minute you relax, they throw their head into your face and squawk as loud as they can. It can be quite startling. Is it just for fun, or to test us to see if we are worthy enough to keep company with them? The only way to win is to catch them off guard and "Boo" them first. This is the favorite game of behavioral consultant Liz Wilson's Blue and Gold Macaw, Sam.

☞ Hit And Run

Many macaws and conures play *hit and run*. From the safety of a playgym, the bird runs across the couch and jabs his owner's arm with his beak. Then, with a maniacal laugh, he runs back to his perch. This is a game intended only as play and not to be mean. Protecting your arm with a throw pillow is one way to avoid injury if the parrot goes into overload and becomes too excited.

☞ The International Food Flinging Competition

Several parrots play this game, but African Greys are the champions. They can fling soft foods to the other side of the room. Non-bird people who visit probably notice, but, to be polite, do not mention the glop blotches on the T.V. screen, the papaya dripping from the ceiling fan, or the desiccated carrot strips limply hanging over the lamp shades. The more you complain about food flinging to your parrot as you scrape the residue off your forehead, the more fun the parrot seems to have doing it. Some day, if parrots get more power, Food Flinging may become an Olympic sport. An additional note: We now have conclusive evidence that it is, indeed, the *greys* who are responsible for the UFFO phenomena we hear so much about (Unidentified Flying Food Objects).

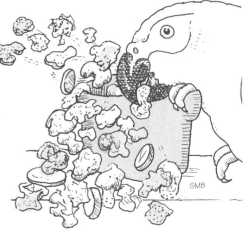

☞ Using Your Words To Get Their Way.

You consistently use the word "UP" to pick up your parrot and, before long, he uses it as a incessant command to get you to come over and pick him up.

☞ The I Love You Mixed Message (or the Sucker Bite)

This is the favorite con phrase for some Amazons. They quickly learn that the phrase "I love you" makes people go all gooey inside. With their softest, most ingratiating voice, they can sound so genuinely sweet saying "I love you" that they easily entice you to come closer so they can give you a good nip.

☞ Playing Statue

You have bragged incessantly to all your friends about your cute parrot. You've told a hundred stories about all the clever phrases he says. Finally, they are coming to see him. He plays mute statue the whole time they are there.

☞ The I Can't Scratch There Game

The parrot has been misbehaving on your shoulder and won't step off for anything. The drama escalates with you flailing your hands around while the bird is chewing on an ear lobe and a mole with a hair hanging out of it. The next step of this game is for the parrot to climb down and hang off your blouse or shirt in that place on your back where, if there is an itch, you can't scratch it by yourself. You can't grab your parrot from this place either.

☞ The Feed The Dog Game

You spend the whole morning slaving over a hot stove to fix your parrot a nurturing, nutritious meal. You pride yourself on your caring and competency because the bowl is quickly emptied as you get ready for work. One morning you peek in and watch your parrot deliberately feed your gourmet offering morsel by morsel to the eagerly awaiting family dog (and we all know how particular most dogs are about what they eat!).

☞ The Blackmail Bribe Game

This game starts out innocently enough. You give your parrot an occasional treat for being good. There is nothing wrong with that. But then you start giving him a treat to get him to behave when he starts acting out. Then he starts demanding a treat before he comes out of his cage. It is easier to oblige him than fight with him so you give in. Pretty soon he won't come out of his cage or go back in or do anything he is supposed to do unless he gets a treat first.

☞ Dance When I Say Dance

This is the favorite floor game of many out-of-control cockatoos. They chase people around the floor and the more dramatic the human dance is, the more the 'too loves to play this game every time he gets on the floor. This game can also be played with the family dog or cat.

Boing Boing Boing

The 8 Legged Parrot

You are trying to get your parrot to go back in his cage. He flops over on your hand and, out of nowhere, grows six new legs. As you try to put him through the cage door opening, all of his 32 toes grab the cage bars so you can't get him into the cage no matter how hard you try. By the time you get one toe pried off the cage bars, the parrot has reattached all of the others making this a totally no-win situation for you, but great fun for the parrot. This seems to be a favorite game for African Greys and cockatoos, although other parrots play it too. There are variations of this game that involve coming out of the cage and trying to pry the parrot off the top or side of the cage or playgym.

The Juggler

This seems to be pretty much a cockatoo game. The 'too takes all sorts of objects, from pellets to toys, and places them on his back or wing/shoulder area. He carefully balances them until they all fall off. He looks for other objects and tries to balance as many as he can. They fall off. Pretty soon everything in his cage ends up on the floor.

The Magician

This is one of the games that gets companion parrots into the most trouble. You leave the room and your parrot screams. You come back and tell him to be quiet. The parrot screams so loudly you are not able to hear him say *"abracadabra."* You rush into the room screaming at the parrot. The drama becomes so much fun that the pattern becomes established. The clever parrot becomes a magician, making you reappear whenever he wants you to.

The Exercise The Owner Game (or Parrot 52 Pickup)

You're sitting there in your easy chair reading and minding your own business with your parrot on his playgym next to you. He picks up one of his foot toys and throws it on the floor. If you don't notice right away, he throws another one down and then another one. Then acts helpless and pitiful, making a little contact call for your reassurance. Without thinking about it, you reach down to pick up the toy and put it back on the gym. Then the precise minute you sit back down in your chair, he throws another toy down — you know, his favorite one that he has to have to be happy. Without realizing the pattern that is being established, you lean over again and return the toy to his stand. Obviously he is concerned about your health, and knowing that you need a little more exercise, your parrot repeats this process over and over until he feels you have burned the proper number of calories.

Nurturing Guidance Tip: Health & Safety

Keeping Your Parrot Healthy & Safe

Understanding the *mechanics* of your parrot and his care is very helpful in keeping him healthy and happy. While all parrots do not have the same exact outward appearance, their anatomy and physiology is similar including *fuel* requirements. When fed a nutritious, varied diet and cared for properly, parrots are relatively sturdy animals with a life-span comparable to ours. However, compared to most other companion animals, parrots can be highly sensitive to toxins, and perhaps to allergens, in the air, water, and their food. With parrots in our household, we must be vigilant about the quality of their environment and the food we feed them. Before we purchase any new items for our homes, it is critical to find out if there is some aspect to them that is dangerous to our avian companions. Without doing this research, we may be exposing our parrots to serious harm and even death.

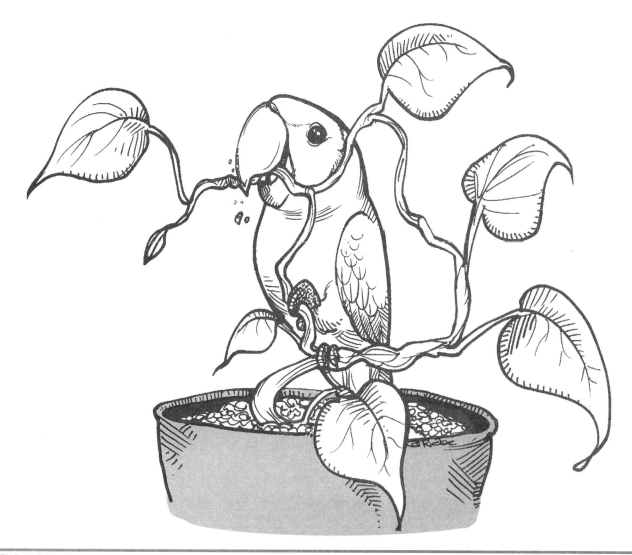

THE GENERIC PARROT

"I am an energetic generic companion parrot. Although I was domestically-raised, I still like to act wild once in a while, but the more I am taught other behaviors, the more comfortable I am as a human companion. This is pretty much true with all of us, from budgies to macaws. Not all parrot-family birds look or act like me. Some are much bigger and some are much smaller. Some have crests and some have long tails. We come in a lot of colors. Although we all are very different, we have many similarities. Most of all, we need for the people in our lives to understand us. The following is a little bit of information about just a few of my parts that make me a parrot."

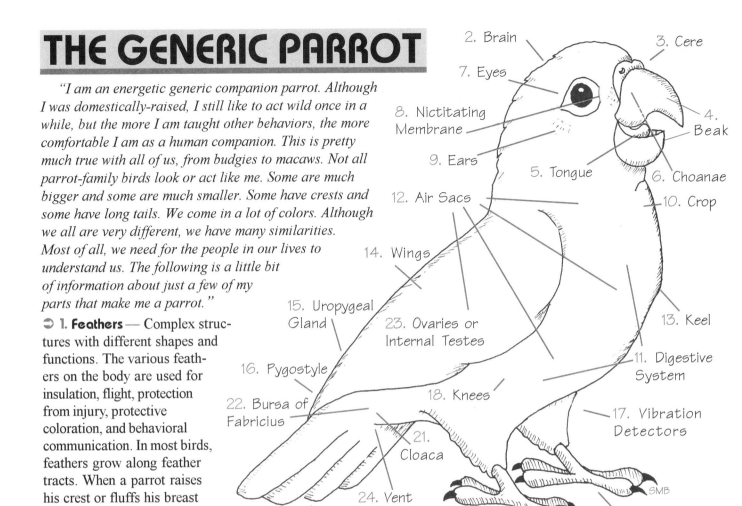

2. Brain
3. Cere
7. Eyes
8. Nictitating Membrane
4. Beak
9. Ears
5. Tongue
6. Choanae
12. Air Sacs
10. Crop
14. Wings
15. Uropygeal Gland
23. Ovaries or Internal Testes
13. Keel
16. Pygostyle
11. Digestive System
18. Knees
22. Bursa of Fabricius
17. Vibration Detectors
21. Cloaca
24. Vent
25. Tail
20. Toenails
19. Feet

➲ **1. Feathers** — Complex structures with different shapes and functions. The various feathers on the body are used for insulation, flight, protection from injury, protective coloration, and behavioral communication. In most birds, feathers grow along feather tracts. When a parrot raises his crest or fluffs his breast feathers, the repositioning of the feathers is controlled by muscles. Baths or showers are essential for feather health, and parrots preen their feathers to keep them clean and properly "zipped." When a bird shivers his feathers after a bath, he is most likely drying the feathers by erecting them along the feather tracts so water drips off of them more readily. Without proper maintenance, feathers do not function properly. Nutritional deficiencies and stress cause problems with feather growth, and may result in *stress bars,* which are breaks or discoloration in the feathers.

➲ **2. Brain** — Insulting someone by calling them a "bird brain" may actually be a compliment when it comes to parrots (and other kinds of birds). Only mammals have a proportionately larger brain than birds, and the parrot brain is one of the most developed of all the birds. Dr. Irene Pepperberg's studies with Alex, the African Grey, have clearly shown that parrots are cognitive and have the intelligence necessary to understand at least basic abstract concepts.

➲ **3. Cere** — The fleshy skin above the beak contains external openings which allow the parrot to breathe with their beak closed. Inside the nostrils (or nares) are little pieces of flesh which may look like a small seed stuck in them. People have noticed these and actually tried to remove these *seeds,* causing damage to the bird's nostril. Check the nostrils often to make sure they are clean with no discharge.

➲ **4. Beak** — The beak is not just a piece of hard plastic-like material. It is a sensitive, growing organ, and the tip has corpuscles, encapsulated bundles of highly sensitive nerve endings. The beak's structure is a continuation of the parrot's skull. The upper beak covers a bone called the premaxilla, and the lower beak covers a portion of the mandible. The part that you actually see is the growing keratin covering called the rhamphotheca (ram-fo-THEE-ka, from the Greek *ramphos*, beak and, *theka,* sheath). Beak condition is influenced by nutrition, but some parrots naturally have rougher beaks than others.

➲ **5. Tongue** — The tongue, which has a "rubber eraser" consistency, has bones and muscles that help it move. While a parrot may not have as many taste buds as we do, they do taste their food. Studies have shown that they may have a natural preference for bitter tastes instead of sweet tastes, but being influenced by the humans in their lives, companion parrots often develop quite a *sweet beak*. The parrot tongue has encapsulated nerve endings which make it very sensitive to touch, and parrots often use the tip of their tongues to explore new textures. Many parrots show affection by touching their owner's skin with their tongues.

⊃ **6. Choanae** — These are the internal nares on the roof of a bird's mouth. Vets often check the choanae to determine a parrot's nutritional status. Vitamin A deficiency can often be determined by the presence of small white bumps there.

⊃ **7. Eyes** — Parrots have eyes towards the sides of their head. Lateral vision allows them to see in front and almost all the way around themselves without moving their heads. To close their eyes, parrots raise their lower eyelids rather than lowering the upper eyelids. Parrots and humans have a similar sense of sight, but parrots can probably take more information into their brain with a single look than we can. Although studies show their color perception is different than ours, it is obvious that parrots have excellent color vision due to the way they use color in their feathers to communicate.

⊃ **8. Nictitating Membrane** — Often called the "third eyelid," this thin, transparent membrane spreads moisture on the eye and acts as *safety goggles* when a bird is in flight. When it is not being used, this membrane is folded up in the nasal corner of the eye. We rarely see it on our parrots, but if we do, the eye looks momentarily filmed over as this membrane blinks across the eye.

⊃ **9. Ears** — We usually don't think of parrots as having ears because there is no external ear. But they actually have excellent hearing, even if their ears are holes on the sides of their heads covered by feathers. Being prey animals, parrots have to hear behind them, and a parrot will fluff the feathers surrounding his ears so he can capture the sounds in his environment. When bathing parrots, we need to be careful we don't get water in their ears. Some parrots actually get waxy buildup and occasionally have to have their ears cleaned by an avian veterinarian.

⊃ **10. Crop** — This elastic pouch is used as a storage area for food before it is gradually digested. In young parrots, the crop is large in order to store the food a baby needs until his parents can bring him more to eat. As the parrot matures, the crop becomes less elastic. Most people think the crop is located only in the front and lower throat area of the parrot, but seeing a parrot who has wet feathers and a full crop will show that the crop may actually extend around the sides of the throat and even down the back.

⊃ **11. Digestive System** — Parrots masticate and manipulate their food with powerful beaks before swallowing it so they usually only ingest the soft parts or small pieces of food. Once in the crop, the food goes through various digestive processes. Food is then broken down by gastric juices in the proventriculus. Then the inside lining of the muscular ventriculus (gizzard) secretes a keratin-like fluid which hardens around food and aids in grinding any hard food. (Grit/gravel is unnecessary because this keratin surface is hard enough to grind foods. Through the years, I have known of several parrots who have become seriously ill from grit/gravel impaction in their digestive system because they have been given free access to it in their diets.) From the ventriculus, food moves into the duodenum where bile secretions continue to break it down. Then it passes to the rest of the small intestine and into the large intestine for additional digestion. Finally, wastes are stored for a short time in the cloaca until they are passed from the body.

⊃ **12. Air Sacs** — Air sacs are balloon-like parts of the respiratory system. They occur in the large humerus bones of the wings, across the chest in the clavicle area on the upper sides of the chest, and in the belly region of the body. It is thought that air sacs are also used in flight and temperature control.

⊃ **13. Keel Bone** — The keel bone is the longitudinal ridge of bone under the sternum in the middle of the upper chest. This area is large in flighted birds because the well-developed chest muscles attach to the keel (or sternum). Many baby parrots with trimmed wings are physically unbalanced and can be clumsy. It is extremely important to keep young parrots off of high places so they are not able to fall or throw themselves down. Landing on the keel bone can cause serious splitting of the tight chest skin, an injury with requires a long healing time.

⊃ **14. Wings** — Wings are not just for flying, but also for balancing. Therefore, both wings should be trimmed equally. Also, parrots hold their wings in specific positions to communicate and display.

⊃ **15. Uropygial Gland** — The bi-lobed preen gland is located on a parrot's back at the base of the spine. When parrots preen they will often rub their beak on this gland and then spread the sebaceous secretion on their feathers. Birds have no sweat glands and only a few sparsely distributed skin glands. The preen gland is their major skin gland. This secretion forms a film of fat over the feathers which keeps them waterproof and helps them from drying out and becoming brittle. The secretion also inhibits the growth of microorganisms. This gland is very well developed in green-winged macaws and budgies, but less developed in cockatiels, cockatoos, lovebirds, African greys, and even blue and gold macaws. Amazons don't have a uropygial gland. At this time, no one seems to know why some birds have more developed uropygial glands than others, or how some birds get along without them. Occasionally, this gland becomes impacted so if there is any inflamation in this area, take your parrot to see his avian vet.

➲ **16. Pygostyle** — The stiff tail feathers used in flight are attached to this bone at the end of the spinal column.

➲ **17. Vibration Detectors** — Herbst's corpuscles are encapsulated bundles of nerve endings occurring on the tongue, beak tip, cloaca, feather tract skin, wings and legs of a parrot. While these nerve bundles create sensitivity to touch, they are considered to be vibration detectors, especially the ones that occur throughout the legs. These nerve bundles make a bird particularly sensitive to movement in a tree or on the ground where they are sleeping, nesting, or foraging, and give them early warning to flee from danger or predators. Herbst's corpuscles may be one cause for traumatic responses to earthquakes. These vibration detectors may also influence night frights common in several species of parrots. Placing these parrots in a secure sleeping cage with padding on the bottom can help prevent night frights and injuries from them.

"Hey, what a cool ride! The vibrations are a lot stronger when you're standing on your feet! Put another quarter in!

MAGIC FINGERS 25¢

SMB

➲ **18. Knees & Legs** — Most people looking at a parrot would think his knees are backwards. But parrots do not stand on the flat part of their feet; they stand on their toes and the tarsus. The long bone going up from the foot is actually what we call our instep. This is called a *digitigrade* stance. So what looks like a parrot's knees are actually his heels. His legs are covered with feathers and his knees are tucked up and held against the body when he is standing quietly. Some ornithologists think that tendons in the leg lock the toes when a parrot is grasping a perch and these tendons supposedly keep them from falling off their perch when asleep.

➲ **19. Feet** — The term for a bird foot, with two toes pointing forward and two toes pointing back is zygodactyl. Parrots have zygodactyl feet which come in handy for tree climbing. Keep your parrot's perches and feet clean.

➲ **20. Toenails** — Parrot toenails are supposed to be like little *pitons* to help them get a secure grip while they are climbing or resting on a tree branch. Make sure your bappy's nails are not trimmed too short!

➲ **21. Cloaca** — The *vat* where the bodily wastes are stored until the parrot evacuates them.

➲ **22. Bursa of Fabricius** — Young parrots are said to have an immature immune system. A gland, called the Bursa of Fabricius, is a pouch on the wall of the cloaca found only in very young birds. This gland atrophies as the bird matures. Along with the thymus, these glands help to form and stimulate the cells of the immune system. It is thought that these glands secrete hormones that stimulate the production of antibodies to infections. Once the bird matures, the immune system of the bird becomes mature and the Bursa of Fabricius is no longer needed to produce extra antibodies.

➲ **23. Ovary or Internal Testes** — In the male, the internal testes enlarge during hormonal activity. In hens, only the left ovary is developed. The fertilized egg develops as it passes through the oviduct and the shell gland, on the way to the cloaca and vent.

➲ **24. Vent** — The orifice where waste passes out of the parrot and the opening for release of sperm and the passage of an egg is called the vent. Sometimes this opening pulsates for a short time after a dropping passes through it.

➲ **25. Tail** — The tail is an important flight tool used as a rudder to steer, a way to increase the lifting surface of the wings, and a brake for slowing and stopping. Many parrots can get enough lift from spreading their tail to fly, even if their wings are trimmed. As with their wings, most parrots spread their tail feathers as a display.

KEEP YOUR PARROT HEALTHY & SAFE

The following are some basic considerations to keep your parrot physically and emotionally safe and healthy:
➲ Feed a varied diet of nutritious food produced for human consumption — preferably organic when possible.
➲ Feed a high quality manufactured parrot diet — preferably one without artificial food coloring.
➲ Do not feed high amounts of fat, salt or sugar in the diet. Junk food is not healthy for parrots.
➲ Do not give your parrot over-the-counter pet shop remedies or *medicines* or feed him supplements or health fad items without checking first to make sure they are safe and recommended for parrots.
➲ If your parrot is still a seed-junkie, gradually work to change the diet to healthier foods.
➲ Keep your parrot's wings trimmed and if choose not to, make sure he does not injure himself or fly away.
➲ Do not take your parrot outside without close supervision at all times.
➲ Don't ever let anyone handle your parrot in an aggressive, threatening manner.
➲ Establish a good relationship with a competent avian veterinarian who you trust to handle your parrot in a gentle manner. Take your parrot in for an annual checkup with his avian veterinarian.
➲ Get into the habit of observing your parrot's physical condition on a daily basis.
➲ Parrots often disguise their illness until they are really sick. If you notice a change in behavior, or a physical problem, consult with your veterinarian immediately.
➲ Do not expose your parrot to unknown birds and their potential diseases.
➲ Keep your parrot's environment and the air in it clean. A quality air cleaner helps.
➲ If you smoke, please do not smoke in the room where your parrot lives, or when you are with your parrot. Parrots have very sensitive respiratory systems.
➲ If you smoke, wash your hands after smoking before handling your parrot. Nicotine can cause contact dermatitis.
➲ Become a careful cook. Almost anything you burn on the stove can cause harmful fumes to your parrot.
➲ Get rid of your nonstick cookware since it can cause fatal toxic fumes for your birds, in some situations even if it is not overheated.
➲ Consider the health and safety of your parrot with any new products you buy. Many cleaning and household chemicals are toxic.
➲ Consider the health of your parrot when you do any home repair or construction. Fumes from paints, adhesives, and other home-repair products can be toxic for your parrot.
➲ Make sure that your parrot's cage has no zinc or lead in the paint.
➲ Do not give your parrot things to play with or chew on without knowing if the materials in them are safe or not.
➲ Bathe or shower your parrot daily or at least a few times a week.
➲ Provide a roomy cage with lots of toys and activity.
➲ Provide a playgym with lots of toys and activity.
➲ Provide full-spectrum lighting for your parrot.
➲ Provide for your parrot's complex social and emotional needs.
➲ Do not punish your parrot or use aggression to train him.
➲ Provide your parrot with lots of healthy exercise and stimulation.
➲ Try to think things through carefully before you do something with your parrot. Think about cause-and-effect — if I do this what will happen?
➲ Prepare ahead for potential large-scale emergencies in the area you live (earthquakes, floods, hurricanes, tornados, and/or fires).
➲ Protect your parrot from theft. Don't let the world know you have a parrot.
➲ Make sure that all interaction with your parrot is trust-building and not trust-destroying. Aggressive quick-fixes can damage the parrot/human bond.
➲ Read the rest of this book. ⸕

"Whatsamatter honey, ya got a bad cough? Maybe I should take you to the vet?"

SMB

A HEALTHY DIET

Opportunistic Omnivores

Most parrots are naturally opportunistic omnivores, which means they eat a great variety of foods available in their habitat. They also spend much of their day involved in food-related activities, including foraging and "unwrapping" nuts, fruits, seeds, and vegetable matter for eating. Food manipulation and a variety of healthy foods provide our companion parrots with not only a nutritious diet but also with much needed stimulation.

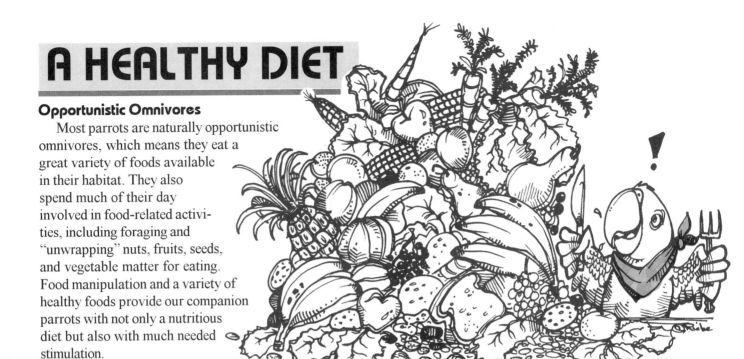

Giving parrots too much of a *Smorgasbird* of all different foods is usually not a good way to get a nutritious diet into them. They will not always choose what is good for them. Put nothing but high vitamin A veggies in the bowl a few times a week so your parrots get this nutrient no matter what they eat. Mashes with healthy ingredients are a good idea because everything is mixed together in such a way that the parrot cannot reject part of his diet. My *glop* recipe is on page 125. If a food is healthy for you, it is most likely healthy for parrots but you have to know what foods are really nutritious. **Percentages given below are approximate and there is some overlap.** Feed a variety of shapes, colors, textures, and sizes of **natural** foods from the following food groups:

⊃ **QUALITY PROTEINS - Up to 20%** Proteins are made up of amino acids. These are the building blocks of life. Many protein sources, including seeds, are of poor nutritional value because they have an incomplete balance of important amino acids. Incomplete sources of protein may be combined with others to form more complete proteins — for example rice and beans. Protein sources include nonfat plain yogurt, nonfat or lowfat cheese in moderation, tofu, nonfat cottage cheese, and very hard boiled eggs. Well-cooked lean chicken, boneless cooked white fish, water-packed tuna, well-cooked turkey, other lean well-cooked meats, or combinations of various grains, brown rice, enriched pasta, corn, nuts and/or various cooked beans are quality proteins sources. Commercially produced meal worms or insect larvae can also be used as a partial protein source. Pelleted diets manufactured for parrots are usually a good source of complete proteins. I do not recommend monkey chow, dog food, or cat food since they have been manufactured for mammals — not birds. The protein/fat ratios are not formulated properly for parrots and most mammal food contains a higher percentage of some minerals, particularly iron, which may not be healthy for parrots. The gut flora of mammals is different than that of parrots. Consequently, parrot foods need a greater control of gram-negative, or disease-producing, bacteria than do mammal foods.

⊃ **VITAMIN A VEGGIES - About 30%** High vitamin A vegetables are some of the most important foods your parrots need. Although some fruits are higher in vitamin A than others, fruits are not generally as good a source as vegetables for this necessary nutrient. Vitamin A is essential for skin and feather condition, eyesight, and helps the body fight infection by keeping the mucous membranes healthy. A general rule of thumb is "the darker the flesh (not the skin) of the vegetable or fruit, the higher the carotene content." Carotene converts into vitamin A when metabolized by the digestive system. The following are good sources of vitamin A:

•**Green Vegetables:** collard greens, mustard greens, turnip greens, kale, spinach, broccoli, dandelion greens, water cress, beet greens, chicory, chard, parsley, green peppers, alfalfa, hot peppers.

•**Yellow-orange Vegetables:** sweet potatoes, yams, carrots, butternut squash, Hubbard squash, acorn squash, dumpling squash, hot peppers, red peppers, pumpkin.

•**Fruits With Decent Vitamin A:** peaches, nectarines, apricots, raw plantain, sour red cherries, papaya, Japanese persimmon, cantaloupe.

Vitamin A is also available from eggs, meat, and many kinds of cheeses in the form of retinol, but these should probably be considered in the other categories listed.

➲ **OTHER VEGGIES & FRUITS - 15 to 20%** While these foods may not be high in vitamin A, they still have other nutritional value or psychological benefit as part of a varied diet. Well-cooked corn on the cob, peas in the pod, bean sprouts, cauliflower, Brussels sprouts, leeks, cooked artichokes, zucchini, green beans, okra, asparagus, beets, tomato, potato, apples, grapes, banana, guava, berries, pomegranates, tangerines, oranges, figs, blueberries, plums, kiwi fruit, cranberries, prickly pear, and pineapple all provide variety and interest.

➲ **WHOLE GRAINS - About 15 to 20%** Avoid high sugar and salt in these products. Whole grain bread or toast, low sugar or unsweetened cereals, manufactured cooking mixes for parrots, whole grain pastas, whole grain "energy bars," brown rice, low fat granola, wheat germ, wild rice, oat bran, amaranth, quinoa, triticale, plus there are whole grain unsalted chips, pretzels, and crackers available from health food stores and some grocery stores.

➲ **FATS - About 5-10%** Digestible dairy products, cheese, nuts, and seeds can provide your parrot with a small amount of fat needed in the diet. Meal worms and insect larvae also contain high amounts of fat. Remember — too many high fat seeds and nuts without lots of exercise make your parrot a perch potato! ✦

MANUFACTURED PARROT DIETS

The development of manufactured diets for parrots has positively changed the bird industry. Far superior to any seed-only diet, these products usually contain processed grains with nutrient supplements added. There is a difference in the ingredient quality of pelleted parrot diets. Some have high quality human-grade ingredients — others do not. Check labels carefully to read what ingredients are in each food. I personally do not feed my parrots any of the manufactured diets that contain artificial coloring.

Most parrot diets are formulated and marketed as a total diet. Although I highly recommend feeding a quality manufactured diet as a portion of a nutritious, varied diet, I do not and will never believe in feeding pellets — no matter how high the quality is — as a total diet. As a person working with parrot behavior for over two decades, I adamantly believe companion parrots (and breeding parrots) need the psychological stimulation of a varied diet that includes foods with different shapes, textures and natural colors.

Although I feed a varied diet with lots of high vitamin A veggies, I particularly love the fact that I can feed pellets on days when I am very busy (like just before the *Pet Bird Report* goes to the printer). With a quality manufactured diet in their bowls, I don't have to worry that I am compromising the nutritional health of my parrots. On these days, they still get their steamed carrot sticks, broccoli flowerets, or baked sweet potatoes. ✦

FOOD PREPARATION TIPS

Buy organic produce whenever it is available. Wash thoroughly. Pam Clark, an African Grey breeder, warns that using plain water is not enough to remove chemicals on vegetables and fruits completely. Fill your sink with cold water. Add 4 tablespoons of salt and the juice of one half fresh lemon. (This makes a diluted form of hydrochloric acid.) Soak fruits and vegetables for 5-10 minutes, 2-3 minutes for leafy greens, and 1-2 minutes for berries. Then rinse well under cold water. Peel skins and rinds unless the produce is organic.

Meat and eggs should always be very well-cooked. Veggies can be fed raw, but are probably more digestible if they are steamed, cooked, or baked. However, overcooking can destroy vitamin content. Do not add salt, sugar, or fat to your parrot's foods.

"My favorite is the sweet potato glop! How about you?"

"I love it but prefer the broccoli with yogurt sauce!"

Make Sure The "SMORGASBIRD" You Feed Has A Healthy Balance Of Nurtritious Foods!

SMB

CONVERTING TO A HEALTHY DIET

⊃ The major reason most people don't succeed in changing their birds' diets is a lack of patience. They give up too soon. Do not expect miracles within a few days or even weeks. The most effective owner knows he is making a lifetime change in the bird's diet. Instead of thinking, "I want my bird to eat this right now," think more realistically — "In a year my parrot will be eating healthier foods and every step I take to improve his diet from now until then will insure that this becomes true."

⊃ A seed-only, or predominantly seed, diet is nutritional abuse. Feeding only seed is a "death" diet no matter what anyone says in their seed mix advertising or packaging. Parrot owners should not rely on the nutrition provided by seed as the base of their bird's diet. A quality seed mix can be a part of a healthy, varied diet but should never be considered the main source of nutrition. Converting parrots from a predominantly seed diet to nutritious foods, combined with a quality manufactured extruded or pelleted parrot diet is essential to a parrot's health.

⊃ Before starting any conversion process with a parrot, have his health checked by his avian vet. Have the veterinarian weigh him and ask what should be a healthy weight range for a parrot his size. Going by a species weight chart may not accurately reflect your parrot's ideal size. Keep track of his weight on a regular basis as you work to change his diet. Either weigh him on a scale or, less effectively, check his weight daily by feeling his keel bone.

Preparing Breakfast For The Multiple Parrot Household

Let's see now, I think it is Smokey who likes yams and hates broccoli and Charley loves broccoli and hates corn but Peaches loves peppers but hates carrots. But is it Pepper who hates peppers? Isn't that strange? Of course, Alex loves anything I feed him as long as it's not green while Joey won't eat anything unless it is cooked but Sammy likes his veggies raw except for mashed carrots — or wait, is it Charley who likes yams and hates cooked squash and Pepper who likes broccoli and totally despises cooked peas. No, no, no — the bro_____ green. Alex acts like I am trying to poison him when I feed _____ must be Joey who likes Brussels sprouts but I think P_____ e just likes to rip them apart so he doesn't want t_____ oked. What about Kiwi? Is he one of my birds or jus_____ o bathe in the collard greens but Alex just likes to_____ Yesterday, I found one hanging off the wall five_____ cept for Peaches who prefers apricots. Joe_____ e red apples and he doesn't like them if_____ the dogs like the pellets so they do_____ hink of what Charley will eat to_____ tely and I am afraid he is _____ special! I think maybe _____ ed with sweet potatoes_____ and carrots would be b_____ on_____ e the yogurt. I have to_____ o cool b_____ Where oranges and Pac_____ ad at me_____ gerator are the straw_____ the almond_____ no! I only and they w_____ for the bird_____ I will be _____ e h_____ lea

SMB

⊃ Don't ever *cold turkey* a parrot — instead, change the diet slowly by gradually replacing the less healthy foods with more healthy foods. Make changes gradually, especially if a parrot has been on a seriously deficient, seed-only diet. Depriving a nutritionally compromised bird can stress him and make him ill.

⊃ Make sure your parrot is getting enough to eat during the conversion process. There is a "Catch 22" — a parrot who is suffering from malnutrition will have health problems which may be aggravated by changing his diet, but if you don't change his diet, he will continue to have health problems. For example, a parrot with liver problems related to malnutrition will most likely become sicker if he does not get enough to eat. The key is to gradually replace the unhealthy foods with healthier foods without compromising the parrot's need for nourishment.

⊃ Pet parrots seem to reflect our food likes and dislikes. If you make an excited fuss about it every time you give your parrot a piece of pizza, he will probably love pizza. (What parrot won't eat pizza?) On the other hand, if you frown every time you try to get him to eat broccoli, it is doubtful that he will eat it no matter how often he is exposed to this nutritious vegetable. I always smile when I give my parrots a new food and they can be quite adventurous in trying them.

⮑ Parrots should not be in control of what they eat. While there may be some truth to the belief that parrots may seasonally select healthy foods, they have to be exposed to these healthy foods on a regular basis for them to select what they need. Because parrots can't whip up a nutritious meal for themselves, they need us to make intelligent dietary choices for them. We also must be vigilant that the nutritious foods we buy and prepare for our parrots actually get into their digestive system.

⮑ Starchy and sweet foods such as corn, grapes, and apples are not the healthiest, but real *seed junkies* may learn to eat them more readily as a transition food to broccoli, sweet potatoes, carrots, and more nutritious foods.

⮑ Parrots are attracted to the color, shape, and texture of foods, so provide a variety until you find a way he will eat a healthy food. For example, carrots can be fed raw, cooked, by themselves or in mashes, whole, diced, sliced, in strips, mashed, grated, pureed, juiced, and so on.

⮑ Make food into toys. Lace greens in the cage bars. Make mashes and wrap foods in other foods — my parrots like a little nonfat cheese wrapped around their pellets. Put veggies and fruits on kabobs. Place large leaves of sopping wet greens (collards, turnip, mustard, or kale) on the top of the cage. Many birds enjoy leaf bathing and may eat the greens at the same time.

⮑ When introducing manufactured diets to parrots, mix several quality pellet brands together in a bowl to give the parrot something to reject. This seems to be important to parrots.

⮑ Plan on wasting food! Parrots are messy eaters and will usually waste a lot of food, especially when you are trying to get them to eat new foods. I have never felt guilty about this since my dogs have always eaten the leftover glop and veggies.

⮑ Parrots are social eaters. Sample nutritious foods as you feed them to your parrot. Smile and act like you genuinely love the food even if you don't. If he is bonded to you, he will usually eat what you eat or what someone feeds you in front of him. Use the Model/Rival technique and have another person feed you in front of your parrot to intrigue him into eating nutritious foods.

⮑ Let him eat healthy food with you. Some parrots are more likely to eat new foods if they are fed away from the cage in a social eating situation. A T-stand by the table works great.

⮑ Pay attention to your parrot's preference and feed the most nutritious foods when he is the hungriest. Some eat best in the morning; others eat best in the early evening. Many are more likely to try new foods when you are eating with them.

⮑ **Be creative. It may take weeks or even months! If at first you don't succeed, try and try again!**

SALLY BLANCHARD'S FAMOUS GLOP RECIPE

This recipe feeds 4-5 medium sized parrots for their morning meal. *Glop* also makes a great handweaning food to finger feed your bappy.

⮑ 1 jar of baby food carrots, sweet potatoes, or winter squash. (I buy organic baby food with high vitamin A veggie varieties. 2-3 times a week, I use baby foods with chicken or turkey. I occasionally use apricot, peach, or papaya.) I also use baked yams, baked winter squash or cooked, mashed carrots.

⮑ 3 slices of coarse whole-grain crumbled toast. (I vary the bread but use the healthiest lowfat bread I can find without a lot of added sugar or salt.)

⮑ 2-4 Tablespoons of nonfat plain yogurt.

⮑ Optional: 2 Tablespoons high quality handfeeding formula or a sprinkle of a natural type supplement.

Put in a large bowl and mash together until toast is saturated with baby food and yogurt, and everything is evenly mixed. Consistency can be changed according to your parrot's preference. Mine like the toast chunky and the mixture thick — about the consistency of turkey dressing. *Glop* is ready to feed — it does not have to be cooked. Anything that is nutritious can be added to the glop for a variety in texture, color, and shapes. I feed it plain or mix one or more of the following: finely chopped collard (mustard or turnip) greens, kale or broccoli, grated carrots, wheat germ, oat bran, no-sugar breakfast cereal, low-salt V-8 juice, grated tofu-cheese, nonfat cottage cheese, chopped nuts or raisins, chopped very hard boiled egg, pasta, brown rice, well-cooked chopped chicken, or powdered parrot pellets. There are also some quality parrot cooking mixtures on the market that can be used as a base for glop. Be sure and add the Vitamin A veggies to them after cooking.

Remember that any soft food will develop bacteria if left too long in the cage. I serve each batch fresh and never use leftovers as ingredients. I never have to worry about this mushy mixture going bad because all of my birds eat it as soon as I put it in their food bowls. My grey, Bongo Marie, loves her *glop*; and my Double-yellows, Paco and Rascal, relish this food, barely coming up for air when I feed it. The nutritious mixture as a part of their diet has kept my parrots healthy for over 20 years. Their feather condition is superb. If you only have one bird and want to make the whole batch, the *glop* can be rolled into balls and/or placed in an ice cube tray and frozen. Thaw as needed but don't overcook. Add any supplement after heating. If at first your bird doesn't like this nutritious mixture — **KEEP TRYING.**

PSITTACINE SCATOLOGY

What Goes In Must Come Out

There are still many outdated books being sold in pet shops, at bird marts, and through mail order that contain very misleading information on parrot droppings. The most common example is the ever present photograph or drawing of the "healthy bird dropping" which is shown as a solid, coiled, wormlike dark green shape with a circle of white paste, surrounded by a clear liquid. It sort of has the appearance of an *alien fried egg*. Truth is that a dropping like this is actually the typical dropping of a bird on a predominantly seed diet. While the bird may be healthy at the time it presented the dropping, it will not stay healthy on a long-term basis on that seed-only diet.

Parrot droppings consist of three components: the solid fecal matter, the urates produced in the kidneys, and the clear liquid urine. These components enter the cloaca (a word which derives its meaning from the Latin word for sewer) and are stored for generally short periods of time until the bird evacuates them in the form of a dropping. The percentage of each component will usually depend on what the bird has consumed. Veterinarians can tell a great deal about both what you really feed your bird, and his health, from looking at the consistency, color, and frequency of droppings over a 24-hour period, so it is a good idea not to change the parrot's paper before a vet visit. If the cage is too big to take (which it should be), just take the paper. (It will give you something to read in the waiting room?) I generally recommend using paper (newspaper, butcher paper, newsprint, etc.) on the cage bottom because you can really read the droppings. (Also some cage bottom materials, such as ground walnut shell and corncob can be dangerous, especially if they remain wet for any period of time because they can harbor fungal and bacterial growth.)

The color and consistency of bird droppings reflect what the birds have been eating and rarely does the dropping of a bird on a varied diet look like the proverbial but inaccurate "healthy bird dropping." If your parrot has an unusual dropping — don't panic. Stop and think what he ate in the last hour or so. Most fruit, particularly apples and grapes, and some vegetables with high water content, will give your parrot watery droppings. On the other hand, grains, cheese, bread, and some pellets will create a firmer dropping. If your parrot has eaten beets, berries, cherries, or pomegranate, his droppings will have a red tinge, or in some cases, be brightly colored enough to worry you that he is bleeding from his vent. Some green veggies may color the droppings bright green. Sweet potatoes, carrots, and winter squash droppings often have a yellow-brown look to them. I occasionally give my parrots a small piece of natural licorice, and you can imagine what that does for my paranoia if I forget I gave it to them. Putting the funny papers in the bottom of the bird cage will also create some weird colors in the droppings as the ink bleeds into the urates.

I am an outspoken opponent of feeding the artificially colored pelleted bird diets. I do not feed them to my birds as I am very concerned about the long-term effects of birds consuming artificial food coloring as a regular part of their diet. Not only do I worry about problems caused by the long-term consumption of these artificial ingredients, it is also difficult to accurately judge what is going on with the multicolored droppings they cause.

From the placement of these droppings I can see that you will meet a tall, blonde woman and fall madly in love.

Pay Attention To Droppings

If your bird has a noticeable change in the color, consistency, or frequency of his droppings that is not food related, check it out with your avian veterinarian. There are certain types of droppings which should cause concern, especially if your parrot's behavior has also changed in any way. Undigested food or seed particles are often a sign of a problem. Certain colors (if not food intake related) are indications of particular health problems. Droppings in which the urates have a pasty lime green appearance can be a sign of Psittacosis, "tomato-soup" whitish-pink to red droppings can signify heavy metal toxicity (unless your bird has been eating tomato soup?), and yellowish droppings can indicate liver problems. While a parrot may strain occasionally to pass his waste material, you should talk to your veterinarian if your parrot seems to have frequent or sudden difficulty evacuating. It is normal in most parrots for the cloacal orifice to pulsate after defecation and this does not appear to be a sign of a health problem. However, protrusion or prolapse of cloacal tissue through the vent requires competent veterinary care immediately.

POTTY TRAINING

I don't recommend rigid training of parrots to pass their droppings only on command. After talking to caregivers who are concerned because their parrot will not pass a dropping without a verbal command, I believe making a big deal about potty training can cause problems. Some parrots who have been so trained will simply not "go" in their cage no matter how long they have to wait. Others are only comfortable evacuating wastes if they are in a certain location. In some cases, these problems become serious enough to need medical care. Rigid potty training may be a causative factor in cloacal prolapse in some parrots, especially Umbrella Cockatoos.

Droppings shouldn't be a big deal if you have a paper towel handy — they come right up and are easy to clean if they dry. Most parrots give ample warning when they have to go. They get restless, a little heavy on the hand, and usually squat down a bit before they go. Some parrots will even be nippy if we refuse to understand their body language. At these times, it is fine to make a comment like, "OK, go potty" and place them over the paper towel or a waste basket. The problem occurs when the parrot begins to think he is allowed to go only with a command or if he begins to associate the act of defecation with verbal praise. Reprimanding him for going when he needs to and taking him out of his cage before he is given a command to pass a dropping can increase the chances of a problem with rigidity.

Fresh, well-washed vegetables and fruits **do not** cause diarrhea in parrots. Yet this myth is still perpetuated. I recently read in a super pet store chain brochure entitled *Caged Bird Care* that "diarrhea may be caused by upsets such as changing your bird's location, but may also be caused by spoiled food; lack of fresh, clean water, *too much fruit in the diet* or bacterial, viral or yeast infections." The truth is because most fruits and some vegetables have a significant amount of water in them, they may cause **polyuria**, an increase in the amount of clear urine in the dropping. This is not diarrhea. The misconception that it is diarrhea (which is an unhealthy condition generally not based on fluid consumption) is unfortunately still one of the rationales people use not to feed their parrots healthy vegetables and fruits. After all, when we feed our birds food from the supermarket, the pet industry loses money in both seed and pelleted diet sales.

Stress droppings are usually very wet, and it is not unusual for parrots to have a few liquid droppings when they are in new situations. A few wet droppings are not necessarily a problem, and some parrots are actually excessive water drinkers for other than health reasons. However, if your parrot continually has wet "squirts," check with your veterinarian. It could be a sign of illness. I personally have not known of a bird who has become so "constipated" he can't evacuate its wastes, although certain foods (cheese, bread, pellets) and a lack of drinking water can cause dense droppings which may be more difficult to pass. Bongo Marie loves her pellets and occasionally her droppings will have the consistency of modeling clay (I am thankful she has no sculptural talent).

Over a period of time, make a point to notice your parrot's droppings so you have a general idea of how many droppings a day are normal or how often your parrot usually evacuates. A decrease in droppings can signify that a bird is not getting enough food, enough water, or in serious cases, has some kind of digestive impaction or blockage. Hens who are egg bound may not be able pass their solid waste material and may produce liquid-only droppings or no droppings at all. It is important to have a basic idea of what is normal for your parrot's droppings. Check with your veterinarian about any sudden or consistent change in droppings, whether it involves continually wet droppings or a change in color, consistency, and/or frequency not related to food intake.

USE CAUSE & EFFECT LOGIC

The Need For Cause-And-Effect Logic

With their combination of high energy and curiosity, most companion parrots could easily be described as *accidents waiting to happen*. As careful as we may be, accidents can and do happen. Spikey Le Bec has a side door on his cage. A quick-link (tightened with pliers) on it kept it locked. I had no idea he had been working the quick-link and had it loosened enough so he could escape his cage and go on a grand adventure. My house cleaner had pushed Spike's cage too close to the window behind his cage. Spike rappelled across the curtains to the kitchen table. Luckily, I was in the other room and heard a crashing sound. I rushed into the living room and found him just regaining his composure from a fall onto the table a few feet from his cage. He was covered from head to toe with chocolate powder, trying to shake it off of his body. He had pried the loose lid off of a can of chocolate powder and fell into it while trying to dip his beak into the powder. The can had fallen too with the contents sprinkling him thoroughly on the way down. While I really enjoy chocolate, I was not very happy about this chocolate-coated caique. I called my avian veterinarian immediately for advice, and Spike had to have a "real bath" as described in the bathing section in this book (pg.110). Since that time, I make a habit of checking the various doors and latches on his doors on a regular basis. I know that he is not the type of highly curious, energetic parrot who would stay alive very long if he was allowed to explore the house on his own. From years of experience with parrots, I know that every time I encounter a new situation, I need to think it out ahead of time — What will happen if I do this? What special preparations do I need to make?

A Long Depressing Book

As the saying goes, "Accidents will happen." But often they don't if we pay attention and anticipate possible risk to our companion parrots. I could write a long, depressing book about the many ways companion parrots have become lost, injured, or killed. In many cases, the owner has taken very good care of his parrot and a totally unexpected accident or incident occurred. In others, the bird's injury or death was a result of a total lack of cause-and-effect logic on the part of the owner. Ultimately, it is our responsibility to keep our parrots safe. We must anticipate problems and do our best to prevent dangerous situations from occurring. We must weigh every situation ahead of time to determine if risk is involved, and if there is unacceptable risk, we must either minimize it or not involve the bird in a potentially dangerous situation. In every new situation we expose our parrots to, we must stop and think — if I do this, what could be the result? What are the possibilities for danger? What is the worst case scenario and how do I avoid a problem? I would never leave my companion parrots outside, even in an outdoor cage without close supervision. I have heard too many tragic stories about cats, dogs, raccoons, and hawks.

Some situations are so potentially dangerous that I would not expose my parrots to them. I would never drive in a car with one of my parrots out of his travel carrier. Years ago, I did with my Amazon, Paco, and she was startled when we went under an overpass. She flew into the windshield and then landed under the brake pedal. The distraction caused me to swerve but I was afraid to stop for fear of hurting her. I was lucky to be able to gain control of my car, pull safely off of the road, and nothing more serious happened.

Even leaving a parrot out of his cage, on his cage or a playgym, without supervision has resulted in the tragic death of many curious parrots. People often tell me, "My bird has never climbed down off of his cage ..." I always want to add the word "yet."

IF YOUR PARROT FLIES AWAY ...

Prevention First!

➲ Anytime you go outside with your parrot not in a carrier, you should make sure his wings are trimmed. Even a few flight feathers partially grown in can make a difference. Some parrots can fly with trimmed wings. This is especially true with slim-bodied birds who do not have the first few wing feathers trimmed.

➲ Microchipping can aid in identification if your bird is found and there is a question about its ownership. There have been situations where owners have found their lost parrots in pet shops and could only prove legal ownership through a microchip.

➲ Always use caution coming in and out of the house when your parrot is out of his cage. Know where your parrot is when you open any doors or windows. Startled birds may fly out open windows and doors.

➲ Install screens on all your windows and make sure your screen doors shut automatically.

➲ Make a recording of the noises of all of your parrots as a precaution. Many escaped parrots stay in the area of their flock if they hear calls, whether they are their own or another parrot within the home flock. Make a recording of your own voice calling him or singing to him so you can play it at higher volume.

➲ If a parrot has previously been taught the "UP" command, its use can be very helpful in getting him to come down from up in the trees.

The Search

➲ Many parrots who fly away are found within the first few hours if you call for them and follow their flight as closely as possible. Some parrots will fly or climb down almost immediately. This is often true with cockatoos, greys, and macaws. Conures and Amazons may tend to stay high in the trees. Most tame handfeds will eventually come down to someone, so letting people know about your lost parrot is essential.

➲ Sometimes another parrot in your home flock can be used as a *decoy*. Make sure he is safely in an appropriate cage or travel carrier and closely supervised at all times. The vast majority of tame handfeds will be frightened but may not know how to fly down to you even if you see them in the trees. Be very patient and reassuring, calling to them continually. Offering favorite food treats, or placing a familiar cage or T-stand near the tree, may encourage them to come down.

➲ As soon as possible, prepare or have someone prepare a lost parrot flyer and place it around your neighborhood in places with high foot traffic, such as intersections with pedestrian crossings, gas stations, restaurants, and grocery stores. Make sure copies go to local veterinarians, pet shops, bird clubs, bird watching groups, and humane societies. Call all these animal-related businesses and report your lost parrot. Ask if someone works with companion parrot recapture in your area. Place ads in the lost and found classifieds of all local newspapers and call local radio and TV stations.

➲ Don't provide people with so much information that *wackos* can call and claim they have your parrot. Save enough information so that if someone calls and says they have found your parrot, you can ask them enough questions to know if the person is legitimate or playing cruel games with you.

➲ Don't lose hope and give up too soon. Many people have had their parrots returned to them days, weeks, and even months after the birds have flown away. ✒

LOST PARROT
Reward for Safe Return

Area: Lost in vicinity of Maple Grove Estates near intersection of 3rd and Maple Streets. May have flown much further than this immediate area.

SMB

Description: African grey parrot. About 11 inches from beak to tail. Grey body with red tail. Says name. Will do almost anything for a slice of apple. Responds to "UP" command. Parrot has been microchipped.

Please call
555-1212 or 555-2121

BIRD THEFT

Something To Be Aware Of

Theft of companion parrots is something all bird owners need to think about. Although most thefts involve large aviaries with rare parrots, the theft of individual companion parrots from people's homes is also a serious problem. One of the sad things in life is that if you have something special, there is always some low-life wanting to take it away from you — if they get a chance. Any monetary loss is insignificant compared to the emotional loss experienced when a beloved parrot is stolen. Regardless of their emotional value or even serious behavioral problems, almost all parrots have monetary value. Thieves can easily sell stolen parrots to unethical buyers, whether they are brokers, stores, or breeders, with no questions asked. I have talked to people who have found their stolen parrots for sale at local pet shops and bird marts.

While hardly anything will stop the determined thief, there are things we can do to make our parrots safer. The number one prevention is not to let the wrong people know you've got birds. While this is counterproductive for a breeder or a bird shop, companion parrot owners may need to make some changes in their lives. A client of mine was proud of his beloved macaw and took him to the farmer's market on weekends. It was great socialization and the bird really attracted attention — not all of it positive. Someone evidently followed him home and the next day broke into his home and stole the macaw. Even though the man loved the macaw as if the bird was his child, the police treated the theft simply as stolen property.

MAKE IT MORE DIFFICULT:

⇒ Have your parrots microchipped and keep numerous identifying photographs of them.
⇒ Don't *advertise* the fact you have birds, and if you do, don't let people know where you live.
⇒ Be careful who you let know about your parrots. Not everyone else who has parrots can be trusted.
⇒ Make sure no one follows you home from a bird club meeting or a bird mart.
⇒ Don't take your parrot places where you can't be in constant control of him and who observes you.
⇒ Don't leave your companion parrots in outdoor cages or unguarded aviaries when you leave the house.
⇒ Lock your parrot cages but make sure the keys are easily accessible to you in an emergency.
⇒ Don't keep bird cages next to windows visible from the street.
⇒ Join a neighborhood watch and have trusted neighbors establish a relationship with your parrots.
⇒ Make your home look constantly occupied by keeping lights and the TV or radio on.
⇒ Keep your doors and windows locked when you are not home (and even when you are home!).
⇒ Leave an extra car in the driveway when you are away from home.
⇒ Get a big watch dog or even a little *foo-foo* dog who barks at strangers and/or post "Beware of Dog" signs.
⇒ Get a home alarm system and use it. Post signs that you have an alarm system.
⇒ Install dead bolt locks in your entry and exit doors and use them.
⇒ If possible, try not to let strangers and service people see your parrots when they come to your home.
⇒ Don't brag to people about how expensive your parrots are. ♪

HOUSEHOLD DANGERS

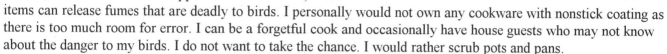

Most parrots are high-energy, curious creatures with an insatiable sense of adventure. Their time out of the cage should be closely supervised! Parrots are the proverbial *accident waiting to happen* — if they are allowed to roam the house by themselves, they will get into trouble eventually. The following are well-documented household dangers:

➲ (PTFE) Teflon™, Silverstone™, T-fal™ and other nonstick coatings used in cookware, stove drip pans (particularly deadly), flame-tamer stove top disks, irons, ironing board covers, bread makers, and other household appliances. When used, these items can release fumes that are deadly to birds. I personally would not own any cookware with nonstick coating as there is too much room for error. I can be a forgetful cook and occasionally have house guests who may not know about the danger to my birds. I do not want to take the chance. I would rather scrub pots and pans.

➲ Self-cleaning ovens and new heaters. These products can release vapors which can be deadly to birds. In many appliances, the heating elements are coated with a rust protector which, when first heated, may cause toxic vapors.

➲ Burning plastic of any kind, overheated plastic pan and pot handles, burning oil, and just about anything burning on the stove or in the household. Nonstick coating is not the only thing that releases toxic fumes when it burns. Some woods burned in the fireplace can create problems, especially if the fireplace is not well-vented.

➲ Fumes from cooking bags, scented candles, plug-in air fresheners, carpet fresheners, hair and nail sprays and products, incense, potpourri. The vapors from the oils in these products can be toxic and even fatal to birds.

➲ Cigarette, cigar, and pipe smoke, marijuana smoke, nicotine on hands and clothing, ingested tobacco and marijuana. Any smoke and/or fumes can be dangerous to birds. Even small amounts of nicotine on hands can cause contact dermatitis, especially foot problems, in parrots. Ingesting tobacco products can make birds sick.

➲ Aerosol sprays of any kind, oven cleaners, furniture polish, air fresheners, carpet fresheners, tub and tile cleaners, cleaning supplies, stain removers, bleach and ammonia fumes, oil-based paint and paint product fumes, tile adhesives, insecticides, flea bombs, fertilizers, fungicides, hair spray, spray-on deodorants, perfumes, colognes, and more. Anything that produces strong odors or fumes can cause health problems and, in some cases, be fatal. It is best to take birds out of a room if it is being cleaned, painted, etc., and only bring them back after the room has been thoroughly aired out and the fumes are gone. Keep your parrots out of the bathroom and kitchen when you use spray products of any kind. New carpeting, carpet pads, and some drapes may emit or outgas harmful fumes.

➲ Keep toilet seats down and do not leave containers of open water around. Stoves, candles, ceiling fans, large mirrors, and open windows can cause serious injury and death. Supervise other pets around birds at all times.

➲ Toxic chewables that can be ingested include some soft plastic or rubberized toys, pressure-treated wood, and paper with heavy concentration of colored inks. The following can contain toxic heavy metals such as lead, zinc, or cadmium: leaded stained glass decorations, some mini-blinds, old paint on woodwork, costume jewelry, curtain weights, lead fishing weights, lead pellets, wine and champagne bottle foil, solder, some artists paints, pencils and chalks, some cage paint & galvanized wire, metal hardware that flakes or chips. If you suspect your parrot has eaten something with any heavy metal, it is essential to get him to the vet immediately. In some cases, an x-ray will show that the foreign object is still in the crop and the crop can be flushed. If the heavy metal goes into the digestive system, it can be a long, involved, and expensive process to get it out and save your parrot's life.

➲ Avocado, chocolate, alcohol, caffeine, rhubarb, fruit pits: these are common foods that I know of that can be toxic and should not be given to birds. Some herbal health-type teas have proven toxic to birds. Also stay away from too much fat, sugar, and salt. Make sure all produce is washed thoroughly to remove pesticides and other chemicals.

➲ Some plants in the home and yard are toxic, especially if a significant amount is consumed. If you do not know which ones are dangerous and which ones are safe, keep your parrots away from plants. Dangerous plants include dieffenbachia, cutleaf philodendron, English ivy, mistletoe, holly berries, sanseveria (or mother-in-law-tongue), poinsettia, oleander, and any bulb flowers (amaryllis, iris, lilly, etc.). Safe ones include aloe, palms, springeri, spider plants, and most ferns. ✐

PLAY & BIRD TOY SAFETY

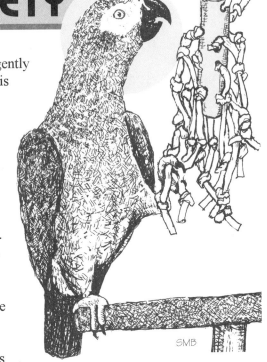

An Essential Part Of Life

Whether a companion parrot plays rough and tumble with his toys or gently manipulates them with his beak and tongue, play is an important part of his daily life. It is essential to provide a good variety of toys and play objects with different sizes, shapes, colors, and textures.

There is no such thing as a 100% safe bird toy for every parrot. Many bird toy manufacturers make their toys with a specific size (and sometimes even a particular species) in mind. Buy the right toy for your individual parrot. As people who share our lives with parrots, we need to take responsibility in determining what toys are appropriate for our parrots. We also need to realize that some toys that are safe when they are new may become dangerous with wear and tear. Many manufactured toys have elements that are generally safe but may become dangerous under certain circumstances. Toys should have safe chain that is the right size for your bird. Make sure frayed or loose fibers from rope and cloth toys are clipped and toenails are trimmed. Toys hung from cable are only safe for birds who do not pick at and separate the potentially razor sharp cable threads. Most hardware and screw eyes on wood toys are generally safe unless they are removed from the chain and wood. All toys should be kept clean or removed if contaminated by food and droppings. Parrots play in many different ways. Some play with great gusto going from one toy to the next, others may concentrate steadily on the intricacies of one toy.

Tips About Play, Toys, And Toy Safety

➲ Many parrots enjoy playing just like a puppy dog. Establishing a play time on the floor is one way to give them high-energy exercise. Roll a ball for them to chase, drag a string with a toy attached at the end, or gently play-wrestle with them on the floor. Place a large sheet on the floor to define their play boundaries. Make sure playing on the floor is your choice and not the parrot's.

➲ If your parrot gets so carried away playing with his toys in his cage or on his playgym that he often loses his grip on *reality* (and his perch), make sure his fall is soft and uncluttered. Wild parrots will fall from branches but quickly right themselves to fly off safely. Our parrots will just fall like lead balloons and may injure themselves if their landing is not safe.

➲ Play with your parrot in a towel to keep him tame and used to being handled (see page 102).

➲ Food can be a wonderful, safe, play toy. Put sopping wet collard greens on top of the cage. Lace greens through the cage bars, hang food in the cage on a kabob-like toy. Provide play-stimulating food or food in packages such as peas in the pod, Brussels sprouts on the stem, unshelled nuts, pomegranates, and/or baked yams in the skin. Food piñatas can be quick fun. Wrap pieces of nutritious food in tortillas and hang in the cage.

➲ Soft stuffed animals are great toys for parrots to wrestle or cuddle with, especially with supervision away from the cage. Keep these toys clean and be sure to remove any small or potentially dangerous parts that may be ingested or cause injury to your parrot.

➲ Observe the way your parrot chews on his toys. Most parrots will not ingest toy particles, but some will. People should be very careful about the toys they give parrots who actually ingest toy particles. Many of these birds should only be given toys made out of either readily digestible materials, or sturdy acrylic, non-shattering plastic, solid nylon, or safe metal toys.

➲ Cockatoos, in particular, have a reputation for being finicky eaters. Why, then, will some of them ingest almost anything they can chew on (except new foods), including their rubber, fiber, and wood toys? Watch carefully to make sure they are not ingesting material from their toys.

➲ Rubber and soft plastic toys are dangerous if a parrot chews on and ingests the soft material. Squeakers in rubber toys may also present a problem. Before any soft rubber/plastic toy disintegrates, remove it.

Sally Blanchard's COMPANION PARROT HANDBOOK

⤶ USA manufactured rawhide is a safe material when dry and clean. Once the material becomes wet and soggy in a water dish, it can become a breeding ground for bacteria.

⤶ There is evidence that pesticides sprayed in the house settle on and are absorbed by the materials often used in children's toys. This may also be true of the materials used in parrot toys. Don't spray pesticides in your home.

⤶ Cloth and rope used in toys should consist of 100% cotton fibers or pesticide-free untreated sisal.

⤶ Colored wood or fiber toys should use nontoxic food coloring or child-chewable safe dyes or paints.

⤶ Colored cloth should be pre-washed several times (most toy companies pre-wash material before making toys).

⤶ Although stainless steel hardware is recommended for heavy chewers and parrots who continually manipulate metal with their beaks, most quality metal hardware is safe for most parrots. The zinc in quality closed plated metal is inert and should not cause health problems unless ingested. Poor quality open plated metal hardware often flakes if you scrape it with a knife blade and should not be used for parrot toys and accessories.

⤶ Quick-links are the safest way to attach toys to the cage. The finish on all quick-links and other hardware used in the toys you buy should not flake or peel. If a parrot spends a great deal of time manipulating hardware with his beak, buy stainless steel hardware for his toys.

⤶ Parrot chew sticks are an easy, safe toy. Clean, untreated pine sticks cut to approximately ½"x½"x6" for smaller birds, 1"x1"x10" for medium birds, and 2"x2"x15" for large ones, can be hung in the cage with a screw eye and a quick link.

⤶ If string, leather, rope, or cloth are long enough for a bird to become tangled, it is essential to either tie the material into knots or cut it short.

⤶ Make sure leather toys use vegetable-tanned, untreated leather that has not been dyed. Suede textured and/or colored leather can be dangerous especially if it is wet or ingested.

⤶ Toy rings should either be too small or too large for your parrot to get his head, body, or wing stuck in them.

⤶ Jingle Bell type bells can be quite dangerous. Any toy (or cage part) with an opening that is wide at the top and then narrows can be a toe, foot, wing, or head trap.

⤶ The split rings (key chain-type rings) can be dangerous, particularly for parrots who want to take every little thing apart. Cockatoos, who like to manipulate toys with their beaks, are particularly at risk of getting these rings caught on their tongues, beaks, and feet.

⤶ If you occasionally make your own bird toys, use care in choosing materials. Do not use any costume jewelry as toy components. Materials used in costume jewelry can be dangerous or toxic to birds.

⤶ In some situations, if a parrot becomes tangled, trapped or caught in a toy, stay calm and remove the toy from his beak, foot, wing, or body if it can be done easily. However, if you cannot detach him from the toy easily, it is safer to support the bird with one hand, remove the toy from the cage with the other, and then try to take the toy off of the bird. If someone is available, have them help you. In some cases, you may need veterinarian assistance. Having a towel handy to wrap the bird in is a good idea, because he may bite if he is trapped and frightened.

⤶ Make sure toys are the proper size for your parrots. Small hard plastic toys like budgie toys and the lead-weighted penguins can be very dangerous for parrots with destructive beaks. Small parrot-family birds are often lost with toys that are too big.

⤶ Many cockatiels love to stick their heads inside their bells. Make sure bird toy bells are the right size for your birds. Large parrots love large bells but make sure they are safe for heavy-duty beaks.

⤶ Instead of letting your parrot chew on your fingers, hold a foot toy in your hand. Let him chew on it.

⤶ High energy parrots, including lories, caiques, conures, Amazons, and cockatoos, love playing with foot toys that they can wrestle with on the bottom of their cages. Hanging a toy from a perch so they can play with it on their backs can also keep many of these parrots entertained. Make sure these toys are kept clean and away from droppings.

⤶ Some parrots, particularly cockatoos, love to hold one toy in their foot and manipulate it in combination with another toy. One of the favorite combinations seems to be wrapping and chewing fabric against hard wood or metal.

TRAVEL & VISITING

Safe, Gradual Introductions

The vast majority of companion parrots can become used to almost anything if it is introduced in a safe, gradual way. Traveling with parrots can often be easier than traveling with dogs or cats, as long as the bird's needs are taken into consideration ahead of time. Spikey Le Bec accompanies me on most of my speaking engagements. At the time of this writing, he has been in 32 states with more visits planned. Most of our trips have been by airplane, but we have also traveled by car up and down the west coast. We have had many adventures together during our travels — most of them good, but occasionally there have been problems. The majority of problems have been caused by people who did not have any accurate knowledge about parrots. Since I always plan ahead and make sure all of Spike's needs are met and all of our paperwork is in order, the problems have not seriously threatened Spike's security or my sanity. Spikey even has his own suitcase which remains packed and ready to go with most of his travel essentials — his folding, portable T-stand and a collapsible travel cage with his perches, toys, and cups. All I have to do is add his various dry foods, a few small jars of organic baby food, bottled water, and some bags of veggies and fruits and we are ready to go. Now if I could just get him to carry it!

➲ Traveling By Air

Spike has more frequent flyer miles than most people. He has visited 32 states with more planned. Over the last decade, we have flown somewhere almost every other month — sometimes more often. Because of this, I have learned the ins-and-outs of flying with a parrot. Advance preparation is essential. Ask the airline and let them know you want to bring a bird on your flight. Some airlines do not allow any pets on board, and if they catch you with one, you will not be able to make your flight. Some airlines allow one accompanied bird in the cabin as long as the carrier fits under the seat. Others word their requirements in specific ways. One airline that has always allowed a bird in the cabin with his owner, now says they will only allow parakeets on board. Ah, but what is the true definition of parakeet? Most of the airline employees have no idea. A parakeet is not just a budgerigar — the definition can include all long-tailed parrots. So have your avian veterinarian refer to your bird as a parakeet on the health certificate. (After all, Spikey Le Bec is really one of those *South American Short-tailed Caique Parakeets* — isn't he?) I think that all airlines require a health certificate signed by a veterinarian, especially for interstate travel, but in the dozens of flights we have boarded, I have only been asked to show one a few times. Regardless, I still wouldn't travel with Spike without one. Most of the time, my flights have gone well. When there were problems, they were usually caused by employees who had no idea what they were doing (or were on some sort of know-it-all power trip). Knowing my paperwork is in order, I ask to speak to a supervisor immediately and that usually solves the problem without further delay. In dozens of flights, I have missed only one flight because of an overzealous ticket agent, but after a great deal of complaining, I turned it into a considerable discount on my next trip.

Again, planning ahead makes a real difference for Spikey's travel comfort. He flies in an acrylic carrier with adequate ventilation. The carrier fits into a loose cloth bag so he has privacy if he wants it. There is a perch which Spike can stand on both in a vertical and a horizontal position, so I can slide the carrier under the seat in front of me. He also has a toy with soft chewing wood and knotted fabric to keep him busy. I put a bit of seed, a slice of apple, orange, and a grape or two in the carrier. Spike has learned to drink water through a pipette or a small syringe inserted into one of the ventilation holes in the carrier. If we have a long layover, I take the carrier into a rest room booth and carefully let him out, clean the cage, and give him some hugging and skritching for a few minutes. I use a small bungee cord to strap his travel carrier on my rolling suitcase, so he gets to go for a fun ride from one gate to the other when I change planes.

Most people who fly with their birds agree that the actual flight usually goes quite well. Spike is usually quiet although he has been known to whistle his off-key rendition of "Yankee Doodle Dandy" as we speed down the runway on takeoff. He will make occasional contact call beeps to keep in touch with me, and all I have to do is nudge the carrier with my foot and say "hi" for him to settle down. He does seem a bit more restless when there is turbulence, but he may be picking up my energy since I am often what could be described as a white knuckle flyer. Spike seems to dance back and forth a bit more when my ears bother me during a landing, but has not shown any lasting problem. One thing for sure — he is always happy to see whoever greets us at the airport.

⊃ Traveling By Car

If you want to take your parrot on a car trip, gradually get him used to the experience a bit at a time. Take him for short rides to help you to predict his needs, then you can acclimate him to car travel so it is not one big surprise. Some parrots can actually get car sick so it is a good idea not to feed them too much before a short car trip. Although Spike and I have been lucky and never had a serious automobile emergency, I plan ahead and am prepared for one. I would never drive with a parrot in my car who was not in a secure carrier or travel cage. When my double-yellow head, Paco, and I were both young and foolish, I learned the hard way. I was just driving to a friend's house a few miles away and I didn't see a need to put her in a carrier. Actually, back then, there were no good carriers specifically for parrots — now there are many. I drove under an overpass which startled her, which in turn startled me. She ended up under the brake pedal as I tried to stop the car. We were very lucky; there were no other cars involved and we just swerved off the road onto a grassy area. No one was injured, including Paco. That was the last time a bird was ever loose in my car while I was driving. Over the twenty plus years since that time, I have heard many tragic stories of loose parrots being injured or killed in cars. I recommend strapping the carrier securely in the back seat with a seat belt. In cars with passenger side air bags, the carrier is best kept in the back seat.

When we travel by car, Spike is usually in a travel type cage where he has lots of room to move around. Several years ago, we were visiting a friend who had a bird toy company in Oregon at the time. My friend noticed that Spike's toys kept bonking him in the head if we turned or stopped. She designed some entertaining toys which attached to the side of the cage and filled the need for safe travel entertainment. Several companies now make this type of cage toy. I still put a few lightweight hanging toys in Spike's travel cage because he seems to enjoy an occasional bonk in the head (as long as it is not too hard!).

Spike's emergency travel kit has bottled water, a large towel or blanket, dry food, bowls, a syringe, spray bottle, flashlight, and a smaller, easily-carried carrier. I did have a flat tire on a very hot day during a trip to southern California and the spray bottle came in very handy to keep Spike cool.

For any interstate car trip, you should check ahead to make sure if the states you are traveling through have any legal requirements for health certificates or proof of ownership. Unfortunately, there seem to be more and more legal restrictions regarding birds all the time. For example, some states do not allow certain parrot species, such as Quaker and Ring-neck Parakeets, and you may not be allowed to enter the state unless you surrender your parrot. Plan ahead so you know what to expect. ⸘

PREPARING FOR EMERGENCIES

⮑ Preparing ahead of time can save your life and the lives of your companion parrots.

⮑ If your bird has not been seen by an avian veterinarian in your area, find the best one and take your parrot in for an introductory visit and exam. If you have an emergency, it will be very helpful if your bird has already been seen by the vet. When you are there, ask about the best place to take your parrot in an emergency if his veterinarian is not available.

⮑ Have a basic first aid kit available. There are several on the market just for birds. Familiarize yourself with the use of the various items in advance of an emergency. If you are putting one together yourself, the important items include blunt-nosed scissors, hemostats, tweezers, Q-tips, a small flashlight, syringes and pipettes, towel, clean bottled water, a wound wash solution or sterile eye wash, sterile alcohol prep pads, Co-flex vet wrap, and corn starch to stop bleeding.

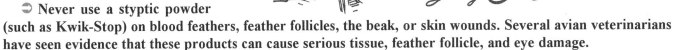

⮑ **Never use a styptic powder (such as Kwik-Stop) on blood feathers, feather follicles, the beak, or skin wounds. Several avian veterinarians have seen evidence that these products can cause serious tissue, feather follicle, and eye damage.**

⮑ In any emergency, try as much as possible to remain calm when removing your parrot from his cage to place him in his carrier. Parrots are easily frightened by a panicked owner, creating even more of a problem. Stop for a moment and take a deep breath — it will save you time in the long run.

⮑ Household fire, smoke, gas, and carbon monoxide detectors and fire extinguishers are essential. In case of fire, smoke, or dangerous fumes, get your parrots to clean air immediately. Don't return them until you are sure your house is completely aired out. If you have called the fire department, ask them when it is safe to enter your home again. If you think your parrots have inhaled smoke or fumes, take them to the veterinarian <u>immediately.</u> Watch closely for changes in breathing, droppings, appetite, or anything out of the ordinary.

⮑ In case of an emergency, make plans ahead of time to house your parrots with a friend, relative, or neighbor who is comfortable with them, and keep extra cages and supplies there if possible. Advise trusted people of your rescue plans for your parrots. They should also have photos and microchip or band numbers.

⮑ Plan ahead for any large-scale emergencies which may occur in your area, such as earthquakes, flooding, firestorms, hurricanes, and tornadoes. A sturdy cage can save your parrot's life. Plan emergency escape routes that are accessible from anywhere in your home. A plan of action can help avoid panic. Practice drills insure that your plan will really work. These drills should include quickly placing your parrots in carriers and removing them from the house. Remember, the calmer you are, the more likely they will be to cooperate with you. Keep an emergency carrier (or evacuation bag) near cages at all times and get them used to being in carriers ahead of time. Keep a towel near each cage and a net nearby for small flighted birds. Store at least a day's dry food and water taped to or near the carrier and at least a week's food (pellets, seed, dehydrated veggies, dry treats) and bottled water in a secure, easily-accessible place. Plan ahead for yourself too — your parrot's safety depends on you. Keep a portable radio with good batteries so you know what is going on. Follow the advice of the emergency authorities. Keep an emergency box ready with warm clothing, blankets, tarps, bottled water, dry foods, and a first aid kit. Keep working flashlights throughout the house. ⨎

BROKEN BLOOD FEATHERS

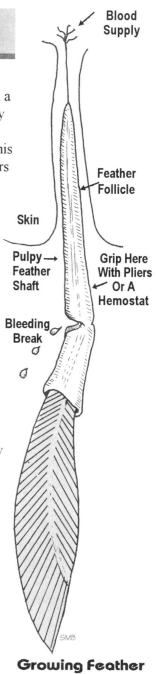

Blood Supply

Feather Follicle

Skin

Pulpy → Feather Shaft

Grip Here With Pliers Or A Hemostat

Bleeding Break

Growing Feather

Normal Molting

Birds normally replace their old or worn feathers through molting. A companion parrot on a healthy diet that contains adequate supplies of vitamin A, calcium, and quality protein usually has no problem growing new feathers. Good lighting is also important. When a bird loses the long-shafted feathers on his tail, wings, and (particularly in cockatoos) the crest and back of his neck, the follicle receives a hormonal message to grow a new feather. These emerging feathers continue to receive a blood supply from the follicle until they are mature.

Blood feathers are perfectly normal and present a problem only if they tear, break, or bleed, which happens if wings are trimmed improperly, if the bird is a feather mutilator, or if the bird injures himself in an accident. Check your bird carefully if you see blood on a perch, in the cage and/or its area, or on the bird itself. Sometimes the feather will be damaged but not actually broken. The bleeding can stop but may start again if the bird moves his wings or tail, as commonly happens when a tail feather is broken.

Sometimes a damaged blood feather will stop bleeding and cause no problems, but some continue to bleed and need to be removed because of the potential for serious blood loss. Consult with a veterinarian or professional groomer if one is available; however, it is possible for the owner to remove a blood feather. It is helpful, but not absolutely necessary in an emergency, to have someone to help you.

Steps For Removing The Damaged Blood Feather

⮕ First, have all your tools ready — a hemostat or pliers and cornstarch or an ice cube. Calm yourself down so the bird doesn't sense your fear or apprehension. Wrap the bird gently in a towel, making sure there is no pressure on the chest and that it fits loosely around the face. Hold the toweled bird against your chest and gently pull the tail or wing out to locate the source of bleeding. If there has been a great deal of bleeding on a dark feathered bird, a small flashlight can be used to help find the broken feather.

⮕ Carefully hold the fleshy area of the wing or tail, and gently separate the broken blood feather from the others so that you can clearly see the break. With your fingers, carefully grip the bird's wing or tail as close to the blood feather as you can without touching the feather itself. (If the bleeding feather is broken at skin level, it will be essential to seek immediate professional care. The bleeding can usually be temporarily stopped with an ice cube or corn starch. **Never use a styptic product like Kwik Stop on a bleeding blood feather, a feather follicle, or on skin wounds.** These products can cause serious tissue damage and should only be used on nail tips, if at all. Apply pressure until you can get to the vet.) If there is enough feather shaft sticking out of the follicle for you to grasp it firmly with a pair of pliers or hemostat, you should be able to remove the feather yourself.

⮕ Grip the blood feather shaft as far away from the skin as possible in front of the break without putting the pliers too close to the break. Securely hold the wing (or tail) so it doesn't move when you pull out the feather.

⮕ Once you have a firm grip, pull the feather shaft out quickly and smoothly using a steady tug (pull). Don't jerk the broken feather or try to wiggle it out because this could result in a break closer to the feather follicle which will require veterinary care.

⮕ Normally the shaft will pull right out, and the bleeding will stop because you have removed the *blood faucet.*

⮕ If the follicle continues to bleed, apply pressure with your finger until it stops. If it still continues, place continuous pressure, an ice cube, or cornstarch (do not use styptic powder) on the opening to help stop the bleeding. A follicle usually does not continue to bleed after the feather is removed. If it does, a portion of the shaft may still be in the follicle and the *faucet* will still be open. In this case, continue to apply pressure and take your bird to a veterinarian immediately. ⸕

The Bird Brain

Series A Diagram 1

Understanding The *Psittachaotic* Mind

"The bird brain is less convoluted than the human brain which means parrots don't have to ask why." Anon.

HIDDEN INTELLIGENCE: Bird IQ is hidden in the "wrong" part of brain, confusing mammalian scientists for years into presuming parrots are not sentient, hence the misnomer "bird brain" as an insult rather than the complement it really is.

OLFACTORY ON/OFF: Identifies pizza from the shape of the box. Causes autonomic response to any new (or green) foods: beak raises from bowl and shakes food across the room, splattering it artistically onto walls.

HYPOTHALAMUS SYNCHRONICITY: Allows such psychic sensitivity that parrot knows exactly how you are going to feel about a situation before the situation even occurs. Just watch the parrot and you will know how you are supposed to feel.

PARROTTINNITUS: Hears the high-pitched whine when your car shifts gears 6 blocks away. Starts call-to-the-flock greeting that shatters neighbor's windows.

SEXUAL IDENTITY SYNAPSE CHASM: Confuses a 150 pound 5'6" human being who has arms, a nose and hair with a less-than-a-pound feathered, beaked parrot of his own species and the opposite sex and commences an intensely passionate seduction.

OBSESSIVE COMPULSIVITY: Obsesses about that hair hanging out of that little mole on your neck or that tiny scab on your index finger. Every available opportunity is spent trying to remove it until it is gone. Parrot will remember location when he is bored in the future.

RIGHT & LEFT TERRITORIAL LOBE: Keeps parrot on duty when there is anyone except for his immediate flock in his territory. Often defends household by chasing intruders around the room threatening to bite their toes if they are barefooted unless they jump around and dance.

GREY MATTER: Resentment in all parrots (except African Greys) that the brain is made up of "grey matter" and not green matter, scarlet matter, or blue & gold matter, etc.

BRAIN KICK START: If parrot feels groggy, he shakes his head and then sticks his toenail into his nostril as far as it will go. Pressure makes contact with "coronal brain start gland" and stimulates hormonal secretions that wake parrot up.

OPTIC ALARM: Senses morning light just before the crack of dawn and screams for the human flock to get up and serve breakfast.

CAUSE & EFFECT LOGIC DEFICIENCY: Establishes and justifies specific reasons to bite when he *bites for no reason at all*. Sometimes says, "Hello, I love you," to confuse *victim* before biting.

LOQUACIOUS SENSITIVITY: Alerts parrot to the fact that a stranger is listening. Talking either ceases immediately or bird purposefully repeats simple phrases over and over, sounding like an idiot who simply knows how to mimic.

SCATSOFRANTIC BEHAVIOR: Number, fluidity, and offensiveness of droppings increases with excitement level, venting all over you.

CLOACAL RETENTIVE: Saves up droppings all day until he steps onto your shoulder or the couch.

CLOACAL EFFUSIVE: Goes anywhere, anytime, especially when company is present.

VACUUM CLEANER CORTEX: Whirring sound simulates waterfall and stimulates bird to squeal with delight and take a drenching bath in his water dish.

THE THREE FACES CONFLICT: Parrot seems to have multiple personalities, behaving differently to everyone depending on what he wants.

SMB

Chapter Eight:
TOOLS & CONCEPTS

Nurturing Guidance Tip: The Right Tools

A job is much easier to do when a person has the right tools and understands how to use them to his or her best advantage. Using inappropriate tools makes the job frustrating and, in some cases, impossible to do right. One of the expressions I often hear in talking to people is, "I have tried *everything* and nothing has worked!" Trying a little bit of this and some of that will almost always result in an even more confused parrot, especially if they use a series of aggressive quick-fixes. To achieve positive changes in your parrot's behavior, people need to use behavioral tools effectively. They need to do the right thing for long enough. Patience and consistency are probably the two most effective tools people can use to build the mutual trust necessary in the parrot/human bond.

KEEPING YOUR PARROT TAME

⊃ VERBAL COMMANDS & RULES

The purpose of the "UP" command is not just to get your parrot to step on your hand. It is to establish and maintain guidance. Getting into the habit of always using the "UP" command whenever you pick your bird up, and the "down" command whenever he steps off of your hand will help you maintain hand control for the life of your parrot. Loss of hand control is one of the first steps in losing tameness in a pet parrot. Many times when a person starts having problems with his parrot, it is often possible to regain control by simply giving the parrot more focused attention and starting to use verbal commands consistently again.

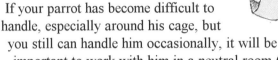

Consistent use of the "UP" command to take your parrot out of his cage makes a tremendous difference in keeping him tame and handleable from his cage. Loss of the ability to handle a parrot near, in, or around his cage is another way people quickly lose tameness in their pets.

If your parrot has become difficult to handle, especially around his cage, but you still can handle him occasionally, it will be important to work with him in a neutral room (a room he is not used to being in, where he has not established any sense of territory). Place him on a T-stand or the back of a chair. Relax and slow down your energy. Make eye contact with the bird and approach him decisively with the back of your hand, pushing your index finger gently against his belly. Say the word "UP." Once he steps on your hand, ask him in the same manner to step on your other hand. Slowly repeat the process several times and do this laddering patterning exercise for a few minutes every day until he is more compliant about stepping up from his cage or any time you request him to. If you start to have problems, repeat this patterning exercise to gain hand control again.

⊃ ATTENTION & AFFECTION

Parrots are highly social animals and depend on us to give them quality attention. There are basically three levels of attention that are necessary for our parrots to remain tame and content.

FOCUSED ATTENTION is the most important level. This is "in-your-face" time that is not shared with anyone or anything else. You are totally focused on your parrot. It is just the two of you. You can spend this time cuddling with him and *skritching* his head. Or you can talk to him and teach him new words or songs. The most important aspect of this time is that he has your undivided attention. Focused

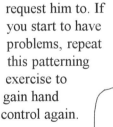

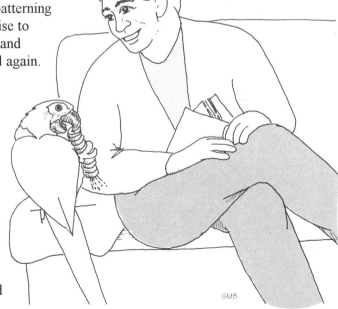

time is the best *medicine* for a parrot who has started to misbehave. I advise my consultation clients that 10 to 15 minutes of focused attention a day is the one "tool" which restores tameness to a parrot who has started to develop behavioral problems.

CASUAL ATTENTION is the second level of attention and occurs when a parrot is with you away from his cage, but he does not have your undivided attention. He may be sitting on your knee or the arm of the couch, or nearby on his T-stand with you reading or watching TV. Even though you are busy and he is busy with toys or treats, you are still handling him or interacting with him from time to time.

AMBIENT ATTENTION is the third level of attention, also called *peripheral consciousness*. You are doing other things but, on some level, are still aware of what your parrot is doing. He is spending time in his cage, perhaps occupied with his toys. When he calls to you, as he would call to his flock, you look up and ask him what he is doing or comment on what a good bird he is without going over to his cage to pick him up. Because it helps a parrot stay in touch with his flock, many parrots remain quite secure with this type of attention even if they are in their cages.

⊃ PREVENTING THE ONE-PERSON BIRD

One of the best ways to keep a parrot tame to more than one person is to pattern him to consistent handling from all the people in his life. Plan to spend a few minutes together each evening. Each person who wants to be involved in the parrot's life should participate. I call this exercise *WARM POTATO,* which means the bird is slowly and gently passed from one person to the next. Each person should hold the parrot for a few minutes, focusing his or her attention on him — talking to him, singing to him, or petting him. Then the next person should verbally get the bird's attention by saying something like "Hi, do you want to come to me?" and using the "UP" command to pick him up, and then giving him focused time for a few minutes. Then the next person picks the bird up with the "UP" command. This process can be repeated several times. Each person who wants to be a part of the parrot's life should participate in this patterning exercise. It is equally important for everyone to also spend individual focused time with the parrot, and provide him with something special that **no one else does** — like a special treat, time-out of the cage, or a shower.

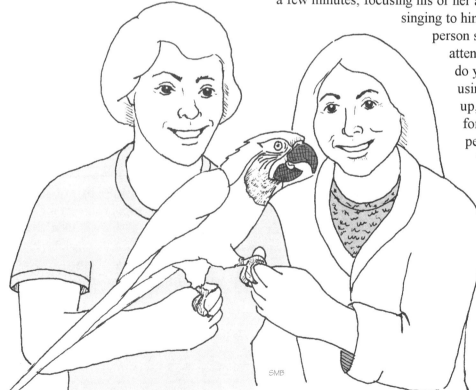

·····→

➲ GENTLENESS & TRUST

Remember that parrots are instinctively prey animals. Because of their instinctive fear of predators, many parrots can become mistrustful and even afraid if they are handled in an aggressive manner or if there is a great deal of stress in their lives. Sustained trauma can be very threatening to a parrot, in some cases even causing phobic behavior. Make sure that no one (even your avian veterinarian) handles your parrot in an overly aggressive manner. While parrots may occasionally have to be in situations that are uncomfortable for them (vet, grooming, etc.), it is critical that the general atmosphere should always be one which is protective and benevolent towards the parrots' needs.

➲ TRUST-BUILDING TOWEL HANDLING

As previously stated, bappies who have become used to being handled gently in a towel for cuddle sessions are far less likely to become afraid of towels when they have to be handled in one. I encourage my clients to continue towel handling and cuddling sessions at least twice a week to maintain the gentleness that this practice fosters. Some birds actually look forward to their towel cuddle sessions before they go to bed at night.

If your parrot is already afraid of the towel, you can teach him to trust being in a towel again. Place a light-colored large towel on a bed or couch in a neutral room. Put his favorite toys and/or treats on the towel and sit down with him. Slowly start to bring up the corners of the towel around his face to play peek-a-boo. As he becomes more used to being in the towel, start to gently pick him up with the towel underneath him and cuddle him against your chest. Make sure the towel is not too tight. Be patient; this process may take some time to work properly as parrots are creatures of patterning and established habits do not change overnight.

➲ STIMULATING PLAY, TOYS & EXERCISE

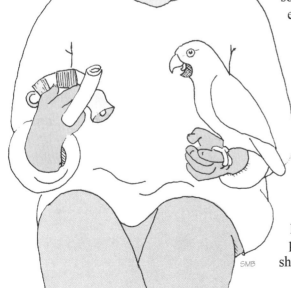

In the wild, most parrots are extremely active and we need to encourage their sense of curiosity and adventure by providing them with a great deal of stimulation and opportunities for exercise. Parrots are capable of learning throughout their lives. Always respect the intelligence of your parrot by teaching him to play with new toys and to safely accept new adventures. Toys and play objects are an essential part of a parrot's life. Birds who are initially afraid of new toys are much more likely to accept them if they are introduced slowly away from the cage area by the person they are bonded to. While most well-adjusted parrots enjoy playing with their toys, there is nothing quite like the games they can share with their human flock. Some parrots, particularly cockatoos,

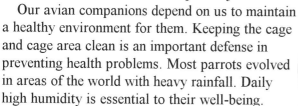

love wing flapping and acrobatics with their caregivers. Many parrots enjoy learning tricks and will often perform them for love and praise from the people in their lives. It is not necessary to deprive birds of food to teach them to do tricks.

⊃ HEALTHY PHYSICAL & EMOTIONAL CARE

To keep your parrot emotionally healthy, provide him with a roomy cage plus multiple perches and toys. For exercise, he should spend time out of his cage on a playgym with several perches and, if possible, a safe, secure outdoor aviary-type cage. Keep him active and stimulated with lots of interactive play and exercise opportunities.

In the wild, parrots spend a great deal of time foraging for and manipulating food. Provide a varied diet with a quality manufactured parrot diet (I do not recommend pellets with artificial food coloring), and lots of highly nutritious food, including high vitamin A vegetables and fruits (carrots, yams, winter squash, broccoli, collard greens, peppers, apricots, nectarines, peaches, etc.), grains, nuts, some seeds, and an occasional bit of very well-cooked chicken or hard boiled egg. Feed healthy foods and stay away from the empty calories of high fat human *and parrot* junk food!

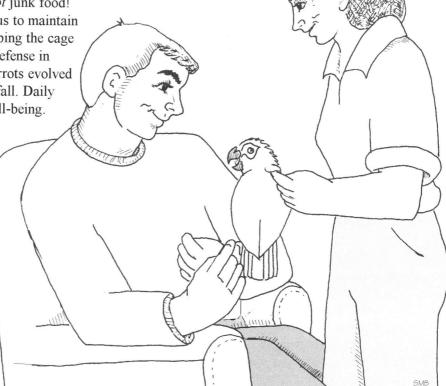

Our avian companions depend on us to maintain a healthy environment for them. Keeping the cage and cage area clean is an important defense in preventing health problems. Most parrots evolved in areas of the world with heavy rainfall. Daily high humidity is essential to their well-being. Make sure your parrot gets a bath or shower several times a week. A good night's sleep along with daily quiet time or an afternoon siesta is also essential for parrot health. Proper lighting is important, as is clean air. Airborne pollutants such as burning nonstick cookware, cooking fumes, cigarette smoke, aerosol sprays, scented candles, carpet and fabric cleaning solutions, and air fresheners can be toxic. Keeping your parrot happy and safe will keep you happier with him.

PUNISHMENT DOESN'T WORK

"I must have reallly been bad, I've been here in the bathroom for over an hour!"

You Can't Punish A Parrot

While immediate, non-aggressive discipline or correction (technically a form of basic punishment) may sometimes be effective in changing a parrot's behavior, complex punishment rarely works. Complex punishment suggests several concepts which make it ineffective with parrots. Parrots don't have a cause-and-effect sense of logic. There is no clear understanding that one event leads to another in the parrot's mind. Parrots do not have the ability to associate misbehavior with a particular punishment. Therefore, they will not avoid misbehavior simply because they want to avoid the consequence. For example, this logic would suggest that they know they will be put in the bathroom if they scream, and if they don't want to be put in the bathroom, they will not start screaming. (Studies have clearly shown that young children do not have a sense of cause-and-effect that is developed enough to understand these concepts of punishment. For example, a child told to stand in the corner for misbehaving does not understand he is standing in the corner because he had been acting up.) We often hear that parrots have the intelligence of a two-to-three-year-old child, yet we often expect our companion parrots to understand they are being put in the bathroom because they were screaming. They don't understand and we can't be upset or disappointed because they can not make the association between their behavior and its consequence.

Immediate Calm Corrections

Most parrots can understand an immediate cause-and-effect correction to misbehavior. A calm "No" and a quick (no more than a second or two) "evil eye" is effective feedback for a parrot. Much more and the person's response is ineffective and may even reinforce the negative behavior by becoming a drama reward, or causing a parrot to become alarmed and afraid. Parrots can become excited by a dramatic response to their negative behavior. If we continually give them immediate dramatic attention for negative behavior, the parrot may find the immediate attention so rewarding he will learn to scream just for the attention. Parrots are flock animals and we should be their *flock leaders*. Parrots look to their flock leaders to define their boundaries and the safety of their world. If the caregiver's response is greatly excited, the parrot may interpret this as a communication that the flock is in danger. Parrots are highly empathic and respond almost immediately to a threat (real or perceived) by fleeing the situation. If they can't get away, they may respond with aggression. Since parrots are instinctively prey animals, if we express alarm by yelling, being aggressive, or being too dramatic, the parrot may respond with alarm and become afraid enough to go into prey mode (the strong aversion and fear response shown by prey animals when a predator is nearby). Repeated fear responses do not create positive behavioral patterns. Confrontation is often met with confrontation. Aggression is usually met with aggression, and excessive aggression will be met with fear, which may result in an aggressive response, or in some parrots, extreme fear. Continued aggressive punishment may create a phobic parrot who becomes afraid of almost everything in his environment. Deprivation of attention or affection as punishment quickly destroys the trust necessary for a positive parrot/human bond and will create a new set of behavioral problems.

Working with the underlying cause of the behavior — finding out why the parrot screams and working to change that — is far more productive than punishment. Most often it is not the parrot's behavior that needs changing first. It is the human flock's interaction with a problem parrot that changes the parrot's behavior.

INEFFECTIVE QUICK-FIXES

Distractions — Not Solutions

Quick-fixes such as those shown in the drawing below do not work to change behavioral problems on a long-term basis because they are simply a distraction from the symptoms — biting, screaming, and so on. They do not treat the underlying cause of behavioral problems which are confusion, realistic needs not being met, and/or a *parrot in control of his own life doing a bad job of it.* At the worst they are confusing, trust-destroying and can severely exacerbate problems, and at best, they do not address the variables in the complex relationship between human and parrot.

After one of my behavioral seminars, I overheard a conversation between two attendees. One person said to the other, "Well, I guess you'll have to stop squirting your parrot in the face with water when he screams." The other person replied, "I know Sally said to stop that, but it's the only way I can stop him every time he screams. You know it's driving me crazy!" She missed my point completely. Squirting her parrot with water had never solved the screaming problem. It had only distracted him from each particular incident of screaming. She had not been dealing with the problem, but only with the symptoms. While they seem easy, in the long run quick-fixes makes life more difficult because the reason the parrot is screaming is never addressed in a way that could actually change the behavior. Her parrot was still a screaming parrot, and the more he screamed, the crazier she was becoming — perhaps eventually, he would drive her crazy enough that she would decide to *get rid of him.* That happens way too often in situations in which there are actually positive methods that could be used to diminish the screaming or other misbehavior. The woman needed to work with the cause of the screaming and, most likely, change her way of interacting with her parrot to make a positive, permanent change in his behavior.

Not Just Ineffective

While some of the quick-fixes I hear recommended are simply ineffective ways of dealing with problem behavior, most will confuse a parrot. Other quick-fixes are severely trust-destroying and some are abusive. Many quick-fix behavioral *solutions* sound too good to be true and they are. Real solutions to behavioral problems take understanding, time, and patience. These intelligent companions deserve people who are willing to work to change the cause of the behavioral problems — not just the symptoms! 🖋

INAPPROPRIATE ABSOLUTES

Black-And-White Thinking

There is a great deal of black-and-white thinking in the world of companion parrots. Most absolutes are inappropriate because of the variables in the personalities of both parrots and people. When you hear a sweeping generalization about parrots, stop and think if it really makes sense. Some basics apply to just about all situations but specifics rarely do. Carefully evaluate every piece of advice to determine if it is actually a logical, positive step to building trust and forming a nurturing bond with a companion parrot. If a statement uses the words *never, always, all,* or *none* — it is an absolute and needs to be carefully evaluated before being accepted.

An example of an absolute rule that has no place in parrot behavior is the statement that "a parrot should NEVER be allowed to touch a person's skin with his beak." While there are most likely some parrots who should never be trusted to touch their beaks to our skin, I think that when people set this kind of rule for all parrots, particularly handfed babies, they are missing some of the most wonderful aspects of having companion parrots. Parrots are highly physical animals with each other and, therefore, will strive to have this type of interaction with the people in their lives. The parrot beak is not innately a weapon simply used to bite intruders. Parrots use their very sensitive beaks much as we use our mouth, lips, hands, and fingers — to explore, to touch, to sense, to manipulate, to preen, and even to give affection with gentle kisses and caresses. If we set absolute rules that say parrots can NEVER touch us with their beaks, we are essentially denying them the natural inclination for allopreening — mutual preening and affection. We can warn them if they are going beyond what is comfortable for us with the words "gentle" or "no bite."

I personally cannot imagine never allowing my Black-headed Caique, Spike, to touch my hands or face with his beak. I pay close attention to his body language, and there are times when I am smart enough to keep him away from my face. There are also times when he is so wound-up, I don't want him chewing on my fingers. But when he is calm and loving, I welcome and completely trust his soft kisses and gentle preening of my hands and face. When she is visiting, it drives my mother crazy when I let Spike preen my face. I know his moods and when I can trust him. He also trusts me to completely encompass his body with my hands and kiss him on the top of the head. Our long friendship has been based on this mutual trust and he knows this as well as I do. My grey, Bongo Marie, is more reserved about physical handling than Spike, but when she is in a mellow mood, she trusts me to hug and pet her. I also pay close attention to her mood and know when it is appropriate to allow her to give me kisses and preen me with her beak.

There is another misconception that is perpetuated by this absolute rule of not letting a parrot ever touch a person's skin. **Beak exploration does not lead to biting**. The exploration a parrot does with his beak, even if it occasionally may be a bit painful to the human flesh, is a totally separate behavior from aggressive biting. It is exploration and sometimes affection. There is no logical progression from allowing a parrot to touch your skin with his beak to aggressive biting. Aggressive biting behavior most often comes from a parrot who has received little or no behavioral guidance and learns to bite as a reaction to fear and/or aggression, or as a way to manipulate or control the people in its environment. If exploratory *beaking* of fingers becomes too painful, the best idea is to find a textured foot toy to stick in the bird's beak instead of your fingers.

When a parrot is in a calm, loving mood, allowing physical affection from gentle beak touching is an important part of the parrot/human bond. Affection should be mutual and if you absolutely know you can trust your parrot to share a gentle kiss with you (closed mouth and beak of course!) — go for it.

ARE YOU REALLY THE EXCEPTION?

Know Which Rules YOU Can Break

There are a lot of rules about having parrots. They are all based on someone's experiences with these intelligent birds. Some rules make sense to most people and others may not. The good rules are based on the parrot's welfare, common sense, and safety considerations. Be aware of these rules and know that most of them apply to you and your parrot unless the two of you are really an exception. Being the exception means that you understand your parrot's behavior and needs well enough to know why and when you can get away with doing something most people should never do with their parrots. People with a young parrot often think they are the exception only to find out the hard way that they were wrong as their parrot matures. Some rules should never be broken, especially those which involve the safety of the parrot. For example, the rule to never leave your parrot out of his cage or outside without close supervision is absolute because we can't control what happens to a curious parrot if we are not there to prevent problems and/or dangerous situations.

Most rules for parrot behavior are written as if companion parrots and the people they live with are all the same. They aren't, and there are exceptions to many rules. However, people have to really know if they are the exception before they break these rules. Use knowledge and common sense to determine if you and your parrot are really the exception! Do you understand your parrot and yourself well enough to know if you are really the exception to the rules about parrot behavior? The following are just a few rules to consider:

➲ **Never put your parrot on your shoulder.** An exception is the woman who called me about her mellow 15- year-old Timneh grey who had always sat on her shoulder in the evening to watch television and had <u>never</u> shown even the most minuscule tendency for aggression even when other people were in the room. Another caller had the same story about a 12- year-old Panama Amazon. The fact that these people could put their parrots on their shoulders for quality time does not mean that every parrot can be trusted there. I have talked with far too many people who thought they were the exception to the rules about parrots on their shoulders and ended up with facial scars (see page 178).

➲ **Never pay attention to a screaming parrot.** Why is he screaming? Did you forget to give him his water and he is thirsty? Most parrots are social eaters — are you eating in front of him when he has no food in his dish? Have you ignored his ritual contact greeting and the only way he can get you to greet him is by screaming at you when you come home? Can you quiet him by calming down so he calms down to match your energy, or redirect his negative behavior with a fun trick you have taught him? Some parrots need attention when they are screaming (see page 183).

➲ **Always trim a parrot's wings.** Almost every day I hear a tragic story from someone who has lost their beloved parrot because he flew out the door or window by mistake. I also hear stories about companion parrots who have been seriously injured flying into windows, but I also know people who trained their birds and take the necessary precautions to have flighted companion parrots in their homes (see page 50).

➲ **Always take a parrot out of the cage with the "UP" command.** This is a pretty firm rule to maintain tameness in a relatively compliant parrot, but what about a bird who has become really afraid when you approach the cage? Or how about a parrot who has gotten into the habit of trying to amputate your digits when you reach in the cage? These parrots need to be worked with in other ways before their owners can reach the point where they can safely reach in the cage to use the "UP" command (See page 172).

AKA: THE HAPPY BAPPY FUNBOOK

OPTIMIZING THE ENVIRONMENT

Providing The Best Care You Can

Changes in the way a companion parrot acts are rarely just physical (environmental) or just behavioral. Changes are rarely that black and white. Negative changes in a parrot's behavior are often a combination of the strong mind/body connection in parrots. Behavioral problems influence physical health and physical health influences behavior. Stress compromises health and poor health creates stress. When a significant behavioral change occurs, the first step is to rule out a health problem or a physical cause with a visit to a competent avian veterinarian. The second step is to carefully evaluate the parrot's physical care and environment to make sure his needs are being met. This is particularly true with the onset of feather picking.

Consider The Following When A Behavioral Problems Starts:

❑ An avian veterinarian examination with necessary diagnostic tests is essential to determine if there is a physical problem. If the parrot has started feather picking, specific tests will help to determine if there is an underlying health problem. Make sure your veterinarian has experience and is competent with parrots. If you have a quality bird shop or breeder nearby, ask them for a reference or call the A.A.V. (Association of Avian Veterinarians) for the name of a veterinarian who has extensive knowledge about parrots.

❑ Misting once a day, with a good soaking (not drowning) once or twice a week with lukewarm WATER only (unless your veterinarian recommends something else) may improve the situation. (Over-the-counter picking sprays are generally a waste of money and may actually cause problems). If feathers are oily or really dirty, a "real" bath with a gentle, organic dish washing detergent or baby shampoo may be necessary. Seek advice from an avian professional before giving your bird a bath with shampoo. Make sure all soap is rinsed from feathers. (See bathing information on page 108-110.)

❑ Plucking can also be caused by skin problems. Make sure your parrot has not come in contact with something that has made his feathers or skin greasy or dirty. I once worked with a 10 month old eclectus who had slipped into a bowl of chicken soup during mealtime. His owners had rinsed him off, but within a few days he was furiously pulling all of his feathers out. The vet put him on hormones and steroids without even noticing that he smelled rancid. When I saw him I noticed his skin was very irritated and questioned the owners who then thought of the previous soup situation. His skin was just covered with bacteria because of the grease from the soup. I gave the parrot a few "real" baths and within a week his feathers were all growing back normally.

❑ The natural law is "preen until you're clean." If a parrot's skin or feathers come in contact with grease or grime they can't clean themselves, overpreening in the form of feather picking may result. Wash your hands often while or before petting your parrot, especially if you are a smoker. Nicotine on fingers can cause contact dermatitis, and is a contributing factor in feather picking in some parrots. Petting your parrot after eating greasy finger foods can also cause feather problems. A client of mine used to watch TV, eat potato chips, and pet his cockatoo. The 'too started feather picking in the areas his owner petted him with his greasy hands.

❑ A humidifier running near the bird's area (or on the furnace) during the winter months when the heat is on and/or during dry hot summers is beneficial. Make sure the water is fresh and keep the humidifier clean.

❑ Consider buying or installing a quality air cleaning or filtration system. (I don't recommend the ozone generator-type air cleaners for use in rooms with birds or people.) Change filters if and when necessary. Make sure there is lots of fresh air with good air flow in the room where the bird lives. Don't believe the old myth that drafts are one of the main causes of health problems in birds. Be realistic — good air flow is healthy — placing the cage under the air conditioner is not. If you are a smoker, please stop smoking in the area where the bird lives.

❑ A clean cage and environment are essential for health. Change papers or cage substrata on a daily basis. Some materials made to cover the bottom of the cage may become disease producing if left too long without cleaning. This is particularly true of ground walnut shell and shredded corn cob bedding if it is not kept dry and cleaned daily.

❑ Good lighting — a full spectrum light about 18 inches to 2 feet above the cage is needed. Keep this additional lighting on during daylight hours only. Replace bulbs according to manufacturer's recommendations.

❑ A few hours of closely supervised time outside in a safe, secure play cage during the day if weather permits will be enjoyed by most parrots. (Always protect parrots from intense sunlight.)

❑ A nutritious varied diet with adequate Vitamin A (yams, carrots, broccoli, etc.) and calcium should be given. Clean drinking water and clean, fresh food without artificial additives are necessary.

❑ Certain foods may cause allergic reactions or skin problems in parrots. Feeding foods with excessive fat, sugar, and salt may contribute to skin and feather problems. Certain additives, including food coloring, may also cause problems for some parrots. Some people believe that feeding peanuts can be a contributing factor in skin problems.

❑ Parrots need lots of stimulation, exercise, and activity with a wide variety of toys, including preening-type texture toys. A large enough cage and a playgym for exercise are essential to keep a parrot active.

❑ Make sure that your cage paint and other items your parrot has access to do not contain dangerous heavy metals (such as lead and zinc) that your parrot may chew and ingest. Most toys made by quality toy manufacturers contain close-plated metal hardware that may contain zinc which does not break down. This hardware is not considered to be dangerous for parrots unless they ingest the entire piece.

❑ Use great caution with any household pollutants including cleaners, aerosol sprays of any kind, air fresheners, scented candles, potpourri, pesticides, and paint products. Stop smoking or smoke outside. Second hand smoke is deadly to birds. If you smoke, ALWAYS wash your hands before handling your parrots.

❑ Ensure that your bird gets at least 9 hours of undisturbed sleep a night. Covering the cage at night or putting your parrot in a sleeping cage in another room can help establish a more secure time for sleeping.

❑ Provide a secure hiding area in the cage. This can be achieved by covering a corner of the cage, putting up a platform with one or two walls, or a tent-like habitat made for parrots.

❑ Make sure that no one in the household is teasing, threatening, or causing the bird trauma. Check around the parrot's cage to see if anything is causing him fear or trauma, such as something new placed into the area or above the cage just prior to the onset of the problem behavior.

❑ Establish *Nurturing Guidance* by setting rules and using verbal commands. Increase predictable, defined, in-your-face attention and affection. Spend time teaching your parrot to play, setting rules, and just having fun together. Provide defined cage-time to encourage independence. If the parrot has become phobic, you may need to suspend any direct attention and establish *Nurturing Submission* (see pages 189-191).

❑ Have you made a change in your appearance (shaved a moustache, acquired a new hairstyle or new glasses, etc.) or has there been a change in your home recently? If so, you need to be patient with your parrot, giving him more time to adjust to it?

❑ Stop and pay attention to your own energy. Are you under a great deal of stress or is there stress in your household which could be causing a reaction in your parrot? Calming yourself down before you give your parrot attention is good for him and good for you.

❑ If there is added stress at work or in the home environment, try to remain calm around your parrot, especially if he is developing a problem. Do not turn an incident into a pattern by rewarding the negative behavior. Your dramatic response or overly-concerned energy may actually keep your parrot in a state of alarm which will intensify the problem.

❑ Seek the advice of a companion parrot behavioral consultant who has a reputation for common sense and practical advice. Do not follow any advice if it seems trust-destroying instead of trust-building. Ask why when you are told to do something specific. Behavioral consultants should be able to give you a logical explanation that makes sense. If they can't explain why they are telling you to do something or their explanation doesn't make sense to you, you shouldn't follow the advice. ✎

TAMING ADULT PARROTS

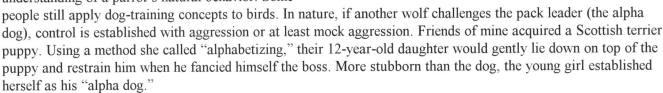

Earning Trust

Taming a bird has nothing to do with aggression; it involves trust. Birds are highly empathic. They often match their moods to those of the people in their lives. Bongo Marie drives me crazy, for instance, when I feel rushed or stressed. She jabbers incessantly, disciplining the dog and the other birds. I learned a long time ago that the only way to have peace and quiet during these jabbering times is to approach her cage, shut my eyes, take slow, deep breaths and hum quietly. As if by magic, she matches her mood to mine, calms down, and whispers softly to me. This is empathy. A wild parrot has no reason to trust us and every reason to be afraid. Slowing yourself down so the bird senses no fear or aggression is the first step in empathy taming.

No Aggressive Taming!

Many of the birds I have worked with were "tamed" with aggression or abuse, and they have remained afraid of humans. Taming problems come from a lack of understanding of a parrot's natural behavior. Some people still apply dog-training concepts to birds. In nature, if another wolf challenges the pack leader (the alpha dog), control is established with aggression or at least mock aggression. Friends of mine acquired a Scottish terrier puppy. Using a method she called "alphabetizing," their 12-year-old daughter would gently lie down on top of the puppy and restrain him when he fancied himself the boss. More stubborn than the dog, the young girl established herself as his "alpha dog."

If done properly, this sort of physical dominance may work with dogs, but it does not create a trusting parrot. In their natural habitats, most parrot species rarely resort to physical aggression. If the parrot's territory is threatened, a defender merely struts and postures unless he or she is so threatened that physical aggression is necessary.

Puffing up his feathers, a parrot communicates with the bright colors on his forehead, wings, and tail. The message is clear — "This is my branch. Go away!" A few loud squawks add emphasis to the message. This is *psychological* warfare, and the bird with the best display usually wins.

As perceptive bird owners know, a pet parrot usually bites only if his warnings go unheeded. If your actions are interpreted as aggression, an empathic parrot may respond with aggression. If your aggression is overwhelming, a parrot may submit out of fear. Fearful birds do not trust people and eventually may become aggressive to them.

I have spent hours working with parrots, particularly Moluccan Cockatoos, who have been traumatized by a training method often referred to as the "love grip." When using this method, a trainer wraps a bird tightly in a towel, leaving the bird's head exposed. He then clutches the bird aggressively with both hands until the bird stops struggling. At this time, the bird may seem tame, but his response is based on fear. In some cases, I believe this treatment is so traumatic that the bird shuts down his personality. Patient owners can undo the damage done to captive birds that have been treated abusively or hit with sticks or hands, but they must understand basic parrot behavior to win their trust.

Allopreening And Bonding

In the wild, parrots allopreen as a form of bonding. "You scratch my neck, and I'll scratch yours!" best describes this mutual preening. A bird cannot reach the back of his head and neck. If you've watched bonded parrots preen each other, you have seen how much they enjoy this attention. The way to a pet bird's heart is through scratching the back of his neck. When parrots preen, they really get into the feathers, down to the skin. Pet your parrot the same way — really get your fingers into the back of his neck, way down into the shafts of the feathers. Don't get too rough with the "skritching" — stay gentle, but just patting a bird's head rarely does a thing for him.

Taming The Military Macaw

As if hypnotized, the Military Macaw lay stretched across my lap on his back. I "skritched" his head and the area where his skin and upper beak join. Stretching his wing, he seemed to beg me to rub his side. With feathers fluffed around his head and eyes half closed, he softly "gronked" in quiet contentment.

Was this bird a sweet, hand-fed baby macaw? No! Less than an hour before this idyllic scene took place, I had removed the screaming, biting macaw from his cage. This imported wild bird had not been out of his cage in at least three years, since he had been purchased from a quarantine station. He had never been handled. Full of doubt, his owners, nevertheless, asked if I could tame their parrot.

When I first saw the Military Macaw in his cage, I wasn't sure I could tame him. As I got closer, he went into full territorial display. Head feathers puffed and he lunged at me against the bars of the cage. Although the cage was an adequate size, the door was small, and I knew taking the bird out of this cage would be traumatic for both of us. I later demanded that the owners get him another cage that provided easier access to him. On this day, however, any progress we might make would be severely jeopardized by the difficulty of removing the macaw through the small door of his cage. My first challenge was to get him out of the cage that had been his only world for three years.

Many parrots remain untamed because their owners start by trying to hand-tame their birds from the perches in the birds' cages. There is little chance of success with this technique because parrots are territorial. If the person working with the bird is not an accepted member of their *flock*, they will defend their cages.

To tame a bird successfully, you must first get him away from his cage. I will use almost any method that is not injurious to the bird to get him out of his cage. Opening the door and letting the bird come out on his own, bribing him onto a stand by placing a nut or favorite treat in a bowl, or even taping or attaching food to the stand and, if the cage is small enough, taking the bottom out of the cage and turning the cage upside down or sideways, are three possibilities. In some cases, it may be weeks before the parrot will venture out on his own. Patience goes a long way, and often, letting him come out on his own will earn more points towards trust than forcing him out and having to deal with his fear.

Sometimes it is necessary to reach in and get the bird out. Owner confidence is essential and it is important to plan ahead — chasing a frightened parrot around his cage is not the way to start a trust-building training session. I often take a large, light-colored towel and throw it loosely over a bird from the front before I pull him out, gently grasping the middle of his body. Usually, if his head is covered with the towel, the bird will not be able to bite. He also is less afraid if he can't see what is going on. I reach for the bird quickly, gently, and decisively. I carefully plan my motion, reach in, and pick up the bird. Trauma occurs if a person must push, pull, and chase the bird all over the cage. With the military macaw, I had little choice. Normally, I refuse to use gloves when I work with birds, and I have rarely been bitten. In this case, with the small cage door, I could not reach the macaw using the towel, so I had to put on gloves to grab him. As he struggled, he bit me quite painfully on my left index finger through the heavy

---

A CALMING TECHNIQUE LEARNED FROM WILD BIRD HANDLING

Years ago, I worked with friends who banded wild birds to help study changes in wild flock populations. I would gently take the small songbirds out of the mist net and hold them on their backs in my closed hand while someone else applied the bands to their legs. In the beginning, I always expected the birds to jump up and fly away the minute I loosened my grip on them. I discovered that if I gently pressed my finger against the top front of their heads, they would stay in my hand as if they were in a trance. To waken them, I would poke them softly on their bellies. Then, apparently comprehending their precarious position, they would fly off chirping and scolding. Time after time, we caught one particular American Goldfinch who obviously wanted his head rubbed. Since then, I have used the similar technique of cupping my hand over a parrot's forehead many times, because it seems to have such a calming effect on many of the parrots I have worked with.

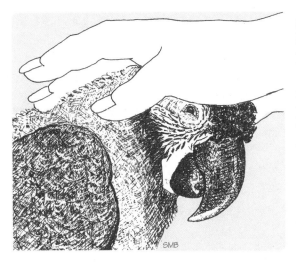

gloves. Bleeding or not, I was still going to work with him since I had already gotten him out of his cage and I did not want to have to put either of us through that ordeal again.

Once he was out, I put a towel loosely over his body and head, removed the gloves and carried the bird into a small room. I put him, still covered by the towel, in a corner and sat on the floor, blocking his exit. I often use a loosely draped towel when taming birds. As with the mistaken cliche about the ostrich burying his head in the sand, what parrots can't see usually doesn't seem to frighten them.

Knowing that the macaw would match my energy level, I began to slow myself down. I stretched out my arms slowly to drain the energy from them, shut my eyes, yawned, and started breathing slowly and deeply. I have never really meditated, but I have used biofeedback to relax. I know that if I can reach a state of relaxation where I show no stress, aggression, fear, or anxiety, the parrots I work with will also relax and not be afraid of my energy. Once I had calmed myself, I reached over and put the macaw on my lap with the towel still draped over him. I gently but firmly cupped my hand over the top of his head just above his beak. (See sidebar previous page.) Applying gentle pressure to the macaw's head calmed him, and I arranged the towel so I could pet the back of his neck.

The Military Macaw immediately responded to facial and neck massage. Within a few minutes I took the towel away from his head and rubbed the sensitive area around his beak. This bird had lived a long time without this essential touching. At this point, as long as I kept rubbing his neck and head, nothing would have distracted him.

While I was still petting the macaw, I managed to slowly upright him and place him on my hand. He was still wrapped in the towel with his head loosely covered and couldn't see that he was sitting on my hand. He was actually too involved in the pleasure of being "skritched" to realize where he was or what was happening to him.

Training The Owner

It wouldn't have done the owners much good if I had simply worked with this macaw, "hypnotized" him, and then left. The most important part of taming a bird is teaching the owner how to finish the taming. Of course, this macaw was not totally hand tamed in an hour. Once he came out of his trance and back to reality, he would still need many taming sessions and consistent gentle handling to become a tame, trusting, pet bird.

One of the owners had watched the whole process, and the second half of the session consisted of her handling the bird under my supervision and guidance. She was able to calm herself and she did well enough for me to be confident that she would continue the work I had started. With some owners however, more in-depth training is needed. Even though I had created a situation in which the bird would not bite because he was so relaxed, an owner may still be fearful, and the bird can sense this. I encourage my clients to spend a lot of time gently handling their parrots in the towel. This not only patterns their birds, it also patterns the owners to handle their pets more comfortably. Most importantly, the caregiver must learn how to become calm and maintain a low energy level so the bird will not become afraid.

The "UP" Command

The Military Macaw responded very positively to the attention I gave him, but he still needed a lot of work before he would step onto his owner's hand. Once a bird I am working with relaxes in the towel, I usually start gently playing with his feet. I rubbed his toes and picked up one foot at a time. If I can maintain a calm energy level, I can often pick up an untame parrot and get him to perch on my hand. As he becomes more and more comfortable, I shorten the time he is in the towel and eventually discontinue its use. Every time I pick the parrot up, I use the "UP" command. In the beginning, if you say "UP" in a clear, firm (but not aggressive) voice each time you put your parrot on your hand, the bird will quickly learn that "UP" means "Get on my hand." You can use any short word as a cue the parrot will associate with the action, but "UP" is an appropriate universal command. As the bird becomes tamer, reinforce the command by playing "ladder." Slowly transfer your parrot several times from one hand to the other, saying "UP" each time. You will find that this command is an important tool in maintaining control of a parrot, even a handfed baby.

Parrots are quite intelligent and usually learn verbal commands quickly. Each time I pick up a bird, I try to hold him a little longer. Once a bird does something over and over, he becomes patterned and will usually accept the behavior more readily next time.

If a bird still bites when I try to hand-tame him, I usually drape the towel over his head so he cannot see my hands. I put the bird's feet on my finger, and when he seems comfortable with that, I slowly pull off the towel. At this point, a parrot may become frightened when he sees he is sitting on my hand and may throw himself onto the ground. For this reason, I prefer to work sitting on a bed, the couch, or the floor in a carpeted area. As the bird gets used to being on your hand, he should stay there a little longer each time. Next, put him on a T-stand or the back of a chair and have him step off your hand onto the perch with the "Down" command. Then pick him up again with the "UP" command. These training steps can go quickly, or they can take weeks. It depends on how much time you spend, how wild the bird is, and how long it takes to win his trust.

Taming A Cage Aggressive Or Cage-Bound Bird

The final step is to train your parrot to come out of his cage onto your hand. Again, patterning is important. If you have trained your companion parrot to act on the "UP" command, the bird should respond no matter where he is. Unfortunately, with some parrots, territorial aggression often becomes an issue when working within a bird's cage. If allowed to become cage territorial, many smaller parrots (Parrotlets, Lovebirds, Gray-cheek Parakeets, *Pyrrhura* Conures, Caiques, etc.) are actually more aggressive around their cages than most larger parrots. If, at first, you do not trust your parrot enough to feel secure that he will step onto your hand from the cage without biting you, you can train your parrot to step on a stick or branch in much the same way I describe above for getting him used to sitting on your hand.

You must begin to gradually establish yourself as flock leader using *Nurturing Guidance*. To do this, keep the bird below your chin level during training sessions. Make direct, but soft, eye contact with the bird during training sessions. In my years of working with parrots, I have rarely been bitten by a parrot I was looking at.

If you watch a bonded pair of birds, generally when one acquiesces to the other, he lowers his head. When Spike, my high-energy Black-headed Caique, gets out of control, I cup my hand over his head and gently lower it. He immediately acknowledges my gentle control. Aggressive dominance is unacceptable and counterproductive.

The "UP" command can also be very effective. Once a parrot is trained to step from a T-stand onto your hand on command, you can start practicing this behavior around the cage. Move the stand closer and closer to the cage, continuing to get the bird to step from the stand on command. Once the stand is next to the cage, start cage patterning by moving the bird in and out of the open cage door, putting him on the stand and then on the perch. With consistent patterning, it gets easier if you ask a little bit more each time. End each taming session on a positive note, with you in control. In the beginning, you may need to bribe him out of his cage with a food treat in a bowl on the stand so you can then take him into a neutral room to work with him.

Establishing rules and nurturing control sets acceptable behavior standards for your pet parrot. Taming a bird with trust and empathy will take time and patience, especially with birds that have been neglected or abused. The reward is a well-behaved parrot that bonds to his owners and enjoys their company.

TRUST IS NEEDED FOR BONDING

Can't Have One Without The Other

A parrot will not form a bond with someone he does not trust. In a relationship with a parrot, trust and bonding need to be a two-way street. We must work to develop the kind of bond where our parrots trust us and we trust them. Without this mutual trust, the bond suffers. If people think their parrot will bite them every chance he gets, then chances are the bird will pick up the apprehension and the person's belief turns into a self-fulfilling prophecy. If a person's behavior is capricious and undependable, the parrot will not know how to respond and may be confused enough to use aggression to get the person to go away.

While the ability to form a strong bond with people is one of the main reasons parrots make such good pets, if that bond is not managed properly, it can be the cause of many problem behaviors. Some parrots may become overly dependent or over-bonded to their owners, or they may form an exclusive mate or sexual bond with their favored person which can result in problems as they mature. The parrot's potential to bond to people could be termed a positive displacement behavior. If an animal's natural behavior is blocked, and that animal substitutes another behavior for what would be normal, it is called a displacement behavior. Certainly, it is not natural for a parrot to bond to a human being. However, if another bird is not available, and care-giving, nurturing people are a constant in a companion parrot's life, the bird easily forms a bond with those people. With *Nurturing Guidance*, proper care, and adequate attention, a human-bonded parrot is content to be a lifelong companion.

It is a generalization to assume that all parrots form the same types of bonds within their family groups or flocks. Some parrots naturally form strong bonds with family and mates. Other species may not form such a strong mate bond, but accept many individuals within their group. A parrot species' "style" of bonding is usually reflected in the way they bond with their human flock. For example, if allowed to, Amazons, greys, and macaws may form a strong exclusive bond with one person in a family, while an Eclectus or an Alexandrine Parakeet may be inclined to form a looser bond with several family members. Cockatoos seem to be less consistent in this matter. Some species and/or individuals tend to be one-person birds while others seem to naturally like almost everybody. The way in which a parrot bonds may be more influenced by early socialization than instinctive traits. Some people like a parrot to develop a strong bond with them but care should be taken so that the bird does not overbond sexually. A healthy sense of independence is a trait that should be developed in all companion parrots. Other people are more attracted to parrots who form a less intense bond because it seems to create less emotional dependence. Even if a certain species does not form an exclusive bond, it is important to realize that any bond can be jeopardized if the bird does not receive consistent attention and affection.

There are many misconceptions about the way parrots bond to people. Over years of working with companion parrots, I have found that these social animals form the strongest bonds with the people in their lives who give them the most consistent guidance. These people are the most predictable and provide the least amount of confusion for the parrot. With parrots, social bonding is not "engraved in stone." Often, the parrot will start out forming a bond with the person who provides the most intense care. During independence stages, that favored person may be more of a play mate or sibling bond — someone who plays with the parrot a lot but may not set rules. But eventually, if a choice is available, the favored person will become the one who provides *Nurturing Guidance*. Flock leadership, focused attention, gentle handling, and infinite patience are important trust-building tools. There are few absolute rules in parrot behavior. However, the following is true almost without exception: "Parrots are most comfortable with the person who is the most comfortable with them."

ANTICIPATION OF NEED

Avoiding Situations That Create Problems

Many of the behavioral problems parrots develop could be easily avoided if people had a better understanding of their parrot's basic needs and how to meet those needs before the parrot has to act up to get them met. A classic example is the family who sits down to dinner without offering their Amazon something to eat first. As with most parrots, Amazons are social eaters. Anyone who eats in front of an Amazon without replenishing his food dish first deserves to be screamed at. If we eat healthy foods, then we can give our parrots some of the same nutritious foods we eat. Many parrots enjoy sitting on a T-stand near the table when their families eat.

Most parrot family birds are flock animals who are strongly bonded to their mates. They communicate through contact calls, ritual greetings, and farewells. Staying in touch with the flock is also very important to a companion parrot. If people get into the habit of acknowledging a contact call with a simple response which says, "Yes, I am here and everything is OK," the parrot retains his sense of flock security. If I am in the living room with him, Spikey makes a beep which sounds like gym shoes on a wooden floor. If I hear it and say, "Hey Spike, what are you doing?" he goes right back to playing. He gives me three chances to respond, and if I don't, he starts screaming at me. At that point, it is difficult to stop him, but it would have been easy for me to prevent the misbehavior. Consistently greeting your parrot when you come home from being gone will usually prevent the bird from developing the habit of screaming until he gets your attention. It also helps a parrot's sense of security to get into the habit of communicating that you are leaving the room with a simple statement such as, "Hey Smokey, I'll be back."

It is funny how many times clients have said something like this to me, "I take him out of his cage and he is happy to see me. We sit down to watch television and I pet him. Everything is fine at first, but he always bites me after four minutes." My initial response is usually pretty simple — just pet him for three minutes. It is usually more complex than that, but if people really start to pay attention to their parrot, they will began to recognize that birds have a fairly short attention span, even for pleasure. This is not to say that some parrots will not allow you to pet them for hours; it is just that they will not be happy if you pet them over and over and over in the same place. The other important element in this scenario is that if you are going to pet a parrot, focus on petting him and not on the television.

Anticipation Of The Human Flock's Needs

Sometimes people need peace and quiet. You need to relax after a hard day at work. You need to study or finish reading an exciting novel. Perhaps people are coming over for dinner, and while you want them to meet the parrots, you want to talk with your friends without a lot of interruption. Avoiding a screaming attack is much easier than stopping it once it starts. While it is abusive to keep a parrot in a back room or covered a great deal of the day, it is not neglectful to plan ahead for special times and situations. Introduce your parrot to your dinner guests. If he behaves, let him stay, but if you know from experience that he will want to be the center of attention the whole time, prevent the dramatic scenario by taking him into a dark, quiet room for a nap or putting him to bed in a sleeping cage after he meets the guests. If you want an hour of peace and quiet when you come home from work, give your parrot a wonderful greeting and then take him into a quiet room with a new toy or a few nutritious treats before you fix him dinner. Anticipating both his needs and yours can make a great deal of difference in avoiding misbehavior that could become patterned.

PATTERNING

Avoiding Problems

UP... Good Bird!

The more familiar we are with performing a task, the more comfortable we are with it. The saying *practice makes perfect* is only true if we practice what we are trying to learn in a positive, productive way. This is most obvious in the world of sports. For example, practicing a proper golf swing will create *neural pathways* for doing it right without even thinking about it. Unfortunately, continually swinging the golf club in an improper way also accomplishes a goal — it entrenches the bad swing so the player has to take more and more swings at the golf ball to finish a round of golf. This is the basis of the concept of patterning. We pattern ourselves by repetition in many aspects of our lives. In fact, we often become so accustomed to performing a task in a particular way that we have to make an intense, concentrated effort to change the habit even if it is causing problems for us. It is just as difficult to change our own negative ways of interacting with our parrots as it is to change their learned behavioral patterns. Just as our own bad habits are hard to change, improving our parrot's negative behaviors also takes time and patience. Negative parrot behavior is difficult, but not impossible, to change. The more we work to pattern good habits, the better behaved our parrots are. That makes us happier and makes them happier, too.

Using patterning exercises with our parrots not only creates positive learned behaviors for them, but also patterns us to do things in a clear, consistent manner. In reality, almost all of our interactions with our parrots will teach them something. The more we repeat an action with them, the more patterned they become to accept it, whether it teaches them something positive or not. Because of this, we must be careful that we are patterning good behavior instead of patterning our parrots to misbehave with excessive screaming or aggressive biting.

A Few Exercises To Pattern Both Person And Parrot Into Positive Interactions

➲ **Neutral room exercises pattern the "UP" and "Down" commands.** Place your parrot on a T-stand in the neutral room. Calmly and decisively approach his lower belly with the back of your hand and use the "UP" command to get him to step on the ridge of your index finger. When he complies, praise him for being a good parrot. Then ladder him to the other hand using the same technique. Then back to the first, saying "UP." After a few more times, place him back on the stand with the "Down" command. Repeat this process a few times, but don't do it so many times you or your parrot become impatient or bored with the routine.

➲ **Patterning a parrot to easily come out of his cage and go back in is important.** Use the same principles outlined above to take a parrot in and out of his cage. If your parrot has recently started refusing to step on your hand from the cage, this is a good way to quickly reinforce the positive behavior.

➲ **Patterning a parrot to go from one person to another involves the game of "warm potato."** The parrot is slowly passed from one person to another. Each one gives him praise and attention before passing him on to the next person. This exercise helps parrots stay bonded to several people.

➲ **Patterning new routines and situations.** Patterning exercises may also be used to get a parrot comfortable with towel handling, teaching your parrot to step onto a stick or branch, and getting him gradually used to new people, change, and new adventures. These are discussed elsewhere in the handbook. ✒

CALM DOWN FIRST

Problems With Overexcited Energy

There is a story I have shared for years in my seminars. Although the details may vary, the story essentially remains the same. The owner lets his or her parrot come out in the morning while he gets ready to go to work. Suddenly, he realizes he is going to be late for work, so a few minutes before the person has to leave, he approaches his parrot in a panic, waving his arms around and yelling something like, "up, UP! C'mon hurry, get in your cage, if you don't hurry, I'll be late for work. Pleeeeeze - HURRY! up, UP!!!" He might as well have run up to the cage screaming like Chicken Little, "The sky is falling, the sky is falling!" With that excitement level, the flock alarm is sounded, and the more excited the person becomes, the less likely the parrot is to go back into his cage. Parrots can be very stubborn, making their owners chase them around the outside of the cage or all over the playgym.

I actually heard from one Umbrella Cockatoo owner whose 'too figured out that she would have to go back in her cage at a certain stage of her owners' preparedness. At that time just about every morning, the 'too jumped down off of her playgym, ran into the bedroom, and hid under the bed. As the woman struggled to get her cockatoo from under the bed, the angrier she became and the less cooperation she got from the cockatoo. When she called me for a consultation, the woman had stopped taking her 'too out for her morning attention. No one wants to be crawling around on the floor under the bed just before they go to work.

Frightened Parrots

Another concern of this section is in dealing with frightened parrots. Working as a companion parrot behavior consultant in earthquake country, I have often talked to people after an earthquake or aftershock. Many parrots become frightened by the instability of the ground below them. They are unable to fly away and sometimes thrash around in their cages. After getting past their own fear and realizing that California has not actually fallen into the ocean, people run to check on their parrots. With panic in their voices, they scream out, "Oh no, Oh God, are you ok?" Rather than being reassured by the owner's presence, the parrot reacts with increased fear and panic.

Parrots mirror our energy, and calm energy is reassuring, especially in times of stress and confusion. The people whose parrots won't go back in their cages need to just leave the room momentarily, calm themselves down, and go back in with a positive change of mood. Once the energy slows down, most surprised parrots readily allow their owners to pick them up and put them back in their cages.

Parrots are far more capable of learning during patterning exercises if we are focused and calm with them. There is a time for excited play and high energy, but that time may be limited before the parrot goes into high energy overload (pg.170). When a parrot is overstimulated, the best way to calm him down is to calm yourself down first.

Lowering Your Energy

When you are stressed or scatter-focused, this isn't a good time to relate to your parrot. Slowing yourself down before you interact with your parrot will make him far more eager to be with you.

A Few Relaxation Techniques:
- Sit down or stand quietly, ignoring distractions as much as possible.
- Visualize a quiet place that gives you pleasure — a rocky beach, mountain stream, or an air conditioned room on a hot day.
- Let your head droop and shut your eyes.
- Sometimes shutting your eyes and slowly rolling your eyeballs around helps relaxation.
- Take several slow, deep breaths and let yourself yawn as you relax. Create a quiet humming noise as you breathe out.
- Listen to and concentrate on your breathing or your heartbeat.
- Let your arms hang loosely at your sides.
- Hold your hands together. Concentrate on the sensation of your pulse in your fingertips.
- Using these techniques for just a few minutes will help you work with your parrot, especially if you are stressed or he is overexcited.

THE "NEUTRAL ROOM"

Territorial Protection

Most parrot species are naturally quite pugnacious in the protection of their established nesting, roosting, and feeding territories. If allowed to, many companion parrots exhibit similar behaviors in regard to their household territories. Without proper guidance and boundaries, a parrot establishes strong cage dominance, and once he becomes comfortable with that, he probably establishes his dominance in all of his cage territory. The cage territory can be any area the parrot can see from his cage or any place he feels the urge to defend. In some situations, a parrot in control of his own life may consider his preferred person his mate and includes this person in his defense. He then defends the area and one person from anyone else. In other situations, even the preferred person is denied access to the cage or other areas of the territory.

If a parrot is always "on-duty" protecting, it is almost impossible to work with him in any area of the home where he is used to being. Over the years, many people have commented to me about how tame their ordinarily aggressive parrots are when they are away from home. This is because the parrot is no longer on-duty — he is away from his territory and is consequently not obsessed with its protection. Another interesting aspect of this is how well-behaved a previously-owned parrot is in a new home for the first week or so. He is in unfamiliar territory and, therefore, has no reason to defend it. Before he becomes familiar with his new home and develops his territorial imperative is, of course, the best time to work with a new parrot. If the new owner can establish behavioral ground rules before the parrot gets too comfortable, the bird may not be able to reestablish himself as ruler of the roost.

A Comfortable Area

Any time a companion parrot begins to challenge his owner, providing focused attention in the *Neutral Room* is one of the most effective tools for working with him. The neutral room is a comfortable area of your house or apartment that is unfamiliar to your parrot — a guest room, a bedroom, the dining room, or any other room the parrot does not perceive as his territory. In the neutral room, be sure he can't see his cage and that you both can be comfortable. I do not recommend the bathroom floor, which, for some reason was often suggested for years as the best place to work with a parrot. Not only is the bathroom uncomfortable, it can be full of germs.

Prepare the *Neutral Room* with the necessary items before the parrot is brought in. For example, a towel placed flat on the bed will usually not frighten a parrot who has been previously afraid of being approached with a towel. If you want to train your parrot to step on a stick or branch, place it on the towel. Treats or toys should also be put on the towel. If you use a T-stand, place it in the room first, unless you are planning to bring the bird in on one. Once you have your parrot in the Neutral Room on the T-stand or the back of a chair, lower your energy by taking a few deep breaths and relaxing. If your parrot is tame but is just being ornery, start slowly laddering him a few times from hand to hand using the "UP" command and giving him lots of verbal praise. Place him back on the stand with the "Down" command and, after a minute or so, repeat the process. The *Neutral Room* is also the best place to introduce strangers to your parrot, and for a less-favored human flock member to win the parrot's trust. It is not just a place for patterning exercises; it can also be a place to teach tricks and to play games with your parrot. *

Sally Blanchard's COMPANION PARROT HANDBOOK

USING DISTRACTIONS TO RETRAIN

Challenge Patterned Behaviors By Changing Your Response

While the advice to never pay attention to a screaming parrot is generally good, there are certainly exceptions to this rule. Sometimes a well-thought-out distraction works well to change negative behaviors. Often negative patterns become so ingrained that both the parrot and the person act in the same manner each and every time. By changing his or her behavior, the person distracts the parrot from the patterned behavior. Once the parrot is distracted, the person has a chance to teach a positive behavior. The key for the parrot owner is to become the **actor** rather than the **reactor**. Rather than reacting to your parrot's misbehavior on an emotional level, instead plan a response which challenges the behavior. Responses can be presented to the parrot in an indirect manner which does not encourage the negative behavior with a drama reward. Distractions usually work better if you do not make direct eye contact with the parrot. Directing your response towards someone else in the room, or even into thin air, gets the point across without taking a chance of inadvertently rewarding the negative behavior.

A FEW DISTRACTION IDEAS

Distractions should never be aggressive or threatening. The purpose is to distract or intrigue the curiosity of a parrot from negative behaviors without giving him direct rewards.

⮞ **Whispering:** Most birds are intrigued by the tonal quality of whispering. It piques their curiosity and distracts them from what they are doing. Years ago, I did a consultation with a screaming Moluccan. He was so loud, I didn't need his home address when I drove down the street. The main problem was that, when his owners left together for work early in the morning, he screamed loud enough to shake the windows. As soon as they picked up their keys or started toward the door, he started screaming. After a few weeks of whispering to each other as they left the house, the man and his wife changed the Moluccan's early morning screaming to early morning whispering. Once he noticed it, he was far too fascinated with the whispering to keep screaming, and eventually substituted whispering because his owners rewarded the whispering with positive attention.

⮞ **Contact Calls:** Contact calls can be any short call — a word or two, a whistle, a resonating hum, or a chipping or clucking sound that the parrot realizes comes from the flock leader. Once established, simple sounds such as these can have great meaning to a parrot and often readily distracts him from negative behavior and/or calms him down.

⮞ **Whistling, Humming and Singing:** Most parrots are musical and love a good tune. Many parrots in the midst of a loud screaming binge will stop and match the level of a gentle, quiet song. The song should not be directed towards them until they quiet down and join in. The nicest part of it is that they don't really care whether we can carry a tune or not!

⮞ **Tricks:** Teaching parrots basic trick behaviors using verbal cues can easily distract them from negative behaviors. When they are in the midst of negative behaviors, simply giving the verbal cue, having them do the trick, and giving the trick verbal praise usually stops the negative behaviors.

⮞ **Adding A New Variable:** One of the best ways to get a previously well-behaved noncompliant parrot out of his cage is to add a new variable — especially if the negative behavior is becoming a pattern or game. If you reach in and say "UP" and he refuses to get on your hand, holding a nonthreatening object (potholder, magazine, shoe, TV remote, etc.) in your other hand usually distracts him from his new pattern long enough for him to step onto your hand. ⸙

SOFT EYE/EVIL EYE

Using Eye Contact To Avoid Problems

Eye contact is one of the most effective ways to communicate with a parrot. There are many ways to establish eye contact. Bongo Marie loves a soft, gentle, smiling steady gaze and it helps her to calm down when she is wound up (this is what we always called "making cow mooney eyes" when I was in college). A quick "evil eye" from me often calms Spikey down if he is acting up. Paco and Rascal become happily excited when I come into their room and make direct eye contact with them, exclaiming how beautiful and handsome they are.

In taming hundreds of parrots, I found that eye contact was an absolutely necessary tool. For example, the vast majority of parrots would not even try to bite me when I was making direct eye contact with them. This did not mean I was staring at them with the "evil eye" in a confrontational manner, or trying to "break them" with aggression. It simply meant they had all my focused attention and I wasn't going to take my eyes off of them. I believe that because of this, they had to direct their total attention to what I was doing (or what I was going to do next) as opposed to biting me.

There were a few parrots that I worked with that I had to make direct confrontational eye contact with, or else I couldn't have taught them anything. I remember one wild-caught Moluccan who was generally a nice bird to his owner, but had started chasing all of the man's friends out of the house. The owner had never established any rules and the bird didn't even understand the "UP" command. I calmly and gently toweled the bird from the front, scratched his head for a while to relax him, and then put him on my hand. Once I removed the towel, I could tell we would have a battle of wills and I needed to maintain strong eye contact with him while he was on my hand. I did not take my eyes off of him. Yes, he saw it as confrontation, but as long as I looked at him, I was winning the confrontation. I spent about 5 minutes teaching him to step from one hand to the other with the "UP" command. He patterned quickly and once he was lifting his foot with the word "UP," I decided my job was done and placed him back on the couch. The minute I took my eyes off of him, he ran over and bit me on the butt, jumped off the couch, and ran back to his cage. It was really quite funny, even though I ended up with a blood blister on my backside. My mistake was letting go of him on the couch and not putting him in his cage. My goal was for the owner to be able to manage him better without being confrontational. I left the room and the man was then able to work with him in a more friendly manner to further pattern him to step on his hand to the command. Because the man was able to establish and maintain hand control of the cockatoo, the bird kept his home. Each consultation I did with a parrot presented a different challenge, and I would not have worked with most parrots the way I needed to with this Moluccan. I believe that the basic concept in working with all parrots should be to build trust. However, there were a few others that needed me to establish a confrontational posture with them to get my point across. I would not have recommended that the owner continue working with the bird in the same manner I did.

In many situations, even the most confrontational parrot responds positively to a quick disapproving look without being confrontational. Spike can be a real dynamo at times. He will be so wired-up that nothing gets his attention better than a quick "evil-eye." I do not continue the look beyond the time he notices it and gives me his undivided attention. If I was to continue the "evil eye" past the time it was necessary, he would perceive it as confrontation.

Parrots are highly responsive to eye contact, both positive and negative. It is one of the best ways to communicate with them. I do not believe in punishing parrots because it is doubtful that they have the cause-and-effect logic to understand the punishment. However, a disapproving look can be used as a very effective quick discipline when a parrot is misbehaving. One of the reasons I do not recommend that people keep parrots on their shoulders is because to make eye contact, they have to make their face vulnerable to a parrot's often unpredictable beak. ∮

CHANGE, ROUTINE & EXPLORATION

Developing A Sense Of Adventure & Exploration

Change happens no matter how hard we try to prevent it. Even if we carefully try to control the routine of our lives, there is always change. It is not change that parrots are afraid of — it is stressful or sudden change. A well-social-ized parrot whose sense of adventure and exploration has been developed when he is a youngster is rarely stressed by change. During the early devel-opmental stages that accompany fledging and food independence, bappies should continually be ex-posed to new surroundings and objects in a safe, nurturing manner. If this is not done, young parrots may develop a fear of change or novelty in their lives. Even with proper early

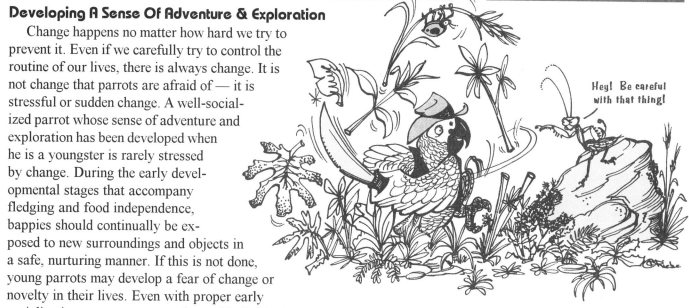

Hey! Be careful with that thing!

socialization, some parrot species and individuals are naturally more wary of change in their lives. These birds may always need special consideration in introducing new situations and objects into their environment. However, parrots of any age can become what Phoebe Linden calls *intrepid explorers* by gradually and safely introducing new adven-tures in their lives. Patience is essential in introducing new situations. If a parrot is even slightly wary of change, the *just-get-used-to-it* attitude can be disastrous — even causing phobic behavior in some reticent parrots.

Examples Of Safe, Gradual Introduction

Rather than just waiting to put a parrot in a new carrier when you have to take him to the veterinarian, get him used to it first. New objects are less threatening when they are introduced away from the cage territory. Place the carrier in a neutral room on the bed or couch. Put some favorite treats or familiar toys in or near the carrier. Bring him in the room, keeping yourself between him and the new object so he knows you are there to protect him. Place him on the bed, point out the carrier, and place the treats inside. Let him explore at his own pace. It may take several times for him to go in and play in the carrier. Give him lots of verbal praise each step of the way. Once he is comfortable in the carrier, close the door and pick it up to take him back to his cage area. Once you get your parrot used to being in the carrier, it might help to place him in it for short rides in the car before he has to go on a longer ride to the veteri-narian or a bird sitter. Be sure to secure the carrier with a seat belt, and if you have air bags, place the carrier in the back seat rather than the passenger seat. Please, for your safety and his, don't let him ride loose in your car.

Any new objects (and people) — including toys, towel play, playgyms, and cages — can be introduced in a similar manner. Placing a new cage in the neutral room for him to visit, then moving it next to his present cage, letting him explore it without removing his familiar cage, is the best way to introduce a new cage. Once he is comfortable with the new cage, remove the old one.

Establishing Routine

While parrots need a sense of consistency and predictability in their lives, the worst thing we can do is establish a stringent, unchanging routine. Once a parrot becomes used to a rigid routine and he expects certain situations to occur like clockwork, then serious problems result if that routine is disrupted. Some parrots can become very rigid about when and what they will eat. Parrots who are rigidly potty-trained may only defecate if their owners give them the proper command, or if they are in the *correct* place. This can cause physical problems.

When a parrot seems afraid of necessary change in his life or a new object that should be a part of his life, it is essential to introduce that very situation or thing he is afraid of in a patient, gradual and safe manner.

READING BODY LANGUAGE

Predictably Unpredictable

Although many parrot species have a reputation for unpredictable behavior, if we pay close attention to our parrots' body language, we can predict how they are going to act in many situations. While parrot body language varies some from species to species, and is not always consistently predictable in individual parrots, certain aspects of psittacine body language remain consistent. But the subtleties of body language can change. Companion parrots often change their behavior and body language according to the responses they receive from their human flock. Consequently, over a period of time, what a parrot is trying to communicate with specific body language may not remain consistent. Observe the changes and additions to your parrot's body language repertoire.

Comfort Behavior Poses

Comfortable, trusting companion parrots do not exhibit the postures associated with the normal vigilance of prey animals. Usually when a parrot fluffs his feathers and seems just a bit pudgy, he is relaxed and comfortable. (Although, if there are indications of illness, continual fluffing accompanied by sluggishness is a reason to consult with your avian veterinarian immediately.) Often a parrot fluffs out his feathers and shakes his tail feathers as a way to express relaxation. A good fluff and shake is the way many parrots communicate they are through with whatever was happening and ready to move on to something else. Beak grinding before a nap or sleep is also a comfort behavior.

A really happy parrot being indulged during a "skritching session" usually fluffs out the feathers in the areas he wants to be petted. Some birds, particularly cockatoos, seem to become *boneless* if they are really enjoying a good cuddle session. If, during these sessions, the parrot's body becomes less relaxed and more rigid, the cuddle session should be stopped. Either the parrot is no longer relaxed or he may be becoming sexually stimulated. Preening is usually seen in a comfortable parrot, although there are some parrots who involve themselves with excessive preening as a displacement behavior when they become nervous or stressed.

Aggressive & Excited Postures

Parrot aggression is shown with threat displays. The difference between fluffed, relaxed feathers and the erect feathers of aggression is noticeable. Fluffed feathers blend together, while erected feathers stand out individually or in groups. Specific feathers on the crest, nape, or other colorful parts of the body are erected as warning and to communicate excitement or aggression. Many parrots show aggression by standing very tall, trying to seem as large as possible. They spread their wings and raise their crest or nape feathers and sway back and forth. The beak is often open with the head forward. In some situations, aggressive posturing is shown by the bird standing horizontally with wings slightly spread — often to show their color accents. In some parrots, the head is lowered with erected feathers on the nape. In others, the head is up with the beak thrust forward. Open beak lunging or lunge biting (when a parrot lunges forward to bite someone) is obviously aggressive behavior. Unless you understand and trust your parrot implicitly, don't *lead with your face.*

Excitement and aggression are two different behaviors, although they may have similar body postures and behavioral results — an overloaded, overstimulated parrot may bite just as hard as an aggressive parrot. An excited parrot is more likely to be screaming than an aggressive parrot. If a parrot is either in overload or exhibiting aggressive behavior, it is best not to handle him without attempting to calm him down first. One of the most evident signs of excitement in most parrots is eye pinning. The pupil expands and contracts as the parrot becomes more stimulated, often becoming just a bare pinpoint. This is not always an indication of aggression — it can simply mean the parrot is excited.

Fear Postures

A companion parrot who is standing stiff and skinny with all his feathers flat against his body is usually stressed or frightened. His head may be held high and forward with his wings held slightly away from his body in a preflight position. In some situations, a stressed bird will jerk his head back and forth. His wings may quiver, and he may repeatedly raise one foot, sway, or shift his weight. Companion parrots are often confused about what to do when they are afraid because their normal fear behaviors of hiding, escape, or fighting do not usually work for them. It is important to pay attention to what causes stress or fear behavior and remove or prevent the causative factors. However, if stress is being caused by something that should be normal in a companion parrot's life, it is best to gradually introduce these factors to the parrot in a gradual safe, manner so they no longer cause negative reactions.

Repetitive Posturing & Impatience

When companion parrots exhibit repetitive behaviors such as bill wiping, toenail chewing, swaying, figure-eighting, or foot stomping, it usually means they are nervous, wary or have a lot of pent-up energy. Usually, these behaviors are a result of frustration and unfilled needs. These parrots often need a program of better care with increased attention and exercise.

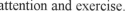

Come Pick Me Up

This very friendly invitation posture may seem similar to, but should not be confused, with aggression. The parrot's posture is horizontal. The wings are slightly spread and usually quivering. The neck is often shortened with the head up. Besides a happy demeanor, the main difference between this and aggression is that the feathers are usually fluffed rather than stiff and tight.

COMMUNICATING WITH COLOR

Flash Colors

Research has shown that parrots do not perceive color in the same exact way we do, but they obviously communicate with their colorful feathers. This alone is evidence they have excellent color vision. Look at the bend of the wing or the tail feathers of an Amazon when he is resting. Usually, you see only a touch of color, but look again when he is excited and displaying with his wings. You see all the color clearly. The same thing is true of the crest of many cockatoo species. Crestless parrots may erect the colorful feathers on their napes and other parts of their heads to communicate. Caiques puff out the feathers on their thighs to form brightly colored pantaloons. The bare patch on a macaw's face often flushes with red when he becomes excited. A Red-fronted Macaw has beautiful orange sherbet colored feathers on the insides of his wings.

This color is seen only when he is in flight or when he spreads his wings. While many companion parrots quiver their wings as a preflight communication to come and pick them up, the red-front often spreads his wings for his human flock to show off how beautiful they are. Who could resist such an invitation for close companionship?

Flash colors are used in many ways. Some are only evident in flight, others warn intruders to leave the territory, and many are direct advertising for a mate. In the world of birds, the ones with the most intricate color displays are often the ones who are most successful in attracting the best mates.

Observe your parrots closely to understand how they use their colors to communicate with you.

HEIGHT DOMINANCE

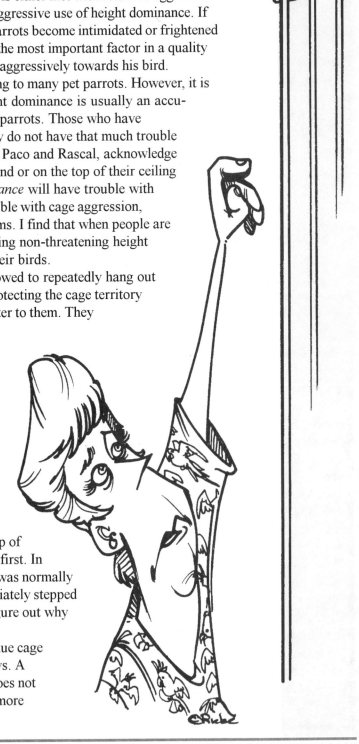

A Barometer — Not An Absolute

The practical advice of keeping pet parrots at or below eye level in order to stop aggressive behavior is effective with many parrots. Why is this true? It may involve many variables. Certainly, when a parrot is encompassed from above and there is no route for escape, the instinct is for the parrot to submit or aggressively defend himself. However, people must not approach their parrots in an overbearing, aggressive manner. Aggression is either met with returned aggression or fear. Many parrots respond with confrontation to the aggressive use of height dominance. If aggressive height dominance is used consistently, some parrots become intimidated or frightened enough for it to damage the parrot/human bond. Trust is the most important factor in a quality parrot/human bond, and trust is lost when the owner acts aggressively towards his bird.

Height dominance can be a significant factor in relating to many pet parrots. However, it is only part of many aspects of *Nurturing Guidance*. Height dominance is usually an accurate barometer of the relationship people have with their parrots. Those who have established a good sense of behavioral guidance generally do not have that much trouble with their parrots even if the bird is higher. For example, Paco and Rascal, acknowledge my "UP" command readily, whether they are on the ground or on the top of their ceiling swing. People who have not established *Nurturing Guidance* will have trouble with height dominance, but they will most likely also have trouble with cage aggression, excessive screaming, biting, and other behavioral problems. I find that when people are having behavioral problems with their parrots, establishing non-threatening height dominance is only one way owners need to work with their birds.

Many parrots become little tyrants when they are allowed to repeatedly hang out on the tops of their cages. They become so focused on protecting the cage territory they may reach the point when nothing else seems to matter to them. They posture and strut, trying to scare away even the most benevolent person in their human flock. Unfortunately, these parrots rarely stay in their homes because they become so difficult to handle. Sometimes, just standing on a step stool makes the owner tall enough to win the power struggle almost immediately. A little bluffing is also helpful for the more timid owner. Sometimes all it takes is for the person to approach the parrot with confidence, and in an assertive enough manner that the parrot doesn't have the time or inclination to refuse his request. Several years ago, I was working in a home with two Sulfur-crested Cockatoos. One was tame and would readily step onto the owner's hand, even off the top of his cage — the other always tried to get a chunk of flesh first. In working with the 'toos, I became confused which parrot was normally difficult and approached him so decisively that he immediately stepped on my hand off the top of his cage. At first, I couldn't figure out why the owner seemed so amazed.

The permanent solution to this problem is to discontinue cage top time which allows a parrot to be king of all he surveys. A high activity play gym and/or multi-perch stand which does not place the parrot above the human flock's height, are far more appropriate places for him to hang out.

DOMINANCE NOT AGGRESSION

Dominance Does Not Mean Aggression

For several years, I referred to my theories of companion parrot guidance as *Nurturing Dominance*, but decided to change the name because of the constant misinterpretation that dominance meant being aggressive with parrots to establish and maintain control. My definition of the term was "teaching with authority," but too many people thought the word dominance implied aggression. I do not believe in using aggression with parrots or any companion animal for that matter. Parrots are highly reflective of our energy and normally aggressive behavior towards a parrot will result in aggressive behavior from that parrot. This is particularly true with parrots who are normally high energy and "full-of-themselves." In some cases, especially with sustained aggression from the human flock, the response will be fear biting rather than aggressive biting. Aggressive behavior towards sensitive parrots will result in fear behavior which could eventually develop into phobic behavioral patterns. Aggression is not trust-building — it is trust-destroying. Trust is essential for a positive companion parrot/human bond.

There is no such thing as a submissive leader — the term is an oxymoron. We must establish our leadership before a parrot will pay attention to us and follow our guidance. Our leadership must be based upon enough authority so our parrots follow our guidance. Our dominance, so to speak, must be based on benevolence and nurturing. Since we are physically so large in comparison to our parrots, we must be careful not to become dominant in an aggressive manner. We don't want our parrots to fear us or perceive us as predators.

Aggression In The Wild?

My observations and research about parrots discount the notion of an aggressive hierarchy in nature. A better concept is "flock leader." We know very little about the actual structure of most parrot flocks. Clearly, in most flock species, there are family groups. Some groups and individuals have better nesting sites, but there may be many different situations that warrant certain birds getting the most desired mates and territories. In many cases, it is probably the genetically more colorful or flashy birds who are dominant, rather than the more aggressive ones. Several reliable ornithological sources indicate that many species of parrots have sentinel birds who sit high in a tree guarding against danger while the rest of the flock forages. These parrots may be "flock leaders" and/or the more dominant birds, but I have never read any reports of these birds establishing this position through aggression. Many parrot flocks seem to base much of their survival on mutual cooperation. Genuine aggression in wild parrots is probably only used as a defense of family and/or territory from predators, and not within the flock.

BAD BIRD!!!

FUN ART *by Sally Blanchard*

"If ya didn't act so dadgum seductive with him, he wouldn't do that regurgitating thang every time he sees ya!"

Nurturing Guidance Tip: The Underlying Cause

Treat The Underlying Cause, Not The Symptoms

We tend to think of companion parrot behavioral problems such as aggressive biting, excessive screaming, and behavioral feather picking as separate issues with individual causes and solutions. However, parrot behavioral problems are only the symptoms of a greater problem — *a parrot in control of his own life and doing a bad job of it.* Without guidance and rules, parrots have no idea how to be good pets. It is our responsibility to interact with them in a way that provides them the guidance they need to lead a contented life as a companion parrot. The more contented our parrots are, the happier we are with them and that is what a human/pet bond should be all about.

IT'S NEVER THE PARROT'S FAULT

Loss Of Pet Potential

Almost all bappies start out with the potential to be a good lifelong human companion. Unfortunately, many are poorly socialized, but in the world of companion parrots, one of the greatest tragedies occurs when a caring person doesn't have or use the *tools* to keep his pet tame. Some people become aware of the problems and choose to work with their parrots, while others give up and make the choice *to get rid of* their pet. Too often, the person blames the parrot and refuses to take any responsibility for the way things turned out. Some people collect one bird after another, never really taking the time to create the exceptional companion parrot. These people are missing out on the positive aspects of living with a parrot. Most of all, many of these parrots are doomed to a life as a "throwaway bird" going from one home to another until their insecurities and behavioral problems become so entrenched they are almost impossible to correct.

Parrots may be intelligent, but it is never a parrot's choice to go bad. At the first sign of a problem, people need to work with the problem behavior. Most of the time, simple measures such as providing predictable, consistent focused attention again, or working calmly in a neutral room to reestablish *Nurturing Guidance* with verbal commands will keep the problems from escalating. Trying to change negative behavior with a series of ineffective quick-fixes, punishment, or forcing your will on the misbehaving parrot with aggressively dominant control, will only make things worse.

It is also critical for the owner not to take biting, screaming, or a perceived transfer of affection to someone else as a personal affront. Even though they may learn to manipulate our behavior to get their needs met, parrots are not trying to punish us, get even with us, or even hurt our feelings with their misbehavior. Negative behavioral changes are most often caused by inconsistency of emotional care, and lack of guidance which results in confusion.

If you genuinely care about your parrot, but are frustrated with his problem behaviors, **the best home he has is still with you.** Too many people get rid of their parrots when there are workable solutions available. Getting help from a competent behavioral consultant, and dedicating yourself to working to correct behavioral problems, will save your relationship with him and keep him from becoming lost in the cycle of the "throwaway bird." Always remember when following any advice, interaction with a parrot should be trust-building and not trust-destroying.

Taking the responsibility for working with your parrot's behavior is the first step towards having a well-behaved, contented parrot and the wonderful bond you wanted when you bought your parrot in the first place. ∮

"Hey man, don't blame me, I came from a dysfunctional flock."

TREAT THE UNDERLYING CAUSE

Treat The Underlying Cause — Not The Symptoms!

Most behavioral problems (such as aggressive biting, excessive screaming, behavioral feather picking, and food rigidity) are actually the symptoms of an underlying problem, rather than the problem itself.

There are three basic causes for most behavioral problems in parrots:

1. A parrot who is not getting his basic physical needs met.
2. A parrot who is not getting his basic emotional needs met.
3. A confused parrot in control of his own life and doing a bad job of it.

Getting Information

When I start a telephone behavioral consultation, my initial questions usually deal with the physical and emotional care of the parrot. I want to assess the caregiver's knowledge. Sometimes, the most basic needs of the parrot are being compromised because the owner doesn't know the proper way to care for his avian companion, or has believed too much misinformation. I go over the steps for *Optimizing the Environment* (on page 148) and make sure the parrot is on a good diet, has an adequate-sized cage with lots of toys and exercise, gets showers or baths on a regular basis, has good lighting and a clean, nontoxic environment. Often, not only does improving the environment help the parrot, but it also gives the owners a renewed sense of concern about their pet. Simply not taking a parrot for granted and by providing him with increased focused attention can make a remarkable, positive difference in his behavior.

As I continue talking to the person, I can usually get a good idea of who is really in control of the household. For example, when we discuss diet and someone continually says, "Oh, my bird won't eat that," I get an accurate idea that the parrot controls most of the other aspects of his life. It is very rare for an out-of-control parrot to have just one behavioral symptom. For example, most people who call me about their biting parrot eventually tell me that the parrot also screams, won't come out of his cage, and/or chases their spouses out of the house.

There are ways to work with problem behavioral symptoms successfully, but for the success to be permanent, the underlying cause must be changed. Bird owners with problem parrots must work to gradually and patiently establish *Nurturing Guidance* by setting consistent rules and guiding the parrot's behavior. As people begin to provide more focused attention (and affection), the parrot becomes more secure within his *human flock*. Consistent guidance creates far less confusion for the parrot and with more predictability in his life, he becomes more predictable. As the human flock starts to guide the bird's behavior, he actually begins to look to his people for more guidance in all aspects of his behavior. If someone has called me about a biting parrot, and after our consultation, they start to use the techniques for establishing guidance, they often report back a few weeks later that not only has the biting behavior stopped, but the screaming has also improved greatly. This is because they are working with the underlying cause — not just the symptoms. *

OVERLOAD BEHAVIOR

Excitement Overload

Keep-away was the Yellow-nape's favorite game. He laughed with delight as he chased after the squeaky ball as fast as his short little legs could carry him. Grabbing hold of the soft rubber ball, he rolled over on his back. Squeezing it excitedly, he squealed in imitation of the shrill, repetitive noise it made. As the ball exploded out from his grasp, his owner grabbed it and tossed it to her friend. The parrot ran after the ball so fast, he tripped over his own feet at least a half-dozen times. Just as he got to the person with the ball, she rolled it back to his owner. He turned and half running, half flying, reached his owner at the same time as the ball. She grabbed it first. The Amazon reached out with his beak and grabbed her hand instead, biting her severely. The fun was over and the parrot's owner was bleeding and shocked. My client wanted to know why her sweet, tame pet had suddenly turned into a vicious, aggressive monster?

The Amazon was not being vicious or aggressive. The playful Yellow-nape had reached the level of excitement I call *Overload*. Most parrot species can become overstimulated and reach a point when their behavior becomes frenzied. Perhaps when a parrot becomes overstimulated, his actions are not simply behavioral, but also hormonal — adrenaline (epinephrine) is secreted into the bloodstream putting the bird into some sort of "super" mode? Adrenaline (a hormone secreted by the adrenal gland) enables an animal to meet sudden dangers and emergencies with physiological changes. Wild parrots who fight to defend family, flock, or territory may be infused with adrenaline. Overexcitement probably sends a confusing message to the companion parrot's brain resulting in overload behavior over which the parrot has no control. Numerous observations of companion parrots who drastically change behavior when there is a great deal of excitement have inspired this theory.

An overloaded parrot will not respond positively to the "UP" command from an assertive owner. The person who attempts to pick up their bird during overload-induced behavior will certainly regret trying (and might as well put a hand in the garbage disposal.) Few modifications can change this overload behavior because it seems to be beyond the parrot's conscious control. However, if the owner recognizes overload as a possibility, changes can be made in the way the parrot is handled during these situations. For example, my client doesn't have to stop playing keep-away with her Yellow-nape. She just has to watch closely and notice when he becomes overexcited. When his squealing becomes more intense, his eyes dilate, and his head feathers stand on end, she now leaves the yellow nape to play with the ball by himself and waits for him to play out his energy and settle down. She also purchased a net to swoop the ball into if the parrot becomes totally out of control. In addition, I showed her how to gently throw a towel on top of her parrot from the front, wrap him up in it, and take him to his cage safely if she needs to before he calms down.

Predictably Unpredictable

Many parrot species have a reputation for being unpredictable. However, often they are predictable in their unpredictability. When people pay attention to their parrot, they will learn to read the barometers of behavior and will prevent situations that create both overload and confusion. Conflict between natural behaviors and the artificial environment can also create confusion which may result in predictable, and therefore preventable, aggressive behavior in certain situations. Although it is true that an owner who has established *Nurturing Guidance* with his parrot will experience far less aggressive behavior, a parrot in overload is not acting in a conscious manner. A pet parrot is not bad or mean because it behaves in a natural, instinctive way in his confusing artificial environment. To guarantee a positive parrot/human relationship, the owner must accept responsibility for understanding and avoiding the situations that produce this kind of problem behavior. ∮

PLAY BITING & HAND CHEWING

Not Based On Aggression

Most biting is not really based on aggression. Remember, the parrot beak is not inherently a weapon, but a sensory organ used to touch and explore. Much of the exploration parrots do with their beaks is not even biting. Bappies particularly love to explore everything around them as part of their learning process. If the exploration gets a little rough, and even painful at times, this beaking and tonguing of our skin, particularly our fingers, is still usually based on play or affection. We need to teach our parrots how far they can go with *beakiness*. Exploration should certainly not be punished or even discouraged, but working with your parrot to keep his beak manipulation gentle will save you some pinches and little *birdy hickeys*. Most bappies can easily be trained to recognize the pain threshold of their human friends. When a parrot gets too excited or rough and starts pinching with pressure, softly say the word "gentle." Be consistent, so he gets the message that this type of beak exploration is unacceptable. If he is too excited to be gentle, slow things down by calmly removing your hands from his beak area.

Unfortunately, many people actually teach their parrots to play bite. Dramatically wiggling your fingers in the face of an excited parrot to try to get him to stop chewing on you makes grabbing and biting fingers more of a game. We teach this game of chewing or biting on wiggling fingers, and it is probably one of the most common games excited parrots play with people. Once the game has been patterned, the parrot will often initiate it by chewing on fingers to encourage the person to wiggle them even more. While this may be OK up to a point, this game can become quite intense if the parrot becomes too excited. Keep a foot toy nearby to stick in his beak to give him something else to chew on besides your fingers. A toy with knotted 100% cotton or vegetable tanned leather usually does the trick. (See below and page 146 for more information on beak exploration.) *

"I AM PACO'S BEAK"

"Some people call me Bill. I hate that! I am an incredibly powerful instrument with a zillion uses. Paco doesn't miss having lips and teeth — they are useless compared to my versatility! I work as both a mouth and a hand. Paco can use me to slice, dice, shred, rip, tear, and demolish almost anything, faster than almost any other animal can without extra tools. Paco also uses me to play-wrestle for fun or even to show affection in courtship. Too many people think just because Paco reaches out with me, that she is going to bite. What nonsense! I often use my beak to explore, or even for balance. Paco doesn't usually use me as a weapon unless she is seriously threatened or given mixed messages. Some parrots, whose human friends don't set rules for them, even learn that their beaks are a powerful tool for getting their way! If Paco does use me aggressively, I am powerful enough to do pretty serious damage!

"I have a great range of dexterity and can also be gentle. Paco uses me to preen, clean, and rezip her feathers together to keep them in tiptop shape. If she has an itch, she can use me to scratch almost every part of her body. I can shell the smallest seed or even feed Paco's tiniest chick. I can crack a nut or carefully snip a delicate flower blossom from its twig. I can carry and hold food or nesting material while Paco flies or climbs through the trees or around her cage. My tip has something called a Herbst's Corpuscle, an encapsulated bundle of highly sensitive nerve endings. This makes me so sensitive that I probably can tell Paco as much about what she is touching as a human can tell by touching something with his finger.

"My structure is actually a continuation of Paco's skull. My upper beak covers a bone called the premaxilla, while my lower beak covers a portion of the mandible. The part that you actually see is the keratin covering called the rhamphotheca (ram-fo-THEE-ka from the Greek *amphos*, beak and *theka*, sheath). If Paco stays healthy, eats a nutritious, balanced diet that includes high quality proteins, calcium, and vitamin A and has lots of fun "stuff" to chew on, I should never have to be trimmed. I have feelings and can even bleed! I hate it when someone grinds my tip back too far, especially using one of those motorized tools — they make my beak hurt and it gets so hot — yuck! I can't touch anything for days!" *

AGGRESSION & BITING

Is Aggression Natural?

Is it natural for a domestically-raised, handfed parrot to become aggressive to people — particularly the people in his human flock? Should every parrot owner live in fear that eventually his tame companion parrot will suddenly turn on him and become aggressive? Can anything be done to prevent this from happening? While aggression does develop in some hand-fed parrots, I do not believe it is necessarily natural for companion parrots to become aggressive. Aggressive behavior and biting in parrots rarely starts as aggression — normally it starts as one or more of the following:

⊃ Confusion in response to mixed messages, inconsistencies, or lack of predictability from the *human flock*. Biting is often the result of lack of guidance.

⊃ A response to changes in life routine — especially a decrease in affection and attention or an increase of stress in the home environment. Parrots often have adverse reactions to sudden changes in their lives.

⊃ The parrots's defense of territory and/or a perceived mate, when he is allowed to control his own life and is doing a bad job of it. Although it may seem illogical, often the favorite person receives the aggression.

⊃ A fear or confrontive response to threatening behavior from people who handle him aggressively or inconsistently. Aggressive behavior towards a parrot is almost always met with aggression from the parrot.

⊃ Overload behavior is a major cause of biting in normally tame companion parrots. Most parrots are easily excited and become overstimulated when playing with people, other parrots, or their toys. Interrupting a parrot who is overstimulated without letting him calm down first is one of the easiest ways to invite a bite.

⊃ Sexual bonding and territoriality when a parrot has become too strongly bonded to one person as a mate. Some, but certainly not all, parrots can become difficult during times of hormonal influence. This is particularly true with what I call "super males." These are cocks (especially cockatoos) who become aggressively dominant during breeding season. Setting a positive foundation, recognizing body language, and being very patient during times of hormonal influence helps caregivers remain lifetime friends with these parrots. Not all males exhibit these behaviors.

⊃ Sometimes parrots just go through cranky moods that their owners need to identify and understand.

⊃ Was he just exploring you with his beak and you overreacted, or was he really biting? (See previous page)

Although guiding a parrot's behavior from the time he is young will most likely prevent serious and permanent aggression, there may still be times throughout a companion parrot's life when he may go through aggressive periods. How we understand and manage these periods of aggressive behavior make a major difference in maintaining the continuing pet potential of our parrots. We need to understand our parrot's behavior and show him that he does not have to resort to biting to communicate with us.

When A Parrot Bites You

⊃ Respond as quietly as possible, without excitement or aggression. Reacting with anger or a drama reward can quickly escalate the aggression and reinforce the behavior. Yes, it hurts, but acting calmly helps keep the parrot from becoming even more overstimulated and biting again. It also does not pattern biting behavior.

⊃ Handle the situation yourself if you can. Don't allow another person — particularly the parrot's favorite person — to rescue you from being bitten. The parrot can quickly learn to bite you in order to go back to another person.

⊃ Place the parrot down on a stand or piece of furniture as calmly as possible. If you are too frightened of being bitten again and need someone else to take control of the parrot, leave the room before he or she picks up the bird and returns him to his cage. Then, get past your fear of being bitten and work with your parrot again.

⊃ Try to understand that it's not really the parrot's fault — most biting situations are beyond his control and are responses to situations in his environment he does not understand.

⊃ Don't punish the parrot — a pain response like "OW!" and/or a quick (no more than a few seconds) "Evil Eye" plus an immediate quick "NO!" are all he needs to know his behavior is not acceptable. Aggressive handling as a response to biting just encourages more aggressive behavior on the part of the parrot.

Sally Blanchard's COMPANION PARROT HANDBOOK

⮑ As soon as you calm down, use cause-and-effect logic to figure out why your parrot bit you. Most of the time there is a reason, and it often has to do with us not being aware of what we (or they) are doing when we approach them.

➤Did you move too quickly or approach him when your energy was too stressed?

➤Were you really focused on him when you tried to pick him up, or doing something else at the same time?

➤Did you not pay attention to his body language before you approached him?

➤Was he already in *overload behavior* from playing excitedly with a favorite toy or defending his favorite food?

➤Did something or someone in the room startle him, causing a fear reaction?

➤Was he protecting you or another person from a perceived intruder?

➤Did you startle him by wearing a red baseball hat or something else you don't usually wear?

⮑ Just because your parrot bit you does not mean he does not love you. Don't take it personally. Biting usually means a parrot is reacting with confusion, or in some cases, fear, or hormonal influences.

⮑ If your bird bites you it does not automatically mean he has become a biting bird and can not be trusted again. Most biting is based on an incident, and does not become a pattern unless you make it one.

⮑ While many parrots are protective of territory and flock, they rarely turn "mean." Normally, parrots who become excessively aggressive on a permanent basis do so for a reason.

⮑ Keep giving him attention or affection. If you need to, find a different way to relate with him in a positive manner until you can work past the aggression problem with him.

⮑ Try not to act differently or fearfully around your parrot. Parrots are highly reactive to our moods and energy and if we act differently, usually our parrots will respond to us differently. This is the way most people turn aggression and biting behavior into a self-fulfilling prophecy.

⮑ Increase the amount of focused attention, *Nurturing Guidance,* and instructional attention. Working with him in a *neutral room* is the best way to reestablish trust without having to deal with cage or territory defense.

A Common Scenario

Almost all parrots, at one time or another, will bite someone, sometime, somewhere. What we do about it will often determine whether biting will be an incident or become a pattern. Why does a tame, sweet, bonded parrot suddenly start to bite? The answer can be both simple and quite complicated at the same time. In a common scenario, the parrot, accustomed to a good amount of handling, becomes agitated when his owner does not give him the focused attention needed to keep him gentle and contented. Parrots don't always know how to ask appropriately, and often respond in ways that actually bring about the exact opposite of the nurturing handling they need. Parrots who are not getting enough attention can quickly become apprehensive, insecure, or simply "out of the habit" of being handled, especially when people are in a hurry or stressed, and don't really focus on their birds. Parrots are highly reactive pets, and a stressed person usually means a stressed parrot. When a parrot becomes petulant, the person becomes less likely to handle him. The confused bird becomes increasingly uncomfortable being handled as the person becomes more uncomfortable. The bird bites. If the person is shocked, takes it personally, and has a dramatic, negative reaction, then the cycle continues with less handling and more biting. Perhaps the caregiver's response becomes more and more dramatic, increasing the excitability of the parrot. The negative behaviors of both the person and the parrot become patterned, and the vicious cycle continues until the owner gets good information on how to get past this cycle or *gets rid of the bird.* Unfortunately, too many good parrots are given up because of confusion and lack of knowledge on the part of the people in their lives. ·····➤

The Easiest Problem To Solve

Although biting is probably the most common behavioral problem in companion parrots, it is generally the easiest to solve. However, this is only true if the person works with his parrot in productive ways. Some fail in their attempts to stop their parrot from biting because they use quick fixes, punishment, returned aggression, and/or drama rewards. There is a rampant misconception that just letting the bird bite and taking them without reacting is the best way to teach a parrot not to bite. All this does is pattern the biting behavior even more. Although there are many complex reasons a parrot bites, the underlying causes are usually the same — *an owner who does not know how to set rules or provide guidance, and a confused parrot in control of his or her own life and doing a bad job of it.*

Parrots do not make good pets if they are not taught to be good pets. Even human-raised bappies do not know how to adjust to life as a pet without a teacher or surrogate parent guiding their behavior. They are not instinctively prepared to be pets, and the behaviors parrots learn from their early interactions with people will be the behaviors they exhibit throughout life, unless work is done to change them at a later time. Because parrots are intelligent animals and are capable of learning throughout their entire lives, teaching new behaviors will require the caregiver to have good behavioral information. Most behavioral changes start with humans changing their behaviors towards their parrot. *Long-term consistency and patience on the part of the owner are essential.*

FUN AD *by Sally Blanchard*

(This cartoon advertisement is only for fun and NOT for a genuine product or service.)

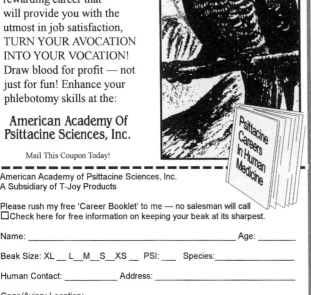
Proper early socialization with *Nurturing Guidance* is imperative for a young bird to develop into a successful human companion. However, even the pet potential of a chick who has been wonderfully prepared by the breeder/handfeeder can be seriously jeopardized by a caregiver who can not or will not provide proper guidance.

Teaching A Parrot To Bite

Much of the biting aggression I see from companion parrots is developed from interaction with their owners. In the wild, parrots are prey animals rather than predators, and it appears that parrots rarely initiate aggression. However, they can become aggressive as a defense if they are threatened. It is a misconception to presume that most biting in parrots is a result of aggressive behavior. Many people remark that their parrots become *mean*. Parrots are not mean because they bite. Biting behaviors normally start because the bird is confused. The vast majority of biting I see in pet parrots develops because the parrot is given confusing mixed messages and is then unintentionally rewarded for biting in his interaction with people.

Once a parrot is in his new home, he either develops his own behaviors or learns from his owners how to behave. A pet parrot will not naturally develop the traits that will make him a good pet. The new human flock must show their pet how to behave in acceptable ways. The problem is that many parrot people do not realize that they are teaching their parrots the traits that make them a "bad" pet bird. A parrot can quickly learn that the best way to get someone to leave him alone is to bite them. The parrot that bites often does so because his caregiver has reinforced or rewarded the bird for biting. Without realizing it, many people are actually teaching their parrots to bite. A caregiver who is aware of the dynamics of aggression and biting can prevent a parrot from developing these behaviors.

THE MYTH OF THE ONE-PERSON BIRD

How It Becomes A Self-fulfilling Prophecy

Several species of parrots are generally referred to as one-person birds. These stereotypes can keep people from buying a certain parrot who may be the right bird for them. While seemingly true of some individuals, usually parrots with whom no one has worked with display this rigid characteristic. Most companion parrots are capable of bonding and rebonding on many levels throughout their lives. In the wild, the mate bond is not the only relationship a parrot establishes with other birds in the flock. As well-managed pets, most parrots are also capable of bonding on different levels to several people in their lives. Parrots may change their bonding preferences from time to time, but these changes are not necessarily permanent. We may not always understand the reasons why a parrot suddenly changes his allegiance from one person to another but people can work with parrots to rewin their trust and affection. Parrots normally form the strongest bond with the person who provides them the most consistent guidance because these people confuse them the least. Not every parrot bond is the same, just as not every human friendship is the same. Some people are not aware of how strongly their parrots are bonded to them because the bird seems to like someone else better.

LOVE ME
LOVE MY BIRD

We work with our parrots to establish patterns necessary for multiple bonding. When people are told their parrots will only bond to one person, and they believe it, and don't do the necessary work which allows the parrot to form bonds with other people, the myth becomes a self-fulfilling prophecy. Some people seem to enjoy the fact that their parrot only likes them. Some even think it is funny that the bird chases their spouses out of the house and some brag that their parrot refuses to be handled by anyone else. These people are asking for serious problems — both with the people and the parrot in their lives.

Defending The Flock

Most parrots are highly social birds. They form ties with their flock and bond strongly to their mates and family group. They can be territorial in defense of their flock and family members. As members of our companion parrot's *human flock* or even as their perceived mate, we will often be defended from others and intruders whether we want to be or not. When parrots are young, they usually allow most people to handle them, especially when their trusted caregiver and protector is there providing safety and assurance. As young parrots continue to mature, unless they are introduced safely to new people on a continuing basis, they often develop either a fear of strangers or a need to defend their perceived territory against them.

Parrots who are properly socialized by being safely introduced to new experiences, objects, and people on a continuing basis will usually not shy away or be aggressive in new situations. If a bird only spends his early development limited to attention from his immediate family or single owner, other people may be perceived as intruders until they are accepted into the bird's human flock. Even people who were perceived as members of the flock when the parrot was young, often become intruders unless they work consistently with him as he matures. Therefore, it is essential for all family members and close friends who want to stay a part of the parrot's life to consistently and comfortably handle the bird throughout his life. Using *Nurturing Guidance*, each member of the human flock should handle the parrot both individually and with other flock members.

Confused Messages From Strangers

A young parrot's mistrust of some family members and strangers is often reinforced by people who don't know how to approach or handle him comfortably, especially when these people have not been around many parrots. When a parrot is continually approached with either fear or aggression, he may become patterned to respond in the same way. The timid person who presents an unclear message for the bird to step onto his hand and then pulls away when the bird responds with confusion may be bitten. This confusion can become patterned into aggression directed towards all people who do not give clear handling messages. This patterning even creates handling problems for previously trusted people. The aggressive person who refuses to listen to the way the caregiver asks them to handle the parrot can also cause serious trust problems — allowing a parrot to be approached by anyone without concern for how they handle the bird can be very trust-destroying. Aggressive handling from strangers may make a parrot mistrustful of all new people in his life.

If You Like Them, They Must Be OK

Introductions are essential. The young parrot perceives us as his surrogate parents and looks to us for defense and protection. In order for companion parrots to accept the family and friends of their owner instead of being wary of them, the new person must be safely and gradually introduced. The introduction is gradual enough for the parrot to perceive the stranger as a new flock member and not an intruder. The way to achieve this is for a trusted flock member to introduce the new person to the parrot. This introduction is more successful if it is done in a *neutral room* rather than in the room where the cage is located. Strangers or people who are not considered part of the human flock should never be allowed to approach the cage, nor should they try to handle the bird without first being introduced. When I visit people with parrots, I always take time to observe the parrot indirectly and then ask the caregivers to introduce me to their bird rather than approaching the bird myself.

Becoming A Member Of The Flock

For a stranger to become a member of the flock, the parrot's friends and family must be willing to work both with their parrot and the new person. The bird should already have a positive trusting relationship with his owners and understand basics like stepping on a person's hand with the "UP" command. Introducing strangers to a parrot properly is essential even if he is a sweet, tame handfed bappy who seems to accept everyone. You want him to stay that way and an unsuccessful, unsupervised introduction which may not work out well can create serious problems.

First, give new people verbal instructions on how to approach your parrot. Let them watch as you confidently handle him using the "UP" and "Down" commands. Show them how you "skritch" or cuddle your parrot. If they listen carefully, they are a good candidate for friendship with your parrot. If they are afraid of parrots, it is not a good idea to have them work through that fear with your pet. If they refuse to listen, perhaps declaring that they don't need to listen to you because they have had lots of parrots, they have no business handling your parrot.

Have the person sit down in a neutral room away from the cage territory. Have them take a few deep breaths to relax. A nervous person will create a nervous, unpredictable response from the parrot. If your friend or family member is frightened or uncomfortable, it is best for them to not handle your parrot unless the parrot is very tame and forgiving. If everyone is relaxed and confident, the new flock member will easily take the parrot from you using the "UP" command. If your friend doesn't feel ready for that step, either place your parrot on a T-stand or your friend's knee.

The knee area is the best place for a parrot to sit. The person can talk quietly to the bird, make gentle eye contact from above, and establish friendly control over the situation. Don't ever place your parrot on the new person's shoulder because this position may put them in jeopardy if a problem arises. The next step depends on everyone's comfort level. If everyone is relaxed and confident, your friend can pick up the bird saying "UP." In some situations, you may want to place the parrot on your friend's hand.

If the parrot has a negative reaction and the friend is competent at handling him, the caregiver may leave the room once the introductions have been made. The parrot may still be reacting out of defense for his favorite person, especially if he is a mature bird. However, many parrots who are aggressive around their cage and family become docile when in the *neutral room*.

Maintaining Flock Acceptance

The parrot's new friend should spend individual time with the parrot in the neutral room. Focused attention, which is time spent giving the parrot instructional attention, goes a long way in increasing the parrot/human bond. Eventually— whether it takes a few hours or a few months, the parrot should learn to trust the new flock member enough to allow handling near the cage. Once the new person is genuinely recognized as a flock member, he or she should be able to take the parrot out of the cage using the "UP" command. It is important to realize, however, if the parrot's behavior is being controlled by hormones during breeding season, it is best to carefully observe his body language before anyone, even a flock member, tries to handle him.

People with infrequent contact with the parrot, especially if time passes between visits, need to repeat the introductory stages to maintain acceptance. This is also an effective way for people who used to be able to handle a parrot to reinstate themselves as a member of the flock.

Family members who want the parrot to stay tame to them have to work at it. Playing *warm potato* a few times a week over the lifetime of the parrot is the best way to pattern a parrot to stay tame to everyone. This involves passing the bird slowly around a circle of family and friends (in a neutral room if the parrot is territorial about his cage) with each person giving the parrot a hug, a *skritch*, and/or verbal praise.

For the parrot to stay tame to them, each person in the human flock must also develop their own individual special relationship with the bird. This involves interactive time spent alone with the bird doing special things such as showering, teaching fun tricks, playing games, and cuddling. Picking a favorite interaction that only the new person does can help to develop a stronger and longer lasting parrot/human bond.

I have worked with many parrots who seemed to have a strong bond with just one person in the human flock. Using the proper techniques combined with patience and consistent attention, even the most hard-core "one-person" bird has learned to accept and enjoy the company of other human *flock members*. However, it is important to realize that there are occasionally parrots and people who are simply not compatible. But before coming to that conclusion, it is worth giving it a concentrated effort for everyone to get along. ✦

PARROTS ON SHOULDERS

The Favorite Perch

One of the most significant mistakes people make with their companion parrots is to allow them to run up on their shoulder. Almost all parrots, even handfed babies, like to be as high as they can. This tendency often results in serious arguments between parrots and people. If the person does not believe in setting rules or providing guidance, the parrot will win easily and his favorite perch will become the shoulder. This may not seem to be a problem in the beginning, but once the parrot becomes patterned it may become difficult to reeducate him not to run up to the shoulder. There are several reasons why this can become a problem. One of the best ways to establish control, or discipline a misbehaving parrot, is with eye contact. If a bird is on your shoulder, it is impossible to make eye contact without making your face vulnerable to beak injury. Also, a parrot on the shoulder is in a more dominant position because his eye is usually level with or above the person's.

Letting the bird climb up on the shoulder seems to be a convenient way to spend casual or ambient time with the parrot. People seem to think they can place their parrot on their shoulder and he will automatically behave himself. One of the reasons we enjoy parrots so much is because of their intelligence and curiosity. These same traits create one of the major problems with shoulder birds. A curious parrot will busy himself looking for things to do. That *bird toy* hanging from your ear, or that little mole on your neck with the hair hanging out of it, is just too inviting. So he starts poking at it with his beak. You turn and say, "Stop it, do you hear me?!" He becomes distracted but soon finds the little silver thing on the frame of your glasses or the loose thread on your shirt sleeve. You admonish him again with increased drama. After a second or so, he remembers that mole again — after all, the hair is still there. You give him more drama before you finally pick him up, telling him what a *bad bird* he is, and put him back in his cage telling him to think about what a *bad bird* he is. He has no idea what you are talking about or that he did anything wrong. He only knows every time he poked at you with his beak, he was rewarded with a wonderful outburst of drama. Parrots love drama and will learn quickly to turn these behaviors into a game so they can get people all excited. As the bird becomes more and more excited, *overload* biting can quickly become a part of this game, with the bird continually being rewarded with the dramatic response. The parrot learns to escape hands by hanging out on the person's back, hanging from the clothing in that totally unreachable place where no one can reach to scratch himself. I have actually watched more than one person take his or her shirt off to try gaining control of their parrot. Unless a person establishes calm, methodical guidance, this bird will become a problem, particularly if he insists on sitting on the shoulder.

Territorial Protection

Parrots who have been raised with rules and guidance present far fewer problems for their caregivers when they reach sexual maturity. However, a parrot who has been consistently allowed to perch on the shoulder may create serious problems as he becomes more territorial. Parrots bond strongly to their primary person's face. If they are sexually bonded to us and we allow them to sit on our shoulder, I believe their perception is one of sitting together with us (our head) on a moving *tree branch*. Our body becomes their territory. If the territory is threatened by any *intruder* (your husband, wife, child, dog, etc.), it is instinctive for the bird to defend that territory. In the wild, a pair of parrots might become very big by spreading their tails and wings, and/or raising their crests to show off all their color. They would pin their eyes and become as threatening as possible. The pet bird may show the same behavior, expecting his *mate* (you) to exhibit the same defensive postures to help scare the intruder off. If you greet the perceived intruder with a cheery "hello" or sit there like a lump on a log, you become part of the problem, not part of the solution. The

Ever wonder why so many pirates wore eye patches?

parrot can't defend his mate and the territory at the same time, so you have to go! So he takes a swipe at you to get you to fly away so he can defend the territory and you can come back when it is safe. If a parrot takes a jab at another parrot, he most likely gets a beak full of feathers. If he takes a jab at you, he gets a beak full of skin. Facial bites can be quite serious, resulting in scarring and even eye injury.

What about the lady with the sweet Timneh grey who has been sitting on her shoulder for the last 15 years and has never shown any sign of aggression? Does she now have to retrain her parrot not to sit on her shoulder? Probably not — she is the exception. Some parrots are well-behaved on their favorite person's shoulder unless there is another person in the area. Unfortunately, many people think they are the exception until they experience aggression when their parrot is on their shoulder. They learn the hard way with a ripped ear, a scar on the lip, a damaged eye, or even facial disfigurement. I once watched a woman with two large macaws on her shoulder at a bird show. She thought she looked cool. The birds were stressed and got into a fight with both of them biting at her face. Would she look so cool with an eye patch?

Retraining A Shoulder Parrot

Start out by placing your parrot on your knee instead of on your shoulder. He can play happily, and you can establish both friendly and disciplinary eye control with him. If he already has the bad habit of running up your arm, simply bring your other hand down your arm and use the "UP" command to have him step on your finger. You may have to consistently repeat this process many times, over a period of time, before he takes you seriously. Make it simple and behave calmly — don't turn it into a game with drama. Do this over and over until your arm is no longer his runway to your shoulder. Do not get into the habit of just leaning over to his cage and having him step on your shoulder. *Maintaining hand control is essential to having a well-behaved parrot.*

The Five Rules For Letting Your Parrot On Your Shoulder

1. The parrot is not allowed on your shoulder unless you have established the proper guidance and rules for him to understand that you are in charge of his behavior when he is there.

2. The parrot is not allowed on your shoulder unless you put him there. He should not be in control of being there. Instead of letting him run up to your shoulder, place him there with the "OK" and "DOWN" commands.

3. The parrot is not allowed on your shoulder unless he will readily step on to your hand with the "UP" command to come off your shoulder.

4. The parrot is not allowed on your shoulder if he has ever shown aggression while he is there. Watch his body language very carefully when other people or pets are in the room. Some birds are OK on shoulders if their *primary bondee* is the only one present.

5. Parrots do not have an on/off button. Don't expect him to behave on your shoulder. Make sure he has something to do (a toy to play with, etc.) while he is there. Don't turn his shoulder misbehavior into a game by rewarding him with drama every time he chews on you.

UNDERSTANDING SEXUAL BEHAVIOR

AN INTRODUCTION TO P-ORNITHOLOGY

① Does this seem to be your parrot's fantasy? Does he really want to settle down and raise babies with you? Of course, the answer is NO — whether your bird is a male or a female, he or she is reacting to strong biological urges towards his or her perceived mate — you. Since companion parrots bond strongly to their human friends, these sexual behaviors are often directed towards them in the absence of a more suitable mate (another parrot!). Many parrots raised with *Nurturing Guidance* do not form sexual bonds with their owners. **Just because parrots are exhibiting sexual behaviors does not mean they need to be placed in a breeding situation**. Nor does it mean that your parrot wants to raise a family. It only means that he or she is exhibiting natural behavior in an unnatural situation. Understanding more about the factors that influence your parrot's sexual behavior as he or she matures will help you provide the guidance he or she needs to be content as a well-nurtured lifelong *celibate* companion.

② No matter what you do, that delightful, sweet, innocent "bappy" is going to mature into an adult parrot with normal biological urges to reproduce. Considering the fact that many people have kept single parrots as contented companions for years, it is obvious that good care and a nurturing environment can override any "need to breed."

③ The key to having a lifelong well-behaved parrot is to establish guidelines and set rules from the very beginning. Although much of a parrot's behavior is instinctive, much of it is also learned. The more intelligent animals are, the more their behaviors are influenced by teaching and example. Parrots, even domestically-raised bappies, have no idea how to adapt to life as a human companion. They do not come out of the egg being good pets — we have to teach and guide them with *Nurturing Guidance*. We need to be their surrogate parents or flock leaders. Parrots who have this type of guidance are less likely to have serious problems when they reach maturity — or start being influenced by their hormones. By giving companion parrots clear messages to guide their behaviors, we can actually override some of the natural behavior that creates problems for them as pets. Using the "UP" and "DOWN" command every time you pick up or put your parrot down, is one of the best ways to give parrots a clear message about what you expect from them.

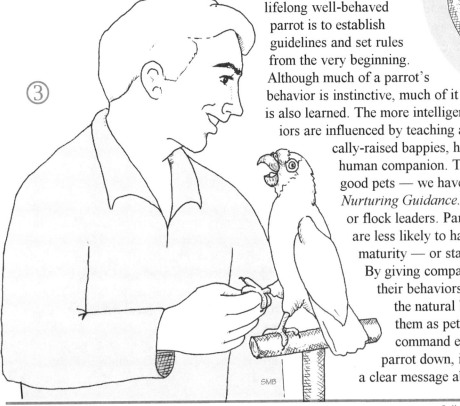

Sally Blanchard's COMPANION PARROT HANDBOOK

④ Everyone who will be involved in the parrot's life needs to spend time with him and develop their own individual bond. A family spending consistent time with the parrot together and separately throughout his life will help prevent him from becoming a "one-person bird." If everyone sets rules and provides guidance, the parrot is less likely to form a mate bond with one person and exhibit sexual aggression towards others. A "neutral room" away from the cage and other family members, where the parrot is not used to being (and therefore does not have a territorial agenda) is a good place for each individual to spend a period of time each day developing his own special relationship with the parrot.

⑤ Just as young children may "play house" long before they are sexually mature, young parrots may begin to "court" their owners long before the birds are hormonal. Just because a parrot exhibits sexual behavior does not mean it is mature enough to breed. Sexual immaturity comes before sexual maturity. One of the first behaviors that may eventually evolve into sexual behavior is regurgitation. It is natural for parrots to feed each other and the fact that your parrot wants to feed you simply means that he has a special bond with you. What a compliment!?

⑥ Sexual behavior in birds has several external influences including light, temperature, humidity, and food sources. In the wild, hormones stimulate birds to breed just prior to the time when food for babies is most plentiful. Food is more available during and after a rainy season. Companion parrots are also naturally stimulated by such factors, and sexual behavior in a mature parrot often starts at about the time the days start to get longer. However, artificial lighting, temperature and climate control in our homes creates stimuli for breeding that may be confusing to both us and our parrots.

⑦ & ⑧ Without realizing it, people may actually be increasing the sexual behavior of their parrots with physical affection or play that is misunderstood by the parrot as sexual foreplay. During the times that hormones are exerting a strong influence on our feathered companions, interactions that would normally be perfectly fine and should cause no problem may cause sexual arousal and serious confusion in our pets. During these periods, in many birds it is best to avoid petting under the wings, pulling on the tail, encompassing the body, putting pressure on the back or rump area, touching near the vent, and beak wrestling.

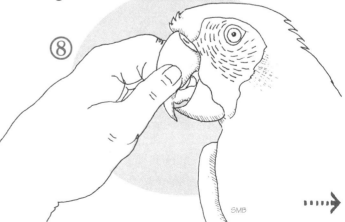

•••••➤

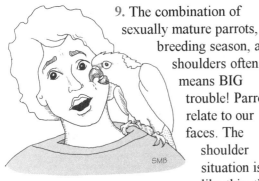

9. The combination of sexually mature parrots, breeding season, and shoulders often means BIG trouble! Parrots relate to our faces. The shoulder situation is like this: the two of you are sitting together on a "moving tree branch." The parrot perceives you as his mate, and an "intruder" (your wife, husband, a kid, or even the dog) threatens the territory you are sharing (your body!). It is natural for parrots to strut and puff to defend the nesting territory. When you don't help, you become part of the problem rather than part of the solution. You get bitten, probably because your *mate* is trying to drive you away. He can't defend both you and the territory and wants you to come back later when everything is safe.

10-11. Many parrots masturbate — some frequently. This will come as no surprise to those who have lived with parrots for some time. After a fairly involved courtship and often frenzied ritual "fore-play," parrot pairs consummate their sexual union by position-ing their vents together. Many sexually mature single parrots derive pleasure by rubbing their vents against almost anything including, but not limited to, their toys, perches, and cage parts. People also receive this type of attention from their parrots. When this occurs, I advise my clients to return the parrot to his cage or stand without making a fuss. This form of sexual behavior in companion parrots is a displacement substitute for natural biologi-cal behaviors and should not be punished. It should essentially be ignored and neither encouraged nor discouraged.

12. During the breeding "sea-son," parrots can be visually stimulated by the presence of a nest cavity or something that resembles one, such as a box, paper bag, cupboard, bookcase, or other dark container with an opening. I know of one Scarlet Macaw who laid eggs when a carpet was rolled up next to her cage during home redecorating. The macaw saw the dark circle created by the rolled carpet as the entrance to a nest cavity. Another client came home to find her Amazon had escaped and was happily sitting on a "nest" of shredded books on the top shelf of a bookcase next to the cage. Paper shredding and increased wood chewing in a mature bird can be signs of nesting behavior, but can also be encouraged as a normal activity.

13. In some parrots, increased aggression is one sign of sexual behavior. Watch for changes in body posture to know if you should be handling your parrot differently than normal. Parrots still need attention during these times, but you may have to relate to your bird less physically until he or she settles down. It is a good idea to train a young bird to step on a stick so if he becomes a problem during breeding season, you can still maintain control without being bitten. Not all parrots become aggressive during breeding season. Some people have reported that their beloved hens have laid eggs in their laps. Caregivers of well-nurtured parrots may not even notice sexual behavior.

14. Parrots make wonderful lifelong companions, but only if people understand and pay close attention to both their physical and emotional needs. Feeding a varied, nutritious diet is essential. Providing a roomy, secure, clean cage environment allows parrots to feel confident and safe. Toys and a playgym are necessary for exercise and activity. Frequent bathing or misting is a must. Proper veterinary care should be provided. But the most important consideration of all is that parrots are highly social animals who need consistent handling, attention, and affection. Provide them the excel-lent care they deserve — the re-wards are substantial.

EXCESSIVE SCREAMING

Screaming Is NOT A Behavioral Problem

I do not consider screaming to be a parrot behavioral problem. Parrots scream. This is a fact of life. They evolved to scream so they could stay in touch with other flock members across vast areas of land. They scream because they are happy to be alive. Perhaps they scream because it feels good. But there is often a problem with too much screaming in our living rooms, and we need to teach our parrots acceptable ways to express their enthusiasm. The major problem we have is not with screaming but with manipulative, excessive, nagging screaming which drives us crazy and often ruins our relationship with our parrots. Most of the time, we are the ones who have actually caused this excessive problem screaming. The worst and most common way far too many people deal with their parrot's screaming is to scream back. Since parrots are highly empathic animals, screaming back rewards the behavior and makes it worse. Any sort of drama reward, such as screaming or running over to bang on the cage or cover it, will most likely accomplish the exact opposite of what we want. If screaming is not a problem, why do so many people think it is? ·····>

THE "PRIMAL PSITTA-SCREAM"

My experience observing wild parrots in Costa Rica clearly showed me just how loud parrot screams can be. As I stood in a rainforest clearing, I could hear the calls of a flock of parrots long before I saw the birds fly over, and long after they were out of my sight. When parrots vocalize, they usually have something to communicate. Loud calls and screaming can signify the importance of what they are communicating. Calls to stay in touch with the flock are an essential part of social interaction for most parrot species. Alarm cries are often loud and high-pitched, assuring that the entire flock is called to attention. In some cases, loud yelling may just be a way to let off steam or let the world know the parrot is happy to be alive. With many species, the first screams are at daylight as a "Let's go eat!" announcement for the flock to fly to the feeding grounds. During the day, screaming becomes a call to the flock to stay in touch or to announce other daily routines. Parrot flocks have their own language — an assortment of many different calls and sounds, each with its own unique significance. Individuals verbalize in many ways with sounds that signify their state of being (apprehension, belligerence, pleasure, affection, and so on) and are used to communicate with their mates, other flock members, and other creatures in their environment. Some are loud and raucous, some are soft and subtle.

Since screaming as a form of communication is such a natural behavior for most parrots, it is both almost impossible and undesirable to prevent all outbursts from a companion parrot. This is especially true with high-energy, excitable birds. However, it is usually easy to prevent screaming from getting out of hand. The first step is to accept normal parrot noisemaking and take it in stride. The more we try to stifle normal calling behavior, the more likely we are to create a screaming parrot. Let your parrot have a time each day when he can become really exuberant and let all that energy out — a sort of *primal psitta-scream* or *happy to be alive scream.* What is acceptable screaming and how does it differ from excessive screaming? The answer to this question may actually depend a great deal on what each individual parrot caregiver (plus his or her family and neighbors) can tolerate. People who can't tolerate any noise at all should probably not own any kind of parrot. Even parrots with reputations for being quiet, such as Pionus, may become screamers or make repetitive noises that can irritate people who are very noise sensitive. Some cockatoo, Amazon, and conure owners may think their parrots are relatively quiet. ⸘

The answer is that parrots learn to use screaming to manipulate their owners. Loud, often repetitive, excessive screaming causes such unhappiness in so many parrot owners. Years ago, when I first became fascinated by parrots, I had friends who were just starting to breed Amazons. The couple had turned a large workshop behind their garage into an aviary. The more, the merrier, and merry is noisy with Amazons. Both people were somewhat hard of hearing, and when they went into their aviary, they simply turned off their hearing aids. This, of course, is not a logical solution for everyone who lives with screaming parrots. EXCESSIVE screaming is one of the major behavioral problems people have with their companion parrots. It may be one of the easiest problems to prevent, but can be one of the most difficult to solve.

Preventing Screaming

Many parrots scream because of confusion and to self-stimulate. It is unusual for a well-socialized, happy bappy to develop a serious screaming problem as long as his physical and emotional needs are maintained. One of the first aspects to consider is making sure the bappy you buy is abundantly fed and weaned to his own timetable, rather than gavage (tube) fed and deprivation weaned. Many underfed, forced-weaned baby parrots start communicating their distress vocally at a very young age with crying, whining, and food-begging. Since new owners are often admonished not to start handfeeding their "weaned" baby or they will "spoil him," they just pick up the parrot to cuddle him rather than feeding him which would solve his hunger and the insecurity it causes. This is a setup for the new parrot owner, and certainly the origin of at least some excessive, manipulative vocalizations. People are often told not to pay too much attention to their new avian companion for fear of overindulging him — but he is a baby and needs lots of instructional interaction. Depriving young parrots of attention can seriously compromise their sense of security. Young parrots use vocalizations to communicate this insecurity and their need for reassurance.

Most new parrot owners do not understand how important vocal communication and contact calls are to their new bird. Some people are so afraid their parrot will turn into a screamer that they come running up to quiet the bird every time he squawks. This, of course, can quickly reinforce the squawking by rewarding it with attention. One of the most

UNDERSTANDING CONTACT CALLS

Vocal & Social Animals

"Yes, you're OK!"

Most parrots are extremely vocal and social animals who use contact calls to stay in touch with their mates, young, and other flock members. Contact "Am I OK?" calls are simple notes, sounds, or vocalizations with specific meanings. Different flocks within the same species have their own dialects — calls that are unique to the members of their flock. Young parrots quickly learn the "language" of their parents so they can fit into the flock. Companion parrot chicks also learn the language of their flock, but this turns out to be the sounds of the calls and responses they hear from their "human flock."

As parrot owners, we can communicate with our avian companions using contact calls. Young parrots should be encouraged to explore their environment by hearing our calls in the form of a reassuring voice saying, "You're OK — I'll protect you." Greeting them when you enter the room and bidding them a farewell when you leave is one way to help guarantee their sense of security.

Consistently returning and initiating contact calls is one of the best ways to prevent screaming in young parrots. This is also a positive way to work with established screaming behavior. Pay attention and learn to recognize the words and sounds your parrot uses to get your attention. Often a companion parrot will start with body language and then communicate with a single call note. If we notice and answer with a simple return call, we can often avoid having them go into a screaming session to get our attention. When I am in the living room and Spikey is playing in his cage, he often stops to check if I am paying attention. He makes a simple one-note call that sounds like a smoke alarm battery. If I ignore him, he will make it again — usually up to three times. Being a social flock bird, staying in touch with me is very important to Spikey. He gives me three chances and then he screams at me — I figure I deserve it!

Sally Blanchard's COMPANION PARROT HANDBOOK

immediate causes of any parrot misbehavior is a change in the amount of attention and affection, or drastic changes in the environment that threaten the bird's security and cause confusion. The problem is often made worse when people become frustrated with their parrot's noise level and use any quick-fix to control the screaming except for really working positively with the underlying causes. Quick-fixes work only as distractions, can be confusing for the parrot, and only stop each screaming incident while they do little to change the reason the parrot screams.

Long-term Ways To Work With Screaming Behavior

➲ Remember with all behavioral problems, there are no overnight quick-fixes. Because most parrots are *reactors* rather than *actors*, people have to change their behavior before the parrot changes his behavior. Long-term patience and consistently working with the underlying causes of screaming are the only way these problems will be resolved. Realize that sometimes the problem may seem to become even worse while you are working to change it. Parrots are creatures of habit, and may increase their negative behaviors to try to maintain the status quo.

➲ Don't create drama rewards by running over screaming at the bird, squirting him with water, covering his cage, or taking him someplace for punishment. These actions do not change screaming behavior — they reward it.

➲ Don't turn your parrot into a magician — making you reappear whenever he screams when you leave the room. Instead call back and forth to him and only pay him positive attention once he has become quieter.

➲ Increase the amount of focused attention, in-your-face instructional interaction, and *Nurturing Guidance*. Often, positive interaction and playtime in the neutral room are all it takes to settle a parrot down.

➲ Lower the energy and the sound level in the room. Parrots not only mimic our energy, they also like to compete with and often outdo the noise in their environment. Turn the music down or whisper instead of shouting to each other.

➲ Make sure your parrot's basic needs — both physical and emotional — are being taken care of adequately.

➲ Anticipate your parrot's needs. For example, parrots are social eaters. Most are not be happy if you eat in front of them without sharing. Keeping track of the *human flock* is also very important. Consistently greeting a parrot when you come into the room, and verbally announcing you are leaving when you walk out, helps prevent and solve some screaming problems.

➲ Learn to recognize contact calls and the body language which precedes your parrot's screaming. Responding to these early communications can prevent screaming.

➲ Pay attention and try to figure out what your parrot is trying to communicate with his screaming. Did you ignore his initial, quieter requests for water, a treat, fresh food, ambient attention, rescue from a threatening situation, or to go back to his cage?

➲ Distract the parrot without rewarding his screaming behavior. Indirect responses do not have the same effect as direct negative responses. Singing, humming, whistling or whispering to yourself or another person can make the parrot curious enough to stop screaming and pay attention to you.

➲ Teach your parrot positive behaviors — tricks like raising his wings on command — and give him the cue for a trick to distract him from screaming. ✒

FEATHER DESTRUCTIVE BEHAVIOR

Consider Physical Reasons First

Although there are many factors influencing feather picking behavior, I believe the main causes are still physical and/or environmental, with disease or injury, improper nutrition, and lack of bathing opportunities at the top of the list. Most feather picking is caused by a complex combination of physical, environmental, and behavioral causes. Parrots need a nutritious diet to *manufacture* healthy feathers and skin tissue. Their feathers and skin must be clean and healthy. When a parrot starts destroying his feathers, the first step is to make sure that his physical and environmental needs are being met properly. For a checklist on improving these aspects of your parrot's life, please read *Optimizing The Environment* (page 148). Since I believe that most feather destructive behavior starts for physical reasons, I encourage a full veterinarian workup at the onset of the problem. Feather picking can be an indication of an injury or disease process (this can include aspergillosis, giardia, heavy metal toxicity, or viral and bacterial infections.) The presumption should never be made that the problem is simply behavioral.

However, even if picking starts for a purely physical reason, behavioral complexities can continue the plucking beyond the resolution of the physical cause. The primary behavioral influence is a drama reward given to the bird when he is picking. A bird who starts plucking because of the irritation of a simple insect bite may develop a habitual pattern if the human family pays attention to him every time he messes with his feathers. While pluckers certainly need nurturing and attention from their caregivers to feel secure, it is important not to give them that attention around their picking behavior.

Behavioral reasons for feather picking usually involve a change in the parrot's sense of security. Some young birds, particularly African Greys, may experience confusion and emotional trauma if they are left during their critical independence stages. For this reason, I recommend that my clients do not plan vacations away from their young parrots until they are well over a year of age. If a vacation or trip is necessary, planning ahead is essential. Getting a young bird used to visiting the place where he will be left and introducing the bird sitter ahead of time makes a big difference in the way the bird perceives being left by his primary human flock. If he has a trusted friend and is in a situation he already knows and is comfortable with, he is much less likely to feel abandonment.

Gradual change by itself should not cause enough of a trauma to start a feather picking episode. However, parrots who have been overprotected and/or poorly socialized may not react well to any new situation, especially if it happens suddenly. If the change seriously threatens the bird's sense of security, phobic behavior may result in feather destructive behavior. In young parrots, traumatic or aggressive handling can also be a factor in picking. It is important to protect a young bird from any threatening experience. Unfortunately, early veterinarian and grooming visits may be very traumatic to a young parrot — particularly one who already has some insecurities. Aggressive handling, cutting toenails too short, perches that are too smooth or large for a young bird's grip, and a botched wing trim may all contribute to balance problems and falling which can have a disastrous effect on a parrot's sense of security. Please see the sections on veterinarians (pgs.44-47) and grooming (pgs. 50-55) for more information on these topics.

Some people drive their parrots crazy. Teasing, aggressive behavior, stress, continual confrontation, or constant arguing from humans can cause insecurity in parrots that can lead to picking. The behavior of our parrots is often a barometer of the human energy and behavior in their household. While human interactions can be difficult at times, our major goal for our parrots should be to help them feel secure in our homes.

Boredom and lack of stimulation do play a part in some feather picking situations. In captivity, parrots are far more sedentary than their evolution prepared them to be. As conscientious parrot owners, we need to provide our parrots with a great deal of activity and stimulation to keep them healthy and happy.

Poor Early Socialization

Parrots are intelligent animals and much of their behavior is learned. Early socialization is not simply the number of people (or birds) that a young bird comes into contact with. It is the process by which parrots learn their social and survival skills. Basically, parrots do not automatically know how to adapt to their life in a living room. We need to teach them how to be good pets. If we don't guide their behavior from the time they would naturally start exploring their environment, parrots raised for the pet trade can begin to show serious behavioral dysfunction. These problems are rarely apparent until the young birds start to reach their independence stages. One of the manifestations of this behavioral confusion can be feather picking. It appears that most (but not all) plucking related to poor early socialization will usually show up in a young parrot by the time he is a year to eighteen months old.

The majority of people who consult with me are under the erroneous presumption that their parrots must be unhappy if they pick. While some feather pickers do have emotional problems, this is not necessarily true for all parrots who exhibit feather destructive behaviors. Many contented parrots play happily, love to be cuddled, chatter loquaciously, and still pick their feathers. The most important advice I give the owners of plucking birds, whether the picking originates from physical or behavioral causes (or both), is to totally ignore their bird when he picks. Give him lots of

THE NEED TO PREEN

If clothes make the man, then feathers certainly make the bird. Feathers are used for insulation, flight, protection from injury, protective coloration, behavioral communication, and attracting mates. The feathers on a parrot are complex structures with different shapes and functions. Healthy parrots are normally fastidious about maintaining their feather condition. Baths or showers encourage preening. Preening is the process of cleaning and "rezipping" all the barbs and barbules so they align properly. During each preening, the parrot will also remove several loose feathers that are ready to molt (see next page). This should not be confused with feather picking behavior. Without proper alignment, the feathers can't do their important job in maintaining the parrot's health and mobility. Many parrot species have a uropygial (preen) gland which secretes a substance used in preening and feather conditioning. Some birds also dust bathe, rub themselves against wet leaf matter, and use acids obtained from rubbing insects on their bodies as *feather conditioners*. Occasionally, companion parrots (particularly cockatoos) will place cloth or other matter (seed, pellets, wood chips) in their feathers, perhaps as a preening aid. It looks weird and doesn't seem to make any sense to us at all — of course, there is no way to know if it really makes sense to the parrot. Parrots may preen sedately at times, and other times they may go at their feathers in what seems to be a frantic manner. Most preening also involves fluffing, scratching and kicking at the feathers parrots may not be able to reach with their beaks, and what looks like it could be called "nitpicking." Some parrots may spend a great deal of time in this often intense scratching process, and parrot novices often wonder if their pet has fleas or some sort of external parasite like lice or mites. This would be highly unusual. (The mite protectors on the market are not only unnecessary but they contain potentially harmful materials.) In twenty-five years of working with companion parrots, the one louse I found was so unusual my veterinarian wanted me to save it for him to see. Many parrots finish a good preen by sticking their toe in their nostrils. My guess is that this is to create a good sneeze to get rid of all the feather dust that has gotten in their nostrils during preening.

Lack of proper preening behavior is usually a sign of a parrot with physical problems. Preening, even occasionally frantic preening, is a normal, healthy parrot behavior and should be encouraged by frequent bathing and showering. Be careful not to show alarm when your parrot is involved in normal preening activity. Showing too much concern and worry about normal preening may actually play a part in the origin of some behavioral feather picking. Over-preening, where the bird clips, breaks, or chews feathers is not a normal behavior and may be a result of illness, nutritional deficiencies, stress, poor lighting, allergies, lack of bathing opportunities, and emotional problems. These can all contribute to problems with skin health and proper feather growth. ∮

affection and nurturing focused attention when he is not plucking but ignore the actual picking process. Parrots can be highly manipulative, and if they receive attention for a behavior, they will continue it. Fussing over a parrot when he picks at his feathers almost guarantees that the behavior will become a habit.

As with all behavioral problems, treating the symptoms is less effective than solving the underlying cause. The underlying cause of most behavioral problems in companion parrots is a confused bird in control of his own life and doing a miserable job of it. With very confused or phobic birds who pluck (see next page for dealing with phobic birds), working to increase their sense of security is essential. Giving clear messages with verbal commands, and defining periods of focused attention and time in the cage for self entertainment, will help develop a sense of independence in spoiled birds. Protecting a parrot from traumatic experiences is essential; however, overprotected parrots who have not been introduced to change in safe, secure ways are often feather pickers. Gradually setting rules, providing behavioral guidance, and teaching a bird to accept change and new adventures under close supervision is imperative to their well-being. As with all behavioral problems, increased focused nurturing attention makes a world of difference in a parrot's sense of security.

Is There Hope?

Many episodes of feather destruction are stopped with dedication from a concerned owner with the right information. But even with conscientious changes and behavioral guidance, we may never be able to stop all feather destructive behavior — especially if it has become habitual. In some cases, parrots have caused follicle damage and feathers may no longer grow in severely picked areas. Even if we can't completely stop habitual feather picking, we can work to prevent it from getting worse or reaching the very frustrating level of skin mutilation. Working with behavioral pickers will usually make a significant difference, but may never completely prevent future episodic picking during times of confusion and stress. Even if your parrot may not look perfect, he is still worthy of affection and appreciation.

MOLTING

As feathers become old and worn, they are released from their follicles and new ones start to replace them (see page 137). This process is called molting (sometimes spelled moulting). Feathers are molted a few at a time in a definite, usually symmetrical, sequence so a bird can maintain proper flight and body protection. Parrots generally molt at least once a year, but the process may occur over a span of several weeks or longer. In companion parrots, molting may not follow a consistent timetable because of the artificial environment our birds live in. Certain conditions such as changes in lighting, length of day, temperature, and diet may influence the endocrine system to send a message to the body to start molting feathers. For example, a sudden increase in temperature may cause an artificial molting process to start. Other environmental and care variables may create particularly heavy molts for some parrots. Some young parrots, particularly eclectus, seem to go through heavy molts when they lose their first feathers and start to develop adult feathers. Generally speaking, it is not normal for a parrot to develop bald patches during a molt or to lose feathers too frequently.

Because several feathers are being grown at one time during a molt, a nutritious diet (particularly quality protein, calcium, and vitamin A) and good lighting are needed. If not supplied, a feather does not have the raw materials to grow properly and may have a weak shaft, stress bars, or abnormalities in the colors. Emotional stress and antibiotics given during feather growth also contribute to imperfect feathers. Extreme danger or fear may cause a fright molt which occurs when a bird loses several tail or wing feathers at one time. For example, a cockatiel in a night fright thrashing episode may lose all of his tail feathers and some of his wing feathers. Presumably, this is to avoid capture by a predator grabbing his tail or wings. If you notice an unusually heavy molt or the abnormal development of feathers on your parrot, have him examined by his avian veterinarian.

PHOBIC BEHAVIOR

"UP!"

Heartbreaking Situation

One of the most frustrating behavioral problems occurs when a previously tame and loving parrot suddenly seems to become afraid of almost everything, including his previously trusted caregivers. Most people are at a total loss about what to do because everything they do with the parrot seems to make him worse. Characteristically, the bird becomes terrified of the person he was most strongly bonded to and often transfers the bond to someone with whom he has had no relationship. Before this behavior started, the parrot did not seem to be abnormally afraid of anything. Perhaps he took awhile to get used to new toys or new situations, but there was little warning that phobic behavior would develop. **Discomfort or trepidation in unusual or threatening situations that passes fairly quickly is a relatively normal reaction with many companion parrots and is not true phobic behavior.** True phobic behavior is long-lasting, and seems to affect every aspect of the parrot's personality. As with all behavioral problems, phobic behavior is not always based on an emotional problem. It can be a sign of physical injury and illness. Phobic behavior may be an indication of a parrot being in pain. A visit with a competent avian veterinarian is always indicated with any significant change in a parrot's behavior. Make sure the veterinarian understands your parrot's situation as much as possible, so the problem is not aggravated by examination and testing.

Phobic behavior can happen with just about any companion parrot, but seems to be more common in a few species. This intense fear behavior seems to be quite rare in Amazons, although I have seen a few who were phobic. As I recall, these birds were also physically ill which was most likely a major causative factor. Phobic behavior is a little more common in macaws, but the greatest number of phobic parrots I have worked with are African Greys, Rose-breasted Cockatoos, and *Poicephalus* such as Senegals and Red-bellied Parrots. I have also worked with several other species of cockatoos whom I would also classify as phobic. Avoidance of people at all cost seems to be the norm with most phobic birds. Thrashing in the cage can cause serious injury. Often, in these birds, this fear-based behavior takes on different characteristics, with fear biting being quite common.

Sustained Trauma: A Major Behavioral Cause

I started to keep track of these phobic parrots and began to notice specific characteristics. My extensive work with phobic birds indicates a common pattern: a sustained trauma (not usually a momentary fear but one that lasts for several minutes or sometimes days) causes the parrot to go into a "prey response." The bird remains in that mode for some time, even after the traumatic situation is over. If they are approached too directly by anyone, the fear becomes even more intense. Consequently, working with them directly often intensifies the problem. Many parrots thrash in their cages if someone even makes direct eye contact with them. It is as if the people they once trusted have become predators and the birds fear for their lives. The threatened parrots avoid new situations rather than be confused or threatened by them. Because of this, some parrots only become rigidly comfortable in their cage because other situations are too threatening to them. A vicious cycle is started because the more they are allowed to stay in their cages without experiencing new situations, the more narrow what they will accept becomes. But if we try to approach them to bring them out of their cage, they can become threatened enough to thrash around the cage hurting themselves. It seems like a no-win situation.

The sudden onset of phobic behavior can be triggered by an event of sustained trauma, such as aggressive mishandling by a veterinarian or groomer, or a new situation that threatens the bird, like an earthquake and its associated aftershocks. A common scenario for phobic greys starts with a botched wing trim and/or toenails being trimmed too short. One macaw became phobic after being dropped down a flight of stairs in a travel cage. A caique became terrified when wild birds he was watching at the window feeder were captured by a Cooper's Hawk. One Senegal became terrified when his owner came home with long red fingernails after a manicure. In a situation with a young African Grey, the teenage friends of the owner's son teased the grey while they tried to feed him french fries. A Scarlet Macaw went into extreme fear posture for several days and would not eat when a brightly-colored abstract painting was hung next to his cage. Once the painting was removed, the macaw quickly returned to normal. However, sometimes the triggers are far more subtle. A change in the caregiver's appearance may also trigger phobic behavior but minor changes such as this act only as a trigger and not the underlying cause of phobic behavior. In many cases, the owner could not think of a specific traumatic event or change.

A Serious Problem With Poorly Socialized Domestically-raised Parrots

Many parrots who become phobic are *accidents waiting to happen*, often because of poor early socialization or deprivation weaning. These are contributing factors (not inclusive) for insecurities, especially when the birds begin to reach their independent stages. Certainly, a lack of guidance and the inconsistency it creates are also contributing factors. It is sad to think of the number of parrots who have gone through this type of personality change. I wish I had the definitive answer as to why some parrots suddenly become phobic when others do not. I doubt if there is just one reason. There are most likely several factors that play a part in the development of phobic behaviors in parrots. First, we have to understand that parrots are prey animals, which means they are attacked and eaten by other animals. This means a parrot who is exposed to a traumatic situation may become threatened enough to go into a *prey response* of extreme fear. Some parrots quickly get over this mode of behavior once the traumatic situation is over, while others remain afraid and even become threatened by aspects of their life that were previously reassuring. Strongly bonded young parrots look towards their human flock to protect them. If a traumatic situation occurs, the young bird may perceive a betrayal of trust from a person he previously trusted.

There are many aspects to raising parrot chicks in captivity that either encourage or diminish their pet potential. Nurturing is teaching with reassurance. Quality early socialization, gradual weaning and abundant feeding, and allowing a parrot to fledge before wing clipping all encourage a sense of security in a chick. Another possible explanation for phobic behavior is poor early socialization. Well-socialized parrots have a strong sense of security and curiosity and rarely become phobic because they have learned to adapt to changes in their environment. A poorly socialized parrot reacts instinctively with fear because he has not been taught to accept change in his environment. The instinctive reaction is normally to fly away but a parrot in a cage can not flee — they can only throw themselves around the cage in fear. Parrots are highly intelligent animals who depend on their parents and/or others in the flock to teach them their survival and social skills. In the wild, a young parrot who does not learn and develop these skills does not survive.

For domestically-raised chicks, this early learning process is just as essential and, in many ways, even more complex. Parrots who are not guided from the time they are very young to adapt to life as a human companion will be at a total loss about how to behave. Life as a pet is in conflict with most of their natural instinctive behaviors. Many poorly socialized companion parrots end up living in confusion because of the conflict between their natural behavior and the alien environment they live in with us. Consequently, if they do not receive early socialization in the form of consistent guidance and instructional attention, they are unable to adapt well to life in our living room.

"You know, Pop ... It's not the flying part that's hard. It's the landing that hurts!"

I believe that some species of parrots simply do not adjust well to life in pet situations unless their sense of independence is developed through quality early socialization. Young parrots usually develop a strong bond to the person they perceive as parenting them. As the bird matures, during his independence stages, it is natural for this strong parental bond to lessen. While many species of wild parrots grow up in strong familial units with extensive parental care, others do not seem to form or maintain strong bonds with their biological parents in the wild. This is true of Rose-breasted Cockatoos and may be true of several *Poicephalus* species, including the Senegal. Even as handfed babies, these species may have negative reactions if people put too much pressure on them to form and maintain a strong bond. This may be why they transfer their favorite person status so quickly to someone who has paid them little attention.

Using *Nurturing Submission* To Win Back Trust

I have had good success in working with phobic parrots. This success rate is, of course, much better if the caregivers have exceptional patience and believe they can make a difference without giving up just because there are occasional setbacks. It may take weeks or months to win a phobic parrot's trust again but it is worth the effort. There are ways to work with phobic parrots to gradually regain their trust. Since these birds seem to view the people they are afraid of as predators, the key is to be indirect and nonthreatening. In most situations, I recommend that people in the phobic bird's life start responding to their parrot in a very submissive manner to encourage his security. I worked with one phobic Rose-breasted Cockatoo who had not allowed anyone to come near him for months. After just a few minutes of indirect submissive contact, he ran across the bed and onto my shoulder. I was a stranger with no history with him and it took much longer for his owners to win his trust, but it was a good start. The purpose of the following exercises are to invite a phobic parrot back into your life, making it his idea to come to you rather than something you are making him do.

⮑ Phobic parrots are much more likely to trust you if you allow them to initiate contact. Do not approach your parrot directly or try to make him come out of his cage.

⮑ Always try to calm yourself before you approach your parrot. Move very slowly and speak softly.

⮑ Approach the parrot with head bowed and do not make direct eye contact.

⮑ If you need to make direct eye contact with your phobic parrot, lower your head to show submission. Do not keep your eyes directly on your parrot for more than a few seconds at a time.

⮑ Sit or kneel down when you need to change his food or water so you are not towering over him.

⮑ Sit by his cage and hum, whisper, or sing without looking at him.

⮑ Sit in front of his cage with the door open, lean against the cage, and read a book or magazine. Be patient. The goal is to subtly invite him to join you without being direct.

⮑ Use your *peripheral consciousness*. Observe him with your peripheral vision rather than looking right at him.

⮑ Often, even after a few days of interacting in this manner a few times a day, the parrot should begin to be more relaxed with you nearby because you are not making any demands on him.

⮑ Many parrots will then venture out of their cage and even onto your arm or leg. Stay calm and relaxed and continue to respond in an indirect manner. If you move too quickly and frighten him back into his cage, be very patient. Go back to square one and start the process again.

⮑ Continued patience and time will eventually return your phobic parrot's trust to you. Even so, continue to go slowly.

⮑ While it is possible to get a phobic parrot past his loss of trust, once he can be worked with again, care should be taken to gradually and safely introduce him to change so that he doesn't have such severe reactions to new situations in his life. Start slowly so you don't overwhelm him. Play *Real Estate Agent* (pg. 104) with him. On a very gradual level take him into new areas so that he experiences safe adventures with your constant reassurance. Gradually and patiently replace *Nurturing Submission* with the principles of *Nurturing Guidance* so your parrot starts to look to you in a positive manner for behavioral cues in his life. Interact with him as calmly as possible.

⮑ Once a parrot has exhibited phobic behavior, avoid situations which could cause this response again. Be his protector and do your best to prevent traumatic or threatening experiences or sudden changes in his life. ⁄

WHEN NURTURING GUIDANCE

Understanding Why

Working successfully to change negative parrot behavior is a process of doing the right things consistently for long enough to make a difference. I am always delighted to hear that my theories of *Nurturing Guidance* and focused attention have helped people to understand and work with their parrots. Feedback about the effectiveness of my techniques is extremely important for me so that I can continue to develop my ideas to help both parrots and people. I know from working with hundreds of people and their parrots that the techniques I use do make a significant difference in improving parrot pet potential.

My goal has always been to teach people to understand how their parrot *ticks* — WHY he does the things he does and WHY people need to relate to their parrots in a specific manner to create positive pet potential. If people understand the basics of companion parrot behavior, they will see patterns and will learn to interact with their parrots in an enlightened manner. They will usually also be able to figure out for themselves how to deal with new problems if they arise. An obvious example is in understanding that a great many behavioral problems start when a parrot is not getting the level of attention he is used to. Knowing this, the human flock can increase the level of focused attention and instructional interaction and see almost immediate positive results. Once people understand and implement the basics, they will be happier with their parrots and the parrots will be happier with them.

Following Advice

One of the most frustrating aspects of doing consultations is when I can tell that bird owners won't follow the advice I provide them. In some cases, people are very direct. One man with a phobic Rose-breasted bluntly told me, "I can tell you right now, I won't do that!" He wanted a miracle that would restore his cockatoo's pet potential but wasn't willing to do any of the work. He wanted me to handle his cockatoo so that she would be tame again and refused to understand that being handled by a stranger would frighten her making the problem worse instead of solving her phobic behavior. He was angry with me because I did not provide him with the ultimate quick-fix. It seems he had purchased the bird primarily because the galah matched the color scheme of his house. Eventually, he sold the bird to a pet shop where she died a few months later.

Sometimes people call me for a follow-up consultation and report that nothing has worked. When I talk to them, I find out that they only worked with the problem for a few days and when nothing seemed to change, they quit. In other cases, people call me for advice, then call a few dozen other people, then ask for help on the Internet. They follow a little bit of my advice and a little bit from all the other people. When I talk to someone who says they have tried EVERYTHING, I become particularly concerned. Even if they were on the right track, they are not consistent enough for a long enough time to make a positive difference. Trying a little bit of everything for a short time can be far more confusing to a companion parrot than not doing anything to work with negative behavior.

Therefore, if you choose to work with a specific avian behavioral consultant, evaluate his or her advice carefully. If it is logical, trust-building information which does not rely on quick-fixes, then follow that advice exclusively for long enough to give it a chance to work. Do not mix and match other people's theories and advice (even if it seems similar) during this period. Only after spending the time and energy to really give it a chance, if it doesn't seem to work, then go ahead and consult with another knowledgeable behavioral consultant.

DOESN'T SEEM TO WORK

Testing, Patterning, And The Desire For Normalcy

Parrots are creatures of habit and patterning. They may go along with a new behavioral protocol for a while, perhaps because it seems novel to them. But often, after a few days or weeks, parrots want to go back to what seems normal. Parrots simply do not understand what is best for them in the long run. They become stubborn and they may balk at your requests for behavioral changes. Sometimes a parrot's behavior actually gets worse before it improves. A bird allowed to establish his own behavioral rules may test you to make sure you are an adequate flock leader, because your adequacy is the only reason he would rightly follow your behavioral cues. During times of testing, you must remain consistent and continue to work through the problems. Unfortunately, many people decide at this time that what they are doing is not working (or in some cases seems to be making the parrot's behavior worse) so they give up just before a major breakthrough occurs.

Changing behavior on a permanent basis is not a linear process. It rarely proceeds from step-one to step-two to step-three, and so on. Working with negative behavior in parrots is usually a two steps forward, one (two, three, four?) steps backward proposition. It is only in hindsight, after the goals have been achieved, that people can really see they were making progress all along, despite setbacks along the way.

Limitations In Human Behavior

Many people are, for one reason or another, clearly unable to work successfully with their parrot's negative behaviors. Some people have an investment in the drama of a parrot that bites and screams. Perhaps having a parrot pushes their own *behavioral buttons* that they have not been able to conquer. The *FooFoo*-type person who refuses to set rules, or the *Macho* types who must dominate aggressively, will not know what it is like to have a mutual bond with a parrot. The *Collector* who goes from one parrot to another will also never be able to fully understand the individual needs and personalities of their parrots. The ego-invested *Know-it-all* will not be able to understand that learning about parrots is ongoing and can make a significant difference in the quality of his relationship with his parrots. People who do not accept responsibility for their own lack of behavioral guidance or aggressiveness towards their parrot, and blame the bird for his misbehavior, will never make progress with changing their pet's negative behavior.

Some problems within the human flock may not be easily alleviated. Bad marriages, a stressful job, family illness, uncontrollable kids, or a boyfriend or wife who hates birds can all contribute to the misery level of a companion parrot. One couple I worked with was clearly using their parrot as a way to communicate their anger with each other. The woman was delighted when her cockatoo chased her husband out of the room, and the man was equally passive aggressive with his Amazon's behavior toward his wife. In another relationship, the husband clearly teased the parrot to make him scream so he could complain to his wife about the noise the bird made. The problem in these situations is not the parrot's behavior — but is it my place to recommend a psychologist or a marriage counselor?

Parrots are capable of learning throughout their entire lives. Changing our behavior and our interaction with them is the first step in having well-behaved lifelong companion parrots. Working with parrot behavior can be a challenging experience but the rewards for a job well done are clearly worth it! From my personal experience, I can assure you, there is nothing quite like a positive lifelong relationship with a companion parrot.

PsittaSitaShoulda
Facial Protector

Stay Close To Your Parrot Without Worrying About Your Facial Security

**From *T-Joy*
The Name
You Trust In
Parrot Products!**

➤ Snug Fit Adjustable Chin Strap
➤ Bulletproof Lucite Facial Guard
➤ No-Grip Helmet (Space Age Materials)
➤ Detachable Dual Parrot Rear Baffle
➤ Busy-a-Bird Toy Hanger On Each Side
➤ Dual Sound Muffler Stereo Earphones
➤ Non-stick Sharkmesh Shoulder Apron
➤ Non-skid Perch Platform On Each Shoulder
➤ Optional Scataguard Protects Clothes (not shown)

SMB

Chapter Ten:
A FEW IMPORTANT ARTICLES

Nurturing Guidance Tip: Use Common Sense

Get The Right Information

Using common sense is one of the most significant factors involved in having a wonderful companion parrot. Whenever you plan a certain action or adventure with your parrot, make sure you think about it ahead of time — "What would happen if I did this?" "What could go wrong?" "Could my bird react in a negative way to this new adventure?" "How do I make this as safe as possible for my parrot?"

There are a number of misconceptions within the parrot literature and people's personal knowledge about parrots. Many of the books on the market contain misinformation or seriously outdated information. Learn to judge the information you read or hear. Before you follow any advice, stop and think whether it makes sense or not. Again, common sense plays a very important role in deciding which advice you will follow or ignore. Think about all behavioral information from the viewpoint of whether it is trust-building or trust-destroying. Most of all, think about advice carefully before you choose to follow it!

COMMON PARROT MYTHS:

⊃ **MYTH • Parrots are "hard-wired" and early socialization is insignificant to their early development.** What a breeder/handfeeder does or does not do has great significance in the personality development and pet potential of a chick. Quality early socialization makes an extremely significant difference in the behavioral development of a young parrot. The absolute biological proof of this is the fact that wild parrot chicks have a long maturation process which involves extensive nurturing and parenting. Without the lessons learned from their parents, they would not survive.

⊃ **MYTH • All ____ are ____.** (Fill in the blanks with any parrot species and any trait.) Stereotypical generalizations rarely apply, because the pet potential of any parrot species depends on the individual traits of each individual bird and the way he is raised and behaviorally maintained. For example, according to stereotypical generalizations, all cockatoos are noisy. Some are, but there are also quiet cockatoo individuals. Not all Moluccans are needy — if raised properly, they can be quite independent. Not all Amazons become aggressive as they mature — some are *love sponges* throughout their lives. Not all greys are excellent cognitive talkers, but some certainly are, especially if they have owners who provide instructional attention. I get tired of hearing how "neurotic" greys are — phobic behavior and feather picking is not a consideration with the vast majority of <u>properly socialized</u> and well-cared for greys. Not every scarlet macaw is aggressive. Not all Hyacinth Macaws are *gentle giants*. Not all *Pionus* are quiet. I could go on listing generalizations for pages … each parrot is an individual influenced by the people in his or her life.

⊃ **MYTH • You have to handfeed a baby parrot for it to properly bond to you.** If bappies are well socialized and learn to trust from gentle and frequent handling, they will transfer their bond to anyone who handles them confidently and comfortably. Handfeeding by inexperienced novices can create serious problems which can seriously damage the potential parrot/human bond. Even worse, an inexperienced handfeeder may create serious health problems for his new baby parrot including, but not limited to, crop burn, aspiration, puncturing of the throat, bacterial infection, fungal infection, malnutrition, dehydration, starvation, and even death.

⊃ **MYTH • You should not pay any more attention to a baby parrot than you will for the rest of his life.** This is nonsense. Baby parrots absolutely need more reassurance through instructional attention and guidance to develop their personality and pet potential. Not giving them proper socialization will limit pet potential. *It is not the amount of time spent with chicks that spoils them; it is what is done during that time.* If baby parrots are just cuddled for hours, they will be spoiled. Time must be spent playing with baby parrots in an instructional manner which develops their independence and pet potential.

⊃ **MYTH • Getting another parrot to keep the first one company will make life easier for people.** It is a fact that two birds are always more difficult to care for than one. In many cases, it is also harder to keep two parrots tame if they are living together and form a strong bond with each other. If continued pet potential is desired from two parrots who relate to each other daily, it will be essential for caregivers to establish and maintain strong *Nurturing Guidance*. Each bird must be given consistent, focused, individual attention plus time together with the people in his life.

WHY THEY DON'T MAKE SENSE

➲ **MYTH • Once a parrot bonds to someone, this exclusive bond lasts forever.** Most parrots in the wild form different levels of bonding with other parrots. Stronger bonds are with parents, siblings, and then later, with mates. Looser bonds occur within the family group, the juvenile flock, and with other flock members. Companion parrots are capable of bonding to different people on different levels throughout their lives. Some parrots are monogamous — but some may be monogamous in the same sense that human beings are ... and we all know what that means.

➲ **MYTH • Change is bad for companion parrots and should be avoided if at all possible.** It is not change that causes problems for parrots — it is sudden, unexpected change that a parrot has not been prepared for that creates problems. Parrots are usually most concerned with changes made in their cage and other perceived territory. They also often have a negative response when one of their human flock members changes his or her appearance or attitude. More problems occur if a person sets a rigid routine and tries to protect his parrot from any change at all. Change is inevitable in life, and if a parrot is prepared ahead of time for any change in his territory or routine, and treated with patience during the change, there should be few problems. Well-socialized parrots who have had their sense of adventure developed when they were young and maintained by their human flock rarely have problems with change in their lives.

➲ **MYTH • You ALWAYS need to be the boss.** If aggression, confrontation, stubbornness, and rigidity are used to control a parrot and to force him to comply with demands, the trusting bond a parrot develops with his owner can be seriously damaged. While it is essential for a person to guide his parrot's behavior, the concept of total dominance can be trust-destroying, especially with sensitive parrots and birds who begin to exhibit phobic behavior. With more secure parrots, dominating confrontive behavior on the part of the person may bring out aggression in the parrot.

➲ **MYTH • Parrots give their caregivers unconditional love.** Generally not true. People have to provide consistent nurturing affection and attention to win and maintain the trust of a parrot. There is no love or bond without trust. Mistreatment and/or neglect quickly damages the trust and bond parrots have with their human family.

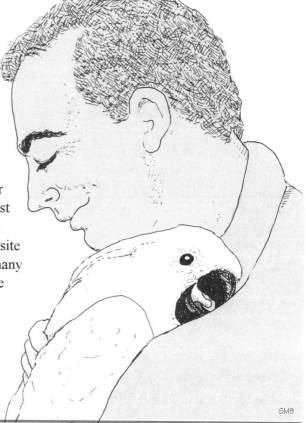

➲ **MYTH • Male parrots bond to women and female parrots bond to men.** This generalization is nonsense! One absolute rule of parrot behavior is that parrots are more comfortable with people who are comfortable with them. Any gender preferences may be formed because of the people parrots are most used to being handled by when they are young. However, if they are then gently and comfortably handled by a person of the opposite gender, the bond can be transferred easily. I have worked with many parrots who are considered women's birds who learn to enjoy the company of men who work to win their trust and vice versa.

➲ **MYTH • People should not groom their own parrots or the birds will hate them.** It is not grooming which threatens a parrot's sense of security. It is the manner in which they are handled. Once a person learns non-aggressive handling, toweling, and grooming techniques, and becomes calm and confident grooming his parrot, there will be no threat to the relationship he has with his parrot.

⊃ **MYTH • Quick-fix punishments stop problem behaviors.** While quick-fixes may distract a parrot momentarily from negative behavior, they will not teach the parrot anything that will change his behavior on a long-term basis. Working patiently and consistently with the underlying causes is the only way to change negative behaviors.

⊃ **MYTH • When parrots become sexually mature, they no longer make good pets and need to be put into a breeding program.** This myth is absolute nonsense, perhaps perpetuated by aspects of the pet industry who want either to sell you a new bird or want yours for their breeding programs. People who are willing to work with their parrots can create contented lifelong companions. A well-socialized, well-loved companion parrot whose owner has established positive rules and guidance rarely becomes so difficult that he or she no longer has pet potential. While some parrots may become more difficult for a few weeks or so each year, for a few years, the knowledgeable bird owner can learn how to deal with these periods of time.

⊃ **MYTH • Parrots who are sexually mature are *happier* in breeding situations.** It depends on the parrot and it depends on the breeding situation. Many companion parrots who exhibit sexual behavior do so because of the strong bond they have with their owners. This does not mean they want to raise babies, and many of these parrots are not happy if they lose their human flock. Some breeding situations do not take proper care of their parrots. Many companion parrots exhibit sexual behavior because of their relationship with the people in their lives — not because they want a parrot mate. Many successful companion parrots are unhappy in breeding programs.

⊃ **MYTH • Once a parrot starts to exhibit problems, the problems can't be solved.** Parrots are capable of learning throughout their lives and, therefore, with consistent instructional attention, even the most entrenched behaviors can be worked with and changed ... but only if the person is willing to change his behaviors first.

⊃ **MYTH • Biting is a natural aggressive behavior in parrots.** Most wild parrots will bluff and strut long before they resort to using their beaks as weapons. People often unwittingly teach their parrots to bite. Pet parrots usually bite only when they have no other means to communicate or when their initial explorative chewing behavior is reinforced in an aggressive way by people.

⊃ **MYTH • Don't let a baby parrot touch your skin with his beak or he will become a biter.** This black-and-white generalization denies a companion parrot's ability to give affection.

⊃ **MYTH • If finger chewing and beak exploration are not stopped, the parrot will turn into an aggressive biter.** Beak exploration and aggressive biting are two entirely different behaviors. A parrot's highly sensitive beak and tongue are used to explore and even give affection. Young parrots who chew too hard should be quietly told to be gentle or given a foot toy to chew on, but never punished for exploring with their beaks.

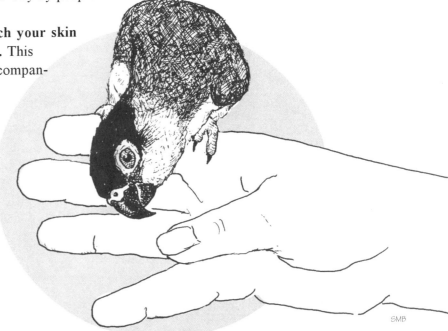

⊃ **MYTH · Breeding birds do not need toys.** To deprive parrots of behavioral enrichment and/or play objects (also defined as toys) because of the mistaken belief that play objects will keep the pair from breeding is absolute nonsense. Exercise, stimulation, and activity are essential to all captive parrots whether they are breeding birds or not. Aviculturists who provide their breeding pairs with behavioral enrichment, including toys, report having better success with breeding and much more contentment in their aviaries than before toys were introduced.

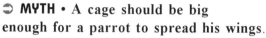

⊃ **MYTH · A cage should be big enough for a parrot to spread his wings**. Cages should be larger than just a parrot's wingspan. Cage size should be determined not only by the size of the bird, but also by his energy level. High energy parrot-family birds such as parrotlets, caiques, lories, and the small cockatoos need larger cages in proportion to their size.

⊃ **MYTH · Dominance is the only way to control a parrot.** If being dominant involves aggressive and/or confrontational behavior towards the parrot, it creates more problems than it solves. *Nurturing Guidance* does not involve aggression. The key to having a successful relationship with a parrot is to create and maintain trust.

⊃ **MYTH · Techniques for training parrots for bird shows such as operant conditioning, clicker training, food deprivation, and food reward are the best ways to work with problem behaviors and teach companion parrots to do tricks.** The basic concepts of rewarding positive behavior and ignoring negative behavior can be effective in working with companion parrots. In some ways, teaching a behavior can be similar to teaching a trick. However, some techniques used in training may not consider the complexities of the relationship between a companion parrot and the people in his life. Food and attention deprivation techniques are trust-destroying and should not be considered by pet owners. Operant conditioning tools such as clicker training can work in a companion parrot situation as long as people understand and take the unique characteristics of the animal they are working with into consideration. Often, it is actually the increase in focused attention which brings about change in the companion parrot and not simply the method of training.

⊃ **MYTH · It is anthropomorphic to believe parrots are sentient, cognitive, or feel emotions.** Anyone who has lived with a companion parrot realizes they are clearly aware of their environment and understand much of what goes on in it. Also obvious is the appropriate manner in which parrots use words and phrases. Anthropomorphism is defined as giving animals human characteristics. However, it is clearly not anthropomorphic to describe parrots using behavioral traits which they clearly possess. The cry of anthropomorphism often seems to be an excuse some people use to treat parrots in a less than humane manner.

⊃ **MYTH · Parrots are "easy-care" pets.** I have lived with parrots for over twenty years and find them to be the most complex animals I have ever shared my life with. Parrots have complicated behavioral needs. While there is little that is easy about living with a companion parrot, the more work you do, the easier it gets. People who do not take the time and energy to create the proper behavioral guidance will probably never know how pleasurable living with a parrot can be. People who are up to the challenge will have a successful relationship with their companion parrots. They are the ones who reap the rewards! ♪

DON'T SPOIL YOUR NEW BAPPY

Too Many Generalizations

As a generalization, parrots who are family pets have a reputation for two traits. One is being "love sponges" who crave and need to be constantly attached like velcro to their owners. The flip side of this generalization is that, if this constant craving is not indulged, they turn into demanding, screaming, biting monsters who drive their human family to the brink of insanity. While there can certainly be some truth to both of these beliefs, whether a parrot fits these stereotypes depends on two factors. The first is the way they have been raised, and the second is the ability of the owner to establish and maintain the guidance that encourages independence in these intelligent birds. Because of the high-production ethic of bird breeding (which includes poor socialization and lack of nurturing) used by too many breeders, a good number of parrots of all species being raised today are actually being raised to be extremely needy. For some time now there has been an absurd philosophy that since parrots can easily become overdependent, it is best to ignore them when they are babies so they become used to this level of little attention and, therefore, will not demand attention as they mature. This is absolute non-sense! I have no patience for the breeders who excuse their production mentality with, "I have too many babies to spend all that time with each one." I have also often heard of breeders who state, "Oh, I don't give them any attention when they are young because I don't want to spoil them (or I don't want them bonding to me so they won't bond to the new owner)." This is some of the most convoluted, erroneous thinking I have ever heard. The result of this lack of nurturing is actually the exact opposite — parrots who have been production-raised with little handling or nurturing usually become very needy and develop serious behavioral problems as they reach their independence stages.

Nothing But "Cuddly Love Sponges?"

Add to this scenario the stereotypical thinking which often mistakenly attracts many people to some species of parrots as pets — the belief that they are all simply cuddly "love sponges" who will always stay that way. Even the most dedicated parrot owner will not be able to tolerate a bird hanging off of him 24 hours a day, 7 days a week, 4 weeks a month, 12 months a year. The problem is that once parrots are raised to be overdependent, they will do almost anything to maintain that level of interaction. If there is a significant decrease in the attention they receive or their owners simply become impatient with their continual demands, the results can include serious behavioral problems, such as excessive screaming and/or whining, aggression as a reaction to unrealistic needs unmet, and in some parrots, behavioral feather picking. In extreme cases, the sense of abandonment or "betrayal" can turn into life-threatening self-mutilation. There are cases of Umbrella and Moluccan Cockatoos who seem to prolapse their cloacas (see glossary) for attention. Most parrots are very intelligent, and this intelligence can be channeled into extremely manipulative behavior. One of the criteria some animal behaviorists use to determine the intelligence of an animal is its ability to deceive other animals. If an animal is capable of improvising and changing its behavior to deceive another, it clearly has a certain level of sentient awareness. Parrots clearly improvise and change their behavior in ways which manipulate their owners.

Sally Blanchard's COMPANION PARROT HANDBOOK

Using this criterion, many parrots can be judged as quite intelligent. Once a parrot perceives he can receive attention, or even a negative drama reward, from the owner for certain behaviors, that behavior is not only likely to continue, it is likely to escalate. Perhaps initially there was a direct emotional or physical cause-and-effect for a certain behavior. The young bird could have been calling to the owner because he was hungry or frightened, but once the owner begins to respond inappropriately, the bird learns to make the same noises to receive attention or drama rather than food or safety from a feared situation. The initial reason is obscured but the attention-getting behavior continues. Likewise, if a parrot has a small injury and every time he picks at it his owner comes running over to admonish the bird for bothering the area, the smart bird puts 2 and 2 together. The resulting skin mutilation may seem to add up to 3 or 5 to us, but the continued and escalated mutilation of the injured area got attention results for the parrot. As intelligent as a parrot may be, there is not necessarily a logical cause-and-effect as we understand it. We can't expect more awareness from a parrot than we can from a person and, of course, many humans also indulge in self-destructive behaviors regardless of the fact they may make no sense if we think about them logically.

Handfeeding Traumas

A psychologically healthy parrot is one who is secure. A needy parrot is too involved trying to get his needs met to become independent. Some parrots, such as macaws, greys, eclectus, and cockatoos are particularly affected by handfeeding and weaning traumas. Production feeding techniques are creating parrots who often have serious eating disorders. Owners often use the term anorexia when referring to their cockatoos whom they can not get to eat properly. Whether this term is appropriate or not, sometimes it seems like an uphill battle to get young cockatoos to eat anything. Traumatic handfeeding situations, such as gavage (tube) feeding into the crop, forced weaning using deprivation techniques at an arbitrarily early age, and poor nutrition, can play havoc with a young parrot's sense of security. I receive far too many calls from parrot owners with supposedly weaned birds who won't eat and food beg all of the time. Food begging involves wing flicking, head bobbing, *gronking* or whining, and crying. One cockatoo breeder referred to this behavior as "singing," but believe me, these are not happy cockatoos. In some cases, the whining birds were gavage fed until they were forced to wean, a situation which creates a parrot who has not learned proper food manipulation. The new owner, after calling the breeder or pet shop for help, is often told that certain parrots are not big eaters anyway, and then often receives the admonishment, "You don't want to spoil him; he is weaned. Whatever you do, don't start handfeeding him again or he will demand that you feed him for the rest of his life, and you will never be able to wean him again." I have read books and articles that advise parrot owners to set up rigid food timetables and never feed their pets away from the cage or they will become spoiled. This is nonsense. While it may be true to some extent that many parrots will accept or even demand syringe feeding well into adulthood, all of above bad advice just perpetuates the parrot's insecurity.

Increasing a young parrot's sense of security has nothing to do with spoiling him! Even if the youngster is already eating some food on his own, for a whining food-begging bappy I always recommend some sort of "regression weaning." The purpose of regression weaning is not just to get food into a bird; it is also to encourage a better sense of security. Although I may recommend using a syringe or spoon again for relatively young birds, this does not necessarily mean returning to the handfeeding which causes the bird to pump for food. It may just mean squirting or even drizzling pureed sweet potato baby food into his open beak. I suggest finger feeding soft, warm globs of food several times a day if possible. Warm cooked yams, oatmeal, a quality commercial parrot cooking mixture, or my glop recipe work well. These birds should also be fed from a large crock full of a variety of nutritious foods. Some parrots seem to eat more readily if their crock is conveniently placed on the floor of their cage. Teach the bappy to play with and manipulate his foods. Let him watch as you take pieces of vegetable, move them around in his dish, pull them apart, and eat some of them yourself. Be patient. It may take some time for the bird to accept being fed from your fingers. ·····➔

The Detrimental Effects Of Gavage Feeding

In many cases, especially with birds who have been gavage fed, young birds will have to be taught to manipulate their food. Gavage feeding involves placing a tube directly into the crop and injecting the food into the bird. This technique is often used by production-type bird breeders for its speed and convenience. There is absolutely no justification for routine gavage feeding as a benefit for the bappy. This technique teaches a young bird nothing about eating or manipulating food. Of course, since he never has food in his beak or mouth, he never gets to taste it, chew it with his beak, move it around with his tongue, or swallow it. While I think routine gavage feeding of baby parrots for expediency is detrimental for their proper development, occasionally a baby parrot will have to be gavage fed temporarily for one reason or another (illness, medication, getting past a difficult period of time, etc.). Therefore, it is necessary for handfeeders to understand how to use the technique safely, properly, and appropriately.

Although eating is certainly a natural enough behavior, aspects of eating such as making good food choices and consistently good eating behaviors are partly learned. Consequently, it is critical for a baby parrot to learn to manipulate food and eat securely on his own before he will become secure enough to accept a sense of independence from his owners. Macaws, cockatoos, and greys seem particularly sensitive to handfeeding trauma. Many macaws who have been gavage fed to weaning tend to food beg incessantly, and these insecure behaviors may be transferred from begging for food to begging for attention as the birds mature. Cockatoos who have been gavage fed to weaning may become almost anorexic in their eating habits and caregivers can have serious problems with them not becoming food independent. These insecure parrots need to be finger fed soft warm globs of food to familiarize them with eating and the pleasure of food.

Love Takes Work

Once a young parrot begins to feel secure around food issues, it is important to work with his sense of independence. The generalization that parrots, particularly cockatoos, are all overdependent only becomes true because people do not work with them to encourage independence. It is not the amount of time spent with parrots which spoils them, it is what is done in that time. Parrot cuddle time is essential, but cuddling alone without nurturing for independence will create spoiled, demanding companions.

Don't let anyone try to convince you it does not take work to raise and maintain a well-behaved parrot, but those people who live with them rarely think of the time and energy they spend setting rules and providing guidance as "work." Love takes work, but when love exists, somehow the work comes naturally and does not seem to be a chore.

Love without respect for an animal's basic needs and future success is just not good enough. Nurturing is not just providing physical affection; it involves teaching and parenting. From the time a young handfed bird reaches what Phoebe Linden calls the "peeking out stage," his behavioral development is greatly influenced by interaction with people. This is the stage where a wild parrot would start to explore and head towards the light at the opening of the nest cavity. Encouraged by the parents, the rapidly-growing baby starts the adventure which leads towards independence months later. Just as the wild parents gradually encourage independence in their chicks, the people in the young companion bird's life must also provide guidance. Although companion parrots will always be dependent on humans for their care, feeding, and emotional needs, it is critical for them to learn that their entire existence does not revolve around interaction with the people in their lives. They need to become secure with adventure, and must learn to initiate their own healthy self-stimulation and to keep themselves entertained.

Highly Active Birds

Our captive-reared first, second, and usually at the most, third generation pets are genetically programmed the same as their wild counterparts. In their natural habitat, parrots are very busy birds, spending much of the day foraging for food, interacting with their mates and flock, and reacting to the happenings in their environment. Wild parrots are constantly bombarded with stimulation and it keeps them active and on their toes. In contrast, the activity level of our pets may not even come close to filling their need for stimulation. This discrepancy and the need for almost constant stimulation is one of the reasons parrots develop so many behavioral problems in captivity. Screaming, feather picking, and even self-mutilation can have much of their basis in a parrot's natural need to be stimulated. We must develop healthy ways to keep companion parrots busy, but these ways should only include interaction with us part of the time. Providing a varied diet with some high activity foods (peas in the pod, well-cooked corn on the cob, Brussels sprouts, pomegranates, broccoli flowerets, greens laced through the cage bars, nuts in the shell, occasional fresh coconut still attached to the shell, etc.), a large cage with multiple perches and swings, multiple playgyms and climbing perches, a great number of preening, *chew 'em up*, and puzzle toys, safe branches with leaves, wadded paper and cardboard to shred, lots of bathing opportunities, radio and TV, and whatever busy activities you can think of will go a long way to keeping a parrot stimulated.

Keep in mind that not all parrot species react to stimulation in the same manner. Some birds, such as the macaws, African Greys, eclectus, as well as Sulphur-crested, Umbrella, and Moluccan Cockatoos generally have a long attention span for puzzle-type toys that require a longer focus, while the smaller conures, Bare-eyed and Rose-breasted Cockatoos, and other high-energy birds seem to enjoy a tremendous variety of stimulating projects where they can go from one to the other. Pay attention to your parrot to see how he likes to play and encourage his particular play tendencies.

At first it may be important to share these adventures with him so that he learns how much fun they can be and gradually partakes in them by himself. Another valuable concept in dealing with parrot behavior is understanding the different levels of attention. This is not a black-and-white issue with the only alternatives being constant, in-your-face focused attention or no attention at all. There are also varying degrees of what I refer to as ambient and casual attention. This is the time spent with the bird in the cage while you are in the room, on the play gym with your supervision, or on the arm of the couch with you sitting next to the bird. You can be a part of his flock without him being on you. Look up now and then and talk to him as he plays. Tell him how great, handsome, beautiful, clever, etc., he is. In all of these situations, occasional verbal interaction can add to a parrot's sense of security.

Teaching A Secure Sense Of Independence

From the time the bappy starts exploring, his sense of adventure should be encouraged. It is, however, essential to provide guidelines and boundaries to the adventures. *Nurturing Guidance* is based on providing these guidelines which add security and take away confusion from a young bird who only knows to follow his instinctive behavioral messages. These instinctive behaviors simply do not work in a pet situation, and we can override these nonproductive behaviors with non-aggressive guidance. Many simple activities and exercises encourage independence and healthy self-stimulation in parrots. Using consistent basic verbal commands such as "UP" and "DOWN" establishes our position of "flock leaders" so the young bird acknowledges our guidance. From the time a parrot starts flapping his wings in earnest, I recommend an exercise I call "real estate agent." This involves taking the bird from room to room. Set him down in safe but unfamiliar locations and reassure him by saying, "you're OK." As he becomes used to the new location, provide him with something to do (a nut to chew on, a toy to play with) and walk away a few steps at a time, providing him with continual reassurance that he is OK. Once he becomes comfortable in safe new areas and starts to nonchalantly eat his treat or play with his toy, your continued reassurance will not be necessary. This exercise patterns him to know that he is safe in different areas without being in physical contact with you.

·····➤

Nurturing time out of the cage with the human flock is essential, but it is also important for a parrot to learn it is all right to be in his cage even if you are nearby. The rule "don't ever pay attention to a screaming bird" needs qualification. If the youngster calls to you, don't just ignore him. Make sure his basic needs have been met. For a bird who is already food independent, these needs are basically water and healthy food in the cage, lots of nurturing attention, a nonthreatening environment, and things to keep him active. If these needs have been met, and he is just looking for time with you, reassure him verbally from whereever you are that he is OK. Don't make him into a magician by magically appearing at his cage front every time he calls for you. Reassuring him by simply returning his contact call teaches him that "ambient" attention is also a time he is secure and loved.

In-Your-Face Time Is Important Too!

Even well-socialized parrots with a healthy sense of independence usually have strong needs for affection. Never punish your bird by depriving him of attention. A parrot who receives little or no physical handling or affection is very needy and insecure, especially if he has been used to this attention in the past. Depriving a parrot of such an integral part of his basic needs creates a vicious circle wherein he becomes increasingly demanding, using any method which seems to work to get his demands met. Consistent, predictable, defined, daily in-your-face attention is one of the best ways to encourage the security which leads to independence. Bring him out with the "UP" command, and tell him what you are going to do. Take a walk around the house with him; let him help you sort the mail (they love this one — finally a use for all that junk mail!); share your favorite music, dancing, and singing with him; watch television with him sharing the plot of the show. Take a short afternoon nap together, but don't fall asleep and roll over on him. And by all means, at least once a day (more if possible) go to the cage, announce your presence, and bring your parrot out with the "UP" command for a wonderful, indulgent cuddle-fest and skritching session. He will love it and it will probably lower your blood pressure.

Not The Parrot's Fault

Can an older, already overdependent parrot be retrained to be independent? I believe the answer is usually yes, but it takes a great deal of change in the owners' behavior first. After all, it is interaction with people that has created the problem in the first place. The unreasonable quick-fix of suddenly denying the spoiled bird attention is certainly not the answer and will create more problems. It may seem to be contradictory, but actually the people in the parrot's life will have to give him more attention to encourage independence. The solution is *instructional interaction* — gradually creating a balance between dependence and independence by setting rules and teaching the bird to entertain himself in the same manner one would prevent the negative behaviors from developing in the first place.

The process is one of creating a self-reliant, emotionally secure parrot using *Nurturing Guidance*, consistently defined and focused affection, and the gradual substitution of healthy forms of self-stimulation. There is no quick-fix that creates necessary long-term behavioral changes in an overdependent parrot. Inappropriate aggressive and quick-fix punishing responses such as shooting a parrot with water for screaming, aggressive handling for biting, ignoring him or denying attention and

Sally Blanchard's COMPANION PARROT HANDBOOK

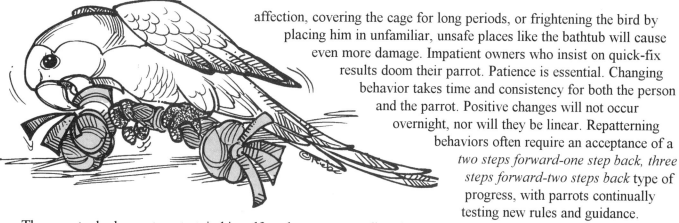

affection, covering the cage for long periods, or frightening the bird by placing him in unfamiliar, unsafe places like the bathtub will cause even more damage. Impatient owners who insist on quick-fix results doom their parrot. Patience is essential. Changing behavior takes time and consistency for both the person and the parrot. Positive changes will not occur overnight, nor will they be linear. Repatterning behaviors often require an acceptance of a *two steps forward-one step back, three steps forward-two steps back* type of progress, with parrots continually testing new rules and guidance.

The parrot who learns to entertain himself, and accepts spending time playing on his own in his cage or on his gym (even with his human flock nearby) is the parrot who has a lifelong home with people who would never consider placing him elsewhere. But it is not possible for the parrot to learn the behaviors which determine this independent nature without positive interaction with nurturing people. And it is certainly not the parrot's fault if he becomes spoiled because his interaction with humans has failed to teach him the lessons he needs to learn to be independent.

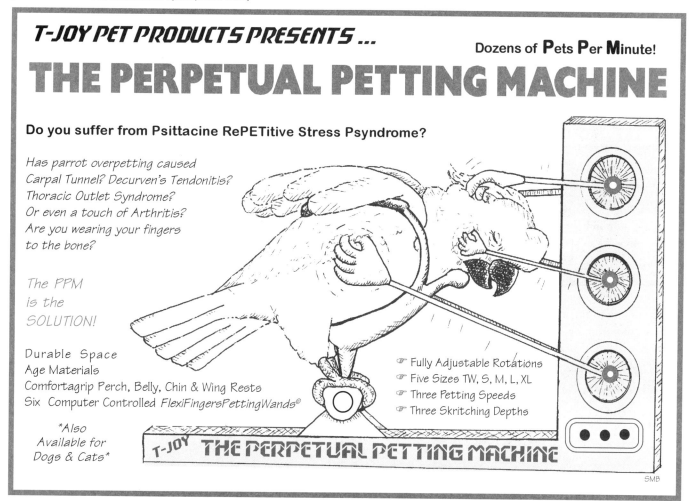

DON'T TURN AN INCIDENT INTO A

A Consultation About A Grey Who Bit His Owner

Talking with people about their parrots usually helps me clarify my own theories about parrot behavior. A long-term Pet Bird Report subscriber called me with a question about her African Grey. For the most part, her grey (who was almost 2 years old) had been a well-behaved, contented parrot causing his owner few behavioral concerns. Her worry was that occasionally, for reasons she was not always sure of, the parrot would bite her. These infrequent bites were rarely hard and seemed more like petulant warnings than mean-spirited aggression In some cases, she had become aware of the fact that he was actually grabbing her finger with his beak to direct her hand because he wanted her to be doing something else. For example, if she was petting him and wasn't paying attention, he would reach over and grab her finger to tell her to pet him more carefully.

If he bit too hard, she dealt with the behavior immediately by giving him a quick disapproving look (*the evil eye*) and saying a firm (but not aggressive or overly dramatic) "NO." Usually the grey would settle down immediately. In some cases, if he seemed overstimulated, she would place him, without further admonishments or drama, away from her, either on the arm of the chair, his playgym, or back in his cage — not as a punishment but to let him calm down.

The reader wanted to make sure these incidents would not become a pattern. Clearly at the young grey's age, the rare biting behaviors were isolated incidents, not part of a habituated pattern. This was most likely true because his owner had dealt with them in a manner which neither rewarded him with drama nor punished him with aggression. My only advice was to try to figure out if there might be some sort of pattern to the biting incidents, keep dealing with the occasional obstreperousness in the same manner, and enjoy her delightful companion.

Prediction, Portent, Prophecy, Prognostication?

Many human beings (not excluding parrot owners) seem to jump to the conclusion that when one bad thing happens, it is an omen of a future full of disaster. (Been there, done that!) Following these prophecies of doom, many a parrot owner goes off the deep end the first time his parrot bites him. Often the first reaction, which is totally illogical is "my parrot doesn't love me anymore!" The grey's owner had saved her relationship with him by accepting his occasional forays into misbehavior as what they were — simply a part of his independence process or a slightly inappropriate communication. She did not erroneously jump to any conclusion that an occasional bite was the beginning of the end, and was therefore able to deal with the behaviors in a rational way.

Will The Real Drama Addict Please Stand Up

I often write about parrots being "addicted to drama." Certainly many of their behaviors (both wild and domestic) can seem quite flashy. However, it is also important to realize we are dealing with a prey animal (one who can become another animal's lunch at the slightest misstep) who also clearly exhibits the importance of being hidden and unnoticed. There are certainly times when a parrot should be as quiet and unobtrusive as possible.

I would like to make the equally accurate observation that we humans also tend to be drama addicts. And our parrots thoroughly enjoy this aspect of our behavior. In fact, our dramatic responses to their behavior are likely to turn an incidental act into a habituated pattern. Our parrots love our drama whether we are attempting to be positive

NEGATIVE PATTERN

or negative. Providing them with a dramatic response reinforces the behavior we are responding to, and this is often the very behavior we would rather not have repeated.

So, in actuality, we are the ones who so often turn our parrot's initial misbehaviors into habituated patterns because we do not deal with them correctly. It is doubtful to me that the grey in this story will ever become a biting bird because at the rare times he does bite only that particular incident is dealt with. He is not rewarded with drama, nor is the single bite responded to as if the African Grey had suddenly turned into a blood-lusting vampire. The incidents will not become a habit.

It appears to me there are actually people who seem to have an investment in their parrot's misbehavior. Perhaps they also love the drama it brings into their lives. Others seem unable, no matter how important it is, to set rules and provide guidance for their parrots. These parrots usually end up with some serious behavioral problems. Most of them end up losing their homes.

Taking It Personally

Another recent call was from a woman whose macaw had *suddenly* become unmanageable at 11 months. While she could still pick up the bird without being bitten, it had become impossible to handle him around the cage. Her husband had been the macaw's best buddy and now the bird was biting him. This made the man angry, and the macaw's biting behavior quickly escalated in response to this anger. The man's attitude was another I hear too frequently: "For no reason at all, my bird suddenly turned mean." There was no forgiveness in his voice and although he would not admit to it, his feelings had been hurt because the bird *had loved him best* and now was aggressive to him almost every time he approached the cage. He did not realize that companion parrots often change their bond as they mature ... but they can change it right back if the previously preferred person interacts with the bird in a nurturing manner. Young macaws often bond strongly with a person who just plays with them but as they mature, that bond often switches to a person who provides *Nurturing Guidance* and causes them little confusion.

His long-term future relationship with the macaw was being seriously threatened, not because the bird had "turned mean" but because the owner was stubbornly refusing to believe his angry attitude was responsible for the escalation of biting behavior. I explained to him that most macaws go through an independence stage at this approximate age where they might become a challenge for their owners, particularly if the birds have had little or no behavioral guidance. While his wife was willing to do almost anything to work on the problem, he was unwilling to accept his complicity in exacerbating the biting pattern. He had discussed the situation with several people who suggested his macaw was exhibiting sexual frustration and needed to be in a breeding program (unlikely because the bird was less than a year old!), a solution he was definitely considering. He also believed, because some "experts" had told him, that he could not change his macaw's recently-developed aggressive tendencies because macaws generally turn *mean* and this aggression is engraved in stone. These generalizations are nonsense and people who do not want to

207

"So what'd you do to end up here?"
"He says I turned mean for no reason at all, but believe me, I had my reasons!"

SMB

work with their parrot grab onto this nonsense as an excuse.

I could not understand (and will never understand) why he was so quickly able to dismiss his relationship with a macaw who had previously been his best buddy. In fact, he was more willing to purchase another macaw (most likely from one of the breeders giving him bad behavioral advice) and transfer his affection to it rather than working with his previously loved bird who he thought had "rejected" him. This is one of the most irritating aspects of the "throw away" mentality I see in some parrot owners. I could imagine this man buying a parrot every year, never providing the proper rules and guidance, blaming the bird, and then feeling justified in "getting rid of" him because he "turned mean for no reason at all." Breeding programs and parrot rescue sanctuaries are full of such birds.

Speaking Of Breeding

Does breeding behavior last forever? No. Once a parrot reaches sexual maturity, the bird is not in a permanent, perpetual state of sexual agitation and aggression. People often dread this time because they have heard so many stories, most of which are based on bad behavioral information. Although some parrots slide through the initial stages of sexual maturity without their owners even noticing, others go through periods of time during the year when they do exhibit serious behavioral problems. Of course, the only reason these behaviors become a problem for the parrots is because they are a problem for the owners. Does this mean a parrot who becomes unpredictable and aggressive during certain seasons of the year no longer makes a good pet? Of course not. Again, the one key is starting out by providing rules and guidance and maintaining it throughout the bird's life. The other key is accepting the fact that parrots will naturally go through some periods in their lives when they might not be what we humans think of as the *ideal pet.* If people have realistic expectations and provide instructional interaction, the negative behaviors will not last forever — live with them, love them, and work with them to get past the seasonal behaviors.

Just A Stage?

"Oh, don't worry. It is just as stage he is going through. He'll be fine when he gets through it." While biting, screaming, and other negative behaviors **may** be

part of a stage a parrot is going through and he **will** indeed get through this stage, it is important to realize that we will be the ones who determine whether or not he gets through it with his pet potential intact. While some people have an overwhelming and inappropriate response to one or two bites, the opposite also occurs. Too many people wait to work with their parrot's behavior until the problems become entrenched. The longer the person waits to get the right information to change his parrot's aggressive biting, excessive screaming, and/or behavioral feather picking, the more difficult it is to change the behaviors.

I strongly advise parrot owners to take each behavioral misadventure as an event by itself and not go *off the deep end* about them. However, it is also important to know how to deal with these incidents so they won't become repetitive patterned behaviors. If the one or two bites do turn into a patterned behavior with the problem escalating, it is best to get good, trust-building information as soon as possible. The parrot will not change his behavior by himself. It is essential for the owner to start interacting with the parrot in a positive way to change the negative behaviors.

FUN AD *by Sally Blanchard*

(This cartoon advertisement is only for fun and NOT for a genuine product or service.)

Who is the Boss, anyway?

THE UPPITY PARROT MANUAL

**Learn to manipulate your human flock!
Advice from the *master of manipulation* —**

Spikey Le Bec

STEP-BY-STEP INSTRUCTIONS:

- Sympathy Poses
- Food Begging Tips
- Intimidating Postures
- Food Flinging Techniques
- Places To Hide In The Cage
- Perfecting Overload Behavior
- Perfecting The Psittacine Strut
- Chewing Value Of Furniture Woods
- Yelling to Make The Flock Reappear
- Biting If You Don't Want To Be Bothered
- Achieving Permanent Physical Attachment
- 100 Different Screams For Drama & Attention
- From Misbehaving To Charming In 2 Seconds

THE UPPITY
PARROT MANUAL

A How To Guide
by Spikey Le Bec
Master of Manipulation

LIFE STAGES & PET POTENTIAL

Why Are Parrots Desirable Pets?

Through the years, I have contemplated the many factors that contribute to parrots being desirable human companions. I have never come up with a definitive answer. I know that they can be wonderful pets for the right people. If they weren't so intriguing, I would not have developed such a lifelong fascination with them. When I know what people's expectations are, I better understand the relationships they have with their parrots. In discussing the reasons parrots are special to many people, the variables are complex. When a person has lived with parrots for a long time, the reasons seem to become even less definable. People who form a strong bond with their parrots rarely make superficial comments. Beauty and intelligence are certainly part of the reason people are initially attracted to parrots. Well-loved companion parrots develop comical, acrobatic personalities which add joy and humor to our lives. Another connection certainly must be their ability to mirror our energy, both in talking and mood. In captivity, parrots are small dependent creatures who are capable of forming strong bonds to people and who need us to care for them. Yet, they often retain a strong sense of independence which many of us respect. The human maternal or paternal instinct is often a very important part of living with a parrot. However, this may create a strong and unrealistic desire for the baby parrot to stay a bappy forever.

Bappies Forever?

For some people, the myth or illusion is that pet parrots stay babies forever. In reality, they are dependent on us their entire lives for proper care and nurturing, but they do mature just like any other living thing. Whether they stay tame and sweet as they grow up depends a great deal on the way that they are raised and handled by their owners. If raised with *Nurturing Guidance* and handled consistently, most handfed parrots have the potential to stay tame and "baby-like" even as adults. In some ways, I still think of my parrots as bappies — even though my Amazons, Paco and Rascal, were hatched in 1976 and 1978. My grey, Bongo Marie, was not a young bird when I bought her in 1976 and Spike, my caique, came to live with me when he was less than a year old in 1989. I also am very aware that they now have the more defined personalities of adult parrots. I raised them with rules and guidance so they are still the kind of pets that I enjoy.

Most Companion Parrots Are Young Birds

From my many conversations with bird owners throughout the country, it is very clear to me that the average person with a companion parrot has birds under ten years of age, with most under five years old. Those people who are taking the time to learn about parrots and their physical and emotional needs will have pets that live up to their potential. Chances are, those people who do not raise their parrots with *Nurturing Guidance* and rules will never know what a marvelous relationship could have been possible. That is tragic for both the person and the parrot. I do meet an occasional parrot caregiver with older birds. I have met several parrots who are 20 to 40 years old. Those parrots who have been treated well by the people in their lives usually have a delightful comical personality which still exhibits many *bappy-like* characteristics. This is not an *accident*, but rather it is due to the long-term relationship people have established with these parrots.

Different "Timetables" For Different Species

The development of a chick into maturity and the life span of a parrot depends on the family and species of parrot. There is a vast range of size, development, and maturation in parrot-family birds. Small parrots such as Budgerigars (commonly and mistakenly called parakeets) and cockatiels usually reach breeding maturity by six months to a year, and may have a possible life span of 15 to 20 years if provided proper care. On the other hand, a wild hyacinth macaw youngster may still be dependent on its parents after two years of life. Although the possible life span of many of the larger parrots is 30 to 60 years, there are documented examples of parrots who have lived over a century. The actual life spans of most captive parrots are much shorter than their potential because so many have suffered nutritional abuse. With increased knowledge about proper care and good nutrition, the average life span of captive parrots is increasing.

"K Select' Species"

Most parrots are included in a group of birds that are called "K Select Species." This term is used to describe a species that breeds at most once or twice a year (or every two years with Hyacinth Macaws) and produces only one or two chicks in each clutch. The altricial chicks produced are dependent on their parents often until the next breeding cycle and, in some birds, even longer. The chick's survival depends on how well his parents teach him life skills. Often in these parrot species, the young parrots remain with their parents' flock. Because the few offspring produced require such long-term parental attention and take such a long time to mature before they produce young of their own, many parrots are unable to maintain viable populations with any pressures on their habitat or breeding cycles. Unfortunately, because of this, many "K Select Species" are becoming endangered or are on the verge of extinction in the wild.

·····➔

Life Stages Of A Parrot

Parrots are altricial birds: they hatch blind, helpless, and naked. As babies, they are totally dependent on their parents for survival. A baby parrot will perish quickly if his parents do not expend their utmost energy attending to his ever-demanding needs. Little or no light filters into the nest cavity and, at first, the nestling's strongest reaction is to touch. (Please take note that it is inappropriate for breeders or handfeeders to keep nestlings in well-lighted aquariums during this stage of their lives.) After the first feedings, the baby begins calling out for food every time he senses motion in the nest. The gangly little blob of silly putty in the eat-poop-sleep stage of development has little or no personality yet. Personality seems to have its origins once the baby's eyes open and curiosity begins to develop. Parents have to forage diligently to satisfy the voracious appetite of the chick, whose body begins to grow and develop rapidly. Soon the pink butterball begins to look more like a pin cushion with all of his new feathers emerging. The bappy starts paying attention and responding to motion, shapes, color, and noises. Sometimes the bappy shows fear or aggression. The reassuring, soothing presence of the parent (whether bird or human) can get the bird past this fear stage quite easily.

Velvet Feathers

As the pin feathers unfold into the perfect, soft, bright, virgin feathers, the baby becomes more active and adventurous. Still not able to fly, he may spend time pacing around in the nest, peering out the entrance. Although there is still some important growing and filling-out to do, about this time the body size of the feathered baby can be almost the same size that the bird will be as an adult. Soon the flapping begins in preparation for the first flight. The rotund chick may maintain his appetite or start to refuse a few feedings. Once the furious flapping and decrease in appetite has created strong chest muscles and a more streamlined chick, he is ready to fly. Encouraged by his parents, the adventurous pre-toddler may climb out onto a branch to do his flapping. His razor-sharp toenails help keep him secure on the branch so that he does not become some predator's lunch on the ground. When he is ready to fledge, the parents, flying from limb to limb, call to him encouraging him to take the plunge. I have heard that some parrot parents, who have become impatient with a trepidatious chick, will actually knock him off a perch to force his first takeoff (I wouldn't recommend this in raising companion parrots!). Once he fledges, the most intense socialization process begins and his most important survival lessons are taught to him by his parents. In captivity, we are beginning to understand that bappies who have been allowed to fledge and fly for a few days and then have their wings gradually trimmed over a few days are far more secure as they mature than bappies who never get to fly.

Critical Learning Time

It would be totally unnatural for a parrot chick to wean before he has fledged. The time between fledging and total food independence is probably the most critical learning stage in both wild and handfed bappies. This is the time their wild parents teach them how and what to eat, how to find their food, what to do when there is a predator in the area, and the skills they need to be a part of the flock. If a baby bird does not learn these lessons well in nature, he will not survive. In captivity, handfeeders, breeders, and new owners must teach bappies social and survival skills and establish *Nurturing Guidance* by providing instructional interaction and rules. Socialization is not just introduction to different people, but involves the development of the young parrot's entire personality. A bappy who learns to look to his owner for behavioral guidelines and has been taught to accept change and new adventure readily will have tremendous potential to stay a tame, loving pet. Without proper socialization, baby parrots may develop serious emotional dysfunction as they mature. Just as there are no juvenile delinquent human babies, most bappies are quite delightful. Behavioral dysfunction rarely shows up until bappies begin to reach their independence stages.

The next important stage in a bappy's life is weaning or food independence. In the wild, a young parrot may learn to eat some foods on his own, long before he is totally food independent. Learning about new food sources and occasional feeding by parents may continue for some time past weaning, especially in the larger parrots. The more the behavior and personality of a parrot species depends on socialization and learning, the longer the species depends on parental guidance to learn its social and survival skills.

The First Major Independence Stage

This critical stage of development usually starts between 5 and 9 months in the average medium-size parrot species (including Amazons and African Greys). Physically, the bappy begins to fill out and looks very much like he will look for the majority of his adult life. Behaviorally, this is often the time that many owners lose the tameness of their bird and the bond between them is jeopardized. As the bird strives for independence, the owner who has not established *Nurturing Guidance* may lose control of his previously sweet pet. Poor early socialization and lack of rules begins to produce behavioral dysfunction in young birds. In the wild, this is a time when young birds who have learned their survival skills test these skills. In the beginning, they do so under the watchful eye of the parent. As the young bird becomes more and more proficient with his survival skills, he has increased autonomy from his parents. This is a very confusing time for a young parrot in captivity. Instinctively, the bappy may feel that he needs to be establishing his own life independently from his caregivers whom he has perceived to be his parents. Yet, the very fact that he is a pet bird means that he will always remain dependent on the people in his life. Young birds may appear very willful, stubborn, and even aggressive at times during this independence stage.

Even the caregiver who has established guidelines and rules may still have some problems with his bappy during this stage. This is especially true if the bird is very intelligent. Maintaining *Nurturing Guidance* is essential to maintaining lifelong pet potential. Although the pet parrot will depend on us for the rest of his life, a degree of independence must be encouraged. Make sure that the bappy spends some time in his cage on a daily basis even if you are there. Additionally, the young bird should learn to entertain himself by playing alone in his cage. At this stage, problems with overdependency may become apparent and these include a need to be with people all of the time, screaming when no one is with him, not playing with toys or being able to entertain himself, and continued baby-like behavior. Overdependency on the constant presence of the human flock may become a serious threat to the bird's emotional health because the bird instinctively feels that he is not prepared to survive on his own and is threatened at the prospect of abandonment by his parents.

Redefining The Relationship

During and after the independence stage, young parrots seem to start a "struggle" to redefine their bond with the people in their lives. In the medium-size parrots, this stage may begin at 12 to 15 months and continue until the bird is around 2 years old. Young parrots no longer respond to their owners as a bappy does to a parent. In an emotionally healthy parrot, his independence may actually result in a less intense bond with his owner just like the wild young bird may form a looser bond with other individuals in the flock during this period of time. Now the bappy is no longer a bappy. This is not to say that a well-trained, well-nurtured parrot will not still remain tame, sweet, and cuddly. He will if the owner works to maintain that kind of relationship.

Playing House

In the next stage of development, the young parrot seems to practice being an adult. One moment he is sweet and cuddly, and the next he may be unpredictable and even aggressive. Just as young children play house long before they are hormonally influenced, the young parrot may start courting his owner and practicing courtship rituals. He or she may start bonding to his owners as if to a mate. There may be an increase in territoriality or aggressive protection, regurgitation for feeding, and dancing and prancing to seduce the owner. Nothing usually comes from this behavior because, after all, at this time it is just practice and the courtship behaviors are fairly benign.

Raging Hormones

BUT ONE DAY... when the light, the temperature, and the humidity are just right, the hormones may start "raging" through his body and the young parrot begins to behave sexually. Actually, Phoebe

Linden refers to this early period as *sexual immaturity* since the parrot may be acting sexually, but certainly is not mature enough to form a strong bond, mate, and raise young. This event usually occurs between the ages of 2 to 4 years old in a medium-size parrot and is the true test of whether or not the caregiver has provided the proper groundwork for a lifelong, well-behaved parrot. If the owner has established a strong *Nurturing Guidance*, then a hormonally controlled parrot should be agreeable as a pet. If raised properly, some parrots never form a sexual bond with their caregivers. In the scheme of things, the person who sets rules is perceived as the dominant partner in the pair bond. The more submissive parrot waits for the person to take the sexual initiative. Most caregivers will not do this purposefully; however, at this time care must be taken to handle the previously docile parrot in a manner that will not be interpreted sexually. This may mean that for a period of time while the parrot is seasonally stimulated by its hormones, people shouldn't pet the parrot in his *erogenous zones*. Many parrots are sexually stimulated by beak wrestling, pressure on the back, petting under the wings or tail, and by someone running his hand down the bird's back to the tail area. The caregiver should be able to continue this kind of physical affection once the parrot's hormones subside. Just because a parrot is exhibiting sexual behavior towards a member of their human flock does not mean he needs to be placed in a breeding program. Most often, because of his strong bond to humans, the young handfed domestic parrot would be just as happy with continued attention and nurturing from his caregivers.

The Cooling Off Period

The first few years of sexual maturity can be quite intense, especially during breeding season. Often, after that, the well-guided pet parrot usually relaxes into more mellow behavior even during periods of hormonal stimulation. The person who gives up on his well-loved young parrot by putting him in a breeding program or selling him because of hormonal aggression, may be missing out on the best years of their lives together.

(Even though I have worked with problem behavior in birds for many years, I really haven't seen great numbers of pet birds too far beyond this stage of life. Although I have certainly worked with some domestically-raised parrots that are over ten or so, the majority of these birds were imported. Too many of these parrots have died of neglect or nutritional abuse. The older imported parrots that have survived have hopefully settled into a good pet relationship with a caregiver who took the time to work with them, or have long since been placed in quality breeding situations.)

The Middle-aged Parrot

Middle-aged parrots become increasingly predictable. Perhaps it is because their human flock have lived with them long enough to finally figure them out. If they are well-cared for and given quality focused attention, they comfortably settle into the routines of their human flock. They continue to learn, but there are few behavioral surprises if their care remains consistent. Bongo Marie continues to learn new words and phrases all the time, and while she has her moods from day to day, she is a very steady companion.

The Elderly Parrot

Through the years, I have had the opportunity to meet quite a few senior psittacines. I have worked with several parrots that are over 30, a few over 50, and one cockatoo that was reported to be well over 60. In each case, I found these birds to be receptive to learning new behaviors. Just as the aging human personality can remain open to change, even an older parrot is capable of learning new behaviors and adapting to changes in his life. Older parrots begin to slow down and may exhibit varying degrees of both physical and mental feebleness. They often show their age with feather loss, swollen joints, decreased mobility, cataracts and loss of quality vision, loss of hearing, and other symptoms of the ravages of time. As parrots age, the benefit of a high quality, nutritionally balanced, varied diet becomes obvious!

Keeping Your Bappy A Bappy

Most new owners start with the same hope that their new bappy will stay sweet and tame throughout their lives together. Because fledged and weaned baby parrots look much like adult birds to the novice, many new owners do not realize that just as all living creatures mature and change, their baby parrots will grow up and behave differently. One of the wonderful traits of a well-socialized domestically-raised handfed baby parrot is that his human parents can do a great deal to shape his adult personality. By setting rules and providing guidance, the owner can establish the *Nurturing Guidance* that will maintain many of the delightful attributes of a bappy into adulthood.

PICASSO'S PARROT

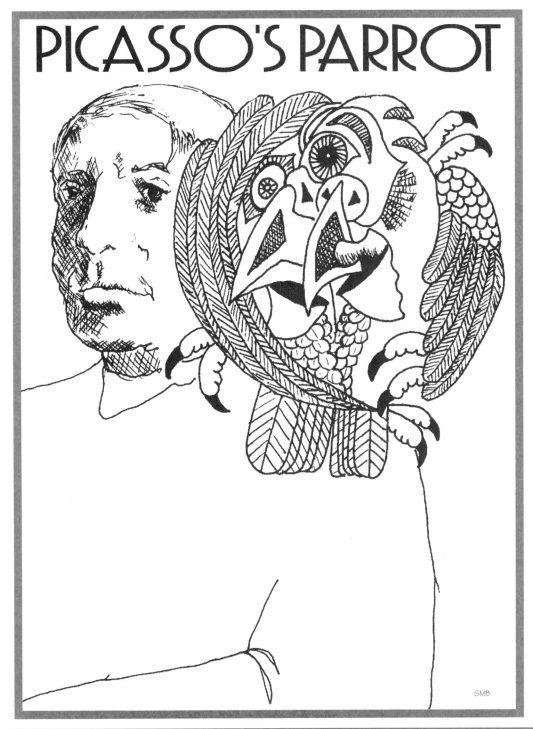

SMB

Nurturing Guidance Tip: The BIG Picture

Think Beyond Your Living Rooms

As companion parrot owners, we need to be aware of the *BIG PICTURE.* There are significant issues which may affect us and our appreciation for parrots. Staying aware and educated about all aspects of the bird industry, government regulations and legislation, and conservation will help us better understand our parrots and know what our rights and privileges are. One of the shortcomings of the bird industry and aviculture has been inadequate grassroots education that provides the general public with information about the positive aspects of bird keeping.

Popular media information may give people a negative idea about the people who keep parrots. Those of us who are concerned about our companion parrots can help educate the public about domestically-raised parrots, their pet potential, and their proper care. If you read an article or see a program that mentions only the negative or is full of misinformation, make a phone call or send a letter and let the writer or the producer know about the positive aspects of keeping companion parrots.

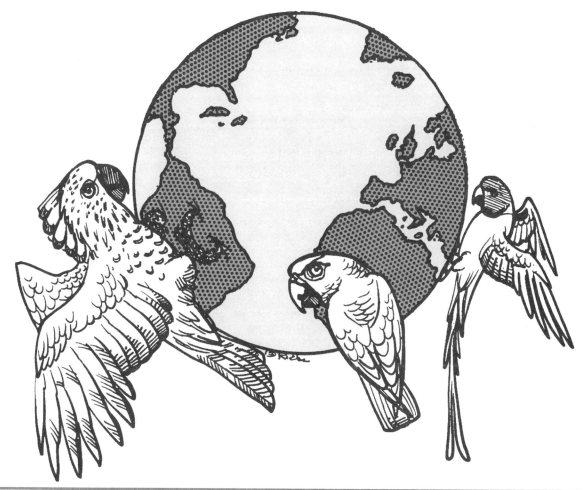

ETHICAL CONSIDERATIONS

The Birds Need To Come First In *The Bird Biz*

Many people who share their lives with parrots are genuinely concerned about doing the *right thing* for these intelligent and sentient birds. There are some quality bird shops and aviaries where all the birds receive optimal care. It is a delightful experience to spend time with breeders and bird shop personnel who raise chicks with benevolent concern for their physical and emotional health. I have visited parrot-related businesses that were so appalling that I felt embarrassed to think that someone might associate me with such an establishment. Of course, like most aspects of life, in bird-keeping there is a range from excellent to horrendous. Judging the quality of care parrots receive is not a black-and-white issue, being all good or all bad. Surprisingly, some of the people do not yet have good information. Others might be willing to try different ways if they really understood why different methods work. Some bird-related businesses learn from their customers and improve the care of their birds or the quality of their products accordingly. Others remain stubbornly ignorant and would never take the time, energy, or money to improve products or provide better care for their parrots. I started the *Pet Bird Report* magazine, partly because I passionately believe in the mutual support of like-minded people. PBR provides support to the entrepreneurs, manufacturers, bird shops, breeders, behavior consultants, and avian veterinarians who put the parrots first. There is a vast difference between earning a successful living with something you love and the exploiting of parrots for money. As consumers, we need to learn to judge the differences for ourselves. There are certain aspects of parrot keeping that I am adamantly against. For example, I strongly believe that shops that still feed only seed and/or wean their babies to a seed-only diet are living in the *Dark Ages* of bird care. Feeding a nutritionally abusive, total seed death diet is evidence of a shop's lack of caring about the parrots they keep. After reading this book, you are most likely aware of other aspects of bird care I use to evaluate the quality of breeders, bird shops, and parrot-related products.

Vote With Your Money

In many ways, the bird industry is still young and growing. As people who love and respect parrots, we have the opportunity to influence a positive growth. Many times, as consumers, we feel relatively powerless. But we really have more power than we think. We can VOTE WITH OUR MONEY to determine whether or not we want to have an industry that truly concerns itself with the welfare of the parrots we care about. **Every dollar we spend with a less than quality bird shop or aviary where parrots are kept and raised in substandard conditions is an investment towards that poor care.** I refuse to spend one penny in a store that offends me with the care they provide their animals. If I want something badly enough, I can find it somewhere else. Please ... spend your money with quality pet stores and breeders who truly care about the welfare of the animals they raise and sell. I encourage the readers of the Companion Parrot Handbook to evaluate carefully where they want their bird care dollars to go. If there is more than one pet shop in your area, but the really good one is several miles out of the way, it is worth driving those extra miles to support quality in bird care. If the only pet shop in your area is one that makes you want to rescue every animal and bird in it, let your friends know why you won't shop there. Order your products by mail or make a special trip a few times a month to a quality shop within a day's drive. You can help keep the quality alive in this expanding bird biz! 🐦

BARGAIN BASEMENT BIRDS
We breed um - U feed um
The younger they are - the cheaper they are

"We deal in quantity not quality. This one is really cheep - get it, ha ha! *cough cough* He's not weaned but he was a bronco chick we had to tame. At these prices, don't ask for any references or guarantees. If you buy more than one, we'll give you an even better price. We've got some jist out of the egg for a really low price. This one here may look sick but he's just a baby - he's jist takin' a nap. With lots of love, he'll be jist fine. Take him home today and we'll give you our special sick or damaged bird discount of 25% off! WHAT A DEAL!

ANIMAL RIGHTS & AVICULTURE

Who Says Parrots Shouldn't Be Pets?

There are people in the United States who think parrots shouldn't be pets, and some of these people are working diligently to ban bird keeping by private citizens. Does this mean we should all become paranoid and live in fear that someday some imaginary *Animal Rights Police* will knock on our doors to confiscate our parrots? I doubt it but there are some potentially scary things going on. This is a serious issue and there is a great deal of legislation being proposed on the local, state, and national level that is considered to be anti-bird keeping. There are fanatics on both sides of this issue. Some people involved with parrots don't think that the government has the right to regulate <u>any</u> aspect of bird care. They will fight all legislation having to do with birds even if it may be beneficial to their proper care. I don't want the government over-controlling my life either, and am well aware of the abuse of power in many law enforcement agencies, but I also am aware of the poor care so many parrots still receive.

Is this all black and white, or is there a grey area? Is compromise possible? Overreaction, propaganda, exaggerations, and lack of accurate knowledge ends up paralyzing many of us with paranoia and keeps us from acting in a positive, productive manner. Try to get the facts before you believe everything on the Internet or the often slanted information put out by the various factions involved. It is essential for parrot owners to stay informed about what legislation and regulation permits us to do and not do in regards to our parrots. We need to be aware of all pending legislation in our cities, counties, states, and countries which may be aimed at restricting our ability to keep birds for breeding or as companions. We also need to evaluate for ourselves if some legislation is needed to benefit captive birds and improve their care.

Animal Rights, Aviculture And The Middle Ground — Animal Welfare?

I am not necessarily for or against all aspects of either animal rights or aviculture — I am profoundly pro-parrot. I believe in continuing education to improve the welfare of companion parrots. I have been referred to as an animal rights fanatic by some people in aviculture and considered a shill for the bird trade by people who are active in animal rights groups. Since many special interest groups often demand 100% adherence to their agendas, I am usually placed in a difficult middle position. There are aspects of the bird industry I have serious concerns about, but I also believe devoutly that parrots can make incredible human companions if people properly nurture them. Because of this, I have devoted my life to providing people with proper care information.

Create Public Awareness

It is also essential for us to create a public (or *grassroots*) awareness of the quality aspects of bird-keeping. Due to a steady stream of animal rights propaganda and public television specials based on the plight of wild parrots and the horrors of poaching and smuggling, many people believe that all companion parrots are still wild-caught or smuggled birds. Rarely do these programs make any kind of statement that the vast majority of, if not all, baby parrots in the pet trade today have been domestically-raised.

Not too long ago when I was traveling, I checked into a small, delightful motel on the California coast with my mother and my favorite companion, Spikey Le Bec. When the owner (an active P.E.T.A. member) saw him, she was appalled and started to give me a lecture about how horrible it was to keep birds in cages. He was in his travel cage and the woman thought that was his permanent cage. I sat down with her and introduced her to Spike. I showed her the *Pet Bird Report* and talked to her about all of the wonderful, caring bird owners and breeders I know. I told her that we knew there were some serious problems in the pet bird trade but that there were lots of concerned people trying to make life better for parrots. I explained that the vast majority of companion parrots were domestically-bred and not taken from the wild. When we left, she had a totally different perspective and even an appreciation of pet birds and aviculture. She had also (at least tentatively) fallen in love with Spike and his happy personality.

One at a time, each of us can do our part to let people know about the positive side to bird keeping. 🖊

A BRIEF TAXONOMY LESSON

Confusing Common Names

Common names for living creatures can get pretty confusing. Even with parrots, there may be several common names for each bird. Although we all are familiar with Moluccan Cockatoos, Rose-breasted Cockatoos, Severe Macaws, and Blue and Gold Macaws, we might not be as sure about Salmon-crested Cockatoos, Galahs, Chestnut-fronted Macaws, or Blue and Yellow Macaws. We might be able to figure out what a Molukkenkakadu or a cacotoes des Moluques is, but how about a gelbbrustara or a rotbugara? Obviously, if people (especially those with a scientific interest) are going to be discussing parrots all over the world, there has to be basic terminology that defines a certain species. Everyone around the world who understands the taxonomy of parrots will understand the scientific names: *Cacatua moluccensis, Eolophus roseicapillus, Ara severa*, or *Ara ararauna*. Often the terminology is not so confusing if you know a little Latin or Greek or pronounce the name aloud — *roseicapillus* translates as rosy-capped which makes sense for a Galah or Rose-breasted Cockatoo. How about an *Amazona ochrocephala*? We can figure the Amazon part out right away and isn't ochre a yellow color? The cephala part is a little harder if we have no medical background, but this word always has something to do with the head. So now we know we have a Yellow-headed Amazon. But how about *Amazon aestiva* or *Amazona autumnalis*? Whoever gave these parrots their scientific names was stuck on the seasons. The Blue-front Amazon with his vibrant green, blue, yellow, and a touch of red was named after Summer — *aestiva*. The Red-lored with his vibrant green, blue, yellow, and a touch of red (different arrangement of colors) is named after fall — *autumnalis*. Not all of the scientific names will make sense to us no matter how hard we try to figure them out. Some animals and plants are named after the people who discovered them, and some have strangely inspired taxonomic descriptions that seem to provide proof that many scientists graduated from Gary Larson's Far Side School of Biology.

Taxonomic Classifications

Even though this is **not a scientifically correct correlation**, we might better understand the scientific designations used to identify birds (as used in Forshaw's <u>Parrots of the World</u>) if we compare them to me and my present address:

Class: Aves (All the birds in the world) — (Continent: North America)
Order: Psittaciformes (All the parrots in the world) — (Country: United States)
Family: Psittacidae (Parrot family) — (State: California)
Subfamily: Psittacinae (Parrot sub-family) — (County: Alameda)
Genus: *Psittacus* (African Greys) — (City: Alameda)
Species: *erithacus* (Congo African Greys) — (Last Name: Blanchard)
Common name: African Grey Parrot (Well, Bongo Marie, my African Grey, calls me *Sawee* and whistles for me as if I was her pet dog, but other people have their own favorite names for me.)

The first grouping includes every bird in the world or everyone who lives in North America. The next step narrows the groupings to parrots and people in the USA. By the time we get down to the genus and species, we are pretty sure we know exactly whom we are talking about. All African Grey Parrots are *Psittacus erithacus*. Of course, bird species are not grouped by where they live as much as by similarities in their physical characteristics and genetic inheritance. ∮

Chestnut-fronted macaw?   Max?   Rotbugara?   Severe macaw?   Maracaná guaçu?   Ara à front châtain?   Hey you!

Ara Severa

PARROT HYBRIDS

Defining Hybridization

Hybrid parrots are the offspring of a male and a female of two different parrot species. Although hybridization does rarely occur in the wild, most hybridization within the parrot family has been done as a human effort. These pairings are often within the same genus. For example, the Scarlet Macaw (*Ara macao*) and Blue and Gold (*Ara ararauna*) combine to create the Catalina macaw. However, the human-created Tracy Macaw is the product of *Ara ararauna* and *Anodorhynchus hyacinthinus*, the Hyacinth Macaw, two biologically different species. Although the hybridization of parrot species in aviculture is most often done with macaw species, cockatoos, conures, Amazons, *Poicephalus*, *Psittacula*, and others are also routinely hybridized in captivity. The molbrella is a hybridization of the Moluccan and the Umbrella Cockatoos — I've often wondered aloud why this bird isn't called the *umbluccan*?

On the previous page, I briefly explained what makes a parrot a species. Generally, a parrot species is distinct from other species because of its unique biological and, in some cases, behavioral characteristics. These characteristics are unique enough to cause the individuals of the species to choose their mates only within that species. In some cases, birds may look physically quite similar but have such different calls or behavioral characteristics, they are not likely to breed with the similar species. An example of this in ornithology are the physically almost identical Eastern and Western Meadowlarks. Their ranges overlap in the United States prairie states, yet they are not likely to interbreed because their songs are totally unique. When there are geographic changes of the habitat or environmental pressures, there may be some interbreeding of similar species. For much of recorded history, the arboreal Baltimore and Bullock's Orioles were separated by a treeless prairie. As people settled the Midwest and planted thousands of trees and shrubs, the ranges of both birds increased until they met. Although both birds are orange, black, and white, their markings are quite different. Yet they readily interbreed and create viable offspring. So they were reclassified as one species — the Northern Oriole.

There is still much more to learn about the biological interrelationships between parrot species. Recently, ornithologists have redefined the genus and species of several parrot-family birds. Much of the scientific thinking on species has been changing due to the ability to study the DNA of parrots defined as similar yet separate species.

"The one on the right is a *Molucacynth* and the one on the left is a *Hyaluccan*. We breed them selectively for the intelligence of the Moluccan and the gentleness of the Hyacinth. Or wait, is it the intelligence of the Hyacinth and the gentleness of the Moluccan??"

Arguments FOR and AGAINST The Hybridization of Parrot Species

Is hybridization a positive or negative aspect in aviculture? It depends on whom you ask. I became involved with parrots through an interest in wild birds and conservation. Although I am personally opposed to the hybridization of parrot species in captivity, I certainly encourage people who have hybrid companion parrots to love, cherish, and take excellent care of them.

➲ *FOR: Everyone else does it.* AGAINST: Many species of parrots, particularly the large macaws, are endangered or becoming seriously threatened in the wild. Ethical breeders who are aware of the "big picture" will not hybridize different species. A large captive gene pool with many healthy and pure individuals of a species may become their best, and even last, hope for survival.

➲ *FOR: There is a good market for them and some people will pay a high price for a unique parrot.* AGAINST: Pure species parrots traditionally sell for as high a price if not more than hybrid parrots. Many people believe that the breeding of hybrids is greedy. Why else would people do it if there was not a financial payoff?

⊃ *FOR: Individuals from two parrot species fell in love and it was not fair to separate them. Against:* Parrots are capable of bonding and rebonding throughout their lives. It is highly likely that parrots who have been paired with different species will eventually bond with a parrot of their own species if placed with consideration for their needs.

⊃ *FOR: We've done it with dogs. Why not with parrots?* AGAINST: This is a common misconception — companion dog breeds that are interbred are not separate species. They are different breeds, but all the same species.

⊃ *FOR: Parrots hybridize in the wild, so it is a natural thing to do.* AGAINST: While there are rare records of separate but similar parrot species hybridizing in the wild, it is not a normal occurrence and often seems to be the result of environmental pressures.

⊃ *FOR: There is nothing wrong with it. They are being created for the pet market, not for conservation or the gene pool.* AGAINST: The gene pool of many captive parrot species may be all that exists in the next decade or so as they become seriously endangered and extinct in the wild.

⊃ *FOR: We can selectively breed a healthier and more desirable companion parrot by hybridizing. A hybrid harlequin will have the best traits of the Blue and Gold and the best traits of the Green-wing Macaw.* AGAINST: Why won't the hybrid parrot develop the worst traits of the Blue and Gold and the Green-winged Macaws? Most breeding of hybrids in captivity is haphazard with no real knowledge of genetics. When mankind messes with a species for their own reasons, they can really mess things up. Consider the health problems so many highly-bred dog breeds have with their joints, skin, and breathing. Do we want to do that to parrots?

⊃ *FOR: Experimentation: what would a hybrid Cape and Jardines look and act like, or a Blue-front and a Yellow-nape ... or a Hyacinth and a Blue and Gold? Or even a cross between a Caique and a Severe Macaw, which has been documented?* AGAINST: What happens to the physical health and emotional well-being of the offspring when we interbreed two species — especially when we are dealing with parrots with varying diets, beak sizes, and/or anatomical adaptations? The species nature created are special enough — why do we humans insist on playing God?

⊃ *FOR: Hybrids make better pets because they don't have so many natural instinctive behaviors. The desire is to produce the perfect companion parrot — what would it be like to create a new hybrid produced from, say, a species with the reputation of talking well and one which generally stays very tame. Would this make having a positive relationship with a companion parrot a more positive experience for the masses?* AGAINST: The pet potential of a domestically-bred parrot has more to do with proper socialization and client education than it does with genetic tinkering. ✦

MUTATIONS IN AVICULTURE

Mutations are caused by changes in the genetic material of the parents which result in hereditary changes in the offspring. In the wild, mutations are unpredictable although some genes tend to produce the same mutations. Cockatiels, lovebirds, budgerigars, Australian grass parakeets, and ringneck parakeets are the parrot species most commonly bred as mutations. Mutations of these birds are selectively bred mostly for their colors, size, length of tail, fullness of crest and other physical characteristics. In aviculture, a mutation is the manipulation of genetic characteristics within a species. Some breeders are knowledgeable about genetics and know which characteristics to develop and which ones not to mess with. Others play *hocus-pocus* just to see what happens — they breed sister with brother, and then breed one of their offspring back to a parent, and then interbreed the bird from that union with the other parent ...

The health and sturdiness of a mutation depends on whether the breeder modulates his desire for interesting physical characteristics with a strong desire for creating a healthy, genetically strong bird. Mutation breeders often keep their best birds for future breeding and sometimes sell the culls (ones that did not work out very well) to the pet trade. Unfortunately, some of the mutations on the pet market today, particularly the budgies and cockatiels, now have genetic predispositions for all sorts of problems. Production-raised budgies have a propensity for fatty tumors. Several cockatiel mutations, particularly albino and lutino 'tiels, seem to have serious problems with night frights and emerging blood feathers. When you buy one of these birds, try to make sure he came from a reputable breeder who is knowledgeable about genetics. ✦

PARROTS & ECO-TOURISM

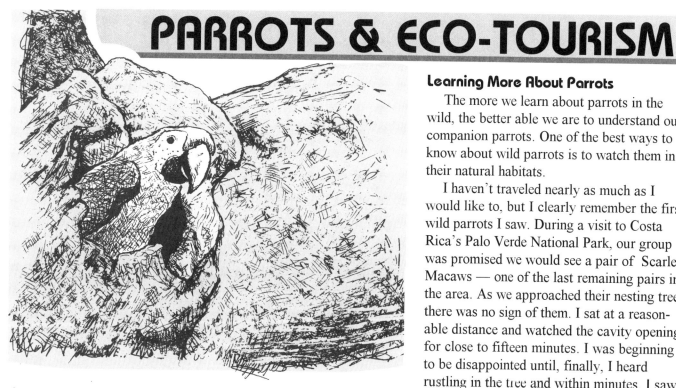

Learning More About Parrots

The more we learn about parrots in the wild, the better able we are to understand our companion parrots. One of the best ways to know about wild parrots is to watch them in their natural habitats.

I haven't traveled nearly as much as I would like to, but I clearly remember the first wild parrots I saw. During a visit to Costa Rica's Palo Verde National Park, our group was promised we would see a pair of Scarlet Macaws — one of the last remaining pairs in the area. As we approached their nesting tree, there was no sign of them. I sat at a reasonable distance and watched the cavity opening for close to fifteen minutes. I was beginning to be disappointed until, finally, I heard rustling in the tree and within minutes, I saw the curve of the upper beak, then the head, and then the body of the Scarlet as she slowly climbed out of the nest. She shook her feathers and launched herself towards the edge of a downslope. I heard her raucous calls through the valley and shortly she was joined by another. Later, as I was intently watching a tiny, fuzzy baby in a green-breasted hummingbird nest, I heard the pair calling in the distance. As they approached the nest, their calls ceased and they both landed on a nearby branch. One climbed into the cavity while the other stood outside watching us. He seemed accustomed to people being around his protected nest site and eventually he climbed into the tree cavity. For some time, we could hear them moving around but unfortunately we had to leave. It is impossible to use words to explain the awe and exhilaration of watching this wild pair of brilliant Scarlet Macaws flying over a lush green valley.

I have lived vicariously through many people who have visited areas of the world specifically to see wild parrots. The clay licks at Manu and Tambopato in Peru are favorite destinations for parrot aficionados. A guided tour of the Pantanal in Brazil allows macaw lovers to see Hyacinths hanging out with cattle and feeding on the ground. A trip to northeastern Australia rewards travelers with neighborhood cockatoos and gregarious lories. There are special birding trips available to several of the Caribbean Islands which are home to severely endangered Amazons. Several conservation and avicultural groups have worked with travel agencies to put together special parrot watching trips. If parrot lovers keep supporting these adventures to parrot habitats, there will be many more planned. There are birdwatching trips planned every year to almost every place in the world, and more and more of them are featuring parrots.

Another Good Reason

Learning more about our domestically-raised parrots is not the only reason to visit the habitats of wild parrots. Traveling to see parrots in the wild also supports eco-tourism and, in many ways, contributes to the conservation and survival of parrots and their habitat. Up until the last few years, the only value native parrots had to the indigenous people was for food or money received from robbing nests for the pet trade. In the last few years, many national and international conservation groups are working to educate native people to respect and protect their wildlife. In fact, some people who formerly poached parrots for smugglers are now the very people who are employed to guard nesting sites. Each country has its own heroes who are dedicated to the welfare of their land and animals. Many of the conservation and educational programs emphasize the financial value of eco-tourism. When tourists come to an area specifically to see the native wildlife, it puts money into the local economy. Local people began to realize that their welfare depends on the protection and survival of the wildlife. It is a win-win situation for the wildlife, the tourists, and the native people. ✒

WILD PARROTS NEED OUR HELP

The Ancestry Of Our Companion Parrots

When I first started working with pet birds over a quarter of a century ago, the majority of the large parrots were imported, wild-caught parrots. Some were older, while others were young birds who might have been handfed by natives after capture. When I started giving parrot care seminars several years later, I would often ask the question, "Where did your parrot come from?" The answer was almost always the name of a local pet shop.

For many years, I created bird sculptures out of a great variety of hardwoods from all over the world. When patrons would ask me where the woods in their sculpture came from, I would provide them with a list of the countries where the trees grew that the lumber came from — not the name of the lumber yard or rare woods store. As I became more and more knowledgeable about the destruction of the rainforests, I became more concerned about using such rare woods.

Accordingly, people need to know and think about the fact that their parrots did not originate from the local pet shop, but actually came from the jungles of Brazil, the arid scrubland of Australia, or the rainforest of west equatorial Africa. Although the majority of our beloved parrots are now aviary-raised in the United States, most of their parents are wild-caught birds. Our companion parrots have a significant natural heritage.

The Sad Truth

I was able to win the trust of many of the wild-caught parrots I worked with right away, while others took time, and some were never tamed. For every imported parrot who reached a good home, there were far more who didn't. Some were lucky enough to go to decent breeding situations, others were bought and sold over and over, never finding a secure place. Some are still being shuffled about from place to place, becoming more confused with each transfer. Far too many died and far too many are still dying. Now most parrots sold to pet homes and breeders are domestically-raised. Each and every parrot in captivity deserves a quality life but, unfortunately, even many of our handfed bappies do not end up in a stable, loving home. Most of the bappies being raised now come from imported parents, but that is changing as more and more domestically bred parrots go into breeding situations. Companion parrot lovers and the entire bird industry owe a dedication to the wild parrots of the world. Without them, there would be no bird industry. People who care deeply about parrots need to help maintain parrots in the wild.

Why Do Parrots Become Endangered And Extinct?

Many bird species throughout the world are becoming threatened, endangered and, in some cases, extinct at an alarming rate. Survival of the nestlings in the most advantageous conditions is *iffy* at best, but compromising situations sometimes tip the odds against survival. Extinction is rarely the result of one event or one aspect of a species' decline, but there are usually several interconnected factors which create pressures on a species' ability to survive.

The consequences of human overpopulation is clearly the number one problem. When increasing numbers of

---

Sally Blanchard's COMPANION PARROT HANDBOOK

people inhabit an area, they put pressure on the natural habitat, both plants and animals. Each increase in population means the land has to support more people. Increased hunting decreases plant and animal populations which are used for food. The natural ecosystem is gradually destroyed to make room for the agricultural crops and domestic animals raised for food. Well-established parrot nesting, roosting, and foraging sites become seriously compromised. Even building a road which separates the roosting and feeding grounds in the rainforest can cause a downturn in bird populations. In modern times, the misuse of fertilizers, pesticides, and other contaminants causes environmental pollution which can seriously compromise the health of adult birds and chicks. In some cases, because of toxic pollution, egg shells do not form properly or chicks hatch out malformed and are unable to survive.

Hunting for food rarely diminishes a species by itself, although when the habitat is seriously compromised, overhunting can deal a more serious or even final blow to a species. The same is true of trapping for the pet trade. Once a species becomes threatened, trapping and poaching can put the species in serious jeopardy — especially when nesting sites are destroyed and nestlings and young birds are taken year after year, threatening future generations.

Man brings other complexities with the introduction of competing or non-native predatory species. Many birds are cavity nesters, and as the nesting sites diminish with human overpopulation and habitat destruction, most introduced animals skew the established balance of nature by competing for food and nesting sites. Birds co-evolved with their natural food sources and with their natural enemies. When the natural patterns change, the flock traditions of a bird species must adapt. Only a few species adapt well and those are usually scavengers or omnivores who can readily adjust to multiple food sources.

Species And Flock Traditions

Some bird species are so specialized that their survival is threatened by even the most subtle changes in their routine and habitat. Birds with strong flock traditions often are the most seriously threatened. At one time, there were so many passenger pigeons that reports say they darkened the skies. It is presumed that their decline into extinction (and that of the Carolina parakeet) had a great deal to do with the fact that courtship and breeding success depended on great numbers within a flock. As the numbers dwindled, the

SOME EXTINCT & ENDANGERED PARROTS

According to world parrot expert, Rosemary Low, companion parrot owners **must** care about the plight of wild parrots for progress to be made in their conservation. "They can aid parrots in the wild by educating others about their plight and by contributing cash to some of the projects which desperately need funding and supporting organizations directly involved with parrot conservation." She also believes that for aviculture to truly contribute to conservation, more breeders need to let the natural parents raise their chicks instead of hand-rearing all the young because of serious problem in attempting to breed hand-reared birds.

EXTINCT — Carolina Parakeet
(Conuropsis carolinensis)

If these golden-headed conures existed today, they would be classified as *Aratinga*, the same genus as the sun conure. The only parrot native to the Eastern United States, the last Carolina Parakeets were sighted in the late 1920s. Some were even kept as pets, but no attempts were made to conserve this species.

PARROTS OF THE CARIBBEAN

The parrots of the Caribbean are in serious trouble. The Cuban macaw and several other island parrots are extinct. Most of the native Amazons are endangered, including the St. Vincent Amazon, Imperial Amazon, Red-necked Amazon, Vinaceous Amazon, St. Lucia Amazon, and the critically endangered Puerto Rican Amazon.

CRITICAL — Puerto Rican Amazon
(Amazona vittata)

The Puerto Rican Amazon is one of the most seriously endangered parrots in the world although much has been done to increase the population. Deforestation, overhunting, and tropical storms have all contributed to the decline of this Amazon.

ENDANGERED — Double Yellow-head Amazon
(Amazona oratrix)

Over twenty years ago when Paco and Rascal first came to live with me, it never occurred to me that their species would become endangered. They were so available in the pet trade. The numbers of this Amazon commonly bred and kept as a pet decreased rapidly, mostly due to the pet trade but also because of habitat destruction. ·····➔

ENDANGERED — Red-fronted Macaw (*Ara rubrogenys*)

Another parrot that is being bred in captivity in good numbers but is declining in the wild. Some aviculturists will not breed them because they do not sell easily enough in the pet trade.

CRITICAL — Echo or Mauritius Parakeet (*Psittacula echo*)

Considered to be the most severely endangered parrot in the world. A captive breeding program has recently had some success breeding echo chicks for release into the wild.

CRITICAL — Lesser Sulphur-crested Cockatoo (*Cacatua sulphurea*)

Another parrot commonly kept as a companion, the Lesser is native to several Indonesian islands which have been deforested. The pet trade has also had an alarming effect on the decline of this species and its four subspecies.

CRITICAL — Red-vented Cockatoo (*Cacatua haematuropygia*)

This cockatoo, which occurs but is unusual in the American pet trade, is native to the Philippines. It has declined rapidly in the last few years due to nest-robbing for the pet trade and habitat destruction.

EXTINCT IN THE WILD — Kakapo (*Strigops habroptilis*)

A very unusual nocturnal flightless parrot from New Zealand. The up-to-seven pound cocks boomed and strutted at *leks* (see glossary) to attract hens. The few remaining Kakapos have been relocated to small controlled islands to try to save the species. ♪

flock traditions were lost and breeding successes plummeted. When a species consistently has greater mortality than breeding successes, the species is doomed.

Although extinction happens on all continents, island species are most at danger because they are a confined microcosm. Island overpopulation and deforestation has been a major cause of the extinction of many bird species. Populations of endemic species occur in small areas and can be quickly decimated by tropical storms or volcano eruptions. This is particularly true of the Amazon parrots of the Caribbean.

Why Are Parrots So Threatened?

At this time, parrots are one of the most seriously threatened bird orders. Most parrots are what biologists refer to as K-select Species, birds who produce only a few offspring once a year. Their young are altricial which means they are hatched naked, blind, and helpless. The road from hatchling to adulthood is perilous, with no guarantee of survival. Parental care is intensive and long-term. Chicks remain dependent on their parents, and the young take at least a few years to become capable of breeding. Most parrots live in flocks with strong traditions involving communication, behavior, and specific nesting, roosting, and foraging areas.

When a parrot species is threatened by any of the above-mentioned pressures, each and every new threat can become critical to its survival. Many of the most threatened parrot species, particularly Amazons and cockatoos, come from islands where the natural environment has been irrevocably altered.

Look Beyond Your Living Room

Is there any hope? With some species the answer is YES, and parrot lovers can help fund and promote studies and programs involving the conservation of parrots and their habitats. Concerned people throughout the world are involved in efforts to increase the populations of many threatened and endangered parrots. They need our help. Through education of indigenous people, habitat preservation, providing artificial nesting sites, natural habitat breeding programs, eradication of introduced competing species, captive breeding of genetically pure and healthy parent-raised chicks for reintroduction into the wild, and eco-tourism there is hope for the recovery of many bird species. The World Parrot Trust and R.A.R.E. are two of many groups throughout the world that are making a difference for the parrots. ♪

ORNITHOLOGY & WILD PARROTS

Fascinating To Study

When the word "parrot" is mentioned, the average person tends to think of a generic green bird that comes from the rainforest, lives in social flocks, eats seeds, nests in tree cavities, and is active during the day. As most parrot aficionados know, *Psittaciformes* actually have an incredible variety in their sizes, coloration, habitats, and behaviors.

Ornithology is the scientific study of birds. Parrots present a fascinating challenge for study because, while we know a great deal about these intelligent animals as human companions, we don't know nearly as much about their natural lives. When I was in Costa Rica a number of years ago, I watched a small group of Yellow-nape Amazons take off from a nearby tree. I asked the ornithologist guide where they were going. His answer was both simple and profound, "To know, you would have to have wings." Of course, this is one of the reasons we know so little about the habits of wild parrots. Also, many parrots live in remote habitats that are difficult for all but the most intrepid ornithologist to access. Unfortunately, natural habitats are being destroyed so quickly throughout the world that we may never know much about the behaviors and habits of many parrot-family birds. Because we know so little about parrots in the wild, there are many aspects to their behavior we may never understand.

There are several concentrated efforts being made by people associated with various universities and ornithological, avicultural, and conservation groups to learn as much as possible about wild parrots and their habits. I am familiar with several research and conservation efforts involving wild parrots, including Amazons in Mexico, African Greys in west equatorial Africa, Hyacinth and Lear's Macaws in Brazil, cockatoos in the Austral-Asia region, the Kakapo of New Zealand, and the Echo Parakeet on Mauritius. Because of an almost total loss of natural habitat, science may never have much information about the natural habits and diets of some parrot-family birds such as the Moluccan and Goffin's Cockatoos. With a better understanding of flock traditions, natural breeding protocols and environmental pressures, some threatened parrots may be saved from extinction. ⨍

Some Unusual Parrots

Kea *(Nestor notabilis)*

This large parrot from New Zealand lives at high altitudes and has a reputation for being very destructive. Campers return from hikes to find their campsites and vehicles totally trashed. What would happen if this unusual parrot turned up in the pet trade? No doubt people would come home to find their houses demolished with the satisfied Kea sitting on a pile of rubble finishing off a table leg.

Pesquet's Parrot *(Psittrichas fulgidus)*

This rare black and red parrot lives in the mountain forests of New Guinea. It has a featherless face reminiscent of a vulture. This unusual parrot feeds on blossoms, figs and other soft foods. Presumably the bare face allows the Pesquet to bury his head in the ripe fruit without getting his feathers dirty.

Hanging Parrots *(Loriculus species)*

Did you know there is a parrot that sleeps upside down hanging like a bat? These unique birds live in India, Indonesia, S.E. Asia and several Austral-Asian islands.

Pygmy Parrots *(Micropsitta species)*

New Guinea is home to the world's smallest parrots. The smallest — the Red-breasted and the Buff-faced — are just a wee bit over three inches long.

Hyacinth Macaw *(Anodorhynchus hyacinthinus)*

With a potential length of close to four feet and a wing span of over four feet, the hyacinth macaw is the largest parrot-family bird. Because of their size, these macaws from Brazil, Bolivia, and Paraguay, are often referred to as the "Gentle Giant" in the pet trade. However, the Hyacinth Macaw only stays tame and gentle with the right kind of guidance and attention from his human flock. ⨍

A FEW INTERESTING PARROT FACTS

FLY BY NIGHTS

Most parrots are active by day (diurnal) and sleep at night. Patagonian Conures nest in burrows in cliffs along river beds and have been observed flying in flocks from twilight to dawn, especially when there is a full moon. This nocturnal behavior may simply be a case of getting to the feeding grounds first or, perhaps, the very *early bird getting the worm*?

THE FULLER BRUSH BIRD

Lories do not just consume nectar from flowers. They have brush-like papillae on their tongues and use these erectile *bristles* to collect pollen from flowers. Pollen is a very important part of the natural diet of most lories.

SENTINEL 'TOOS

According to Sam Foster, a cockatoo behavioral consultant who lived in Australia, "Several cockatoo species rely upon designated sentinel birds, within the flock, to act as lookouts during foraging and roosting. In Australia, we witnessed this phenomenon with Greater Sulphur-cresteds on several occasions when, upon sensing danger, a sentinel (there are typically several sentinels within a large group) would sound the alarm with a harsh, unmistakable cry, sending the flock up into the sky for safety. There are also recorded instances where these sentinels have actually pursued a predator, giving chase until it was a good distance away and no longer perceived as a threat to the flock."

KINDERGARTEN COCKATOOS

Sam Foster has also observed that "Rose-breasteds are raised unlike any other cockatoos. As soon as the young fledge they are guided to a creche tree, where all the juvenile galahs within the flock are taken by their parents. There, they are watched during the day and night by designated 'nannies' (single adult rose-breasteds), who also provide valuable lessons in flock protocol and survival. Parents may continue to go to the creche periodically during the day to feed their own young until they are completely weaned, but that is the only contact they have with them. When the majority are food independent, the chicks form a juvenile flock and fly off together."

ACOUSTIC ADVERTISING

The male Palm Cockatoo increases his noise potential with the use of a tool. He breaks off a branch, shapes it just right, and then advertises to his mate by banging it rhythmically against a hollow tree trunk to communicate his territory and readiness to breed. In response, the female flies to him and the pair start to caress affectionately as prelude to mating.

SMB

Nurturing Guidance Tip: Keep Learning

Works In Progress:

You may have noticed that this book isn't titled 'The Complete Total Guide to Everything You Will Ever Need To Know About Companion Parrots." The luckiest companion parrots in the world live with people who keep learning because they have a never-ending thirst for knowledge. Both you and your parrot should continue to be "works in progress." There are always new ideas and theories about parrot care and behavior. Some make a lot of sense and some are absolute nonsense. Talk to people, attend seminars and conferences, watch videos, learn to recognize reliable information on the Internet, and most of all, read all the good information you can.

BE A THINKER!

Is the advice you are getting worth following?

- Think about it — does it make sense when you use common sense cause-and-effect logic?
- Is it based on rampant generalizations or stereotypical thinking about parrots?
- Is it punishing or based on ineffective or aggressive quick-fixes?
- Is it trust building or trust destroying?
- Think of *the why* of this advice. Why would it work? If the advice doesn't fit a basic parrot behavioral concept, it probably won't work.
- If it doesn't seem to make sense or it seems trust-destroying — don't follow the advice no matter who it comes from!

Please notice that the index and glossary also contain important information about companion parrots and their study.

SALLY BLANCHARD

AUTHOR & ILLUSTRATOR

Sally Blanchard's name is one of the most recognized among parrot lovers. This reputation is well deserved, for her contributions to our body of knowledge about the proper care and behavior of companion parrots have revolutionized our theories of how to live successfully and happily with our household birds. Her theories, more than any others, and the very effective manner in which she shares them, have improved the quality of life for companion parrots and their humans alike. Her interest in birds was first sparked by an experience many of us have. A childhood friend, Mickey Finn, a charming and talkative budgie, introduced her to the magic a bird can bring to our lives ... and to the disappointment so many of us feel when a lack of information causes the early loss of such a pet.

Sally & Spike

Her interest in birds grew and Sally became an avid bird watcher. Her approach to this science was unique, in that she focused, not on numbers, but on interactions and behaviors, asking herself continually why the birds she observed did the things they did. This interest has continued to be a strong one now for over 30 years and serves as a broad base of knowledge, from which many of her ideas about companion parrots and their behavior are born. Consistent with the innovative slant she brings to all things, she takes her observations of wild birds and asks herself how they are pertinent to the lives of our companion parrots. Trained as a high school art teacher, Sally had considerable artistic talent, and she chose to focus this on the birds she so loved. She began carving birds from rare hardwoods, and became well-known for her beautiful hardwood-inlay bird sculptures. This talent finds its outlet today in many of the illustrations that appear in the Pet Bird Report and in the book you hold in your hands.

Sally is also an innately avid student, who searches out the information she needs rather than waiting for it to come to her. Today, this is reflected in her collection of bird-related books, publications, and artwork, which exceeds 4,000 pieces. She has also, over the years, taken college-level classes in animal behavior, biology, field ecology, zoology, anthropology, sociology, ornithology, psychology, childhood development, and teaching, which have served to round out the knowledge that helps her to understand companion parrots and the people in their lives.

Two specific incidents combined to play a part in narrowing the focus of her interests onto parrots. First, she had the opportunity to help care for a friend's numerous Amazon parrots. Second, she undertook an expedition to Costa Rica, where her firsthand experiences of seeing wild parrots contributed to the development of some of her later theories about avian behavior. Before too long, Sally was sharing her life with Paco and Rascal, two intelligent and exuberant Double Yellow-head Amazons, whom she still has today. In short order, her interest in parrots became her life's love. Soon thereafter however, the injuries she incurred in an automobile accident forced an end to her successful career as a bird sculptor and she made the transition into a full-time career working with parrots. And thus, her life's love became her life's purpose.

When she first acquired Paco and Rascal, Sally had been astonished to find a real scarcity of information on the proper care of parrots in the home. Knowing that experience is the best teacher, Sally began to create for herself learning opportunities, from which she would eventually be able to formulate ideas about the needs of parrots in the domestic environment. She began taming wild-caught parrots for pet stores and individual owners. She also offered her services handfeeding babies for others, and began providing in-home and telephone behavioral consultations. From that period until the present, Sally has worked in most areas of the field of psittacine behavior and care, and her resulting ideas have irrevocably shaped our understanding of parrot behavior.

Sally's early articles in Bird Talk magazine began in 1988. They were the first to emphasize the importance of using non-aggressive taming methods with wild-caught parrots. Other ground-breaking ideas at the time included the importance of early socialization for domestically raised chicks and the positive use of verbal commands, such as "UP" and "DOWN" in maintaining a parrot's pet potential. Further, she went on to develop ideas about eating and foraging as social behaviors, the development of food independence, the differences between imprinting and social bonding, empathic response in companion parrots, behavioral dysfunction as a result of poor socialization and weaning trauma, and methods for developing pet potential in hand raised babies ... ideas which heretofore had remained unrecognized. These concepts today comprise her highly respected theory of *Nurturing Guidance*. Unique in her field, Sally was the first to emphasize the need to base all principles and practices on building trust between parrot and caregiver.

In 1991, Sally began publication of the Pet Bird Report, a bimonthly magazine devoted to the optimal care of companion parrots. This magazine has grown steadily in size, reputation, and number of subscribers since that date. Within the pages of the PBR, writers, including Sally, continue to explore, explain, and expose the depth and subtleties of the parrot/human bond.

Today, Sally shares her home in Alameda, California with several companion parrots, three dogs, and two cats. She is currently working on other parrot-related books, one concerning the different parrot personality profiles, and the second focusing on African Greys. Sally is also working on a series of publications about preventing and solving specific behavioral problems.

JEFF RIEBE

HUMOROUS ILLUSTRATOR — *by Sally Blanchard*

In 1995, the Pet Bird Report received some cartoons in the mail from a PBR subscriber. Included among these was a note from the artist, wondering if the PBR might be able to use his humorous illustrations. The response was immediate — YES! Jeff Riebe's cartoons are not only accurate depictions of parrots and their personalities, they show a marvelous comprehension of both the fun and irony to be found in living with these fascinating and complex companions. Jeff has been drawing cartoons for the PBR ever since and was the perfect choice to co-illustrate the Companion Parrot Handbook.

Jeff lives in Ohio with his Blue-crowned Conure, Wallie, and works as a humorous illustrator. He has been drawing cartoons for the Pet Bird Report since 1995, and specializes in producing artwork for a variety of books and other publications. However, his real enjoyment is found when coupling his love of birds and animals with the pleasure he takes in his artwork.

Animals and art have always been a part of Jeff's life. His first introduction to the enchantment which birds can bring to our lives arrived when he was faced with the task of raising a couple of orphaned house sparrows, who were eventually released once they were flying around the house and feeding themselves. Thereafter, as so often happens, a variety of other birds, mammals and reptiles found their way into Jeff's care. Once healed, those that were injured were either released or taken to a wildlife rehabilitation center to be cared for there. Jeff is a licensed falconer and shares his knowledge of these birds of prey by giving educational volunteer programs to audiences in both churches and schools. For several years each spring, he has led owl-watching walks for local nature groups. Jeff is a member of the World Parrot Trust and the Nature Conservancy and has at times helped with both parrot rescue and rehabilitation.

As the author, I feel grateful to have the opportunity to work with Jeff Riebe. As he readily admits, living with parrots has helped him communicate the joys and challenges of caring for companion parrots through his artwork. I think that his artwork in turn helps all of us to get closer in touch with the joys our parrots bring to us.

Jeff & Wallie

BONGO MARIE 19?? - 1999

Anyone who knows me and my work, also knows of my parrots, especially my African Grey, Bongo Marie. She was an important part of my life for almost a quarter of a century. The lessons she taught me and the stories I have left from her life with me are a significant part of the Companion Parrot Handbook, which is only fitting. I had no idea how old Bongo Marie was when she first came to live with me. I knew she was an adult, perhaps even an older bird. When I first brought her home, she had a massive, chronic respiratory infection and my veterinarian was surprised we managed to restore her health. However, she did regain full health, and graced my home for over 20 years with her undaunted spirit and the peculiar viewpoint that only an African Grey can bring to life. I will never fail to smile when I remember how she would greet visitors with the question, "Who do you are?" or "Where's your poodle?" She was probably responsible for more of my laughter than any other creature on earth.

In the last few years, it became obvious that, even with excellent care and veterinary support, her health was failing. In January 1999, the quality of her life diminished to the point where I had to make one of the most difficult decisions of my life. With the gentle urging and support of friends and Dr. James Harris, my avian veterinarian, Bongo Marie was euthanized. Although it left a tremendous hole in my existence, I feel fortunate to have had her with me for as long as I did. Everyone who met Bongo Marie knew what a special bird she was — mostly because she was so full of life and *full of herself*. She observed and commented on every aspect of my life on a daily basis. I miss her very much, particularly her larger-than-life attitude and sense of humor. The quiet in my house after her passing was deafening.

During the final stages of preparing this book, Julie Murad of the Gabriel Foundation called to express her condolences and tell me, if I was ready, she had a marvelous young African Grey who needed a new home because he had become a biter. Julie has quoted me many times as saying "biting is the easiest behavioral problem to solve," so she knew I would be up to the challenge. A coincidence — the Grey's name is Bongo. He arrived in March and we are bonding nicely — he is quite the handsome boy and is also *full of himself*. He hasn't bitten me yet and has become quite the cuddle boy! I need to get to know him well enough to think of an appropriate middle name for him. He is a very different parrot than Bongo Marie and I will always miss her but I look forward to developing our friendship and the adventure of spending the rest of my life with him!

INDEX & GLOSSARY

parasites. Sun bathing is also a favorite pastime for some birds who spread their wings and posture to take advantage of the light and warmth.

Beak — 118, 146, 171

(The) Beak as a Tool — 171

Beak Grinding (as a Comfort Behavior) — 162 — Often parrots grind their upper and lower beak together as they relax to go to sleep. The common explanation is that this behavior keeps their beak trimmed. While this may be true, since the beak has nerves that transmit pain and pleasure, this may actually be a comfort behavior to help the bird relax and prepare him for sleep.

Beak Grinding (to reshape beak) — 46, 52, 53

Beak Exploration (Beaking) — 80, 146, 171, 198, 206 — Natural and normal chewing and exploration with the beak often as a form of affection.

Beak Lunging (Lunge biting) — 162

Beak Notching — 46, 52, 53 — Drastic beak mutilation used as a quick-fix to prevent feather picking and, in some cases biting, behavior. Should never be used or only as a last resort.

Beak (bill) Wiping (A displacement behavior which often indicates discomfort or aggression) — 163

Beak Wrestling — 181

Behavior — 18 — The actions and reactions of animals under given circumstances.

Behavioral Consultants — **58**, 149, 168, 192

Behavioral Dysfunction (in Companion Parrots) — 25, 74, 102, 213 — The inability to function in an emotionally stable manner. This can lead to an unhealthy bond to the people in their lives.

Behavioral Enrichment — see Enrichment

Behavioral buttons (pushing our) — 193

Behavioral Stages — 81, 208, 210

Bells (in toys) — 133

Betrayal of Trust — 190, 200

(The) **Bird (Pet) Business (Industry)** — 25, 37, 61, 218, 219

Bird Room — 66, 88

Bird Sitting — 56, 75

Bird Shops (judging quality) — 57, 218

Birdwatching — 223

Bitey (nippy) — see Beak exploration

Biting (aggressive) — 18, 21, 29, 61, 73, 82, 80, 146, 160, 164, 169, 170, 171, **172-174**, 179, 198, 200, 206, 207, 209 — The use of the beak as aggressive communication.

Black and White Thinking — 30, 31, 61, **146**, 198, 203, 219 — Generalizations, stereotypical thinking which states that <u>all</u> parrots of a certain species are alike or that certain parrots <u>always</u> do the same thing. Advice based on this type of thinking is rarely helpful.

Blood Feather — **52**, 54, 137 — An emerging growing feather. Usually one of the long shafted tail or wing feathers but can also occur on the crest and sometimes other parts of the body. Blood feathers are normal but a damaged blood feather can create problems.

Blow Dryers — 109, 110

Blue and Gold Macaw (*Ara ararauna*) — 30, 51, 220, 221

Blue-fronted Amazon (*Amazona aestiva*) — 29, 50, 163

Body Language — 22, 78, 83, 162, 173, 179, 185 — Facial expressions and the movement of body and feathers can be used to communicate or interpret a parrot's mood and/or intentions.

Bond (Parrot/Human or Human/Parrot) — 13, 16, 22, 32, 34, 35, 36, 38, 69, 72, 73, 82, 98, 154, 164, 175, 196, 197, 210 — The cohesive connection based on trust between a parrot and a person.

Bongo Marie — 6, 16, 17, 28, 34, 72, 100, 105, 107, 110, 112, 127, 146, 150, 160, 210, 215, 220 — Sally Blanchard's African grey parrot

Books (parrot-related) — 61

Border Collie — 100

Bottle Fed — 37 — A method of handfeeding using a squeeze type bottle. This is a positive way of feeding bappies unless the same squeeze bottle is used indiscriminatingly to feed many parrots from unrelated clutches.

Bowls and crocks (food and water) — 67, 108, 201

Brain (bird) — 113, 118, 138

(The) Brick Wall — 20-23 — The metaphor used in the theory of *Nurturing Guidance* to describe the artificial environment a parrot lives in as a human companion.

Budgerigar (*Melopsittacus undulatus*) - 33, 35, 51, 211, 222

Bursa of Fabricius — 120 — A gland in the wall of the cloaca of young parrots. It is believed to produce antibodies as resistance to diseases. Once the bird reaches maturity, the gland has absorbed back into the cloacal wall. At this time, it is assumed that the young parrots immune system is developed.

-C-

Cages — 67, 80, 149, 199

Cage Aggression (See cage territory)

Cage Bound — 153 — A parrot who is comfortable only in his cage and will not readily come out without aggression or fear is considered to be cage-bound. Losing hand control of a parrot is the first step in losing cage control which helps to create a cage bound parrot.

Cage Location — 66

Cage Sharing — 18, 69, 82 — The concept that rather than establishing dominance and forcing a parrot to come out of his cage, we share the cage territory as a flock member (or flock leader) so we are not intruding on a parrot when we reach into or gain access to him in his cage.

Cage Territory (Cage aggression, Cage Control) — 18, 66, 69, 80, 82, 108, 147, 151, 156, 157, 158, 164, 176 — The cage and the area around it where the parrot establishes or tries to establish a territorial dominance. Being able to ask your parrot to step on your hand when he is in the cage and have him consistently and readily comply is essential to keeping him tame.

Cage Time — 80, 213

Caique (*Pionites melanocephala* or *P. leucogaster*)— 16, 17, 29, 31, 34, 67, 72, 93, 106, 107, 109, 133, 134, 135, 146, 153, 155, 160, 163, 184, 190, 210, 219, 221

Cajole — 80, 82 —To coax, to attempt to persuade by flattery or cunning. I like applying this definition of cajole to the gentle manipulation which we must use to gradually get our parrots used to new situations and objects.

Calming down — see Empathy

Cape Parrot (*Poicephalus robustus*) — 222

Carolina Parakeet (*Conuropsis carolinensis*) — 225

Caribbean Islands — 225, 226

C.A.S. (Certified Avian Specialist) — 44, 47 — A pet industry designation for someone who has taken a four hour class and taken an open book test on bird husbandry.

Casual Attention — 23, 92, 141 — One of the levels of attention we give our parrots (see page 95). Casual attention is the time we spend with our parrots with us while we participate in other activities such as conversation with others, reading, or watching TV.

Catalina Macaw — 221 — Hybrid of scarlet and blue and gold macaws

Cats and Parrots — 16, 72, 64, 115

Cause-and-effect Logic — **128**, 144, 160, 201

Cere — 40, 118 — The fleshy soft membrane above the beak which contains the nostrils.

Change (in parrot's life) — 149, 161, 172, 186, 188, 190, 191, 197

Children and parrots — 51, 73

Choanae — 118, 119 — The internal nares in the roof of a bird's mouth. Veterinarians often check this area to help determine the nutritional status of a parrot. Vitamin A deficiency can often be determined by the presence of small white bumps on the choanae.

Cigarette (cigar, pipe) Smoking and parrots — 66, 109, 121, 131, 143

Clark, Pamela — 64, 123

Clicker Training — 199 — A method of operant conditioning that uses the sound of a clicker as a bridge between stimulus and behavior. While this method may be successful in training specific behaviors and tricks, it rarely takes

The Main Reason Parrots Are Not As Profoundly Introspective As Most People

They Have No Navel To Contemplate

into consideration the many variables in the personalities of companion parrots and the people in their lives.

Climbing Ladder — 67, 79, 101

Cloaca — 45, 119, 126, 200 — The common passage where wastes (urine, urates, feces) and sperm or eggs pass out of a bird.

Cloacal Prolapse — see Prolapsed Cloaca

Closed Aviary — 48 — An aviary that considers its parrot population to be complete and that does not allow new birds on the premises for any reason. A truly closed aviary will not allow visitors into the aviary or nursery areas without extreme, but necessary, quarantine procedures.

Clutch — The total number of eggs laid by a hen during one nesting period.

Cock — 172 — Term used (usually by breeders) to identify male birds.

Cockatiel (*Nymphicus hollandicus*)— 33, 35, 51, 70, 125, 188, 211, 222

Cockatoo (*Cacatua, Callocephalon, Calyptorhynchus, Eolophus, Probosciger*) — 30, 31, 33, 35, 38, 40, 41, 51, 61, 67, 70, 82, 100, 109, 113, 115, 116, 129, 133, 150, 154, 157, 160, 162, 163, 164, 183, 187, 193, 196, 201, 202, 220, 221, 223, 226, 227, 228

Collector Personality — 193

Color (Communication with) — 150, 163

Color of droppings — 41, 126-127

Comfort Behavior — 162 — Used to describe behaviors that have to do with the maintenance of the body. In some cases, such as beak grinding before sleep, the bird may be grinding the upper and lower beak together because it feels good but keeping the beak trimmed is the practical result of this pleasurable behavior.

Comfort Level — 88

Common sense — see cause and effect logic

Companion Parrot — Another way of saying pet parrot. Companion parrot has a more *politically correct* sound to it because it seems to define a more benevolent relationship.

Confrontation — 144, 160, 186

Compatibility — 34, 35, 177 — The ability to get along and relate to each other successfully.

Confusion — 21, 170, 172, 173, 175, 190

Conservation — 17, 223, 224-227 — The preservation of the flora and fauna of the world and their natural environment.

Consumer Interests — 218

Contact Calls — 80, 81, 95, 135, 155, 159, **184**, 185, 204 — Simple notes, calls, or vocalizations between pairs, families, and members of a parrot flock, used to stay in touch and to communicate.

Contour Feathers — Feathers that form the outline of the bird's body.

Conure (*Aratinga, Pyrrhura, etc.*) — 31, 51, 101, 110, 114, 129, 133, 183, 221

Conversion (to new foods) — 78, 79, 90, **122-125**

Cooper's Hawk — 190

Co-parenting — 32 — The simultaneous raising of parrot chicks by their natural parrot parents and people.

Corella — see Bare-eyed cockatoo and slender-billed cockatoo

Costa Rica — 108, 183 , 223

Covering the Cage — 70, 101, 149

Coverts — 54 — Feathers which cover the top of the wing and the tail.

Creche — 82 — A nursery or area in the wild where young birds are gathered for parental or flock care. Rose-breasted cockatoos are raised in a creche.

Crepuscular — 228 — Term used to describe birds who are active at twilight. A few parrots seem to be crepuscular including the Patagonian conure.

Critical — 225, 226 — used to describe a species in imminent danger of extinction.

Crop — 40, 119, 196 — Enlargement of the esophagus most evident in the front neck region which functions as a storage area for food before digestion. The crop is most developed in young birds where a great deal of food may need to be stored before it can be gradually digested.

Crop Burn — 40, 196

Cuddle Wrestling — 101 — Gentle play wrestling with parrots; macaws, cockatoos, caiques, and conures particularly love this type of interaction.

Cuddling — 22, 78, 79, 92, **98**, 103, 104, 162, 176, 196, 202

Cull — 222 — A term often used in breeding for animals or birds who are separated from the others because they do not exhibit the characteristics the breeder is trying to achieve. For example, in the breeding of cockatiel mutations, birds that do not have the desired physical characteristics are usually sold into the pet trade rather than kept for future breeding.

Curiosity (Development of) — 38, 161, 190

-D-

Decoy — 129 — A live bird or effigy of a bird used to attract other birds. This is effective because many birds are flock animals.

Deprivation Weaning — 74, 184, 190 — Weaning parrot chicks by depriving them of handfeeding to force them to eat on their own. This technique may cause weaning trauma which creates insecurity and may make babies more difficult to wean. Deprivation weaning can damage pet potential.

Deprivation of attention — 204

Depression — 101

Derbyan parakeet (*Psittacula derbiana*) — 98

Diarrhea — 127

Dimorphic — 15 — Genders within a species do not look alike.

Discipline — 160 — Discipline is considered to be a form of punishment, however, in regards to parrots, I prefer to think of discipline as the use of a short verbal cue and short evil eye to communicate immediate disapproval for unacceptable behavior. (See page 144)

Displacement Behavior — 20, 21, 154 — Replacement behaviors developed as a substitute when a natural behavioral response can not be completed. Displacement behaviors are common in companion parrots who continually have their instinctive behaviors blocked.

Distracting (negative behavior) — see redirecting negative behaviors

Diurnal — 228 — Active during daylight. Most parrots are diurnal.

DNA — 221

DNA Sexing — 15 — Genetic sexing of birds using blood or feathers.

Dog Food (Feeding to parrots) — 122

Dogs (and parrots) — 16, 64, 72, 80, 84, 100, 101, 105, 115, 150, 178, 182

Domesticated — 13, 20 — Dogs and cats are domesticated companion animals. This means that their instincts and personality have been altered by hundreds or thousands years of living with and being bred by human beings.

Domestically-raised — 20, 24, 74, 81, 90, 190, 215, 219 — Parrots who are raised in captivity.

Dominance — 22, 178, 197, 199 — (see aggression also) Although most people associate dominance with aggression, the use I prefer is one of establishing authority.

Double-yellow Head Amazon (*Amazona oratrix*) — 16, 51, 72, 98, 101, 135, 225

"DOWN" — see Verbal commands — The verbal cue used to get a parrot to step off of your hand. However, the major importance of this command is to maintain hand control of a parrot throughout his life.

Drafts — 57, 148

Drama Addict — 18, 178, 206 — A term coined by Sally Blanchard to describe a parrot's excited response to and encouragement of dramatic response from their human flock.

Drama Reward — 172, 174, 178, 183, 185, 186, 206 — positive or negative responses which may be dramatic enough to provide a reward which encourages rather than discourages negative behaviors.

Droppings (Defecation) — 29, 41, 42, **126-127** — Occurs when the waste matter in the cloaca is passed through the vent.

D.V.M., Dip-ABVP, Avian Practice — 47 — The title used by Board certified (American Board of Veterinary Practitioners) avian veterinarians.

-E-

Ears — 119 — Small opening below and to the back of the eyes. The auriculars, or feathers that cover the ear, are often a slightly different color than other feathers in that area of the head.

Earthquake — 157, 189

Easy-care pets — 12, 199

Echo Parakeet (*Psittacula echo*) — 226, 227

Eclectus — 15, 30, 33, 35, 80, 98, 99, 154, 188, 201, 203

E-coli (*Esherichia coli*) —A gram negative bacteria causing illness in parrots.

Ecology — The study of the interrelationship of animals, plants, and the habitat they live in.

Ecosystem — 224-227

Eco-tourism — 223, 226 — tourism based on observation of natural habitats and its wildlife.

Ectoparasite — 187 — A parasite that lives on the outside of a bird's body. Although these are common in wild birds, they are rarely a problem for companion parrots.

Egg Binding — 101 — a problem with egg production where the egg remains in the body instead of being properly laid. Nutritional deficiencies, lack of exercise, and genetics are all possible causes of this possibly life-threatening problem in sexually mature hens.

Egg Laying — 101, 182 — The presence of a male parrot is not necessary for a hen parrot to be stimulated to lay an egg. There have been many situations where companion parrots have laid eggs for their owners, sometimes in their laps. Egg laying should not be a problem if a parrot is on a good diet and gets plenty of exercise.

Elderly Parrots — see older parrots
Emergencies — 19, 136, 137
Empathic — 17, 18, 22, 40, 88, 136, 149, 150, 151, 157, 173, 176, 183, 185, 191, 207, 210 — Closely matching the energy and mood of another being. Many companion parrots are highly empathic to the energy of their human flock.

Endangered — 221, 222, 223-227 — A living organism in danger of extinction.

Energy Level — see Empathic
Enrichment (Environmental or Behavioral) — 23, 106-107, 199 — A term to describe all that we provide to captive animals to enrich their lives and provide them with stimulation.

Environmental Enrichment — see Enrichment

Ethical Considerations — 57, 218, 219
Ethology — The biological study of animal behavior.

Evil Eye — see Eye Contact
Exceptions to the Rules — 51, **147**
Exercise — **101**, 142, 149
Expectations — 22, 77, 113 — Realistic expectations are realizing and accepting the actual pet potential of a parrot.

Extinct — 224-226 — a living organism that no longer exists.

Eye Contact — 22, 38, 80, 144, 153, 159, **160**, 172, 177, 178, 189, 191, 206 — One of the ways to communicate, both positively and negatively, with your companion parrot.

Eye Pinning — 162, 170 — the dilation and contraction of the parrot's pupil as a sign of excitement and in some cases, aggression.

Eyes — 15, 41, 64, 102, 119

-F-

Facial Bites — 178, 179
Falling In Love — see Impulse Buying
Fats (in parrot diet) — 122-123
Fault (not the parrot's) — 19, 89, 168, 193, 204
Fear — see Phobic Behavior
Fear Behavior and Postures — 163, 189
Feather *Conditioner* — 187
Feather Destructive Behavior (Picking) — 18, 21, 46, 70, 81, 109, 148, **186-188**, 196, — Any feather destructive behavior such as feather plucking, feather shredding, feather pulling, and feather snipping.

Feather Fluffing — 162
Feather Follicles — 137, 188
Feathers — 40, 108, 118, 187, 212 — Complex keratin structures used for flight, body protection, coloration and behavior.

Feathers and Health — 40, 187
Feet — 64, 109, 120
Feral — An animal or bird that has been raised and kept in captivity that has become wild.

Figure-eighting — 163
Finger Feeding — 36, 74, 75, 79, 201 — Using fingers to feed soft, warm pieces of food or handweaning pellets to baby parrots.

First Aid — 136, 137
Flash Color — 163 — A color pattern on a bird that is distinctive and identifies that bird from a distance. These color patterns are also used to communicate.

Fleas — 187 — External parasites such as fleas, mites, or lice are so rarely a problem with companion parrots that products such as Mite Protectors are useless and can be dangerous.

Fledge — 24, 25, 37, 51, 74, 82, 190, 212 — To fly for the first time. Flight skills.

Flight and Flight Skills — 24, 50, 51 — Skills learned after fledging from actual flight experience and parental observation and teaching.

Flock — 13, 66, 88, 89, 165, 175 — A social group of birds.

Flock Hierarchy — 71
Flock Interaction — 13 — The time a flock spends interacting with each other. In companion parrot terms, the focused time a person spends with his or her parrot.

Flock Leader — 19, 34, 69, 144, 165, 193 — A term particularly used with companion parrots to define the human who provides the most *Nurturing Guidance.*

Flock Member — see Human Flock
Flock Traditions — 24, 225 — the normal established patterns and routines of a flock in their natural habitat.

Floor Time — 67, 79, 101, 105, 132 — Closely supervised and pre-planned time spent playing with a parrot on the floor or flat surface.

Focused Attention — 13, 23, 73, 83, 88, 92, **95**, 140, 158, 168, 169, 173, 185, 188, 192, 199, 203, 204 — In-your-face attention totally focused on the parrot. Companion parrots need at least 10 to 30 minutes of consistent focused attention each and every day to remain secure.

Fomite — 48, 49 — Substances that can absorb, hold, and transmit infectious germs. These can include your body, clothing, hair, shoes, and possibly even items purchased at a bird mart.

Food Allergies — 149
Food as Toys — 90, 106, 110, 122, 125, 132, 201
Food Begging Behavior — 39, 74, 75, 78, 184, 201 — Postures and calls used by baby parrots to let their parents know they need to be fed.

Food Coloring (artificial) — 121, 126, 149
Food Deprivation — 40, 184, 199 — The technique in which baby birds are encouraged or forced to wean by withholding handfeeding and providing only food they eat on their own. Most baby parrots will actually wean more securely and readily if they are fed abundantly and exposed to a wide variety of nutritious foods at the same time.

Food Independence — 24, 37, 74, 161, 202, 203, 213 — A parrot chick becomes food independent when he no longer depends on his parents or other adults for any part of his feeding. Since some parrot species continue the process of feeding after their young are capable of eating on their own, total food independence occurs after a bird is weaned.

Food In Foot (Holding) — 75
Food Insecurity — 36, **75**, 202
Food Rigidity — 124, 169, 202
Food Throwing (Food Flinging) — 28, 114 — It is normal behavior for many parrots to throw their food around their cage area.

FooFoo personality — 193
Foot Stomping — 163
Foot Toys — 133, 146
Forage (Foraging) — 88, 90, 101, 203, 212 — The process of feeding and moving from area to ara in search of food. Parrots spend a great deal of their day foraging for food.

Forced Weaning — 74, 184 — depriving a parrot chick of food in an attempt to make him eat on his own. This technique usually causes weaning trauma which may decrease pet potential.

Foster, Sam — 228
Fresh Air (the importance of) — 148
Fright — see Phobic Behavior
Frightmolt — 188 — When frightened or attacked some birds will molt their tail feathers and other feathers. The feathers actually appear to be let loose from the follicles all at once. This may be a way to shed feathers that are most likely to be grabbed by predators or may even act to distract the predator while the bird escapes.

Frugivorous — An animal who normally eats fruit as the major part of their diet.

Fruits (in parrot diets) — 123, 127
Full Spectrum Lighting — 66, 148 — Lighting which contains the entire spectrum of natural outdoor lighting. Parrots who do not have normal exposure to natural sunlight (glass in windows block some of the normal spectrum), should have some sort of full spectrum lighting in their environment.

Fun — 12, 13, 23, 104, 107
Fun Ads — 26, 42, 76, 86, 174, 185, 205. 209 — Fun ads for nonexistent humorous parrot-related products and services.

Fun Art — 166, 216

-G-

Galah (see Rose-breasted Cockatoo)
Game playing — 69, 79, 97, 104, 114, 170, 171, 178, 179
Gavage Feeding — 37, 61, 184, 201, 202 — Also called Tube Feeding. Feeding by inserting a tube down the throat and into the crop. This method bypasses any manipulation with the beak and teaches bappies nothing about eating.

Gender Characteristics — 15, 197
Generalizations — 28, 30, 196 — see black and white thinking) Blanket, stereotypical statements about parrots such as All ___ are ___.

Genes — 221 — The hereditary units of a

chromosome.

Genetics — 221, 222 — The scientific study of genes and heredity.

Genus — 220, 221 — A group of species with similar physical characteristics. They all have a common ancestor.

Gentling Exercises — see Patterning

Giardia — 186

Gizzard — 119

Glop Recipe — 123, **125**

Goffin's Cockatoo *(Cacatua goffini)* —227

Grains (in parrot diets)— 123

Grass Parakeets — 222

Grates in Cages — 67

Gray-cheek Parakeet *(Brotegeris pyrrhopterus)* — 52, 153

Greens — 110, 125

Green-winged Macaw *(Ara chloroptera)*— 75, 221

Greeting — 155

Grief — 85

Grit — 119 — Ground rock, shell, or gravel which is sold as a digestive aid for birds in captivity. Grit (or gravel) is not necessary for parrot-family birds and may actually be harmful. Parrots masticate and manipulate their food with their powerful beaks before swallowing so they are usually only ingesting the soft parts or small pieces of food. Once swallowed, the food goes through various digestive processes. In the proventriculus, gastric juices break it down. Then the inside lining of the muscular ventriculus (gizzard) secretes a keratin-like fluid which hardens around the food and aids in grinding any hard food. Grit/gravel is not necessary since this keratin surface is hard enough to grind foods that parrots eat. I have known of several parrots who have become seriously ill because of grit impaction in their digestive system because of free access to grit in their diets.

Grooming — 46, 50, **52-55**, 94, 103, 189, 197

-H-

Habitat — 223, 224-227 — Natural environment in which an organism lives.

Half-mast Eyes (See Eyes and Health) — 41

Hallander, Jane — 107

Hand Control — 18, 82, 87, 96, 97, 179 — The ability of a person to have their parrot readily step onto their hand with a simple verbal command or cue regardless of where the parrot is.

Handfed (Handfeeding) also see food related topics — 64, 75, 196, 201 — Babies who are fed and weaned by humans instead of their natural parents are referred to as handfed. Buying a handfed baby doesn't necessarily guarantee a well-socialized baby parrot.

Handfeeding Traumas — see Weaning Trauma, Food Deprivation, Crop Burn, Handfed

Handicapped Parrots — 33

Handling (mishandling) — 43, 79, 96, 97, 176

Handweaning Foods — 74

Hard-wired Behavior — see instinctive

Harlequin Macaw — 222 — Hybrid of Green-wing and blue and gold macaws

Hanging Parrots — 227

Happy to be Alive Scream — 33, 183

Harnesses (for parrots) — 51

Harpy Eagle Looking for Lunch — 52, 89, 102 Sally Blanchard's description of the way most companion parrots are still toweled.

Hawks (as a danger) — 104, 190

Hawk-headed Parrot *(Deroptyus accipitrinus)* — 51

Health Considerations (signs of illness)— 23, **40-41**, 78, 121, 126, 127, 202

Hearing — 102

Heavy Metal Toxicity — 186

Height Dominance — 164, 191 — The theory that we have much more control over our companion parrots if we are always taller than they are and therefore they have to look up to make eye contact with them.

Hen — 15, 120 —A female parrot.

Herbst's Corpuscles — 70, 102, 120 — Encapsulated nerve endings which occur in a bird's leg joints and other parts of the body. These bundles of nerves are thought to be used as vibration detectors.

Hereditary — see Genetics, Mutations

Hinsz, Barbara Jo — 100

Hormonal behavior — see Sexual Behavior

Household Dangers — 66, 67, 72, 131, 136

Human Flock — 21, 66, 69, 88, 169, 172, 176, 177, 184 — The people who form the family group in a companion parrot's life.

Human/parrot Bond — 13 — The bond a person develops with his or her companion parrot is just as important to a successful relationship as the bond the parrot develops towards the person.

Humidity — 108, 148

Humming (as a distraction) — 159

Hyacinth Macaw *(Anodorhynchus hyacinthinus)*— 113, 196, 211, 221, 223, 227

Hybrid — 221-221 — The offspring resulting from breeding two different and separate species.

Hypnotize — 150, 151

-I-

Immune System — 37, 49, 120

Impaction of foreign material — see ingestion

Imperial Amazon *(Amazona imperialis)* — 225

Imprint — 32 — A behavior term often used to describe an *instantaneous bond* or rapid learning in young animals. For example, certain species of birds will follow the first relatively large object they see within a short time of hatching. This happens during a specific time frame and if it doesn't occur during this "window of opportunity" it most likely will not happen. Parrots do not form relationships through imprinting but through bonding.

Impulse Buying — 27, 33 — "Falling in love" and buying a parrot without any consideration about how it will fit into your life ... sort of like meeting someone in a singles bar, falling in love and getting married the same night. The chances of it working out are about the same.

Incubator-hatched — 37 — Eggs hatched in a heated, moisture controlled device with no parental brooding or care of the hatchling.

Independence Stages — 24, 81, 82, 154, 190, 191, 200, 202, 206, 213 — Various somewhat predictable stages baby parrots go through on their way to maturity. These include fledging, food independence, and gradual independence from parental supervision to integration from the family unit into the flock. Proper learning, socialization, and reassurance is essential during these stages. Understanding something about these stages will help in understanding the behavioral development of companion parrots.

Ingestion of foreign material — 132

Infectious Disease — 48, 49

Insecurity — 74, 81, 184, 190, 202

Instinctive Behavior — 13, 18, 24, 90, 180, 190, 196, 203 — Innate behavior which is inherited and generally species related rather than learned behavior which is acquired through an individual's life.

Instructional Interaction — 12, 22, 64, 78, 81, 92, 99, 100, 105, 184,192, 196 — Focused time spent with a parrot teaching new behaviors through play and patterning.

Intelligence — 13, 16, 21, 91, 100, 106, 112, 113, 153, 168, 174, 200

Integument — 40 —The fairly thin skin and feathers covering a bird.

Internet — 28, 31, **60**, 192 — Both a wonderful and horrible source for parrot information. Learn to know the difference.

Intrepid Explorer — 161 — A term coined by Phoebe Linden to describe a well-socialized parrot who readily accepts adventure and change in his environment.

Intrinsic Value — The essential or inherent value of an animal generally meant to indicate that the value is not based on financial worth.

Introducing New Adventures — 161, 163, 175

Introducing New Birds — 71

Introducing New Foods — see Converting to new foods

Introducing New Toys, Objects — 19, 82, 161, 175

Introducing New People — see Strangers

-J-

Jardine's Parrot *(Poicephalus gulielmi)*— 222

Jingle-bell Type Bell — 133 — A dangerous bell for bird toes because a parrot's toe or beak can become entrapped in the wide opening and then slide into the narrow area.

Job (Give your parrot one) — 100

-K-

Kakapo *(Strigops habroptilis)* — 226, 227

Kea *(Nestor nobabillis)* — 227

Keel Bone — 119

Keratin — 119 — Material forming the structure of feathers, beaks and nails.

Kiss (beak) — 146

Knees — 120

Know-it-all Personality — 193

K-Select Species — 24, 211, 226 — A bird species that breeds only once a year or every two years. Chicks are slow to mature and require extensive parental or flock care and teaching.

-L-

Kwik-stop — 136, 137 — Never use a styptic powder like Kwik-stop on any part of a parrot except the tips of the toenails. Corn starch stops bleeding just as well and styptic powder can cause serious tissue damage.

Laddering — see Patterning exercises
Ladder over the Brick Wall — 21 — The metaphor used to describe *Nurturing Guidance* and its steps to guide the behavior of a companion parrot.
Language — see Verbal Communication
Larson, Gary — 220
Laughter — 16
Leaf Bathing — 109, 125 — Bathing on wet leaf matter that may contain specific oils which assist in cleaning or preening.
Learned Behavior — 24
Lear's Macaw (Anodorhynchus leari) — 227
Leather on toys — 133
Leg Band (removal) — 52
Legs — 120
Lek — 226 — An area that male birds use as a stage to attract females by booming and strutting. The near extinct Kakapo performs at a lek to attract the females.
Lesser Sulfur-crested Cockatoo (*Cacatua sulphurea*) — 113, 226
Lice — External parasites such as mites and lice are very rare in companion parrots.
Life Span — 117, 211
Life Stages of a Pet Parrot — 210
Lighting — 66, 148
Linden, Phoebe Greene (Santa Barbara Bird Farm) — 30, 61, 74, 161, 202, 214
Lories — 109, 133, 228
Lost Parrots — 129
Love — 16
Lovebirds (*Agapornis*) — 31, 153, 222
"Love Grip" Taming — 150
Love Sponges — 30, 31, 200
Low, Rosemary — 225
Lowering Energy — (see Empathic) — Lowering our own energy is an effective tool to lower our parrot's energy.
Lunge Biting — 162
Lutino — 222 — A color mutation in cockatiels and other species bred to be predominantly yellow. Some lutino 'tiels have serious problems with feather production and health.

-M-

Macaw — 30, 31, 35, 51, 82, 101, 114, 129, 154, 163, 179, 189, 190, 201, 202, 207, 221
Macho Personality — 193
Magic Fountain — 105 — A game to get your parrot used to being sprayed.
Malnutrition — 41, 124, 196, 211
Manipulation (behavioral) — 113, 114, 168, 183, 188, 200 — To influence or manage successfully. Although this work may have a negative connotation to some, it may be applied both to the negative way some parrots relate to us and the positive way we should be relating to them. In many ways, working with a parrot involves

the skills of observing, understanding, and managing their behavior. Unfortunately, many parrot/human relationships are based more on the parrot manipulating the human through negative behaviors forcing dramatic reactions.
Manu Clay Licks (Peru) — 223
Marion Zoological — 74
Maroon-bellied Conure (*Pyrrhura frontalis*) —110
Masturbation — see Sexual Self-stimulation
Meadowlark — 221
Metal on toys — 133
Meyer's Parrots — 82
Microchip — 129, 130 — A minuscule identification chip place in the muscle tissue of a parrot's chest. Microchip readers can accurately identify that the bird is a specific registered bird.
Military Macaw — 150-153
Mimicry — The ability to imitate sounds and even words.
Misconceptions — see Misinformation
Misinformation — 28, 60, 61, **196-199**— There is a lot of out-of-date, inaccurate misinformation about parrots.
Mirrors as Toys — 107
Misery Level (of parrots) — 193
Mites (Mite Protectors) — 187 — Companion parrots rarely have external parasites and products sold for mites and lice are not only unnecessary but can be dangerous.
Mixed Messages — 83, 172
Model/Rival — 91, 125 — A technique used to elicit predictable behaviors by using a rival for the parrot's affection as a model for that behavior.
Molt — 137, 188 — The natural shedding of old, worn feathers and their replacement.
Moluccan Cockatoo (*Cacatua moluccensis*) — 38, 70, 71, 100, 150, 160, 196, 200, 203, 220, 221, 227
Monomorphic — 15 — Genders look the same.
Mood — see Empathic
Moustache Parakeet (*Psittacula alexandri*) — 98
Multiple Parrots — 34, 71, 196
Mutilation — see Self-mutilation
Mutation — 222 — Hereditary changes in genetic material which creates new characteristics in offspring.
Myths (about Parrots) — see Misinformation.

-N-

Nanday Conure — 33
Nares — 44, 48, 118 — Bird nostrils located above the beak on the cere.
Naughty Box — 91 — The ineffective and abusive quick-fix of putting a parrot in a small, dark box as punishment.
Neglect — see Abuse
Neonate — Term for a newly hatched chick.
Nest Substitute — 182
Neutering Parrots — 46
Neutral Room — 18, 73, 79, 82, 91, 95, 102, 156, **158**, 161, 168, 176, 177, 181 — A room the parrot is not familiar with where he has estab-

lished no territorial imperative. It is much easier to work with most birds in a neutral room.
Nictating Membrane — 119 — The seldom seen third lid of a parrot's eye. It is used to clean and moisten the eye without interfering with vision or light. It is stored in the nasal corner of the eye when it is not in use. This lid also may act as "aviator goggles" to protect the eye from wind and weather during flight.
Night Frights — 70, 188 — Several species of parrots are prone to traumatic night frights, particularly cockatiels and African greys. Night frights usually involve a bird thrashing around in his cage in extreme fright. These may be a response to vibrations or lights flashing through the windows into the bird's room.
"No" Command — see Verbal Commands
Nocturnal - 226, 228 — An animal that is active at night. A few parrots are nocturnal besides the rare Night Parrot of interior Australia and the Kakapo. Patagonian conures are often seen flying at night.
Non-stick Coatings — see PTFE
Nurturing Dominance — 165
Nurturing Guidance™ — 12, 17, **18-23**, 25, 28, 31, 34, 50, 72, 73, 80, 83, 84 , 85, 149, 154, 164, 168, 170, 173, 174, 180, 191, 192, 199, 203, 204, 207, 210, 213 — Sally Blanchard's theory of guiding parrot behavior by teaching.
Nurturing Submission — 149, 191 — Used in the context of *Nurturing Guidance*, "submissive" has the connotation of being a follower to a flock leader. In the case of phobic parrots who have become afraid of the previously trusted people in their lives, the people must behave in a submissive indirect manner, at least temporarily, to regain their parrots' trust.
Nutrition — 37, **122-125**, 143, 146, 215

-O-

Obesity in Parrots — 101
"OK" Command — (see Verbal Commands) — A command or verbal cue to let a parrot know you are giving him permission to do something he is not normally allowed to do.
Older Parrots — 32-33, 85, 93, 111, 150, 215 — Companion parrots who are over the age of twenty are generally considered to be older parrots although their potential life-span is much

greater.

Omnivore — An animal who eats almost anything. Most parrot-family birds are considered to be *Opportunistic Omnivores*. This means they will eat almost anything edible they come across while they are foraging for food.

One-person Bird — 90, 141, 175, 181 — (see strangers also)

Operant Conditioning — 199 — Using a reward which creates a reduction of need to train new behaviors. For example, operant conditioning is used to train performing birds in bird shows. The bird's food is closely measured to keep him in a state of hunger before a show. When he performs a trick properly, he is given food as a reward to teach him to associate that trick behavior with the food reward. While this type of training may be successful for trick birds, it has no place in companion parrot training as food deprivation can be trust-destroying.

Opportunistic Omnivore — An animal who takes advantage of almost all food sources in its environment and eats almost anything that doesn't eat him first.

Optimizing The Environment — **148-149,** 169 — Making sure that all aspects of a parrot's physical environment and emotional care are the best possible.

Organic Foods — 106

Oriole — 221

Ornithology — 15 — The scientific study of birds.

Ornithologist — 15 — A biologist who specializes in birds.

Outside Aviaries for Companion Parrots — 104

Over-dependency — 213

Overload Behavior — 101, 157, 162, 170, **172,** 173 — Excited and often aggressive behavior resulting when a parrot becomes overstimulated.

Over-the-counter-medications — 46, 148

Ovaries — 120

Ozone-generating Air Cleaners — 148

-P-

Pachecos — a highly contagious fatal disease usually diagnosed by necropsy.

Paco — 16, 51, 72, 101, 107, 135, 160, 164, 210 — Sally Blanchard's hen double yellowhead Amazon hatched in 1976.

Pajama Party — 105 — A game to play with your parrot where he gets to go visit a trusted friend or relative overnight to get him used to being in new situations.

Palm Cockatoo (*Proboscigar aterrimus*)— 113, 228

Pantanal (Brazil) — 223

Parent-raised — 32 — Raised in captivity by natural parrot parents.

Parrot-family Birds — for the purposes of this book — any bird in the order Psittaformes including the smaller parrots; cockatiels, budgies, and lovebirds.

Parrot/human Bond — 32 — The bond the parrot develops with a human being in place of a normal bond with another parrot.

Parrot Rescue, Rehabilitation and Adop-
tion — 33, 41, 59

Parrotlets (*Forpus*)— 31, 153

Passenger Pigeon — 225

Patagonian Conure (*Cyanoliseus patagonus*) — 228

Parrots in the Wild — 223, 224-228

Patience — 23, 93, 124, 161, 191

Patterning (Patterned Behavior) — 21, 23, 96, 103, **156,** 157, 158, 175, 206 — (see Patterning Exercises also) A process that involves learning through repetition. Performing a behavior over and over makes that action, task, or behavior easier to perform the more it is done.

Patterning Exercises — 23, 79, 82, 91, 103, 104, 157, 193 — (see Patterning also) Specific exercises and routines uses to teach, encourage, and pattern certain positive behaviors and traits in a companion parrot.

PBFD — 45 — Psittacine Beak and Feather Disease

Peanuts — 149

Peek-a-boo — 104, 102 — A game to play with your young parrot to get him used to being in a towel. Place the towel flat on a bed or couch, place him on the towel and playfully bring the corners up to hide your face and then gently place the corner over his head.

Peeking-out stage — 202 — As defined by Phoebe Greene Linden, the preflitting stage where a nestling starts to explore the opening of the nest and the area around it.

Pelleted Diet — 67, 123, 127 — Manufactured diets for parrots that are formulated to contain optimal nutrition. Although they are a major breakthrough in parrot nutrition, they should not be fed as a 40-60% of the parrot's diet along with nutritious natural foods and not as the total diet. Not all pelleted diets contain the same quality of ingredients. Some may contain artificial food colorings and preservatives which may, if fed as a total diet for long periods of time, contribute to health problems.

Pepperberg, Dr. Irene — 118

Perches — 67, 101, 164, 186 — A variety of appropriate materials, sizes and shapes are important in the cage.

Perch Potato — 101 — A sedentary parrot.

Peripheral Consciousness — 141, 191 — Being aware of the total environment — the proverbial *having eyes in the back of their head.* Very important for prey animals and for people interacting in a nonthreatening manner with parrots who are afraid or phobic.

Personality Change — 190

Pesquet's Parrot (*Psittichas fulgidus*) — 227

PET BIRD REPORT — 12, 60, 71, 74, 123, 206, 218 — The Companion Parrot Magazine started by Sally Blanchard in 1991.

Pet Potential — 18, 25, 27, 31, 64, 74, 79, 85, 168, 215 — The unique combinations of quality early socialization, abundance feeding and weaning, Nurturing Guidance throughout a companion parrot's life increases his pet potential or ability to remain a successful human companion.

Pet Trade — 25, 218, 225

Phobic Behavior (in parrots) — 43, 46, 73, 89, 161, 186, **189-191**

Physical Examination — 41, 44, 124

Picking up a Parrot — see Handling

Pigmentation (see Feathers and Color) — Coloration of skin and feathers. Most feathers, except for blues, violets, and greens are pigmented with pigments. Blues, violets and greens are perceived because of light refraction.

Pin Feathers — 99

Pinioning — 46 — The permanent immobilization of the wing by breaking or removing bones.

Pionus (*Pionus*) — 183, 196

Plastic on toys —

Play — 101, 103, 106-107, 132-133, 142

Playgyms — see Perches

Poicephalus **Parrots** — 82, 189, 191, 221

Poisons — see Toxic Substances and Household Dangers.

Polyoma — A highly contagious disease which commonly effects young parrots but can also be contracted by some adult parrots, particularly caiques. There is now a highly recommended vaccination for Polyoma.

Polyuria — 127

Potty Training — 29, **127,** 161

Power Feeding — 37 — The forced injection of handfeeding formula into the back of the mouth and crop with a syringe.

Predator — 24, 72, 73, 89, 102, 107, 188, 189, 190, 191, 212 — An animal who eats another animal as food although parrots are often referred to as seed predators.

Predator Response — see Predator

Predator Skills — see Survival skills

Predictability — 23, 161, 172 — Consistent behavior from people which encourages a parrot's sense of security.

Preening — 24, 99, 108, 110, 148, 152, 162, **187** — Cleaning and "rezipping" of the feathers to keep them functioning properly.

Preparation (bringing bappy home) — **63-** 73, 78

Pressure Point on Forehead — 152

Prey Animal — 24, 89, 141, 144, 162, 174, 190 — An animal who is attacked and eaten by predators. Birds of prey are the most common parrot predators although eggs, young, and some adults are also eaten by other animals, including snakes, monkeys and other birds.

Primal Psitta-scream — 76, 183

Primary Feathers — 54 — The first ten flight and longest feathers on a parrot's wings. In most parrots, only a few to several of these feathers should be trimmed to prevent flight.

Privacy Shelter — 67 — A three sided box or platform in a parrot's cage, usually towards the top, where he can hide for security.

Production Values — 36, 64, 200 — The value system of those people who raise baby parrots with little concern for their socialization, pet potential, or healthy emotional development.

Production-raised — 36, 218 — Baby parrots raised with little concern for their socialization, pet potential, or healthy emotional development.

Prolapsed Cloaca — 127, 200 — The pushing or extension of the cloacal tissue out of the vent. Along with cockatoo mutilation, this is one of the most confusing physical/behavioral problems that occasionally occurs in cockatoos (mostly Umbrellas and Moluccans). It is usually thought to have physical causes, but may become a reoccurring problem because of the dramatic reaction and attention the 'too gets. It is also thought by several veterinarians and behavioral consultants that stringent potty training may be a causative factor in some cloacal prolapse.

Proteins in parrot diet — 122

Proventriculus — The bird's glandular stomach.

Psittaciformes — 220 — The parrot order.

Psittacine — A bird in the parrot family.

Psittacosis — 41, 45 — Chlamydiosis, ornithosis, parrot fever. An infectious parrot disease which can be contracted by humans.

Psittacula — 35, 98, 99, 221

PTFE — 66, 109, 131 — Nonstick coating commercially called Teflon, Silverstone, T-fall. Toxic to parrots if overheated.

Puerto Rican Amazon *(Amazona vitatta)* — 225

Pulsate (vent) — 127

Punishment — 58, 69, 80, 89, 91, 92, 96, 105, 108, **144**, 160, 168, 174, 204, 206 — A normally ineffective disciplinary reaction to negative behavior. Parrots lack the comprehensive long-term sense of cause and effect required for punishment to successfully change negative behavior to positive behavior.

Purchasing A Parrot — 36, 39

Pygmy Parrots — 227

Pygostyle — 120 — The fused vertebrae at the end of the spine where the flight feathers (rectrices) of the tail attach.

Pyrrhura **Conures** — 153

-Q-

Quarantine — 48 — The separation of new birds in a given location from the birds that are already there to prevent the transfer of infectious diseases.

Quiet (cage) **Time** — 78, 80

Quick (Nail) — 54 — The growing area of a nail which contains blood.

Quick-fix — 17, 18, 58, 61, 89, 92, 105, 108, **145**, 174, 185, 192, 198, 204 — Any behavior technique that treats the symptoms rather than the underlying cause. Quick-fixes are ineffective in changing negative behavior and may actually create more negative behavior because of the confusion they cause in the parrot.

-R-

Raffle Birds — the use of live birds to earn money through raffling at bird clubs and other bird-related organizations. Generally speaking, the PBIC discourages raffling life birds for profit.

R.A.R.E. — 226 — A conservation agency working to save endangered birds. Their educational programs developed with Paul Butler in the Caribbean Islands have given many of the severely endangered Amazons a new lease on life.

Rascal — 16, 51, 72, 98, 101, 160, 164, 210

— Sally Blanchard's double yellow-head Amazon cock hatched in 1978.

Real Estate Agent — 79, 104, 107, 191, 203 — A patterning game developed by Sally Blanchard to develop the curiosity and a sense of adventure in a young parrot. This game involves taking the bappy from room to room and placing him in unfamiliar, but very safe, situations providing him with continual reassurance.

Realistic Expectations (Unrealistic Expectations) — See Expectations

Reassurance — See Insecurity

Rectrices — The long flight feathers of the tail

Redirecting Negative Behavior — 82, 97, 100, 104, **159**, 185

Red-bellied Parrot *(Poicephalus rufiventris)* — 189

Red-fronted Macaw *(Ara rubrogenys)* — 163, 226

Red-lored Amazon *(Amazona autumnalis)* — 220

Red-necked Amazon *(Amazona arausiaca)* — 225

Red-vented Cockatoo *(Cacatua haematuropygia)* — 226

Regression Weaning — 75, 201 — Parrots who have experienced weaning trauma and/or have been forced to wean too young may start excessive food begging behavior. Starting to feed them again with a syringe, or finger feeding them warm, soft foods can help their sense of security. Most chicks who are regression weaned will wean themselves once they become more secure.

Regurgitation in Parrots — 74, 166, 181, 214 — The bringing up of partially digested food from the crop or stomach to feed unweaned young. Some parrots also regurgitate for their mates as part of bonding and if the mate is unable to leave the nest to get food. Companion parrots, particularly macaws and caiques, often regurgitate for the specific members of their human flock.

Reinforcement —Providing a reward to increase the likelihood of a specific response or behavior.

Repetitive Calling — 75 — A food begging behavior in young birds

Repetitive Posturing and Actions — 101, 163

Rescue — see parrot rescue

Respiration (and Health) — 40, 52, 101

Response — 18, 19

Rigid Routine — (see routine) — Always doing everything the same way at the same time may create such a rigid routine for a parrot that he will not accept or may become insecure with any variation in the routine.

Ringneck Parakeet *(Psittacula krameri)* — 98, 222

Ritual Greeting — see greeting

Roost — 70 — An area where a flock usually rests or sleeps.

Rope on Toys — 132

Rose-breasted Cockatoo *(Eolophus roseicapillus)*— 82, 100, 189, 191, 192, 203, 220

Rotating Toys — 106

Routine — 79, 161, 197

Rubber on toys — 132, 133

Rules — 147

Rungs of the Ladder — 21-23 — The metaphor in Nurturing Guidance to describe the steps to provide guidance for a companion parrot.

-S-

Safety — 66, 80, 93, 117, 121, 128, 131, 132, 134-135, 149, 161

St. Lucia Amazon *(Amazona guildingii)* — 225

St. Vincent Amazon *(Amazona versicolor)* — 225

Scarlet Macaw *(Ara macao)* — 30, 190, 196, 221, 221, 223

Scenic Bird Foods — 74

Screaming — 18, 21, 29, 76, 83, 116, 147, 159, 164, 169, **183-185**, 200, 203, 209, 213 — One of the major problems people experience with their companion parrots. Some screaming is a natural part of being a parrot and should not be considered a behavioral problem. It is excessive, manipulative screaming that is a problem. (see page 183)

Scrollwork — 67 — Although decorative scrollwork on parrot cages may be attractive to some people, it can be extremely dangerous to the parrots.

Secondary Feathers — 46, 54 — The shorter flight feathers closer to the body. These should not be trimmed except with very light bodied birds. Do not trim the secondary flight feathers closest to the body.

Seed-only Diet — 37, 123, 124, 218

Seed Junkie — 93, 124 — A parrot-family bird who was either weaned to a seed-only diet or acclimated to one while receiving poor care. They may be difficult but not impossible to convert to a healthier diet.

Self-fulfilling Prophecy — 80, 98, 173, 175, 206

Self-mutilation — 201 — The gouging of skin, most often on the upper chest in cockatoos. Can also occur in Amazons who seem to develop a problem with their feet and legs. One of the most difficult problems to solve in cockatoo behavior. Most likely starts for physical or environmental reasons but can then become behaviorally habituated through increased attention and/or dramatic responses.

Senegal Parrot *(Poicephalus senegalus)*— 82, 189, 190, 191

Sense of Humor — 23

Sentinel Birds — 89, 228 — Birds within a flock who stand guard while other birds forage. Sentinel parrots sound an alarm if there is a perceived threat to the flock. Some parrot species (such as sulfur-crested cockatoos) seem to have specific birds who stand guard. In others, such as African greys, part of the flock feeds while the others stay in the trees watching for danger. In nature, there are species of birds which all the birds in a location pay attention to for predator warnings. In Costa Rica, I was told that all birds, including parrots, feeding in an area carefully watched the Scarlet-rumped Cacique (a bird in the oriole family) as the sentinel bird.

Severe Macaw (*Ara Severa*) — 220

Sexual Aggression — 173, 177, 182 — Aggressive behavior that is usually hormonally induced and based on the companion parrots protection of his perceived territory and mate.

Sexual Behavior — 83, 162, 177, **180-182**, 198, 207, 208, 214, 215

Sexual Bonding — 180

Sexual *Frustration* — See Sexual Behavior

Sexual Organs — 120

Sexual Immaturity — 83, 181, 214 — A term coined by Phoebe Greene Linden to describe companion parrots who have started to be influenced by hormones but are not yet ready to breed. Behavior is often inconsistent and unpredictable during this time.

Sexual Maturity — **180-182**, 198, 214 — A parrot has reached sexual maturity once he has become consistent and predictable during hormonal periods and is mature enough to breed. Many parrots are put into breeding situations long before they are mature enough to breed.

Sexual Self-stimulation — 181, 182

Shank, Chris — 51

Shared Territory — see Cage Sharing

Shoulders (Birds on) — 97, 104, 147, 160, 177, **177-178**, 182

Silverstone Cookware — see PTFE

Singing (as distraction) — 107, 159, 185, 201

Skritch — 83, **99**, 103, 113, 152, 176 — The way one scratches or pets a parrot. This often involves a deep, yet gentle, circular ruffling of the feathers to get to the skin.

Sleep — 38, 66, 70, 78, 79, 149, 204 — Generally speaking it appears that active birds sleep more soundly than more sedentary birds. There is a great deal of anecdotal evidence that parrots need a good 8-10 hours of interrupted sleep to stay healthy. Nap time for diurnal prey birds rarely involves deep sleep as they must maintain awareness of predators in their area.

Sleeping Cage — 70, 155 — A small, secure cage for sleeping and nap-times. May also be used for time-outs but not ever as punishment.

Sleeping Tent — 67, 149 — A fabric tent-like product that hangs in a bird's cage which provides privacy and a sleeping area.

Sleeping Tube — 67 — A fabric tube-like product that hangs in a bird's cage which provides privacy and a sleeping area. Generally preferred by smaller parrot-family birds such as lovebirds, conures and caiques.

Slender-billed Cockatoo — 52

Slender-billed Conure — 52

Smoking and Parrots — See Cigarettes

Smuggling — 31

Social Eating — 90, 107, 125, 155, 183

Socialization — **24-25**, 27, 29, 36, 89, 113, 161, 168, 174, 186, 187, 190, 196, 212, 213 — The process by which all young animals learn their survival and social skills.

Social Skills — See Survival Skills

Social Relationship — 177, 181

Species — 220, 221 — The most basic category of living organisms besides the individual.

Spikey Le Bec — 17, 29, 34, 67, 72, 93,

106, 107, 134, 135, 146, 155, 160, 184, 210, 219 — The Celebrity Caique, Sally Blanchard's companion caique who works as a "visual aid" and travels with her to seminars and conventions.

Spoiling a parrot — 78, 184, 196, 200, 213

Spoon-feeding — 37, 64, 94 — A method of gentle handfeeding using a small spoon. Sometimes the sides of the spoon are bent inward to accommodate the shape of the beak.

Squirt Bottle (Squirting with water) — 105, 108, 110

Stages (behavioral) — See Behavioral stages and Independence Stages

Stick (or Branch) Training — 82, 94

Stimulation — 23, 101, **106-107**, 149, 186, 202, 204 — Companion parrots need a great deal of stimulation to remain healthy and happy. They need for the people in their lives to keep them active and provide them with many stimulating sources for exercise, play, and entertainment.

Stimulus — 20, 21 — An observed or sensed thing, event, or situation which causes and encourages a response or reaction.

Strangers (Parrots and) — 19, 38, 69, 73, 79, 80, 158, 175

Stress — 52, 55, 149, 163, 172

Stress Bars — 40, 188 — Breaks, lines, or discolorations in new feathers caused by illness, malnutrition, or poor lighting during feather growth. Antibiotics given during feather growth may also contribution to the formation of imperfect feathers.

Stunted Parrots — 41 — A chick who is has not developed properly and is too small, out of proportion, has other physical problems such as bulgy eyes, and is often mentally underdeveloped.

Submissive — see Nurturing Submission

Sulphur-crested Cockatoo (*Cacatua sulphurea*) — 113, 162, 164, 203, 228

Sun Conure (*Amazon solstitialis*) — 50, 163

Super Male — 172 — In some companion parrots, particularly cockatoos, there seems to be very dominant male birds who are more challenging for the people in their lives especially during periods of hormonal influence.

Supervision — 72

Surgical Sexing — 15, 46 — A method of determining the sex of birds by making an incision in the belly and looking at the internal organs with an endoscope. This is a surgical procedure and should not be performed at bird marts. DNA sexing is much safer but the results take longer and may not indicate the health or condition of the reproductive organs if these facts need to be known for breeding purposes.

Surrogate Parent — 111 — A substitute parent. Parrot breeders and handfeeders who think of themselves as the bappy's surrogate parent generally are more concerned about proper early socialization.

Survival Skills — 24, 90, 102, 212, 213 — All the innate and learned skills that allow animals to survive successfully in their natural environment, those used to avoid being captured and eaten by a predator.

Sustained Trauma — 19, 46, 52, 73, 102,

149, 186, 189 — Any traumatic event that lasts long enough to create enough fear that a parrot may perceive himself as losing his life due to a predator attack. Sustained traumas are often the major trigger for phobic episodes in sensitive parrots.

Swings — 67, 101, 203

Syringe-feeding — 37, 94, 201 — Most baby parrots are handfed formula with a syringe. Food is placed in the syringe and then placed into the bird's mouth by pushing the plunger down.

-T-

Tail — 120

Taking it Personally — 173, 206

Talking Parrots — see Verbal Communication

Tambopata Clay Licks (Peru) — 223

Taming — 17, 150, 153

Taste — 118 — Because parrots have proportionately less taste buds than most mammals, it is presumed that they do not taste food as well. While this may be true, it doesn't mean they have no sense of taste. There is much evidence that parrots do have food preferences based on the way the food tastes.

Taxonomy — 220 — The science of classification.

Teasing Parrots — 69, 73, 149, 186, 190

Teflon — see PTFE

Television (and Parrots) — 70, 107, 203, 204

Temperature (Food) — 94

Temperature (Household) — 66

Territoriality — 18, 69, 91, 158, 172, 173, 176, 178, 214 — The protection and heightened awareness of intruders into the perceived nesting, individual or flock territory of the parrot.

Testes — 120

Theft of Birds — 121, 130

Thick-billed Parrot (*Rhynchopsitta terrisi*) — 24

Thrashing — 21, 188, 189 — Some frightened and/or phobic parrots will throw themselves around their cage during episodes of great fear or night frights.

Threatened Species — 222, 224-227 — A species that is not yet considered to be endangered or extinct yet is experiencing environmental pressures and declining numbers.

Throwaway Bird — 168, 208 — Many people are not willing to establish a quality relationship with a companion parrot. They blame behavioral problems on the bird and *get rid of him*. Eventually if this happens enough the bird can develop such serious behavioral problems that he loses any pet potential and becomes a throw away bird.

Time-out — 69, 80

Timneh African Grey (*Psittacus erithacus timneh*) — 107, 179

T-Joy Parrot Products — T-Joy in the Fun ads stands for "The Jokes On You"

Toenail Chewing — 163 — A common behavior with some parrots. It may be to trim the toenails or it may be a nervous displacement behavior in some parrots.

Toenails — 46, 52, 54, 67, 94, 120, 186,

190, 212

Toes in Nostrils — 187

Tongue — 118, 228 — Parrot tongues are muscular and thick with sensitive corpuscles (encapsulated nerve endings) that are used to manipulate and explore food and other items. Lory tongues have "brushes" on them used to extract pollen and nectar from flowers.

Tool-use — 113, 228 — Considered to be a sign of intelligence in animals. Many parrots create and use tools to help them with specific tasks.

Total Diet — 122-123 — In the wild, most parrots are omnivores spending much of their day foraging for a varied diet of fruits, vegetable matter, natural seeds, nuts, grubs, insects, and other foods. Feeding a total diet of just one food (whether it is seed or pellets) does not keep a parrot stimulated and may cause health problems.

Touch — Because of sensitive nerve endings on their skin at the bases of their feathers, birds can even tell when the tips of their feathers are being touched.

Towel Acrobat — 104 — A game to increase a young parrot's balance skills and get him used to friendly towel handling.

Towel Handling — 46, 79, 94, **102-103**, 104, 142, 151, 158, 170 — Parrots are not naturally afraid of towels. It is usually the way they are toweled that makes them so threatened by them.

Toys — 67, 68, 101, 106-107, 132, 133, 142, 169, 182, 199, 203 — Play objects are absolutely essential for companion and breeding parrots.

Toxic Substances — 66, 95, 106, 117, 121, 131, 143, 149, 225

Training (for bird shows) — see trick training

Traumatic Handling — see Aggressive handling and Sustained Trauma.

Travel to See Wild Parrots — 108, 183, 223

Traveling with Parrots — 80, 128, 129, **134-135**

Trick Training (for companion parrots) — 16, 58, 93, 105, 107, 159, 185, 199

Trust — 13, 16, 17, 141, 150, **154** , 189, 190, 191 — Confidence, firm reliance, knowing you can depend on someone. Mutual trust is an essential element in the parrot/human bond.

Trust-building or Trust-destroying — 12, 18, 55, 58, 61, 89, 145, 149, 165, 168, 208 — An action which strengthens the bond between parrot and human and an action which weakens or destroys the bond between parrot and human.

T-stands — 68, 73, 95, 107, 153, 158, 176

Tube Feeding — See gavage feeding

-U-

Umbrella Cockatoo (*Cacatua alba*) — 113, 127, 157, 200, 203, **221**

Unconditional Love — 16, 197 — Love which has no conditions. Many people think that their companion parrots provide them with unconditional love. I think that love from a parrot is very conditional and depends greatly on the consistency and guidance of the people in the parrot's human flock.

Underlying Cause — 169, 174 — A parrot in control of his own life doing a bad job of it is usually the underlying cause of most companion parrot behavior problems.

"UP" Command — see Verbal Commands — The verbal cue used to get a parrot to step on to your hand. The purpose of this command is not just to get the bird to step on your hand but also is one of the tools used to establish and maintain hand control and a parrot's pet potential.

Urates — 126-127

Uropygial Gland — 119, 187 — The preen gland just above the base of the tail on the bird's back. Most parrots have these but some are more developed than others and they are lacking in Amazons.

-V-

Vacuum Cleaners — 108

Vegetables (in parrot diet) — **122**, 127 — In a parrot's diet the high vitamin A ones are most important.

Verbal Commands or Verbal Cues ("UP, Down, OK, No" etc.) — 19, 20, 22, 69, 78, 79 82, 87, 91, 93, 97, 129, 140, 147, 153, 158, 159, 160, 164, 176, 180, 203 — Commands or cues given to a parrot who has been patterned to know what they mean and therefore, complies with the request.

Verbal Communication — 16, 22, 92, **111-113**, 129, 183, 184, 215

Verbal Praise — 16, 100

Vent — 41, 120, 182— The opening of the cloaca.

Veterinarian Care — 28, 44-47, 124, 126, 148, 161

Ventriculus — 119, 126, 127 — A bird's grinding stomach or gizzard (see grit)

Vibration Detector — 70, 102, 120 — it is thought that Herbst's corpuscles are used to detect vibrations rather than for touch purposes.

Vicious Cycle — 173, 189

Vitamin A (in parrot diet) — 122

-W-

Walnut Shell (as substrata) — 126

Warm Potato — 73, 79, 90, 103, 104, 179, 141, 156, 177 — The game developed by Sally Blanchard for getting parrots used to being handled by several people.

Wasteful — 91 — Parrots are wasteful eaters often only consuming a small portion of what they are fed.

Wean — 25, 36, 37, 39, 64, **74-75**, 81, 82, 212 — To encourage a parrot to eat on his own and become food independent.

Weaning Trauma — 39, **74-75**, 201, 202 — The insecurity and dysfunction caused by deprivation and/or forced weaning, gavage feeding until weaning, and inadequate nutrition.

Whispering (as a distraction) — 159, 185

Whistling (teaching or as a distraction) — 112, 159, 185

Wild-birds and Wild Bird Handling — 17, 151, 224

Wild-caught Parrots — 17, 150-153, 224

Wild Parrots — see parrots in the wild

Wilson, Liz — 51, 114

Window of Opportunity — A period of time in a young bird's life when certain learning must take place or the lessons may not be learned or learned as competently.

Windows (dangers of or cage placement) — 107

Wing Flapping — 101, 212

Wing Quivering — 163 — One of the physical signals used by chicks to beg for food. It is also a preflight posture. In companion parrots, wing quivering can be a way the bird says "Come pick me up."

Wing Trimming — **50-55**, 94, 129, 147, 190

Wings — 119, 199

Word Cues — (see Verbal commands) — Words which a parrot associates with a particular action.

WORLD PARROT TRUST — 226 — An organization founded in 1989 to help the endangered and threatened parrots of the world. Recently the WPT has become more involved in the plight of unwanted companion parrots. http://www.worldparrottrust.com)

-X-

X-ray — Used in avian medicine to determine many problems including foreign body ingestion and heavy metal toxicity.

-Y-

Yams — 122, 126, 149 — Another word for sweet potatoes, an excellent source of vitamin A in a parrot's diet.

Yawning — Parrots yawn both for physiological reasons and as a comfort behavior. However, excessive yawning (or gaping) may be a sign of a health problem.

Yellow-collared Macaw (*Propyrrhura (Ara) auricollis*) — 100

Yellow-naped Amazon (*Amazona auropalliata*) — 108, 170, 227

-Z-

Zygodactyl — 120 — A description which means two toes forward, two toes back. Parrots have zygodactyl feet.

The Main Reason Most Parrots Are Not Mathematically Inclined:

They Can't Count Past 4 Without Falling Off Their Perch